Dr. Melvin Loewen
1706 Kentfield Way
Goshen, IN 46526-4675

W9-DCJ-050

CONFLICT, CONQUEST, AND CONVERSION

Conflict, Conquest, and Conversion

TWO THOUSAND YEARS

OF CHRISTIAN MISSIONS

IN THE MIDDLE EAST

Eleanor H. Tejirian and Reeva Spector Simon

COLUMBIA UNIVERSITY PRESS   NEW YORK

COLUMBIA UNIVERSITY PRESS

Publishers Since 1893

NEW YORK   CHICHESTER, WEST SUSSEX

cup.columbia.edu

Library of Congress Cataloging-in-Publication Data

Tejirian, Eleanor Harvey, 1938–

　　Conflict, conquest, and conversion : two thousand years of Christian missions in the Middle East / Eleanor H. Tejirian and Reeva Spector Simon.

　　　　p.   cm.

　　Includes bibliographical references and index.

　　ISBN 978-0-231-13864-2 (cloth : alk. paper) — ISBN 978-0-231-51109-4 (ebook)

　　1. Missions—Middle East—History.　I. Simon, Reeva S.　II. Title.

　　BV3160.T45　2012

　　266.00956—dc23

2012017416

Columbia University Press books are printed on permanent and durable acid-free paper.

This book is printed on paper with recycled content.

Printed in the United States of America

c 10 9 8 7 6 5 4 3 2 1

Jacket design: Liz Cosgrove

References to Internet Web sites (URLs) were accurate at the time of writing. Neither the author nor Columbia University Press is responsible for URLs that may have expired or changed since the manuscript was prepared.

CONTENTS

ACKNOWLEDGMENTS

We thank the Middle East Institute at Columbia University for its financial and moral support of the project since its inception. The interlibrary loan services at Yeshiva and Columbia Universities made access to a large variety of sources that would have been difficult to obtain otherwise. Particular thanks are also due to the Rockefeller Foundation, whose invitation to Bellagio provided validation of the project at a critical juncture. We are grateful to all the scholars who participated in the conferences and panels of the project; their work pointed us in directions we might not otherwise have considered. They include Fatma Al-Sayegh, Lisa Anderson, Peter Awn, Andrea Bartoli, Dale L. Bishop, Richard Bulliet, Randi DeGuilhem, Mehmet Ali Dogan, Eleanor Doumato, Ellen Fleischmann, Carolyn Goffman, Yvonne Haddad, Linda Herrera, Eileen Kane, Ruth Kark, Samir Khalaf, Hans-Lukas Kieser, Ann Lesch, Ussama Makdisi, Bruce Masters, Eden Naby, Inger-Marie Okkenhaug, Jean-Marc Oppenheim, Andrew Porter, Thomas Ricks, Aron Rodrigue, Paul Sedra, Heather Sharkey, Marcella Simoni, Elizabeth Thompson, Devrim Umit, John Voll, Steve Weaver, Robert Woodberry, and Michael Zirinsky. We appreciate the research by Eitan Kastner and thank the copyeditor, Annie Barva, and the editors and staff of Columbia University Press, especially Wendy Lochner and Christine Mortlock.

Credit for the entire project should also be given to Benson and Eleanor Harvey, whose tales of missionary life in the Philippines from 1926 to 1945 sparked their daughter's curiosity about the meaning and complexities of the missionary experience. Finally and most important, we are grateful to our husbands, Sheldon Simon and Edward Tejirian, who have been extremely patient throughout the project and will surely be glad to see the finished product.

This history of Christian missions in the Middle East is an outgrowth of a project called "Altruism and Imperialism," begun at the Middle East Institute of Columbia University in 1998. At the time, the idea that missionary activity was relevant to the history and politics of the Middle East was just beginning to become acceptable. Few courses were offered that covered the missionary enterprise, even in religion departments and seminaries, except at evangelical institutions, despite the fact that major universities house important mission archival collections.

In fact, until quite recently, in the story of the Middle East in modern times missionaries have been marginalized, and in the story of the missionaries the Middle East has been marginalized. This is odd because it was the Middle East—the land of the Bible—that was most privileged by the missionaries themselves, in particular the Protestants, whose enthusiasm became the catalyst for missionary revival in the nineteenth century. Yet there is little in the literature of either the Middle East or missions that examines the entire landscape of Western missionaries—Roman Catholic as well as Protestant, European as well as American, their impact on the region, and the effect of their activity on other aspects of Western involvement in the Middle East.

We began the project with panels at the meetings of the Middle East Studies Association conventions in 1998 and 1999 and participation in a workshop held at the Watson Institute of International Affairs at Brown University in 1999. The subject of missionary activity in the Middle East soon elicited broader interest. The Rockefeller Foundation invited us to hold an international conference at its center in Bellagio, Italy, in August 2000, and Columbia University's Middle East Institute published in 2002 an edited selection of the papers presented at the Bellagio conference as *Altruism and Imperialism: Western Cultural and Religious Missions in the Middle East*. Another workshop, focusing on the period following World War II and on the relationship between religious missions and faith-based nongovernmental organizations (NGOs), a subject that had animated all of our work, was held at Columbia in December 2005.

In the decade since the publication of *Altruism and Imperialism*, interest in the subject has grown, with an ever-increasing number of dissertations produced and more conference panels organized. In the United States, the focus has been primarily on Protestant missionary efforts in the nineteenth and twentieth centuries.[1] Scholars in a number of disciplines have begun to use missionary sources to investigate such issues as the status of women,[2] the impact of Western education and technology on the people of the Middle East,[3] and even the relationship between religion and international politics.[4] Israeli scholars have published on missionary work in the Holy Land.[5] With the resurgence of interest in imperial history, British scholars have been particularly active in reanalyzing the complex relationships among commerce, trade, mission, and imperial control.[6] Although European scholars from countries that are primarily Roman Catholic or Orthodox have incorporated material on Roman Catholic missions and even Russian missions, they, too, tend to write from national perspectives.[7] As a consequence, despite this burgeoning interest in the general topic, it became increasingly clear to us that research in these areas had been targeted to specific groups and topics related to the subject with little sense of the overall historical and religious context of the missionary enterprise in the Middle East, one that dates from the earliest days of Christianity. Furthermore, by focusing on Protestant missions, American studies have neglected the long history of Roman Catholic efforts in the region and the relationship between the Eastern and Western branches of Christianity, just as Europeans have neglected American missions.

The purpose of this book, then, is to provide a benchmark narrative that tells the story of Christian missions to the Middle East from the beginning of Christianity to the present. It is an effort to fill the gap in the story of the Middle East by examining the missionary phenomenon in the region in the context of political events. By contextualizing this phenomenon, we hope to provide a frame of reference for a systematic study of the interaction between proselytization and conversion with political change that focuses on the modern period but looks both backward to the Muslim conquests and the Crusades and forward to the cultural and religious evangelism of today, taking into account the domestic roots of the missionary enterprise as well as its international outreach. We are concerned in particular with the interaction between politics and religion as well as with missionaries' political and social impact on the region. As explicit proselytizing and the work of faith-based NGOs have increased in the region along with Western military and political influence, we need to understand earlier efforts and their effects both on the Middle East and on the countries from which these organizations have come.

The concept of missionary activity has been central in theological terms and in practice to both Christianity and Islam from the earliest days of their existence. Christianity expanded through the Roman Empire, eventually *becoming* the Roman Empire. Islam developed within the context of the breakup of the Roman and Persian empires and spread by military conquest. Both religions began in the Middle East, expanding outward from there, and, as a result, their holiest places are there. Both are founded on the holy books of Judaism, and the three together constitute the Abrahamic religions. However, their closeness both religiously and geographically has produced more conflict than mutual understanding.

Our story starts with the Great Commission of Jesus to his disciples, which established the universality of his message, and the journeys of St. Paul, the most important of the earliest Christian missionaries. It was these disciples who spread the Christian Gospel throughout the Roman Empire and beyond, focusing first on the Jewish communities, but with Paul's universalization of the Christian message moving outward across the Roman world. With the legalization of Christianity by the Emperor Constantine in the early fourth century, the new religion became increasingly institutionalized and absorbed into the political fabric of the empire. As Rome and then Byzantium weakened, however, coinciding with the weakening of the Persian Empire, space in the Middle East opened sufficiently to allow military conquest by the Arabian tribes under the banner of a new religion, Islam. Over a period of three hundred years, from the seventh century through the tenth century, much of the population from Spain and North Africa to Persia and beyond gradually became Muslim, shrinking the area dominated by Christianity to western Europe and the ever-smaller Byzantine Empire.

Thus, this is a story of shifting momentum. From the crucifixion of Jesus, traditionally dated to 33 CE, until the rise of Islam in the mid–seventh century, Christianity expanded steadily throughout the Mediterranean and contiguous areas, as far north as the British Isles, east to Persia and India, and south to Ethiopia. With the rise of Islam, however, missionary momentum shifted dramatically. Western Christianity was all but moribund following the Germanic invasions, and Eastern Christianity was forced by the Muslim challenge into what was at best a holding pattern. Islam made major inroads into the Christian communities of the eastern Mediterranean, Spain, and North Africa. In the eleventh century, however, the tide began again to turn as Western Christianity expanded north and eastward, the reconquest of Spain proceeded, and, with the Crusades, Europe began a process of increasing its influence on the Middle East. This process was arrested by the rise of Turkish power, culminating in the Ottoman conquest of Constantinople in 1453, and for the next three hundred years the boundary between Christianity and Islam was essentially the boundary between the Ottoman Empire and Europe. Both Christian and Muslim missionary activity in the region diminished until the eighteenth century, though religious interchange continued, particularly as the Roman Catholic Church maintained its contacts with Christians in the Ottoman Empire.

The Crusades, preached in France by Pope Urban II in 1095, mark the first attempt by the Roman Church to retake the Holy Land, Jerusalem, and the Middle East, although the Crusaders were interested primarily in conquest rather than in conversion. This first foray, lasting two hundred years, was ultimately a failure, and Islam consolidated its hold on the region, expanding it with the rise of the Ottoman Empire. As the Ottomans spread their control over the eastern Mediterranean and pressed Europe on its eastern borders, western Europe began to explore the world to the west. Spain and Portugal in particular extended their reach to the Americas, taking with them Roman Catholic missionaries. As western Europe increased its political and military power, projecting it throughout the world and carrying Christianity with it, the Church of Rome fragmented under the challenge of Protestantism. By the end of the eighteenth century, Islamic political power, represented primarily by the Ottoman and Persian empires, had weakened, and the West, including Western Christianity both Catholic, which had never left the region, and Protestant, was moving in to replace it.

Most of this book covers the period of Western hegemony in the Middle East and the rise of nationalism that coincided with the so-called Great Awakenings. These Protestant revival movements of the eighteenth and nineteenth centuries began in America and spread to Britain and the rest of Protestant Europe, inspiring the sending of missionaries throughout the globe. In the Middle East, Protestants first focused on the Holy Land and on conversion of Jews. At the same time, Roman Catholic and Orthodox powers had their religious protégés whom they could use to leverage their imperial relations with the Ottomans, Egyptians, and Persians. For most of the nineteenth century, commerce, religion, and imperial strategy dominated the Europeans' policy in the Middle East and Central Asia in what was known as the "Eastern Question"—or what to do with the Ottoman Empire as it declined—and in the Anglo–Russian competition in Central Asia known as the "Great Game." For Russia, Germany, and even secular France, missionaries were used as instruments of imperial policy. The British generally dissociated missionary work from state policy, but they were able to parlay their support for the Ottoman Empire against Russian incursions in the Middle East into the establishment of an Anglican presence in Jerusalem and to gain official status for Protestants in the Ottoman Empire.

At the same time, initial American Protestant attempts at missionary work in the Middle East were discouraging. With the British already established in the Holy Land and in Egypt, American Protestants began to work in Lebanon and Anatolia, where they focused on education and medicine. Their missions saw Eastern Christians as targets if not for conversion, then at least for modernization. Unlike the Roman Catholics and the Orthodox, whose missionaries were directed from Europe through orders resident in the region, American Protestants often went to work in the Middle East as individuals or families and may or may not have been associated with missionary organizations in the United States. By the end of the nineteenth century, as Protestant evangelical organizations transformed and proliferated, their diversity was mirrored in the Protestant organizations in the Middle East.

The decade preceding World War I was the high point of Western missionary work in the Middle East. Roman Catholic missions proliferated in the Middle East and North Africa, and the Russians bolstered Greek Orthodox institutions in the wake of the Protestant challenge. Among evangelical Protestants, religious fervor generated by revival meetings on both sides of the Atlantic, concern for Christian victims of war in Greece, Bulgaria, and Lebanon, and Muslim uprisings in India and the Sudan sparked renewed interest in converting Muslims. Meetings in Britain and organizations such as the Student Volunteer Movement motivated youth to mission. This euphoria occurred at a time when the focus of the Protestant mission in mainline churches was shifting from conversion to support of indigenous churches, education, and humanitarian assistance.

The consequence of this change is what scholars look to when they wish to assess the impact of the missionary enterprise on the peoples of the region. The establishment of schools and colleges, the institution of Western curricula with their space for intellectual challenge and questioning, and interest in biblical and pre-Islamic archaeology at a time of burgeoning nationalisms throughout the region lead many to see a correlation between the missionaries' work and the development of local nationalist movements.

World War I destroyed the Protestant missionary enterprise, just as this enterprise had developed under the patronage of the European powers in the nineteenth century. Although the Middle East was never subject to Western imperial control to the same extent as India and Africa, the missionaries nevertheless benefited from European protections and were clearly part of the cultural encounter between East and West that characterized the period. With the rise of nationalisms in the former Ottoman and Persian empires during the interwar period, the resulting conflicts with the Western powers that had been granted mandatory authority in the former Ottoman Empire by the League of Nations affected missionary activity.

The ideological and theological developments within the missionary movement itself, brought about by the changing circumstances both in the Middle East and in the West, have caused a shift from an emphasis on conversion to one of cooperation with existing churches and the indigenization of the missionary churches. This shift has resulted in the strengthening of the Eastern Christian churches even as their members emigrated the region in greater numbers, leaving the Middle East a more thoroughly Muslim world than at any time in its history. For the mainline Protestant churches, missionary zeal has increasingly been channeled into affiliated, faith-based NGOs, and the evangelical mission has been taken up by other evangelical and Pentecostal Christian groups. It is the latter who continue the work of the Great Commission.

CONFLICT, CONQUEST, AND CONVERSION

ONE

The Spread of Christianity

The First Thousand Years

As he walked by the Sea of Galilee, he saw two brothers, Simon who is called Peter and Andrew his brother, casting a net into the sea, for they were fishermen. And he said to them, "Follow me, and I will make you fishers of men." Immediately they left their nets and followed him. (*Matthew* 4:18–19 RSV)

Now the eleven disciples went to Galilee, to the mountain to which Jesus had directed them. And when they saw him they worshiped him; but some doubted. And Jesus came and said to them, "All authority in heaven and on earth has been given to me. Go therefore and make disciples of all nations, baptizing them in the name of the Father and of the Son and of the Holy Spirit, Teaching them to observe all that I have commanded you; and lo, I am with you always, to the close of the age." (*Matthew* 28:16–20 RSV)

The first story recounts Jesus's recruitment of the first missionaries, the twelve disciples who followed him during his lifetime. Peter and Simon were followed by two more brothers, James and John (the "sons of thunder"), and then by Philip, Bartholomew, Thomas, Matthew, James (the Less), Thaddeus (called Jude), Simon the Zealot, and finally Judas, later accused of betraying Jesus to the Romans. The stories of the travels of the first eleven, though perhaps apocryphal in many cases, give us a clear idea of the lands to which the Christian message was thought to have been carried in the first century, the apostolic period. The second story, referred to as the "Great Commission," is the touchstone for the evangelical foreign missions of the nineteenth, twentieth, and twenty-first centuries.

Peter preached first in Jerusalem and then in Rome, where he was martyred in 67 CE. His brother Andrew is reputed to have gone to Thrace, Constantinople, and Macedonia and was martyred in Patros in Greece. There is also a tradition that he traveled to Georgia in the Caucasus and preached to the Scythians near the Caspian Sea. By tradition, James was martyred in Jerusalem in 44; his brother John remained in Jerusalem until just prior to the Jewish revolt against Rome in 66–70, when he went to Ephesus. He is reputed to have remained in exile on the island of Patmos until his death in 100, writing several of the books included in the New Testament canon: the Gospel According to John; the letters designated First, Second, and Third John; and the final book, Revelation. Philip is thought to have gone from Galilee to Galatia in present-day Turkey and was martyred at Hieropolis at the age of eighty-seven. Bartholomew also went to Hieropolis, then variously to India and Armenia, where he is thought to have been martyred at Derbend, on the west coast of the Caspian Sea, in 68. It was Thomas who went to Babylon and may have established the first Christian church there. From there he is thought to have gone on to Persia, India, and even as far as China. He was martyred in India. Matthew, the author of the Gospel, is also thought to have traveled to Persia and may have been martyred there or alternatively in Egypt. Mark, regarded as the founder of the Coptic Church, is said to have proselytized in North Africa.[1] There are few traditions concerning James the Less, though he may have been the first bishop of the Syrian Church. Jude is also thought to have evangelized the region of Armenia in Anatolia, around Edessa (modern Urfa), which emerged as a major center of early Christianity. However, there is also a tradition that he worked in northern Persia as well, where he may have been martyred and buried near Tabriz.

The focus of these traditions on the eastern Roman world and the realms even farther east beyond Roman control is striking evidence of the dispersion of Jewish communities throughout the Roman and Persian empires, which were the disciples' first targets. Only Peter, who with Paul went to Rome, and the last disciple, Simon (the Zealot), are thought to have gone west. Tradition indicates that he went to Egypt, Mauritania, and even Britain, though even he is thought to have gone also to Persia.

Peter clearly emerged as the leader of the disciples from the beginning, and the enumeration of the countries in whose native languages his message was heard in Jerusalem provides further evidence of the scope of the earliest missionary enterprise: "And how is it that we hear, each of us in his own native language, Parthians and Medes and Elamites and residents of Mesopotamia, Judea and Cappadocia, Pontus and Asia, Phrygia and Pamphylia, Egypt and the parts of Libya belonging to Cyrene, and visitors from Rome, both Jews and proselytes, Cretans and Arabians, we hear them telling in our own tongues the mighty works of God?" (Acts 2:8–11 RSV).

From the beginning, the primary target of the disciples' mission was fellow Jews, scattered throughout the Roman Empire, for Jesus regarded himself as the fulfillment of the prophecy of a Jewish messiah. Whether and how the message should be extended also to non-Jews was a major source of contention within the nascent church in the first century.

Omitted from this list of the twelve disciples are two major figures of the early expansion of what came to be called Christianity. One is James, the brother of Jesus, who obviously knew Jesus but was not one of his small band of followers. The other is Paul, originally called Saul. Paul's "conversion" on the road to Damascus is one of the seminal stories of the New Testament.

> At midday . . . I saw on the way a light from heaven, brighter than the sun, shining round me and those who journeyed with me. And when we had all fallen to the ground, I heard a voice saying to me . . . Saul, Saul, why do you persecute me? And I said, "Who are you, Lord?" And the Lord said, I am Jesus whom you are persecuting. But rise and stand upon your feet; for I have appeared to you for this purpose, to appoint you to serve and bear witness to the things in which you have seen me and to those in which I will appear to you, delivering you from the people and from the Gentiles— to whom I send you to open their eyes, that they may turn from darkness to light and from the power of Satan to God, that they may receive forgiveness of sins and a place among those who are sanctified by faith in me. (Acts of the Apostles 26:13–18 RSV)

Paul was probably born in Tarsus in Cilicia, a cosmopolitan city founded by the Persians in the fourth century BCE and conquered by Rome in the second century. His family appears to have been tent makers and Roman citizens, though Jews. His daily language would have been Greek, though he would also have known Aramaic. When he went to Jerusalem in 28 to study to be a Pharisee, he took the name "Saul." This was his first conversion—

from Diaspora Judaism, which owed much to Greek thought, to Pharisaic Judaism as practiced in the Temple in Jerusalem.[2] After spending four years in Jerusalem, he was sent to Damascus to counter the increasing influence of the Jesus cult there, at which point he had the vision described earlier.

As we think about missionary practice in early Christianity, it is important to understand that Paul's conversion did not come about as a result of missionary preaching, but from what he felt was a personal experience with Jesus. Unlike later conversions that resulted from his preaching and that of the apostles, he himself was not the object of missionary preaching. He did not begin to preach immediately but instead spent three years in "Arabia" (probably Nabatea) and then returned home to Tarsus. Thus, he does not appear to have regarded the charge on the road to Damascus as an immediate demand that he go out to convert the Gentiles. However, that charge does seem to have implied that he could endeavor to convert Gentiles directly to "Christianity" without first converting them to Judaism.

Paul undertook his first missionary journey in 42 CE, ten years after his conversion, and from then until his execution in Rome in 64 he crisscrossed the Roman Empire from Jerusalem to Asia Minor to Greece, establishing churches in many centers as reflected in the letters contained in the New Testament. He went first to Cyprus and then to Antioch on the Orontes, far from Jerusalem. However, by 46 sufficient controversy had arisen within the small Christian communities over the requirements for salvation that Paul found it necessary to return to Jerusalem to meet with Peter and James, the brother of Jesus, who had assumed leadership of the Jerusalem community. At this meeting, spheres of influence in proselytization were established: "Peter, Barnabas, and those like them would direct their attention to Jews and God-fearers [pagans who accepted the Jewish God] in the synagogues of Israel and lands contiguous with Israel." Paul could make his way outside that large region (into Asia Minor, for example) with what he calls the apostolate "of foreskin"—that is, for Gentiles.[3]

Thus, Paul left Jerusalem for Philippi in Greece and then went on to Thessalonika, Athens, and Corinth, where he remained until 52. During this period, he began to write the letters that were eventually included in the New Testament and that represent the earliest written Christian literature.

In 52, Paul returned again to Jerusalem to try to achieve agreement with James on issues of conversion. James continued to insist that acceptance of the Jewish Torah was required for baptism, a position that Paul opposed. Peter, working in Antioch, accepted James's position, and in 53 Paul left Antioch for Ephesus, where he remained for three years, becoming "an apostle for the faith of the Gentiles in the Diaspora."[4] In 57, Paul paid a final visit to James in Jerusalem, and when they were unable to reach agreement, Paul was thrown out of the Temple, beaten, and arrested by the Romans. As a Roman citizen, he asked to be taken to Rome for judgment, where he continued to preach. He no longer depended on synagogues for preaching, and he felt no dependence on Jerusalem. In 64, Nero, blaming the Christians for the great fire in Rome, launched persecutions during which Paul was beheaded, and Peter, who had also come to Rome, was crucified (upside down, according to tradition). Paul had already cut his ties with Judaism.

Although Paul himself had not been converted by a human agent, his method of conversion of others was preaching, frequently in synagogues or the homes of believers. Several aspects of his life and preaching resonate in the Protestant missionary enterprise of the nineteenth and twentieth centuries. First, Paul's own conversion experience led him to regard it as being "born again," represented by the ceremony of baptism. Second, James and Paul found it necessary to divide the territory of their proselytizing to prevent confusion and conflict, as Protestants would do in the nineteenth century. Third, repeatedly in his career Paul fell back on his family's trade of tent making as a way of earning a living while continuing his preaching. The concept of "tent makers"—that is, missionaries who adopt another working identity to enable them to continue to proselytize—has become very important in evangelism since the late twentieth century.

After Paul, however, there appears to be no formal missionary mechanism within the Christian Church. We find no names of active missionaries until the age of Constantine in the fourth century, despite the fact that Christianity was emerging as the fastest-growing religion in the Mediterranean region. As hope for the imminent End of Time and the Second Coming of Jesus declined, and as a church hierarchy developed, the initial force that drove the first missions receded. Local versions of Christianity, each with its own language and theological variation, developed throughout the empire. Once imperial patronage was established, however, Constantine and his successors would address this heterogeneity in the councils of the early Catholic Church.[5]

To understand Paul's mission, it is necessary to understand the environment in which he operated. The Middle East, together with the rest of the empire, was a world of intellectual and religious ferment—soul searching, interest in mystery cults and other alternative religions,[6] as well as "apocalyptic zeal, intense mysticism, and incipient violence."[7] With the establishment of the Roman Empire under Augustus (27 BCE–14 CE) and the subsequent institution of the cult of the emperor during the first century, religiopolitical loyalties had become more complicated. For pagans, the priests and the sacrifices to the Roman emperor, whose impact on daily life was as divine as their gods, meant the addition of more festivals to the calendar and the opportunity to construct monuments and to fund tributes. Imperial religion deified emperors, who outlawed the Eastern religions that many nevertheless continued to practice. For monotheists, refusal to participate in emperor worship meant disloyalty to the state. To the Romans, it also smacked of atheism.

Judaism was one of the religions from the East that proved attractive to many Romans in this period. Paul's travels took him to areas of the Jewish Diaspora where Jews were one among any number of spiritual and intellectual communities spreading the good word about their particular belief systems during the early Roman Empire. It is only in the first century that we read of a general interest in Judaism's beliefs and practices. Before then, we rarely hear about actual converts to Judaism. By the second century, however, we hear of Christians who are attracted to full-fledged Judaism, in particular women, who did not need to be circumcised.[8] Rabbinic sources provide no evidence of an official doctrine or methodology related to proselytizing. It seems that individuals brought others into the faith, and conversion was personal and spontaneous.[9] Roman authors write of Jews being expelled from the city of Rome because so many people from the Roman upper class were attracted to Judaism that it became somewhat of a fad to follow Jewish customs. Sympathizers who abstained from eating pork, did not work on the Sabbath, and even underwent circumcision were derided. Interested Gentiles did not deny paganism totally but rather venerated the God of the Jews and selected those Jewish rites they wished to observe. More of these "Godfearers" were to be found in areas outside of Judea, especially in Asia Minor among Jews in the communities of the Jewish Diaspora. Early Christianity at its inception was a movement within Judaism directed to Jews.[10]

This intellectual ferment existed in a Roman Empire fraught with internal dissension and the almost constant rebellion along its frontiers from Britain to Judea, the Caucasus, and the eastern marches. Tyrannical rulers found in the adherents to Christianity who brooked no compromise in their monotheism convenient scapegoats for imperial instability. Nero's condemnation of Christians for setting the fire that destroyed much of the city of Rome in 64 came at a time when the emperor faced senatorial plots against his rule and had to call in troops to suppress the rebellion in Judea that would outlast his reign.

Persecutions of Christians occurred again during the reign of Domitian who faced rebellions along the Rhine and assassination. Attacks on Christians during the second century after adherence to Christianity became illegal were sporadic and were often the result of local mob violence rather than imperial decree.

After the Romans destroyed the Second Temple in Jerusalem in 70, however, the split between Christianity and Judaism grew. Christians, who believed that the Messiah had come, did not participate in the Jewish rebellion against Rome (66–70), which was both political and eschatological. Despondent at the loss of Jerusalem, most Jews rejected Christian overtures and continued to await the arrival of the Messiah.

The fact that Christians were not persecuted after the Jewish rebellion under Hadrian is evidence that the Roman authorities differentiated between Jews and Christians and that the split between Christianity and Judaism had become irrevocable. The Bar Kokhba revolt in 132–135, as this rebellion is known, with its messianic overtones led to Rome's decision to sever the ties between Jews and their homeland by renaming it Syria–Palastina. Jerusalem became a pagan cult center called Aelia Capitolina, and Jews were forbidden to enter the city except on the anniversary of the Temple's destruction (the ninth of the Jewish month of Av), when they were permitted to sit at the last remnant of the Jewish Temple, the Western Wall (also known as the Wailing Wall) and mourn. Events of the second century also marked the dispersion of the Jews throughout the world from Central Asia to Spain, where they became one minority among many in the empires where they lived.

Economic and political instability continued as the Roman Empire's traditional mechanisms for political control eroded. The emperors, with few troops under their direct command, relied on client peoples living on the periphery for defense of the imperial heartland, but that reliance began to break down toward the end of the second century. Despite the lengthy and stable tenures of both Antoninus Pius and Marcus Aurelius, drawn-out wars of rebellion by the tribes along the Rhine and Danube river borders and losses in the east against the Parthians severely taxed Rome's prestige and precarious economy. The spread of Christianity across the Roman Empire in the first and second centuries was paralleled by the expansion of the empire itself. Nevertheless, in Rome the old gods still ruled, reinforced by the cult of the divinity of the emperor himself. Both Jews and Christians suffered persecution, torture, and death.

By 200, the Roman Empire had reached its greatest extent, stretching from Britain to North Africa to the Caucasus to the borders of Persia. Fifty years later, however, the empire was in crisis. Civil war over imperial succession led to short reigns by military commanders, whose border origins seemingly provided them with experience at combating the increasing tribal invasions by consortia of Goths, Franks, and Visigoths from the Ukraine to Spain who settled within the borders of the empire. Such stop-gap economic revitalization measures as imperial citizenship (212), however, led more often than not to tax evasion and did not impede the decline of trade and monetary devaluation that accompanied the road to imperial bankruptcy. Urban decline, decentralization of imperial rule, economic stagnation more in the agriculturally based West than the more urban, wealthier East, and major incursions into Mesopotamia by Persians under a newly empowered Sassanid dynasty led Diocletian to create the Tetrarchy in 293, splitting the empire into eastern and western administrative components ruled by two emperors, Diocletian and Maximian, with two subordinate caesars, Galerius and Constantius. With the abdication of both of these emperors in 305, however, what was intended to be a smooth power shift when the caesars were promoted to emperors became a political free-for-all when no less than five military commanders were elevated by their troops to imperial office. The six-year civil war that ensued brought Constantius's son, Constantine, to power in 306.

Throughout this period of political chaos, Eastern mystery cults were a source of spiritual refuge for Rome's citizens. Christianity was certainly among the religions that benefited from the political situation, and it ultimately won out. The change in the character of the empire's leadership from the old imperial elite to a new military caste made acceptance of a new religion easier.[11]

Tradition has it that Constantine attributed his victory over imperial competitors to Christianity. His vision of the Cross in 312 at the Milvian Bridge ended the immediate persecution of Christians that had begun a decade earlier, but his "conversion" and the subsequent legalization of Christianity throughout the empire in the Edict of Milan still leave historians divided about Constantine's personality, his imperial motives, and his relationship to Christianity.[12] What is clear is that in the year 300 North Africa was the major home of Latin Christian literature, and 10 percent of the estimated fifty million people in the Roman Empire in 313 were Christian.[13] By the second half of Constantine's reign, the empire was not only reunited, but became synonymous with Christianity, and the emperor's authority was supreme politically and religiously.

Constantine set Christianity on its course not only by legalizing the faith and establishing Constantinople as the center of Christianity, but also by imposing imperial authority and gradually, through the mechanism of the councils of the church, official theological orthodoxy.

The city laid out by Constantine in 324 was dedicated in 330 as his new capital. Constantinople outshone Rome and the other patriarchates at Antioch, Alexandria, and Jerusalem, and it confirmed the gravitational pull of the empire to the East. It was strategically located on the Bosphorus midway between the Danube and the Euphrates. A center of Greco-Roman culture, it became a magnet for pagan and Christian alike, even though imperial largesse would now be directed to Christian rather than to polytheist institutions as support was slowly withdrawn from the Roman imperial cults. With legalization of all religions, Christians, who had begun to form their own bureaucratic organizations, found it easy to fill the positions available in the new imperial bureaucracy. Constantinople was to draw together a new ruling elite from the eastern Mediterranean into a single political community with a common interest: one god, one empire, and one emperor.[14]

With the official recognition of Christianity came a large building program for the new religion, accompanied by neglect of the old Roman temples. There was also an awareness of the significance of the Holy Places and the importance of visiting the sites that commemorated Jesus's life, preaching, and death. According to the church historian Eusebius, Constantine's mother, Helena, made a pilgrimage to Jerusalem around 325 and brought back part of the True Cross on which Jesus had been crucified. She also began the building of the Church of the Holy Sepulchre in Jerusalem and the Church of the Nativity in Bethlehem, both of which immediately became places of pilgrimage along with other sites in the Holy Land.[15] People began to travel not only to visit the sites but to take relics home in order to provide a sacred link between the places where Christianity originated and those towns to which it had spread. Although such church fathers as Jerome—who settled in Bethlehem and founded a monastery, where he spent time translating the Bible into Latin and writing biblical commentary—Augustine, and John Chrysostom disapproved of pilgrimages and the acquisition of relics, the lay public journeyed enthusiastically to the Holy Land. By the sixth century, itineraries and guidebooks had been produced to the Christian Holy Sites, the more than three hundred monasteries, and the numerous hostels that had been established as part of the pilgrimage service industry. Passage from Europe was relatively easy: Syrian-owned ships plied the Mediterranean between Provence or Visigothic Spain and the ports of Egypt or Syria, and caravans traveled the Middle East.[16]

Although Christianity had always been a missionary church, from the beginning missionary work was carried out by individuals, often merchants and tradesmen such as St. Paul and traveling preachers or "wanderers" who not only preached to the urban poor but also journeyed to remote rural areas. They talked about their faith, exorcised evil spirits, invoked divine wrath about sin and the world to come, and healed the sick through laying on of hands. For people accustomed to magic and miracles, this appeal led to the emotional embrace of Christianity and baptism.[17]

Some individuals attracted audiences by their ascetic piety. In the mid-fifth century at a spot forty miles east of Antioch, for example, Theodoret, bishop of Cyrus, witnessed an astonishing sight—a man standing on a pillar:

> [Even the Bedouins] in many thousands, enslaved to the darkness of impiety, were enlightened by the station upon the pillar. . . . They arrived in companies, 200 in one, 300 in another, occasionally a thousand. They renounced with their shouts their traditional errors; they broke up their venerated idols in the presence of that great light; and they foreswore the ecstatic rites of Aphrodite, the demon whose service they had long accepted. They enjoyed divine religious initiation and received their law instead spoken by that holy tongue (of Symeon). Bidding farewell to ancestral customs, they renounced also the diet of the wild ass or the camel. And I myself was witness to these things and heard them, as they renounced their ancestral impiety and submitted to evangelical instruction. Once even I was in the greatest danger: for he himself (Symeon) told them to approach to receive a priestly blessing from me, declaring they would draw the greatest benefits therefrom. But, in a most savage way they gathered at a run, and some snatched at me from in front, some from behind, others at my sides; and those a little removed, following on top of the others and reaching out with their hands, seized my beard, or took hold of my cloak. I would have suffocated under this enthusiastic onrush of theirs if, by his shouts, he (Symeon) had not put them all to flight.[18]

The base of Simeon the Stylite's pillar is still visible today, and so pillar sitting as a sign of piety (and an encouragement to pilgrimage) spread throughout the region.

Others, at first taking their cue from the Egyptian St. Antony to become hermits and monks, left their monasteries. Gregory the Wonderworker traveled through north-central Turkey. Monks worked among desert tribes from Sinai to southern Palestine and from Transjordan to Mesopotamia. Some of the most notable were Hilarion, from a monastery in Gaza, who earned reputation of miracle worker among Bedouin, and a monk called Moses, a hermit in the Sinai. These monks were instrumental in converting tribes along the periphery of the empire and created important source of military manpower for the Roman Empire. The monastic movement moved westward as well, with St. Benedict of Nursia founding the great monastery of Monte Cassino (site of a major battle in World War II) in the early sixth century. From there, monasteries following the Benedictine rule spread throughout western Europe.

Constantine's lifelong goal was the reunification of the empire following the chaos and divisions of the late third century. By legalizing Christianity, he attempted to use the early church councils as a tool in this effort to create both political unity and religious orthodoxy. In political terms, the councils, convened not by church leaders but by the emperor, were decisive power plays to ensure that the new capital of Constantinople be the seat of both imperial power and ecclesiastical authority. However, for the church itself, what they accomplished by the establishment of Christian orthodoxy was the codification of division rather than unity. These divisions, although usually presented as doctrinal splits, also represented linguistic and political differences. By 325, Rome, Antioch, and Alexandria had already eclipsed Jerusalem in ecclesiastical importance and not only represented different theological positions but were also vying for political supremacy within the church. The results of the church councils at Nicaea (325), Constantinople (381), Ephesus (431 and 449) and Chalcedon (451) can be seen as decisive power plays that in the end left Constantinople and Rome supreme, rejected Antiochene Nestorianism, and marginalized the Alexandrian Copts. What this meant in practical terms was the creation of a Greco-Roman Christian orthodox normative doctrine that rejected the other Eastern churches. They would look for converts in Persia and points east.[19]

There were four councils in the early period: the First Council of Nicaea, convened by Constantine himself in 325; the First Council of Constantinople, convened by Emperor Theodosius I in 381; the Council of Ephesus, convened by Emperor Theodosius II in 431; and the Council of Chalcedon, convened by Emperor Marcian in 451. It should be noted that at this period the councils were convened by the emperor (or empress)—that is, by the representative of political power rather than by the ecclesiastical power, either the pope or the patriarch, as would become the case in the second millennium. The importance of this conflation of imperial and ecclesiastical power is seen also in the emergence of the bishops as the secular political power in their cities, towns, and provinces in late antiquity and, most important, in the union of sacred and temporal power in Constantinople itself. The first seven councils are regarded as "ecumenical"—that is, they included representatives from the Eastern and Western branches of Christianity— whereas the medieval Lateran councils, which took place after the "Great Schism," involved only those churches that acknowledged the authority of the pope in Rome.

With the defeat of Licinius in 325, Constantine was in control of the entire empire, and in the same year he convened the First Council of Nicaea. All 1,800 bishops of the church were invited—1,000 from the East and 800 from the West—but only about 250 representatives actually attended, all but 5 of whom came from the East. The archbishops of Alexandria, Antioch, and Jerusalem were there as well as clergy from as far away as Persia, Armenia, Abkhazia (present-day Georgia), and today's France. The imperial importance of this council is indicated by the fact that Constantine himself offered to pay the attendees' expenses.[20]

One can see in the subjects discussed by the council Constantine's desire for unity and his use of the church to reinforce it. A firm distinction was drawn between Christians and Jews by separating the celebration of Easter, the central event in the Christian calendar, from the Jewish celebration of Passover. The council discussed and rejected Arianism, the teachings of Arius of Alexandria, who lived during the fourth century and preached that Jesus was not co-eternal and co-equal with God. Even after the council's rejection, however, Arianism continued to attract followers and became particularly important in the Germanic areas of western Europe and in Spain. Debates over the nature of Christ and the Trinity continued until the First Council of Constantinople, convened by Theodosius I in 381. This council was much smaller in scale than Nicaea, attended by only 150 church leaders, and was essentially the completion of the earlier council's work. Its revision of the Nicene Creed became the version still in use today and made firm the church's definition of the Trinity. However, the Christological argument was not yet decided and formed the basis for the discussions of the next two councils and the divisions that resulted from them.

The Council of Ephesus, convened by Theodosius II, grandson of Theodosius I, in 431 was attended by about two hundred church leaders, including representatives of the pope in Rome, who at this period acknowledged the primacy of the Constantinople patriarch. This council took place following the sack of Rome by Alaric in 410. The main topic of debate was Nestorianism, and the council concluded by declaring Nestorians and their beliefs anathema. Nestorius, patriarch of Constantinople from 428 to 431, held that Jesus had two distinct natures, human and divine, and he therefore objected to the description of Mary as "mother of God." The choice of Ephesus as the site of the council alluded specifically to that controversy because Ephesus is the traditional site of Mary's house after she fled Jerusalem following the crucifixion. The council essentially reflected a conflict between the theology of Antioch, represented by Nestorius, and the theology of Alexandria, represented by Cyril, bishop of Alexandria, who was supported by the emperor.

A result of the Council of Ephesus, which anathematized Nestorianism, was the splitting off of those who adhered to Nestorius and the See of Antioch and whose language was Syriac from the Greek Church, both in Alexandria and in Constantinople. Christianity had come early to Mesopotamia and thence to Persia, and Edessa became the center of Eastern, non-Orthodox Christianity.[21] From Edessa, capital of a border kingdom established in the second century BCE by the Semitic, Syriac/Aramaic-speaking Lakhmid tribes of northern Arabia on trade routes just outside the boundary of the Roman Empire, the Nestorian Church of the East spread eastward into the Persian Empire, and by 225 CE there were more than twenty Christian bishoprics in Mesopotamia.[22]

The real importance of Edessa for Christianity was the establishment there in 363 of a school called the School of the Persians, which educated the Christian youth of Persia. The school had moved from Nisibis, farther to the east, when that town was conquered by Persia. The language of the school, as of the town, was Syriac, and the earliest Syriac manuscripts for which dates can be firmly ascribed come from the fifth century. The Nestorians were also instrumental in spreading Christianity from Persia eastward to India and along the Silk Road as far as China, carried primarily by merchants and traders. The Nestorian Church, properly called the Church of the East, did not anathematize Nestorius, though the church continues to insist that it does not accept Nestorius's view of the dual nature of Christ, and in 1994 the church signed a declaration with the Roman Catholic Church in which both recognized the legitimacy of each other's theological positions.

The fourth council of the early church was held at Chalcedon, near Constantinople, in 451. It was convened by Emperor Marcian, and, like the Council of Ephesus, focused on the definition of the nature of Christ. Again, it resulted in a split in the church that remains unhealed to this day. Five hundred delegates attended the council, which was presided over by the papal legate, and they confirmed the doctrine of the dual nature of Christ, promoted by Pope Leo I and Flavian of Constantinople. This determination was unacceptable to many of the Eastern churches, hereafter referred to as "monophysite," including the Armenian Apostolic Church, the Coptic Church, the Ethiopian Church, the Syrian Orthodox Church, and the Jacobite Syriac Church, and they remain out of communion with the Roman Catholic and Greek Orthodox churches.

In essence, the Council of Chalcedon in 451 completed the alienation of the Syriac-speaking churches from the Greek church of Constantinople. A few years later the monophysite Syrian church, based in Antioch, and the Nestorian church split, and by the end of the fifth century Emperor Zeno (471–491) closed the school at Edessa and expelled Nestorians from the Roman Empire. In 498, the Nestorian catholicos assumed the title "Patriarch of the East," based in the Persian capital of Ctesiphon, and the church continues to call itself the Church of the East to this day. The school of Edessa was moved back to Nisibis.

Like the other monophysite churches, the Armenian Apostolic Church retained its own language, and it is virtually unique in Christianity in not having any missionary impetus or activity. Armenia was converted to Christianity by Gregory in the early fourth century, and as far as we can tell, the Armenian Church never tried to convert anyone else. Thus, it considers itself the first national church. Christianity had begun to come in from Syria as early as the first century through Jewish settlements in southwestern Armenia, where there is evidence of an organized Christian community by the mid-third century.[23] Armenian tradition dates the conversion of the nation to Christianity from the arrival of Gregory from Hellenized Caesarea in Cappadocia and his conversion of King Trdat III in 301. It is this tradition that led the Republic of Armenia to celebrate seventeen hundred years of Christianity in 2001. Scholars now agree, however, that conversion probably took place in 314, immediately after the Edict of Milan in 313. The early liturgies used in Armenia were in either Syriac or Greek, depending on whether conversion had come from Syria or Cappadocia and on whether the region was under Persian or Roman control. Neither language was understood by the people, so the priest would translate relevant portions into Armenian.[24] The invention of the Armenian alphabet in the early fifth century and the subsequent translation of the Bible and the liturgy into Armenian resulted in a flowering of Armenian literature and was critical to the emergence of a sense of Armenian nationality, linking Armenians whether they lived under Roman or Persian control. The language and the church became the connectors that bound Armenians together into a "nation" in spite of their location on the ever-shifting frontier between the Roman Empire and the Persian Empire. Even when Armenians were divided on both sides of this frontier, the fact that they shared a church and a language codified by its own alphabet created a unity and exclusivity that was unique in the region.

The political division of Armenia in 387, which left most of it in Persian hands, was followed by the split of the Armenian Church from the Roman–Greek orthodoxy at the Council of Chalcedon in 451. Although the royal family had been converted by Gregory in the early fourth century, the conversion of the population was a much longer process, probably effected by "unknown and unorganized missionaries" and "the unorganized activity of wandering holy men."[25] The Armenian Church, in large part because of its use of Armenian as a liturgical language, remained the province of Armenians and did not seek to spread beyond them. Its role was to buttress the border nation of Armenia, not to spread Christianity.

All four of the first church councils focused primarily on what we now regard as Eastern Christianity. This should be no surprise, considering that the first council was part of Constantine's effort to integrate the empire as he moved his capital from Rome to his new city of Constantinople and that Rome itself was sacked by Alaric in 410. The language of the councils was Greek, not Latin, although Constantine's own language was Latin and his speeches had to be translated into Greek. The divisions in the church that were finalized in the first four councils were based not only on theology, specifically the definitions of the nature of the Trinity and of Christ, but also on language. The groups that deviated from the orthodoxy of Constantinople spoke other languages: Syriac, Arabic, Persian, Armenian, Coptic, and, of course, Latin, though the split between the Greek and Latin churches did not occur definitively until the middle of the eleventh century. To some extent, the boundaries of Christianity mirrored imperial boundaries. Christianity spread to Mesopotamia in its earliest centuries, but that form of Christianity was not necessarily the Christianity of Constantinople. The councils of the early church formalized divisions that paralleled the political and linguistic ones, but they also established the statements of belief that continue to be accepted by both the Greek and the Roman churches to this day.

Although the Roman Empire imposed religious orthodoxy under Christian rule after the brief interlude of paganism under Julian, political unity was elusive. By the end of the fourth century, the empire was divided once again as military usurpers seized power in the West and tried to suppress the increasing local rebellions against Roman rule. Rome, the "Holy City" of the pagan Roman Empire, would become the Holy City of Christianity, but all new ideas were expressed in Greek and brought to Rome from the East.[26] Although the empire in the West existed but in name only, the empire in the East, although undergoing political upheaval, emerged restrengthened under Justinian (527–565), when the Roman Empire, now based on Constantinople, reached the greatest extent it would achieve for the next thousand years, stretching from Britain in the north to North Africa, Ethiopia, and Yemen in the south, to Persia, and even to China in the east. Emperor Justinian had restored the Roman Empire but in the process left it exhausted and beset by challenges on all sides.

To the north and west, the empire continued to be pressed by Germanic tribes, many of which had adopted some form of Christianity as they moved south, though the northernmost regions remained pagan. In Britain, Christianity had been known in the second and third centuries, but it was now pushed to the Celtic regions in the west and particularly to Ireland, which became the repository and preserver of monastic learning. In 596, Pope Gregory I sent missionaries to Britain to convert the Anglo-Saxon population, and these Christians then returned to the Germanic areas of northern Europe to convert that population.

To the south and east, Byzantium was pressed by the Persian Empire, which, under the Sassanid dynasty, reached the Mediterranean in the Levant and conquered Jerusalem in 614. For more than a thousand years, Greeks and Persians had been in almost constant conflict. Since the Persian Wars of the fourth century BCE, Greeks, Macedonians, and Romans had fought in Asia Minor and the Middle East against the various dynasties that ruled the Persian empires of the Iranian plateau. The border between them shifted constantly in the region between Mesopotamia and the Mediterranean, with the Persians occasionally penetrating as far as the Bosphorus, although the Greeks (or the Greco-Roman Empire) rarely moved into Mesopotamia itself after Alexander the Great. The Sassanid Persian capital, Ctesiphon, was located near what later would be Baghdad, and Mesopotamia served as the breadbasket and economic center of the Persian Empire. In this frontier zone between East and West, the syncretic religion of Manichaeism developed in the third century, incorporating features of Christianity, Zoroastrianism (the Persian state religion), and Buddhism, sending missionaries to Spain by the fifth century and China by the seventh.

A number of Arab tribes living in Syria and Mesopotamia acted as military surrogates for the major powers, and many converted to Christianity. Despite their alliance with the Byzantines, however, the Syrian Ghaznavids were monophysites, retaining their faith even after the Council of Chalcedon, when the Jacobites and Copts were branded as heretics. The Arab Lakhmids, who lived on the Persian border, adopted an anti-Byzantine Christianity and became Nestorians, advancing Christianity to the east. Although it was true that the Greek Orthodox Christianity of the Byzantine Empire dominated imperial domains, in the contest with Islam that would soon occur, Eastern Christians, at times persecuted by the dominant Greeks, played a not insignificant role in the Arab conquest.

At the beginning of the sixth century, Persia, abandoning its traditional Central Asian orientation, built itself into the cultural and financial capital of the region, and in 603 Khusro II invaded the Byzantine Empire. By 614, Persia had taken Jerusalem, Egypt fell in 619, and in 620 Persian forces were within sight of Constantinople itself. Persia's dream of uniting the Fertile Crescent seemed achievable. But Byzantium roused itself as Emperor Heraclius joined with the Khazar Turks of southern Russia to attack Persia from the north in 627, and in 628 Khusro II was assassinated by his ministers. War and a major outbreak of bubonic plague that decimated urban areas of the Middle East weakened both empires, left the settled areas of the Fertile Crescent in ruins, and set the stage for the Islamic conquests.

Muslim tradition holds that Muhammad was born in 570 in Mecca and at the age of forty began to preach monotheism to the Arabs. His flight from Mecca to Medina in 622 (hijra) marks the beginning of the Islamic calendar and the creation of an Islamic socioreligious polity that at the death of the Muslim prophet carried the new faith, Islam, out of Arabia into the Middle East, across North Africa, and into Europe. Both the Byzantine Empire and the Persian Empire were in disarray, having exhausted each other in battle, their populations depleted by war and disease. Both empires had also neglected the alliances and the fortresses that had defended the settled areas from the desert. After suppressing domestic rebellion, the Arab armies exploded out of the Arabian Peninsula, conquering much of the Middle East and North Africa by the end of the seventh century. Military acumen, religious zeal, and outright luck contributed to Arab victories against the Byzantine and Persian empires. Defeat of the Byzantine army in 636 at the battle of Yarmuk and the subsequent surrender of Antioch and Jerusalem within two years opened Syria to Arab armies and forced the Byzantines back into Anatolia. In 653–654, Muslim armies reached the shores of the Bosphorus. Yet despite repeated Arab attempts to take Constantinople, the Byzantine imperial capital survived with the support of its Christian Armenian allies of Cilicia, eastern Anatolia, and Armenia to the northeast.[27]

Meanwhile, Muslim victories over the Persians at Qadisiya led to the collapse of the Persian Sassanid Empire to the east. With control of vast new territory came the formation of the first Arab Empire under the Umayyad Caliphate and the shift of the Islamic political center from Arabia to Damascus. Less than one hundred years later, the Abbasid dynasty centered their regime at a new capital at Baghdad, just north of the old Persian capital of Ctesiphon in order to rule an empire that now stretched from Iran west across North Africa. Alexandria fell in 642, but it was another fifty years before Carthage was taken in 697. In 711, a combined Arab and Berber army from North Africa, led by Tariq bin Zayd and owing allegiance to the Umayyad caliph in Damascus, defeated the Visigoths in the battle of Guadalete, near Gibraltar (Jebel al-Tariq), killing the Visigothic king Roderick, and Spain lay open to them. The small Muslim army moved inexorably northward, taking Cordoba and the Visigoth capital Toledo virtually without a fight, and by 715 controlled most of Spain. It was not until 732, just a hundred years after Muhammad's death, that the Arab advance northward in Europe was stopped at Tours, only 150 miles south of Paris.

It would be a mistake to regard the Arabs who moved north into the settled areas of Syria and Mesopotamia as strangers to the region. They spoke Arabic rather than Greek, so their language was similar to the Aramaic spoken in the area; many of them were related to the Arab Christian tribes that acted as surrogates for both the Byzantines and the Persians. They were also part of a commercial continuum that stretched from Mecca and Medina to Petra and Palmyra through areas where both Christians and Jews lived. Islam and the Qu'ran were part of the intellectual mix of sacred texts and religious practices of Zoroastrianism, Christianity, and Judaism. Peoples in the region shared the same pilgrimage sites, most notably Jerusalem.[28] The expansion of Christianity around the Mediterranean, however, came to a halt. Now it was Islam's turn to roll back the Christianization of the old Roman Empire. The momentum of conversion had shifted.

Although today we think of the Middle East as part of "the Muslim world," the conversion of the population from Christianity to Islam, much like the Christianization of the region, took several centuries and was never fully completed, particularly in Egypt. When the Zoroastrian-linked Sassanid regime in Iran fell, Persian converts saw benefits in forging a connection with the new rulers. Meanwhile, in Iraq, which became the seat of the new Muslim Abbasid Empire with links from Persia to Spain, conversion took a bit longer, with the process in Syria even slower, lagging perhaps 150 years behind Iran. In both Syria and Iraq, there was a considerably greater Christian presence than in Iran. Few residents of Syria had converted to Islam before the end of the eighth century, and by the end of the ninth century there was still a significant Christian population in place, which, even though not Muslim, had become Arabized as Arabic spread as the language of official business.[29] A similar process occurred in Egypt, where the ninth century appears to have been critical in the conversion process, though Coptic Christians were still in the majority in Egypt until the tenth century.[30]

The pace of the Arab conquest and the expansion of Muslim rule shocked the Christian residents of the Middle East. To some, the defeat of Christian forces was punishment wrought by God against those who were lax in their beliefs and signified the advent of the apocalypse. The End of Days would begin with the arrival of the "Ishmaelites," who would defeat the Greeks, wrote the Syrian called the "pseudo-Methodius," whose writings in Syriac were later translated into Greek and Latin. The Israelites, in turn, would be delivered by the "King of the Greeks," who would inflict incalculable suffering on the Arabs and usher in the Second Coming.[31] Others saw the Arabs as divine agents sent to punish those who flirted with heretical beliefs, be they the Arian Visigoths in Spain cited by the Latin Chronicle of 754 or, in the eyes of the Nestorian John bar Penkaye, both the Byzantine and monophysite churches.[32]

As Islam became entrenched and the End of Days did not occur, Christian writings about Arabs, Islam, and Muslims shifted from the apocalyptic to disputations of the faith and its legitimacy and provided descriptions of Muhammad and Islam that found their way into northern Europe. These works were written primarily by Christians living under Islamic rule, notably the eighth-century John of Damascus in Syria, who contended that Islam was a primitive form of Arianism brought to the Arabs by a false and licentious pretender.[33] Likely the earliest Greek polemic against Islam, John's *De haeresibus* did not have a counterpart in the West until the Spanish martyrs' movement in the ninth century, when some Catholics deliberately and publicly denounced Muhammad and Islam.[34]

Islam, for its part, had an ambivalent view toward Christianity. As monotheists with a revealed text, Christians were considered a "People of the Book" and thus to be accorded toleration. In truth, however, the Arabs and the Byzantines were at war. Nevertheless, a system of religious accommodation evolved as Muslims came to rule over an area where most people were Christian.

As a minority in a sea of Christians, the Muslim conquerors had to come to terms with the population they ruled. Over time, policies were adopted to safeguard the new faith, to protect the Islamic community, and to enforce the domination of the Muslim rulers over the subordinate Christian, Jewish, and Zoroastrian populations. Often referred to as the "Pact of Omar," policies toward non-Muslim monotheists (*dhimmi*) evolved that stipulated that in exchange for legal protection they could not join the army. They were not allowed to proselytize, to build new houses of worship, or to renovate those in disrepair, and they had to wear clothing that distinguished them from Muslims. In addition, minorities paid a head tax, or *jizya*, to the Muslim authorities. Built into this system of coexistence that was designed to safeguard the integrity of Islam and to keep the faith-based communities separate was religious autonomy for Jews and for Christians of all denominations.

Christians functioned in various ways in the new, Muslim-controlled society, often very successfully. For example, the centuries following the Arab conquest marked the zenith of the Nestorian Church at a time when the church in the West was in decline. Not only had the Nestorian Church's members held important positions in the Persian and later Abbasid courts, but the church had also mounted one of the most remarkable Christian missionary expansions to the east. Between the sixth and eighth centuries, Nestorian missionaries had spread Christianity throughout the Persian Empire and east to India, Central Asia, and even China. Nestorian missionary efforts were based on monasticism, as later Western missionary activity would be. Nestorian monasticism dates from the fourth century but after a decline was reformed and revived in the sixth century by Abraham of Kashkar (491–586), who had been trained in Coptic monasteries in Egypt. The monastic rule emphasized "celibacy, chastity, poverty, fasting, silence, prayer, manual labour and study,"[35] and the monasteries that spread particularly in the sixth and seventh centuries provided a corps of educated civil servants for the Persian and Abbasid empires as well as an army of dedicated missionaries who spread outward along the Silk Road and accompanying the Muslim conquests. Whenever a new bishopric was set up, a school, library, and hospital were also established.

The first Nestorian mission to China took place in 635, just prior to the Muslim conquest of the Persian Empire. In 1625, Jesuit missionaries found a stone monument in Shensi Province in western China describing the first visit of a Persian monk and including an outline of the Bible and Christianity in Chinese. Christian—that is, Nestorian—influence in the East peaked in the seventh through ninth centuries. The Nestorian Christians provided the means of transmission of Hellenic learning from the Roman Empire to the Muslim Empire, although their language was Syriac rather than Greek. Treatment of the Christians under both the Muslim and Chinese empires varied, with persecutions taking place periodically, particularly as the balance of conversion began to tip increasingly toward Islam. However, Nestorian clergy served the caliphs in important ways, even carrying out diplomatic missions to Constantinople and Rome.[36]

The decline of the Abbasid Empire and the increasing chaos along the Central Asian trade routes caused by the Mongol invasions diminished the role of the Nestorian Christians in the East. There is little documentation of Nestorian presence in China after the ninth century, when the Chinese emperor forced priests and monks to return to secular life, and after the fourteenth century the Nestorians sank into poverty, ignorance, and seclusion until they reemerged in the nineteenth century—not as missionaries themselves, but as the objects of Western missionary attention.[37] We ultimately cannot know to what extent Nestorian Christianity and the monasteries established along the Silk Road converted the resident population or primarily served the traders who came from Persia and Mesopotamia. There is some evidence of conversion of the Mongol elite, but that conversion did not last. By the nineteenth century, the only remaining Nestorian communities were in the mountainous border areas of Kurdistan between the Ottoman and Persian empires and in south India, where the Church of Saint Thomas, known as the "Church of Saint Thoma," survives to this day.

As the Muslim Arabs consolidated their control over much of the Mediterranean world, the remaining Christian powers, Byzantium and Rome, were forced to look elsewhere for support. Rome looked north and west to the rapidly developing Frankish kingdoms, and the Byzantines, in search of political as well as religious alliances, looked to the Slavs north of the Black Sea in Bulgaria, Russia, the Caucasus, and the Caspian. The Franks also looked north, to Scandinavia and the Baltic states.

Scholars debate whether Muslim control of the Mediterranean and its sea trade severed links between Rome and Constantinople and caused a major economic and cultural contraction in Western Europe that shifted the center of power to the north because of Muslim pressure on southern France. Regardless of cause and effect, it is clear that Charlemagne's short-lived revival of the Roman Empire (800–814) fragmented after his death because of the disintegration of the imperial state and attacks by the Vikings. Nevertheless, relations between East and West were never totally broken because the Muslims accommodated Christians' requests for safe travel to the Holy Land.[38] By the end of the ninth century, however, visitors to Jerusalem reported that the hostel facilities there had become shabby. Arab conquests in Crete, Sicily, and southern Italy and the Norse invasions in northern Europe had made travel dangerous and expensive.

The decentralization of church authority that accompanied the collapse of Charlemagne's western European empire resulted in secular control over areas of the church. By the early tenth century, the sale of church offices and indulgences as well as the issue of married clergy were areas increasingly coming under scrutiny by some clerics and their lay supporters who advocated change. The abbey at Cluny, founded in 911 by William of Aquitaine, which practiced a modified form of the Benedictine rule, became the catalyst for the centralization of church authority under the leadership of a strengthened papacy in the context of what came to be known as the Cluniac Reforms. The Cluniac Reforms of the ninth and tenth centuries brought the monastic movement and its considerable lands under papal authority. With this new economic power base, not only did the papacy became involved in struggles with the European monarchs over issues of ecclesiastical authority, but the church was able to become involved in Italian and Byzantine politics and to authorize a missionary effort to Spain to convert Muslims to Christianity.[39]

The political situation in the Middle East brought the two parts of Christendom together once again. Muslim political unity had already disintegrated in the eighth century when dynasties in Spain declared their independence from Baghdad imperial rule. As Muslim power weakened in the tenth century, the Christian reconquest of Spain began. At the same time, not only had Shi'ite dynasties taken power in areas of Persia, but the Ismailis, a schismatic Shi'ite sect, had overrun North Africa and ruled Egypt as the Fatimid dynasty. Establishing their capital at Cairo, the Fatimids extended their rule north to Syria and took control of the Muslim Holy Cities of Mecca and Medina, seriously threatening the Abbasid hegemony of Sunni Islam. The arrival of the Turks from Central Asia west through Iran, Iraq, and eastern Turkey signaled zealous Sunni incursions into both Byzantine and Muslim territory.

In the East, although by the tenth century the Byzantine Empire sought merely to survive because it lacked the political will and military resources to challenge the Muslims to the south and east, the policies of Emperor Basil II resulted in renewed vigor. Conversion of the Russian Slavs to Greek Orthodoxy was proceeding. At the same time, expansion of imperial domains in the Balkans into Hungary and an enlightened policy toward the newly converted Bulgars that permitted them their own Christian rite and language provided the empire with a secure western heartland when the Seljuk Turks began to overrun eastern Anatolia, where Basil's eastern policy left the empire undefended. By breaking the power of the landed magnates and bringing the Armenian kings under Byzantine control, Constantinople forcibly removed Armenians from the eastern frontier to southern Asia Minor, where they established the Kingdom of Cilicia, leaving a political vacuum that facilitated the Seljuk incursions after the Byzantine defeat at Manzikert in 1071. Byzantine relations with the West were also complicated by tension over the designation of the Holy Roman Empire in Catholic Christendom and Rome's presumption of catholic authority; but the threat both to the pope and to the Byzantines by the Norman conquest of southern Italy and Sicily brought East and West together.

The reform popes of the second half of the eleventh century reinterpreted the relationship between the Western church and the church of Constantinople.[40] Both churches regarded themselves as the rightful successors of the Roman Empire, and both were confronting Muslim challenges on their borders. Yet their responses to these challenges were quite different. In the West, the Spanish *reconquista* steadily pushed Muslim control south, whereas in the East the Byzantine Empire and with it the Greek church turned inward, choosing not to build on the momentum of its successes in the tenth century. A new Muslim threat was rising to the east of Byzantium in the form of the Seljuk Turks, and Constantinople sought to preserve itself by making alliances against them.

In 1054, Pope Leo IX, the first of the reforming popes, sent Cardinal Humbert and Frederick of Lorraine to visit Constantinople in an effort to establish an alliance against the Normans in Sicily. The cardinal and the nobleman found the patriarch Michael Cerularius irritating and placed a bull of excommunication on him, though they apparently got along much better with the emperor, Constantine IX (1042–1055). This excommunication, afterward described as the "Great Schism,"[41] had little effect either on Rome or on Constantinople, but the preparation for the journey had led to a rethinking of Rome's relationship to the Greeks. The pope came to regard the patriarch as his son and the Church of Constantinople as the daughter of the Church of Rome. As a result of this new view of the Byzantines, after their defeat by the Seljuk Turks at Manzikert in 1071, which brought the Turks to the doorstep of Constantinople, Pope Gregory VII launched a military expedition in 1074 to assist the Eastern Christians. Ultimately, in 1095, Emperor Alexius I Comnenus sent envoys to the council of Piacenza to ask Pope Urban II for aid, a request that led directly to the pope's famous sermon in Clermont in November of that year proclaiming the First Crusade.

TWO

The Latin West in the Middle East

Pilgrimage, Crusade, and Mission

After the seventh century, Western efforts at conversion in the Middle East centered primarily on members of the Eastern churches to Catholicism rather than Muslims to Christianity.[1] Taken together, the Great Schism of 1054, the Crusades, and the Sack of Constantinople in 1204 marked the changing relationship between Eastern and Western Christendom. As a result of the Muslim conquests of the seventh century, the gradual conversion of the population of the Mediterranean basin, Mesopotamia, and Persia to Islam, and the conversion of northern Europe to Christianity, most Christians were living in western Europe. In response to this new situation, in the second half of the eleventh century the reform popes redefined the relationship between Rome and Constantinople, regarding the relationship between pope and Greek patriarch to be like father and son and that of Rome and Constantinople to be like mother and daughter[2] and regarding the Eastern churches not as part of the orthodox church, but rather as proper objects of missionary concern, though not of conquest. In other words, the popes believed it necessary to "convert" Eastern Christians to Western orthodoxy, as defined by the pope in Rome. In light of this relationship, how do we view the Crusades?

Although the Muslim conquest of the Holy Land impeded pilgrimage, travel to Jerusalem and Christian sites never ceased altogether. Expensive though such travel may have been during a period when sea voyages in the Mediterranean were imperiled by pirates, individual pilgrims ventured eastward for the adventure, but also, it should be noted, to receive pardon for the sin of murder. By the eighth century, the number of pilgrims from different parts of Europe had increased to the point that Charlemagne requested and was granted permission by the Abbasid caliph of Baghdad, Harun al-Rashid, to build a hostel in Jerusalem. As a result of the Norse invasions in northern Europe as well as Arab conquests in southern Italy, Sicily, and Crete, there was a lull in travel in the ninth century, but when conditions in the Mediterranean improved, travel resumed.

By the tenth and early eleventh centuries, pilgrimage traffic was revitalized, in no small measure a result of disunity in the Muslim world. Safe travel by sea from Italy to the Syrian coast was achieved when the Byzantines suppressed piracy in the eastern Mediterranean, and the Italian maritime republics opened trade with Muslims. In addition, the land route from Byzantine Anatolia south was opened for pilgrimage to Jerusalem when the Fatimids, a Shi'i dynasty, gained control over Egypt and the Levant. In their confrontation with the Sunni Abbasid dynasty in Baghdad, the Fatimids worked with Constantinople to add the Muslim Holy Cities of Mecca and Medina to their territory. In 1019, after Hungary converted to Christianity and the Byzantines annexed the Balkan Peninsula, it became easier to make the journey from Central Europe or Flanders to Syria.

At first, the sporadic problems that did occur were not severe enough to inhibit travel. The Egyptian caliph al-Hakim's short-lived persecution of Christians and the destruction of the Church of the Holy Sepulchre in 1009 produced no major Christian reaction, and the church was speedily rebuilt under his successor. As conditions improved, the numbers of European pilgrims increased, in part because travel was more secure, but also in part because the Cluniac Reforms popularized pilgrimage to the Holy Sites as a means to expiate sin. By the eleventh century, ecclesiastically authorized pilgrimage had become so fashionable that Charlemagne as well as King Arthur were said to have gone, though in truth neither ever set foot in the Holy Land. Hostels were built, routes were marked, and a service industry to provide food and lodging emerged as thousands of Europeans—rich and poor, nobles, kings, and commoners—made the trip. The Norman count of Anjou and some forty Norman pilgrims made the pilgrimage during the first decade of the eleventh century. It was said that in 1065 some ten thousand (probably more like seven thousand) men and women came as part of a German pilgrimage contingent.[3] By the last quarter of the eleventh century, there was a sustained European interest in the Holy Land and the road to Jerusalem. The successful Seljuk Turk invasions of Byzantine territory did not initially interfere with pilgrimages. However, when the Turks blocked routes to Jerusalem during the last decade of the eleventh century, Byzantine calls for aid were reinforced by European reaction, resulting in the First Crusade.

Although the Crusades embody the beginning of a power shift from East to West in Christianity and mark the reentry of the West into politics of the Middle East, they must also be seen in the context of European power politics. The conflict between church and state over whose rule was supreme and the maneuverings of European princes to accumulate territory resulted in what would become the modern states of Europe. By 1095, Europe had undergone major political changes. The area of Christendom had expanded north and east into Germany and the Slavic lands, and the Christian reconquest of Spain was under way. Charlemagne's now-disintegrated vision of Roman unity was being replaced by new monarchies and with them the church's participation in European politics as both church and state struggled to increase and consolidate power. The contest over which authority was supreme—spiritual or temporal, pope's or king's—was played out in a number of ways: church reform; papal involvement in competing feudal loyalties; the election of the Holy Roman emperor, whose domain stretched from eastern France and Germany into Italy; and the appointment of Catholic clerics in the domains of the kings, counts, and bishops. By the end of the eleventh century, the Cluniac Reforms, which had begun in the early tenth century as a monastic revival movement, produced a church hierarchy of papal legates or agents designated to carry out the pope's will; prelates who heard cases in the name of Rome helped consolidate papal power over Europe. Nevertheless, Pope Gregory VII and Pope Urban II remained enmeshed in political struggles with the kings of England and France as well as with the Holy Roman emperor, all the while attempting to use their authority to curtail the violence that plagued medieval Europe. The Crusades, among other things, were a papal attempt to divert the violence from western Europe to the East.

Urban II's call to Christians at Clermont in 1095 did not come out of nowhere. It followed an appeal from the Byzantine emperor Alexius I Comnenus in March of that year for assistance against the Seljuk Turks, who had defeated the Byzantines at the battle of Manzikert in 1071, conquered Jerusalem, and moved close to Constantinople itself. There are numerous and somewhat contradictory accounts of the spectacle staged in central France, especially with its sermon provoking enthusiastic cries of "God will it" from the participants, who then took vows to take back the Holy Land from the Saracens. Questions remain about the text of Urban's sermon as well as about his actual intention. Why were these wars fought? To assist Eastern Christians against Muslims? To save Jerusalem? To protect pilgrimage routes? To establish a Latin presence? To bring Eastern Christians under Roman ecclesiastical hegemony? Or to convert Muslims? Depending on time and place, all of the above. The important point is that the First Crusade established a paradigm for relations among Western Christendom, the Eastern Christian churches, and the Muslim Middle East for centuries to come.

The embassy sent from Byzantium in 1095 arrived at a council already in session at Piacenza, composed of bishops from France, Italy, and Germany. The ambassadors brought with them an appeal from the Byzantine emperor Alexius I Comnenus to the pope, encouraging Westerners to help defend the Eastern church against the Turks, who were making successful inroads into Byzantine territory in Anatolia. Later that year Urban replied to this request with the sermon at Clermont, urging men not only to assist the emperor, but to liberate the Eastern churches from Muslim tyranny and Jerusalem from Muslim occupation. "The justification for the crusade, therefore, was the reconquest of Christian territory, and especially Christ's own patrimony, which had been usurped by the Muslims, and the pope's appeal was presented in such a way that it conformed to the criterion of a just cause."[4]

For the feudal knights of Europe's warrior class, a military aristocracy that worked both to safeguard the church and to advance secular political interests, the sanction of a "just war" by Augustine of Hippo, and a legitimate authority for defense or recovery of property justified violence for religious purposes, even though murder was a sin. At times accompanied by priests, the knights fought against the pagan Saxons and Avars to the north and east. In the Spanish marches, Christians, in their reconquest of Iberia, steadily pushed the Muslims south. They also wreaked havoc in Europe, fighting each other over territory and becoming a threat to the public order. Attempts by the church to curtail military violence through the "peace of God" and the "truce of God" that stipulated protection of noncombatants and periods when hostilities ceased had limited success, especially when they were brought to bear at the same time that the church was changing the definition

of war. Popes enlisted secular allies in their political struggles, offering abso-
lution for sins so that war, like pilgrimage, became an act of penance. This
relationship set a precedent for later, when Crusaders would fight against
Christians in the struggle against heresy.[5]

From Urban's perspective, Christian unity was a prerequisite for the papal
vision of Rome's role within the church, but Constantine, Constantinople,
and the Holy Land, in particular Jerusalem, held tremendous symbolic significance for the pope. After his speech at Clermont, Pope Urban spread his
message of crusade around France, bringing with him from Constantinople
to Rome pieces of the True Cross, giving them to the churches he dedicated.
In this way, "in the Lateran palace and thanks to Constantine and his mother,
the popes lived in the midst of relics of the Holy Land and of Jerusalem.
They were an ever-present and potent reality."[6] But once the First Crusade
got under way, relations with the Eastern church receded in importance as
the taking of Jerusalem became the primary goal.

The First Crusade set the norms for relations—between Catholics and
Greeks, between Catholics and the Eastern churches—for the next two hundred years. Disputes between Greeks and Catholics had always been based
more on political than theological concerns. Popes repeatedly sought rap-
prochement between the churches. They insisted that the Byzantines recog-
nize Roman hegemony, but the Byzantines were still a political power and
remained important players in Middle East politics. Rome, however, considered the other Eastern churches—with the possible exception of the Armenians—beyond the pale, heretical, and requiring conversion to the true faith.
Nevertheless, conversion was not the objective of the Crusaders who set out
for the Holy Land in 1096.

Three forces set out from Europe to the Middle East. The first, the "People's Crusade," led by followers of Peter the Hermit, marched through Germany in 1097. Departing before the regular army was constituted, they began the crusade against the infidel by massacring Jews in communities along
the way. After being denied entry into Constantinople by the Byzantines,
who feared for the safety of their city, most of the force was annihilated by
the Turks in Asia Minor. Next, the regular armies—one led by nobles from
northern and southern France and the other the Norman conquerors of Sicily—converged in Constantinople, where the leadership met with Byzantine
emperor Alexius I.

Alexius, recovering from the shock that the approaching Latin armies
numbered in the tens of thousands instead of the hundreds of mercenary

troops he was expecting, feared for his empire. So the Byzantines, as they had for centuries in the face of external threat, employed time-honored strategies to meet their never-changing goal of safeguarding Constantine's city and the integrity of the Byzantine Empire. Power, panoply, bribery, and diplomacy— with war as the last resort—came into play in Byzantine–Latin negotiations during the spring of 1097. Emperor Alexius exacted an oath that Crusader leaders would return any conquered lands that had been part of the Byzantine Empire. In return, Alexius was to provide weapons, food, and expertise as well as to assist the Crusaders through their passage from Asia Minor to Syria. But the Byzantine behavior smacked of perfidy to the Crusaders. The Greeks outmaneuvered the Latins at the Battle of Nicaea in May and secretly took control of the city. They later neglected to send troops to Antioch during the winter and spring of 1098 when it seemed that the Turks would overcome the Crusader siege at Antioch. Feeling betrayed, the Crusaders carried anti-Byzantine propaganda back to Europe, despite Greek protestations that Byzantine decisions to keep their troops at home were based on intelligence that the Crusaders were losing at Antioch. From their side, the Byzantines had distrusted the Latins, who in direct contravention to their oaths incorporated Antioch into the Latin kingdoms to be ruled by Bohemond the Norman—erstwhile enemy of the Byzantines in southern Italy and Sicily. Subsequent Byzantine diplomatic dealings with the Muslims added to mutual suspicions and would play a role leading to the Latin sack of Constantinople in 1204.

By 1098, then, with Latin–Greek relations deteriorating, the goal of the Crusade had decidedly become to take Jerusalem. Poor planning and logistics; lack of money, food, and supplies; and difficult travel over mountains in harsh weather took their toll on the men who had been on the road for three years. Atrocities against Muslim communities marked the Crusader march through Syria. After the fortuitous discovery of the Holy Lance during the siege at Antioch, the Crusaders renewed their religious fervor and took Jerusalem—massacring the Muslim and Jewish inhabitants until blood was up to their ankles.[7] By the end of the First Crusade, with physical Jerusalem in Christian hands, concerns about the needs of Eastern Christendom hardly figured in subsequent lore about the First Crusade.[8]

For the Crusaders in 1099, the conquest of Jerusalem was not only a miraculous event, but a real example of divine intervention and proof that the Crusade was what God had wanted. In truth, it was a combination of military skill, luck, and Muslim political disunity that resulted in the establishment of the Frankish–Crusader kingdoms in the Levant: the county of Edessa (now Urfa), home to Nestorian, Armenian, and Jacobite Christians, located in eastern Turkey, strategically east of the Euphrates; the Armenian Kingdom of Cilicia, located in southern Anatolia, astride the Crusaders' route to Jerusalem; the principality of Antioch, located in northern Syria, linked to Byzantium by trade and to Armenian Cilicia by military influence; the county of Tripoli in Lebanon, with its considerable Maronite population on the Levantine coast north to Beirut; and the Kingdom of Jerusalem, whose territory extended east across the Jordan.

For the first time since the Muslim conquest, Christians ruled the Levantine coast and had access to commerce and proselytization in areas of the Middle East long abandoned to Islam. The Crusades were the first example of western Europe's projecting power into the Middle East since the classical Roman Empire—and the last until Napoleon's invasion of Egypt in 1798. For almost three hundred years, beginning in 1098, when Baldwin of Boulogne veered off from the main army of the First Crusade to take control of Edessa, and lasting until the fall of the Armenian Kingdom of Cilicia in 1375, the Crusaders managed to conquer and control territory in the region.

The Crusades ultimately failed because not enough Europeans would come to the Middle East and stay. In spite of papal urgings, the European population of the Levant was never sufficient to defeat the eventual unified Muslim reconquest. Edessa, the farthest east of the Crusader advance and therefore the most exposed to Muslim attack, was the first to fall. An early target of a revivified Islam, it was conquered by the Muslim ruler of Mosul, who proceeded to Mardin and then to Aleppo. With Aleppo and Mosul under his control, Imad al-Din Zengi took Edessa in 1144. Cilicia, however, which was based on a more or less indigenous Christian population, held out until 1375. Known as "Lesser Armenia," the kingdom had been established in 1080 by émigrés from eastern Anatolia who had fled Seljuk Turkish advances in "Greater Armenia" and had been resettled in Anatolia by the Byzantine government.

Coveting Armenian territory, both the Byzantines and the Crusaders courted the rulers of Cilicia. Although the Crusaders initially made no attempt to bring the Armenians into communion with Rome, the Byzantine annexation of Cilicia in 1137 and the threat to the Latins brought the two groups together in 1141. Later, during a similar era of political turmoil (1172–1375), the Cilician Armenians turned this time to the Byzantines and almost united with the Orthodox Church. Reverence for Rome, cooperation with the Latins, and a royal family whose social status provided opportunities for intermarriage with the European nobility led to close relations between Armenians and the rulers of the Crusader states.[9]

In Syria, where the principality of Antioch was also established in 1098 following initial Crusader successes, the indigenous Christians were primarily Jacobites and Armenians who now owed political loyalty to the Franks and were granted religious autonomy. Spread throughout former Muslim-controlled territory, they became part of the diplomatic relations between Latins and Greeks that would characterize the early years of the Christian conquest. As Syrian monophysites, the Jacobites had links with the Coptic Church of Egypt, whose jurisdiction covered Syria and Egypt. Living under either Christian or Muslim rule, Jacobites and Copts became players in Syrian politics as facts on the ground changed. At one point, the Byzantine emperor asserted Greek protection and even union with the Jacobites living in northern Syria. The Jacobites demurred. After Edessa fell to the Muslims in 1151, however, the Christian population east of the Orontes River had to deal with a different political situation. Coptic influence expanded after Saladin took Jerusalem in 1187, and Egypt became the strategic focus of the thirteenth-century crusades.

The Maronites of the Lebanese mountains were attracted to communion with Rome. After 423, when the Council of Chalcedon divided Christendom, the Maronites had sided with the Greek Church rather than with the monophysites, but when the Greek patriarchate at Antioch fell vacant in the early eighth century, the Maronites elected their own patriarch without consulting Constantinople. Following the Great Schism of 1054, the Maronite patriarchate allied not with Constantinople, but with Rome. The Crusader chronicles of the next two centuries attest to the Maronites' support of the Franks' crusading armies. However this history is interpreted, it is clear that the Maronites viewed themselves as Uniate Catholics from at least 1180, but it is not certain whether they were "converted" by the Crusaders or had felt themselves subject to Rome before the arrival of the Franks.[10]

Most important from the Crusaders' point of view, however, was the Kingdom of Jerusalem, established by the successful First Crusade in 1099. The Kingdom of Jerusalem would survive for nearly two hundred years despite the fact that the city reverted to Muslim control for most of that time. In 1187, when Saladin took the city, the kingdom's capital moved to Acre, and the Crusader state clung to a narrow strip of coast until the fall of Acre in 1291.

With the Crusaders' capture of Jerusalem, most of them saw their objective attained and went home, leaving the remaining defenders to sustain the Latin kingdoms. A Christian minority among Christians, the Crusaders taxed Muslims, imposed a Roman Catholic ecclesiastical presence in Jerusalem, and instituted feudal rule, leaving no doubt that the church was subordinate to the state. Crusaders seemed to be tolerant of the many other confessions that owned churches and chapels in the city and its environs, for they confiscated only those churches and chapels that had been destroyed before the Latin conquest; they also encouraged pilgrimage and respected other Christians' pilgrimage sites. In fact, though, the popes still sought union with the Greek Orthodox Church—under Latin hegemony, they permitted direct access to the Church of the Holy Sepulchre only to the Greek Orthodox, who had a substantial presence there.

Relations between the Latin Catholics and other churches were pragmatic, more "like extending official recognition to an ecclesiastical diplomatic corps, since most of these [other] groups had few or no adherents in the rest of the Frankish east and were present merely to cater to the needs of pilgrims of their own faith who visited the holy places."[11] Although the Eastern churches did not pay a minorities' tax and in theory the Latin church maintained interest in bringing them into the Catholic fold, there was little doubt that they and Rome distrusted each other. Through trade and commerce, both in the Middle East and with the outside world, indigenous Christians were important for the economic sustainability of the Crusader states. Yet, with the exception of the Maronites, they were never treated as equals, having been marginalized by a church that was becoming ever more militant in its struggle against heresy. For example, although Jacobites were allowed a chapel near the Church of the Holy Sepulchre, they were not permitted direct access to the church.[12] As a result of the First Crusade, Jerusalem was depopulated, but attempts to invite Syrians, Christian Arabs from across the Jordan, and Armenians to settle in the Kingdom of Jerusalem were met with disapproval by the Latin church, which did not want a strong presence of eastern Christians in either Jerusalem or Antioch. When King Amalric was offered the transfer of thirty thousand Armenian warriors with their families to the Kingdom of Jerusalem, he was interested, but the church's response was clear: "We have expelled the Turks and the pagans, but as to the heretics, Greeks and Armenians, Syrians and Jacobites, [we] were unable to chase them out."[13]

The Crusaders gave little thought to conversion of either Muslims or Eastern Christians, even though, with the passage of time, issues about the status of both would need to be clarified. There were some Muslim converts to Christianity during the course of the First Crusade and instances of individuals who held important military positions becoming Christian, but in general the Crusaders were not interested in converting Muslims for economic reasons. Although Muslims were needed for agricultural work, slaves who converted, according to church law and to the chagrin of their Christian owners, were automatically manumitted. Converts were also exempt from the tax Muslims paid to the Christian authorities. This reversal of the Pact of Omar was intended to keep the populations apart, even though on one level it was hoped that Muslims would be led to the true faith.[14]

For the most part, however, European Catholics were not concerned with proselytizing in the Middle East. Jerusalem was in their hands, and Muslims and non-Catholics were too far away from Europe to be of major concern. Spain, being closer, was where the missionary enterprise came into European consciousness. As Christians advanced in their reconquest of Muslim Spain, reports were amplified and spread throughout Europe by the popular chansons de geste, which embellished the exploits of knights and preachers, telling tales of Muslims converting to Christianity "singly and en masse."[15] Gregory VII had sent a mission to Spanish Muslims in 1074, the same year when, following the Seljuk victory at Manzikert, he authorized a military expedition to the east; and Urban II encouraged "by word and example to convert, with God's grace, the infidels to the faith"[16] but did not advocate conversion as a goal of the Crusade.

Fifty years later, as Latin ecclesiastics began to critique "crusade," the subject of mission or peaceful conversion of Muslims was raised once again. By 1141, the translation of the Qur'an sponsored by Peter the Venerable was available to the West, and the renowned cleric advocated winning over the Saracens "not as our people [so] often do, by weapons, not by force but by reason, not by hate but by love."[17] Bernard of Clairvaux, in his call for a Second Crusade, advocated a peaceful approach while paradoxically supporting the Knights Templar, the newly created military order. Nevertheless, at the end of his life he deplored the lack of missionary work, exhorting Pope Eugene III to send preachers to Muslims: "Are we waiting for faith to descend on them?" he asked. "Who [ever] came to believe through chance? How are they to believe without being preached to?"[18]

This debate over whether to combat Islam or to convert Muslims arose during the Third Lateran Council in 1179. The church sanctioned crusades against Christians for the defense of Christendom, thereby justifying the Albigensian Crusade, which was intended to "extirpate heresy in Languedoc and dispossess its adherents, promoters and protectors."[19] Discussions also concerned the question of the intermingling of minority groups and the dominant Latins in the Holy Land.[20] How, then, were good Christians to be prevented from being led astray by the large numbers of Muslims who might not only aid other heretics, but, according to an emerging opinion, were now considered heretics themselves?[21] The issue of whether to regard Muslims as pagans to be conquered or heretics to be converted, however, became moot when eight years after the Third Lateran Council was held, Saladin united Syria and Egypt, retook Jerusalem, and the Christian capital was moved to Acre.[22] The issue emerged once again with political and theological overtones during the tenure of Pope Innocent III.

The urgency of the heresy issue became increasingly apparent in the apocalyptic writings circulating at the end of the twelfth century. Innocent III's vision of a united Christian world achievable through crusade invoked "the 666 years of the beast of the apocalypse"; "he saw in the completing of six hundred years since the rise of Islam a sign that Divine Providence would respond to the Christian hope for the liberation of the Holy Land."[23] This vision of world history had been developed in the writings of Joachim of Fiore, a Calabrian priest whose prophecies were taken more seriously after his death. In his view, Muslims were key agents in the apocalyptical view of history that predicted Muslims' persecution of Christians during what he termed the "Fourth Age" of history and their defeat by Christians during the beginning of the Sixth Age. But now, at the cusp of what was eagerly awaited as the holy Sabbath Age of the Holy Spirit, Muslims once again threatened Christendom. On the way to the Holy Land in 1190, Richard the Lionheart stopped at Messina, where Joachim prophesied that Richard would defeat Saladin. When the Third Crusade failed, Joachim blamed the Crusaders for their lack of devotion.[24]

Almost immediately upon his accession to the Holy See, Pope Innocent III called for a new crusade. In the psychological context of the day, contemporaries viewed the Sack of Constantinople in 1204 during the Fourth Crusade and the subsequent establishment of the Latin kingdom there on the one hand as a misdirection of the Crusades, but on the other as a step forward in the church's goal of reuniting East and West. Scholars still debate whether Innocent III actually played a role in the crusade, but his pleasure at the outcome has been duly noted. For many, the diversion of the Fourth Crusade to Constantinople, where Christians were attacked, as opposed to war in Jerusalem, where infidels would have been targeted, was hypocritical.[25] In response, the pietistic movements that were embodied in the Children's Crusade (1212), seemed to wrest leadership from the church. Despite its failure, the Children's Crusade signaled "ecclesiastical unease" and a movement to "return to apostolic simplicity."[26]

Much like subsequent periods in Christian history, the early thirteenth century was a period of apocalyptic urgency when the perception of a need for reform of the church spawned a new spirituality and renewed missionary thrust. Francis of Assisi spoke to this spiritual environment. We will see a similar effect again in the sixteenth century at the time of the Reformation and later in the "Great Awakening" that led to the Protestant missionary movement of the nineteenth and twentieth centuries.

At the Fourth Lateran Council in 1215, Pope Innocent III set out not only to reform the church and to liberate the Holy Land, but also to "end the schism and then deal with enemies of the faith."[27] Innocent was convinced that another crusade not only would free the Holy Land and unite Christendom but would bring Jews and Muslims to Christianity, thereby ushering in the End of Days. Despite the council's metaphysical overtones, it nonetheless reflected the pragmatism of the pope and of his Paris-trained group of ecclesiastics who institutionalized crusade, while simultaneously laying the foundation for institutionalizing mission to the East.

In western Europe, the missionary enterprise was essentially complete. All of western and northern Europe was avowedly Christian, with many people converting en masse as their leaders were baptized. Christian Germans had moved into eastern Europe and the Baltic, and Greek Orthodox missionaries had spread the faith northward from Constantinople into Russia.[28] However, European political discord, threats by Muslim empires and "Greek schismatics"[29] on the frontiers, heresy within, and apprehension that the End of Times was approaching led the pope to call for a new crusade as well as for church reform. In addition, Rome continued to hold out hope for the Middle East and beyond. Like Pope Gregory VII before him, Innocent III sent papal letters urging Muslim and Eastern Christian leaders to convert to Roman Catholicism, still maintaining the belief that if leaders converted, the people would automatically follow. Written from positions of relative Christian strength, these missives to the sultan of Iconium and rulers of Aleppo and Morocco nonetheless elicited no positive response.[30] With the Muslim Almohad retreat in North Africa, prospects for converts in Tunis, Algeria, and Morocco seemed even more feasible, but they went nowhere.[31] When a few decades later the Mongols threatened Islam, and the Crusader states were on the verge of collapse, there would be a flurry of diplomatic and missionary activity to garner the support of these "new" Christians against the Muslim foe.

The problem was that in 1215 European politics were in flux. Richard I of England was dead, and not only were England and France at war, but their rulers—John of England and Phillip II of France—were under excommunication as church and state remained at loggerheads in their conflict over spiritual and temporal supremacy. The pope was also mired in Italian politics over the choice of a successor to Holy Roman Emperor Henry VI. By offering indulgences for those who fought with him in support of the infant heir who would become Emperor Frederick II, Pope Innocent advanced the legitimacy of Christians crusading against Christians, and he launched the Albigensian Crusade in southern France. At this critical moment, when Muslim political unity in the Middle East so deftly organized by Saladin had fractured under his successor, and succession issues in Outremer (the Crusader kingdoms) portended a dire future for the Latin states, no royal leaders were available to initiate new crusades for the purpose of recovering Jerusalem and securing the Holy Land.

One response to the spiritual crisis that was also crucial to the development of the missionary enterprise was the founding of the mendicant orders, specifically the Franciscans and the Dominicans. For more than five hundred years, missionary work had come primarily from the monasteries. Monasticism had existed in Egypt since the third century and by the sixth had become important in the West with the development of the Rule of Benedict. Monks as missionaries had been important in Nestorian proselytization in Central Asia and China. But both the Dominican and the Franciscan orders, founded in the early thirteenth century with the specific goal of proselytization and conversion, made this a central mission of the church. The Dominicans, followers of the Spaniard Dominic Guzman, were dedicated to preaching ("Order of the Preachers") against heretics, especially the Albigensians in southern France. Sanctioned by the pope in 1215, the Dominicans were entrusted with the responsibility of the Inquisition and had a significant impact on education. For their part, the Franciscans, established by Francis of Assisi, were devoted to work among the poor. They sent missionaries to the Middle East in the wake of Saladin's call in 1187 for the Muslim reconquest of Jerusalem as well as the subsequent failure of the Third Crusade to retake Jerusalem. By 1217, the order had already sent contingents to Spain, Central Europe, and the

Holy Land, preaching the appeal of Christianity to all. Two years later Francis himself traveled to the Middle East. He succeeded in crossing Christian–Muslim lines during the Crusader siege of the Egyptian city of Damietta during the Fifth Crusade (1217–1221), and he met with Saladin's successor, al-Kamil, the Ayyubid ruler of Egypt. Francis engaged the Muslim in religious debate, and al-Kamil allowed him to preach openly to his subjects. In what would become the beginning of a long-term commitment, the Franciscans included as their goals converting the "Saracens and other unbelievers"[32] and securing custody of the Holy Places.[33] Although al-Kamil himself did not convert, he did offer Jerusalem to the Christians. The papal legate Pelagius refused the offer, however. Officially sanctioned by the pope in 1223 and for the next two hundred years, Dominicans and Franciscans would be dispatched throughout the Middle East and Central Asia.[34]

The Fourth Lateran Council provided an opportunity for missionaries from all fields to meet and compare notes on techniques for recruiting and proselytizing. Missionaries were enlisted to preach crusade.[35] Propaganda and preaching manuals were standardized. Recruitment, logistics, supply, finance, and rewards such as indulgences were prepared for a crusading theology set to redeem Latin Christendom. At the same time, what had been distinct concepts, crusade and mission, were now merged: "I believe," wrote James (Jacques) of Vitry, "that many of the heretics dwelling in the east, and many of the Saracens as well, might easily be converted to the Lord if they heard sound doctrine preached."[36]

By the 1220s, the mendicant missionary orders were working in tandem with the papacy.[37] Gregory IX and Innocent IV expanded the pope's jurisdiction canonically by virtue of natural law to enforce conformity in faith among all human souls. Gregory did not deny the right of non-Catholic rulers to govern their lands, recognizing that they, like all men, had the right to earthly governance, but he did assert the church's authority for religious guidance to all. Missionaries were sent to Muslims as well as to schismatics — Bulgarians, Georgians, Armenians, and Nestorians in the East. Assuming that missionaries would be welcome to proselytize in Muslim lands, Catholic prelates wrote letters to Muslim leaders in North Africa and later to Mongol rulers in Central Asia, enjoining them to allow Christians to evangelize in those areas.[38] At the same time, they forbade Muslim missionary work in Christian lands.[39]

The belief that Christianity was the true faith provided Francis of Assisi and later French king Louis IX the rationale for face-to face missionizing during the Seventh Crusade (1248–1254) and Eighth Crusade (1270), thereby extending proselytization well beyond the borders of Christendom.[40] James of Vitry and Oliver of Paderborn, head of the cathedral school of Cologne, both of whom had been recruited by the papacy to preach against the heretical Albigensians, joined the Crusaders in Egypt, hoping to transplant the models that worked in Europe, with the same result in combating Islam in the Middle East.[41]

Missionaries initially had easy access to populations in Muslim lands because the rulers tolerated holy men. However, the earlier missionaries' experience had been limited to Spain and North Africa, so they not only lacked accurate information about the Middle East but did not speak the local languages. Some worked through interpreters, but by 1237 there is evidence that Friar Philip, the Dominican provincial of the Holy Land, and several of his brethren were studying and preaching in Arabic.[42] They had to work with care in Muslim-controlled areas because if they denounced Muhammad, then they would be attacked and possibly killed but for "the miraculous protection of God."[43] The Franciscans, who adopted a life of sacrifice, used the tactic of confrontation, standing as "witness to Christ by word and example," with martyrdom the crowning achievement and supreme evidence of religious devotion. Evoking the "Martyr Movement" of ninth-century Muslim Spain, the new movement attempted to preach in Spanish and North African mosques. For these activities, many Franciscans were exiled; some were publicly executed; and there were at least eighteen Franciscan martyrs in the Middle East between 1265 and 1289.[44]

It soon became apparent that success would come only in areas under Christian control. In 1216, James of Vitry, bishop of Acre, preached throughout Syrian areas under Christian rule without difficulty, baptizing Muslim child captives from Outremer or Damietta and then having them raised in orphanages in Christian-controlled Acre.[45] During a temporary truce (1229–1244), both the Franciscans and the Dominicans used the Latin occupation of Jerusalem to establish missions in Jerusalem; the Dominicans had cloisters in Acre and Tripoli, and the Franciscans established convents in Acre, Antioch, and Tripoli. Although the orders were initially sent to serve the needs of the Latin community, they soon moved on to missionary work.[46]

Innocent III died before the Fifth Crusade got under way in 1217. His successor, Honorius III, continued to preach crusade, but the military campaign was plagued from the beginning by lack of strong leadership. Preoccupied by his own domestic politics, Holy Roman Emperor Frederick II of

Hohenstaufen, who had taken the cross as a Crusader, never arrived with the imperial army, and the Crusader troops that invaded Egypt were bogged down for more than three years in a siege of Damietta on the Egyptian Mediterranean coast. During the truce of 1229–1244, secured by Frederick in the Sixth Crusade (1228–1229), Christians once again established a presence in Jerusalem, albeit under Muslim rule, but after that Crusader territory gradually shrank as Muslims went on the offensive. When the conquest of Jerusalem eluded European troops, they focused on Egypt and North Africa until the fall of Acre to the Mamluks in 1291.

As the map of the Middle East began to change in the mid-thirteenth century, Latin Christians modified their approach to Muslims and Eastern Christians in the region. The Egyptian–Syrian unity that had enabled Saladin to take Jerusalem from the Franks disintegrated under the political maneuverings of his Ayyubid successors. At the same time, the westward expansion of the Mongol Empire from China to Europe, begun in the 1220s under Genghis Khan and ended with the death of Kublai Khan in 1294, sparked renewed European interest in the East.

The Mongols controlled the most extensive land empire in history, an area that encompassed most of the territory from Southeast Asia to Central Europe. The fact that the Mongols were not Muslim seemed to afford Christians opportunities not only for alliances against their enemies in the Middle East, but for missionary work in new areas. Rumors spread west of a powerful Christian power in the East, that of the legendary Prester John, considered a Christian David who could aid the Crusader states in their struggle against the Muslim Goliath. The pope sent missionaries and diplomats (the distinction was not always clear) to the East with the goals of inviting separated Christians back into the church and soliciting aid from the Mongols, some of whom, according to rumor, had converted to Christianity.[47] Whether these stories of conversion were actually about the Central Asian Nestorian Christian community that had been settled on the borders of China since the seventh century, exaggerated tales of powerful eastern Christians sparked an optimistic European response for diplomacy and missionary work, one that endured for more than twenty years. The actual results of the missions undertaken from the late 1240s through the 1260s were negligible, however. One Franciscan mission returned without having met with the Mongols. A second, undertaken by John of Piano del Carpine, returned to Europe with the Mongol khan's demand for total subjugation of all Christian rulers in exchange for cessation of hostilities.[48]

In 1244, a group of Muslim Khwarism Turks, moving in advance of the Mongol onslaught, turned southwest and took Jerusalem, thereby precipitating another crisis in Christendom that resulted in both Christian and Mongol diplomatic efforts and missions to Eastern Christians. In preparation for a new crusade to the East, Pope Innocent IV and French king Louis IX initiated diplomatic activity to secure a military alliance with the Mongol conquerors against the Muslims. For Christians, the prospect at last of defeating Islam was euphoric. Louis, encouraged by the reports of Dominican friar Ascelino and Andrew of Longjumeau, whom he had sent east a few years earlier, ordered Andrew of Longjumeau back to the region, just as Hulagu and his Mongol armies were moving against Baghdad. The khan's political strategy is still a subject of historical debate. More likely than not, his interest in working with the Christians lay solely with opportunities to advance Mongol conquests, but defeat at 'Ayn Jalut in 1260 by the Mamluk forces, now firmly in power in Egypt, changed the political map of the Middle East once again. For the next thirty years, the Franks faced a more powerful Muslim adversary, one zealously dedicated to their expulsion from the region.[49]

At the same time, the establishment of Mongol rule along the Silk Road from eastern Turkey to China provided security for trade and cultural exchange to develop across Central Asia. Franciscan and Dominican missions sent to the East opened the world to Europeans and sparked new interest in the Armenians, Jacobites, and Nestorians. At Mosul, Andrew of Longjumeau met with Jacobite clerics. Nestorian prelates accompanied him to Central Asia. His reports encouraged Louis IX to send the Franciscan William of Rubruck, who had participated in the Seventh Crusade in 1248, as a missionary to the Tartars five years later. William made few converts, but he was able to connect with the Nestorian Christians and suggested that the pope send more missions. Soon afterward, Marco Polo, his father, and his uncle were traveling eastward on trade missions to the Mongols, and in 1266 Grand Khan Kublai sent back to Italy with them a representative asking the pope for Christian missionaries in his kingdom.[50] In 1289, the pope dispatched the Franciscan John of Monte Corvino—who had been working in Armenia urging Jacobite, Nestorian, Georgian, and Armenian prelates to conform to Rome—to the court of the khan at Khanbalik (Beijing), where in 1275 a Nestorian bishopric had been established. In 1307, John was named archbishop and primate of the church in Tartary and patriarch of the Orient with jurisdiction from eastern Europe to the Pacific.[51]

The fall of Acre to the Mamluks in 1291 signified, for all intents and purposes, the end of the Crusades and missionary work in Palestine. Franciscans in the Holy Land noted that the Saracens "had closed off for themselves the way of salvation; they do not want to hear anything that seems to be contrary to the sayings of their prophet Machometh, and should someone say anything contrary, he is killed without mercy."[52] Accompanying the Muslim backlash against Christians, some Christians converted to Islam. The area that had been predominantly Christian for centuries was now predominantly Muslim, with Christians in the minority. Cilician Armenia to the north, under continuous attack by the Mamluks, was overrun in 1375, and its ruling family, long intermarried with the Frankish Crusaders, took refuge in Europe.

Even though European hold on territory in the Holy Land had ended, the work of the Franciscans and the Dominicans laid the foundation for Catholic mission organization in the Middle East, and Muslim authorities permitted a Franciscan presence in Jerusalem. Pope Clement VI appointed them custodians of the Holy Places. Instead of crusade, the church turned to mission, replacing military arms with sermons and public disputations. To that end, Raymond Llull, whose mission work took him to North Africa, worked to convert the Saracens and to establish schools teaching Arabic, Hebrew, Syriac, and Greek. Programs were set up at several European universities, but in the end these languages were taught only in Paris.[53]

As commercial ties between Europe, Central Asia, and China developed, Franciscan and Dominican mission stations (to use the later term) were established in eastern Turkey and Persia for the purpose of preaching to Eastern Christians. The restoration of Greek control in Constantinople in 1261 and the temporary union with Rome in 1273 enabled Latin missions to continue along the northern coast of the Black Sea and in Armenia, where they would record their greatest achievements. In 1335, a young Armenian named Nicholas converted at Kaffa, went to Florence, and returned a Dominican missionary. Other examples of Armenian–Latin contact followed, marking the Armenians as an important point of future contact with Western Christianity.[54]

Throughout the fourteenth century, the two mendicant orders alternately cooperated and competed with each other over jurisdiction, organization, and mission. Franciscans, institutionally organized by vicariate, were active in areas of northern and western Anatolia: the Crimea, Trebizond, Armenia, Azerbaijan, southern Georgia, and Mesopotamia. They established stations in Constantinople, Trebizond, and Tabriz. In contrast, Dominicans, who were not connected with regular convents (*fratrum peregrinantium propter Christum*), were organized as a society, proselytizing in Turkey as well as in parts of Greece, Egypt, Nubia, and all of Asia except Palestine and Syria. When during the 1320s some Franciscans were under fire for their doctrine concerning the extreme poverty of Jesus, Pope John XXII sent Dominicans into Central Asia, roughly defining for the two orders a "north–south" division of responsibility: the eastern Mongol Empire for the Franciscans and Anatolia, Persia, Transoxiana (Samarkand), India, and Ethiopia for the Dominicans.[55] The pope was also responsible for the Catholic presence in Persia among the Armenians. Despite the fact that quantitative success rates of conversion to the Church of Rome were meager, the church persisted and allowed accommodations for local liturgy and custom.[56]

Catholic musings of more crusades in the East still worried the Byzantines. Despite restoration of Greek Orthodox rule at Constantinople after fifty-seven years of Latin occupation (1204–1261), emperor and patriarch had to contend not only with the after-effects of the Union of Lyons (1274) and the relentless Latin effort to bring Eastern churches into the fold, but also with the systematic Turkish advance from the east that was bringing Anatolia under the sway of Islam. Theological considerations and church reform were uppermost in the minds of the clerics, but the existential threat of a Muslim conquest of Anatolia preoccupied the emperors even more. With no choice but to use Italian mercenaries, imperial policy once again raised the specter of a Latin threat. This was at a time when renewed plans for crusade projected Constantinople, instead of Egypt, as the jumping-off point for retaking the Holy Land and when the Venetians and Genoese, whose wealth and prestige increased during the Latin occupation of Constantinople, controlled the Byzantine food supply.[57] The issue became moot in 1453 when, after two centuries of steady encroachments on Byzantine territory through conquest, marriage alliances, and diplomacy, the Ottoman Turks conquered Constantinople and made it the capital of a new Islamic empire.

Ottoman successes in Anatolia came in the wake of the dissolution of the Mongol conquest, which the Mamluks had halted in Syria. While the Turks were consolidating Sunni control of Asia Minor, tribal confederations emerged on the Turks' eastern border as a result of the disintegration of the Mongol khanate. As a result, the direct line of communication to the East was disrupted, and European Christians now faced a formidable Islamic military adversary from the European Balkans to Central Asia. In this new world, of nation-states, this control of territory translated into a political instead of a theological confrontation, one that would endure until World War I.

Despite church politics back in Rome that hampered papal initiative, the scourge of the Black Death that wreaked havoc from Central Asia to the Mediterranean as well as in Europe in the mid-fourteenth century,[58] and the interdiction by Muslim authorities against Christian proselytization, the legacy of these early missions endured. Pilgrimages to the Holy Land continued;[59] and despite the few converts, the renewed interaction between Catholics and Muslims, on the one hand, and Catholics and Eastern Christians, on the other, was sustained. Scattered sources portray the work of individuals, report on attempts to train native clergy, and describe plans for language schools to teach missionaries the region's languages. The institutionalization of the missionary movement, which conflated crusade and mission, would follow the church and inspire the missionary enterprise to the far reaches of the globe. It inspired Christopher Columbus as he set sail from Spain in 1492.[60]

THREE

Disintegration, Revival, Reformation, and Counter-Reformation

1450–1800

Two dates define Muslim–Christian relations in the fifteenth century. The first is 1453, the conquest of Constantinople by the Ottoman Turks, who already held the territories of the eastern Roman Empire. The second is 1492, the completion of the *reconquista* that resulted in the expulsion from Spain of all Muslims, most of whom relocated to North Africa, and of Jews, who settled primarily in Muslim lands on the Mediterranean littoral and in areas directly under Ottoman rule.

From the founding of the Franciscan and Dominican mendicant orders in the early thirteenth century and the Fourth Lateran Council in 1215, the missionary enterprise of the Roman Catholic Church was carried forward by monastic orders under the pope's direct control.[1] This practice is in sharp contrast to the later Protestant evangelical projects, which were frequently carried on by voluntary societies rather than by organized churches and which by the nineteenth century were supported by local parishes and even individuals.

The death of Louis IX in 1270 and the fall of Acre in 1291 completed the failure of the Crusades to conquer the Holy Land and reunite the Mediterranean world, although the Armenian Kingdom of Cilicia, whose ruling family had intermarried with the Frankish Crusaders, managed to hang on until 1375, when their rulers finally took refuge in France. The fourteenth and fifteenth centuries saw disintegration in both Europe and the Middle East. In the East, despite the Mongol invasions that destroyed settled urban life in many areas, the territorial contiguity left in the wake of the Mongols' conquest reinvigorated trade connections and enabled the rapid westward expansion of the Turks, who consolidated their empire in Anatolia and became an existential threat to Europe.

The Western church was in crisis with the papacy's efforts to exert temporal as well as spiritual power in a single pope to replace the rivals in Avignon and Rome. Meanwhile, efforts to consolidate Christianity in the Baltic states continued, as did the reconquest of Spain, but in France, Italy, and England attention to the expansion of trade eastward into Asia and southward in the Mediterranean was replaced by internal conflict and state building rather than to the spread of Christianity. Half-hearted attempts to launch crusades in support of the Cilician Armenians or Venetian commercial interests in the eastern Mediterranean garnered little support. Venice, Naples, Genoa, Hungary, and Cyprus, for example, ignored Pope Gregory XI's wish to launch a crusade in 1374. So although crusading remained the province of the papacy, exercised through the activities of the preaching orders directly responsible to the pope, the Dominicans and the Franciscans, it required the state's economic and military resources, which were not forthcoming. Several popes attempted to raise a crusade to regain Constantinople after its conquest by the Ottoman Turks in 1453 or even to retake Jerusalem from bases in North Africa. None of these ventures came to fruition. By the end of the fifteenth century, renaissance and recovery had begun, and the pieces were coming into place for expansion of both the Muslim and the Christian worlds.

By the end of the first millennium, the migration of the Turkic peoples from Central Asia toward Europe had begun to made its presence felt in the Middle East. One group of Turks, the Ottomans, gradually subjugated Asia Minor and created an empire that threatened Europe. By 1390, the Byzantines were effectively the Ottomans' vassals. Defeat and succession problems at court halted the Ottomans' expansion in the early fifteenth century, but they regrouped and in 1453, under the leadership of Mehmet II the Conqueror , took the prize that long eluded them—the Byzantine capital city, Constantinople. By this time, what remained of the Byzantine Empire—the hinterlands of the Byzantine capital both east and west of the city—was under Ottoman control. The Christian powers, however, paid scant attention to the loss of Constantinople. Poland and Lithuania, the Habsburgs in Central Europe, and the English and the French were enmeshed in continental wars and their own local political struggles. The capture of the city itself was as much symbolic as real because much of the Christian population had already fled to Italy in the wake of the Fourth Crusade, leaving Constantinople virtually depopulated when the Ottomans took the city. Even the Byzantine emperor's agreement to union with the Roman Catholic Church at the Council of Florence in 1449, four years earlier, albeit with no Orthodox clerical support, was not enough to bring the European powers to the city's aid. Only Venice still had real interests in the eastern Mediterranean.[2]

The areas of Ottoman conquest in the fourteenth and fifteenth centuries were primarily Christian, but the Christian majority gradually diminished in these areas, especially the Anatolian territories, because of conversion and migration.[3] The Ottoman Empire continued to control a large Christian population in the Balkans until the twentieth century. However, it was not until after World War I and the demise of the empire that Anatolia became almost totally Muslim. Until then, large Greek-speaking and Armenian- speaking Christian populations remained. Ottoman conquests continued under Suleiman I with the fall of Belgrade in 1521 and the island of Rhodes, which had been under the control of the Catholic Knights of St. John, in 1522. Over the next century and a half, the remnants of Catholic control over the Greek islands, which dated to the time of the Crusaders, were gradually brought to an end by the Ottomans—to their Greek inhabitants' great relief. Only in 1669 was Crete finally taken.

A few years later, however, the tide turned. In Europe, the Turks fought wars with Venice and the Habsburgs; the failure of their third attempt to take Vienna in 1683 marked the beginning of Ottoman retreat in Europe. As Russia expanded under Peter I and Catherine II , who looked not only to the West for cultural synergy but also to the Black Sea and the Caucasus as areas of Russian strategic and religious interest, the Ottomans were threatened in the Balkans and close to Constantinople (Istanbul) itself. The Ottomans' almost constant war with Austria and Russia during the eighteenth century resulted in Russian hegemony over the Crimea and the right to build a Greek church in the Galata section of Constantinople. Under the Treaty of Kuchuk Kainarji (1774), the czar claimed the mantle of protector of Greek Orthodox Christians in the Ottoman Empire, a role that France claimed for the other Eastern Christian communities. Russia would assert this right not only in the Caucasus and in Constantinople, but also in Jerusalem.

In the western Mediterranean, the quasi-independent Islamic regimes in North Africa eventually rebuffed Spanish attempts to control North African ports and became a serious challenge to European shipping in the Atlantic.[4] The corsairs, much like the English and French privateers that raided Spanish ships, attacked European ships, taking their captives and loot to bases on the southern Mediterranean coast. A threat until the early nineteenth century, the "Barbary pirates" gave rise to the fear of Islam that predated European imperial ventures in the region.[5]

The papacy attempted again to mend the schism between the two branches of Christianity at the Council of Florence, which met in various locations until 1449. Pope Eugenius IV persuaded representatives of the Greek church to attend, led by the Byzantine emperor John VIII Palaeologus and Patriarch Joseph of Constantinople , who were desperate to get Western assistance against the Ottomans. Although an agreement was reached, it was recanted as soon as the Greeks returned to Constantinople. Similar reconciliations were reached with representatives of the Armenian, Coptic, and Syriac churches, but, like the accord with the Greeks, these agreements were recanted when the representatives returned home.[6]

The Ottoman conquest of Constantinople solidified the schism between the Greek and Latin branches of Christianity. As the Ottomans gradually absorbed the Eastern Christians into the empire's structure, all possibility of reunion with Rome disappeared. Latin Catholic communities of Italian merchants lived in Constantinople and around the Black Sea, and the remnants of the Roman Catholic Crusaders lived on the Greek islands. It mattered little to any of them whether they were ruled by Greeks or Turks. At the same time, the Greeks themselves tended to prefer Turkish rule to that of the Latins on the islands. Thus, the task of the Latin church became to try to attract members of the Eastern churches to Catholicism to establish so-called Uniate churches—that is, segments of the Eastern churches that accepted the primacy of the pope in Rome. For the next five hundred years, this task would be the major thrust of Roman Catholic missionary activity in the Middle East.

The papacy's immediate response to the Ottoman conquest of Constantinople was to attempt to launch a crusade. Pope Nicholas V commissioned a fleet to sail to the East and called a meeting of representatives of the Italian cities in Rome. No agreement could be reached at the Rome meeting, and, in the meantime, the Venetians negotiated a trade agreement with Mehmet II. Pope Nicholas V died in 1455, having been unable to do anything to recapture Constantinople. He was succeeded by Calixtus III , who was committed to a crusade to recapture not only Constantinople, but also Jerusalem. Calixtus raised a fleet, which sailed to the Aegean in 1456 and succeeded in retaking Lemnos and

Samothrace as well as in defeating a Turkish fleet off Lesbos in 1457. However, these successes were not followed up, and the fleet returned to Italy. Calixtus died the following year and was succeeded by Pius II , who in 1458 called all the princes of Europe to meet in a congress in Mantua. The pope traveled to Mantua the following year, but none of the princes appeared—eliciting a desperate reaction from Pius at the lack of papal theological credibility: "People think our sole object is to amass gold. No one believes what we say. Like insolvent tradesmen we are without credit."[7] Finally, in December 1458, delegates from France, England, the Holy Roman Empire, and the Italian cities assembled and reached agreement on the raising of forces for a crusade. However, further Ottoman successes in the Aegean seem to have created such discouragement that the forces were never raised. Pius II tried persuasion rather than force in writing a letter to Sultan Mehmet II suggesting that he convert to Christianity. The sultan did not reply. In 1464, Pius himself took the cross and set off for Ancona, intending to lead a crusade, but he died soon after his arrival, and all who had assembled went home. By the time Bayezit II succeeded Mehmet II in 1481, "the appeal [for a crusade] had been heard so many times before that it was counted a mere rhetorical formality."[8]

The princes of Europe were simply more concerned with their own issues, in particular their commercial interests, than with the somewhat discredited papacy. The Avignon Captivity of the popes by the French kings, followed by the pope's return to Rome early in the fifteenth century, had weakened the papacy's secular power as the princes became increasingly concerned with their own national interests rather than with the universal interests of Christendom. The economic pressure that the sultan was able to bring to bear on the Vatican was probably the most important reason why the West did not launch a major crusade in the fifteenth century.[9] Within fifty years, just as the Ottoman Empire was reaching its greatest extent, Christian Europe began to fragment along religious and national lines, and efforts at conversion to Christianity became far more complicated.

Ever since the twelfth century, there had been controversy about the goals and methods of crusade. Should the goal be conquest or conversion of the Muslims in the Holy Land? Should conversion be accomplished by force or by preaching? By the thirteenth century, the Dominicans and the Franciscans had professionalized the preaching of crusades and developed standard sermons for the purpose. It was, of course, these orders that led the missionary efforts of the Spanish and Portuguese conquests in the New World from the sixteenth century on.

By the fifteenth century, goals and methods of crusade had changed. "The Crusades of the High Middle Ages . . . could be seen as a failed attempt on the part of the papacy to establish a monopoly of the means of violence within Christendom. By the fifteenth century this monopoly was clearly passing to Europe's secular princes."[10] The rise of the European nation-state changed the means and goals of the spread of Christendom. Attempts to recover the Holy Land were either put on hold or used as pretexts for marching into European territory or abandoned altogether, and the goal of crusade became instead the recovery of Constantinople. That is, after 1453 the goal of the crusading popes, rather than to convert (or reconvert) the Middle East population to Christianity, was to reunite Christianity under Latin authority by recovering Constantinople, the seat of the Greek patriarchate. But even as popes were calling for crusade, princes used the summons for the recovery of Constantinople or even the retaking of Jerusalem as pretexts for political maneuvering in Europe. In 1494, Charles VIII of France claimed that landing his army in Italy was the first step toward a crusade against the Turks. The struggles of the papacy against French incursions in Italy, the consolidation of power by the Habsburgs in Europe, and Ottoman expansion into Europe and the Middle East left little opportunity for a religious crusade. When Pope Leo X called for a crusade against the Turkish advances in Egypt and Iraq in 1518, Holy Roman Emperor Maximilian I and Francis I of France paid lip service, but nothing happened. As Catholic emperor, Charles V spent most of his reign (1519–1556) consolidating Habsburg power, suppressing rebellions, and fighting the French, who at times were even allies of the "Terrible Turk" despite the Turk's practice of recruiting Christian boys to serve in the elite Ottoman military corps and imperial bureaucracy.[11] By the end of Charles V's reign, France was wracked by wars between Protestants and Catholics, and in 1559 Charles divided the Habsburg realm between his son Philip II (of Spain, the Netherlands, and the Americas) and his brother Ferdinand I (king of Austria Hungary, Bohemia, and northern Italy).

Ottoman expansion in Europe continued through the sixteenth century. Now, for the first time, the Turks ruled over as many Christians as Muslims. Blessed with twelve rulers of military skill and administrative acumen, from Mehmet II through Suleiman I, the Ottomans ruled territories from the Balkans to Persia and supported fleets in the Mediterranean and the Persian Gulf. In 1516–1517, Selim I, responding to the Portuguese threat in the Persian Gulf, sent the Ottoman fleet to assist the Mamluks in the area and in the process took control of the Levant and Egypt, with Iraq becoming the border between the

Sunni and Shi'i empires. But just as the expansion of Western Christendom eastward was halted by the rise of the Ottomans, the Ottoman eastward expansion was stalled by the rise of another Turkish dynasty, the Safavids, in Persia.

Like the Ottomans, the Safavids moved into the power vacuum left by the withdrawal of the Mongols. They came from what is now Azerbaijan and, led by Shah Isma'il I, established their first capital in Tabriz in northern Iran in 1501. By 1510, the Safavids had expanded their control to cover all of present-day Iran and beyond, from Herat to Baghdad, and for the next two hundred years the Ottomans and the Safavids contested a long border region that stretched from the Caucasus (present-day Georgia and Armenia) through Kurdistan and Iraq to the Persian Gulf. The Safavid Empire also included a large Christian population—Armenians, Georgians, and Nestorians—that had had continuing relations with Western Christians, particularly through Jesuits and Franciscans, who sought to bring these Eastern Christians into a relationship with Rome. In that mountainous region of ethnic and religious diversity, local rulers sought Russian assistance in their struggles against conquest by either the Ottomans or the Safavids.[12]

Both the Armenians and the Nestorians found themselves on the frontiers of empires, moving back and forth between the Ottomans and the Persians, and as the Russians pushed south, that empire, too, vied for control of these Christian groups. Both were also located on the land route to the East used by Roman Catholic missionaries. In the fourteenth century, the Vatican had assigned China, areas under Mongol control, Jerusalem, and the Holy Land to the Franciscans and had given the Dominicans Iran and Central Asia.[13] The breakup of the Mongol Empire in 1368 resulted in the decline of the Roman Catholic missions, but they were revived after the founding of the Jesuit order in the sixteenth century. From the mid-sixteenth century, contact with the Nestorians and Armenians was continuous, and organized church hierarchies connected with and subservient to Rome were established in the region with help from Franciscan and Jesuit missionaries. In the 1550s, with assistance from Franciscan missionaries in Mosul, the Nestorian monk Hanna Sulaqa traveled to Jerusalem and on to Rome, where he was received by the pope and consecrated the first Uniate patriarch. Upon his return to the Middle East, the patriarchate was established at Diyarbekir.[14] The Armenians, whose territory lay squarely on the route used by Catholic missionaries to the East, had continuous contact with the missionaries.

Christian Europe's territorial expansion to the East had been halted by the Mongol invasions of the fourteenth century and the devastation caused

by the Black Death. The rise of the Ottoman Empire in the fifteenth and sixteenth centuries diverted a resurgent European desire for expansion from a
land-based expansion to expansion westward by sea. Europe was embarking
on the "Age of Exploration," and if Jerusalem and Constantinople could not
be retaken by going east, the thinking went, why not expand Christianity and
incidentally increase trade by sailing west?

In the early fifteenth century, the Portuguese, under the leadership of
Henry the Navigator, had begun to explore the western coast of Africa, looking for a route to the Indies. Pope Nicholas V, who had failed to raise a crusade after the Ottoman conquest of Constantinople, in 1454 recognized the
right of Portugal "to the peaceful occupation of all lands of the unbelievers
that might be discovered along the west coast of Africa."[15] Two years later his
successor, Calixtus III, extended these privileges by granting to a Portuguese
order spiritual authority over all present and future Portuguese territories.

Christopher Columbus's voyage westward in 1492 under the banner of
the Spanish Crown challenged that arrangement. Not only was 1492 the end
of the *reconquista*, finally driving Muslims and Jews from Spain, but it was
also, as we all know, the date of Columbus's voyage across the Atlantic to the
Americas. Although both the Portuguese and the Spanish explorers wanted
to find a sea route to the spice-laden East, plans for the reconquest of Jerusalem from North African bases liberated from Muslim rule—with or without
the assistance of the elusive Prester John—remained in Christian consciousness.[16] These goals were not to be achieved, but voyages to the New World
opened to the papacy and the Western church an enormous new missionary field that continued and expanded the tradition of the *reconquista*, not
to Jews and Christian heretics, but to "benighted and inferior peoples." The
Franciscan Geronimo de Mendieta would later note,

> As Ferdinand and Isabella were granted the mission of beginning to ex-
> tirpate those three diabolical squadrons, perfidious Judaism, false Mo-
> hammedanism and blind idolatry, along with the fourth squadron of the
> heretics whose remedy and medicine is the Holy Inquisition, in like royal
> successors; so that as Ferdinand and Isabella cleansed Spain of these wick-
> ed sects, in like manner their royal descendants will accomplish the uni-
> versal destruction of these sects throughout the whole world and the final
> conversion of all the people of the earth to the bosom of the church.[17]

All of the missionary orders worked assiduously in the Americas under the
aegis of the Roman Catholic Church.

In 1493, for the purpose of evangelism, Pope Alexander VI (1492–1503) divided the world between Spain and Portugal, drawing a line from north to southwest of the Azores, giving spiritual authority west of the line to Spain and east of the line to Portugal. (The line was adjusted the following year, allowing Portugal to exercise authority over Brazil.) This arrangement was clearly inadequate because it did not take into account the fact that east and west would eventually meet in the Pacific or that other European countries would become active players in the European expansion, but it does explain why most of the Americas were Christianized by Spanish missionaries and why Portugal established a foothold in the Persian Gulf, to the Ottomans' surprise, and in such places as Goa and Macao. It also explains why the Portuguese involved themselves in the struggle for ecclesiastical authority over the Chaldean Church in India, which continued to maintain ties with and receive its bishops from the Church of the East in Mesopotamia.[18] In the Middle East, however, the Muslim Ottoman Empire blocked any attempt at conversion either of Muslims to Christianity or of Eastern Christians to Western Christianity.

Although active in spreading the faith throughout the world where the Catholic explorers sailed, the church faced problems at home as European monarchs challenged the pope's authority and rebellions arose among the Christian faithful. The ideas of Martin Luther and the Reformation reflected controversies that had swirled in the church at least since the eleventh century and were related to the controversies over the rationale for and goals of the Crusades. These controversies included the sale of indulgences that promised reward for participation in the attempts to recover the Holy Land, the worship of saints and the Virgin Mary, and the role of the monastic orders. By the fourteenth century, conflicts between church and state had arisen questioning the proper relationship between the pope and secular authority, particularly in connection with property. Scholars in the universities of Paris and Oxford, most notably John Wycliffe , the fourteenth-century English philosopher and cleric, promoted many of the ideas that would later be enshrined by Martin Luther and other reformers. Most important for those concerned with the Protestant missionary enterprise as it later evolved was Wycliffe's emphasis on the importance of the Bible and its accessibility to all. It was Wycliffe who first translated the Bible into English so that it could be read by everyone.

Four strands of what came to be called "Protestantism" need to concern us here because they became important in later missionary history. The first

is that founded by Jan Hus, based in what is now Czechoslovakia and coming to be called "Moravian." The second is Lutheranism, which espoused
the teachings of Martin Luther and was concentrated in Germany and Scandinavia. The third is Anglicanism, which derived from King Henry VIII's
dispute with Pope Clement VII and was based in England and transmitted to the English-speaking countries of the British Empire. Finally, there
is Calvinism, founded on the teachings of John Calvin and important in
Switzerland and as Presbyterianism in Scotland and Puritanism in England
and North America.

Jan Hus, born in Bohemia in 1370, predated Luther by nearly a century
and, like William of Ockham and Wycliffe, was an influence on him. Like
Luther, he was particularly distressed by the church's use of indulgences to
raise money. In the midst of the papal schism in 1411, Antipope John XXIII
preached a crusade in Prague against the king of Naples, who was acting
as protector of Pope Gregory XII, with indulgences being offered by the
church. Hus, basing his objections on Wycliffe, held that no pope had the
right to take up the sword in the name of the church but should only pray for
his enemies. That is, he held that Jesus Christ, not the pope, was the proper
head of the church.

Although Hus was unable to elicit support from his university colleagues
in Prague, "Bohemian Wycliffism" spread into Poland, Hungary, Croatia,
and Austria, and in January 1413 the writings of Wycliffe were condemned
by a council in Rome and burned. At the Council of Constance, convened
in 1414 to resolve the papal schism, Hus was investigated by a committee of
bishops appointed by the pope, tortured, tried, convicted of heresy, and in
July 1415 executed. His legacy lived on, however, in the Moravian Church,
which was organized by his followers in villages east of Prague and established its own ministry in 1467. Following persecutions in the mid-sixteenth
century, the church grew in Poland, Bohemia, and Moravia, but after military
defeat in 1620 its bishop, John Comenius, was exiled to England and Holland. The Moravian Church, as it became known, was revived in the early
eighteenth century by Count Nicholas Ludwig von Zinzendorf and became
important in Protestant evangelical missions.

The reforming ideas of Wycliffe and Hus clearly represent the rise of national consciousness in areas on the fringe of Christian Europe. But it was
Martin Luther, nailing the Ninety-Five Theses to the door of the church in
Wittenberg in 1517, and Henry VIII of England, denying the pope's authority, who, for very different reasons and in very different ways, mounted the

most serious challenge yet to the authority of the papacy, a challenge that would remake the map of Europe.

Martin Luther was ordained a priest in 1507 and began teaching at the University of Wittenberg the following year. His study of the Bible led him to the conviction that the church had lost its way. In 1517, Luther wrote to the archbishop of Mainz protesting the sale of indulgences, and tradition says that he nailed a copy of his challenge to the door of the *Schlosskirche* in Wittenberg the same day. The Ninety-Five Theses were written in Latin but were quickly translated into German, printed, and within two weeks had spread throughout Germany and from there, within two months, throughout the rest of Europe. In 1520, Pope Leo X issued a papal bull warning Luther that he might be excommunicated if he did not recant some of his writings, but Luther publicly burned the bull in Wittenberg. In January 1521, he was excommunicated.

Through his teaching, Luther had become convinced that salvation came through faith alone, the so-called doctrine of justification, which was a direct attack on the practice of giving or selling indulgences as a means to salvation. His attacks on the church gradually broadened to include rejection of the saints and of the requirement of confession to a priest. Although in Luther's eschatological conception of redemption, the pope was the Antichrist, the religious enigma presented by the steady advance of Islam in the European heartland had to be explained. In what would become a bifurcated vision of the Antichrist, the spiritual malignancy in the church represented by the pope was seen to work in tandem with Islam, which was now viewed as the worldly manifestation of the corruption within Christianity. Luther interpreted the Turkish invasions of Europe as the scourge of God brought to bear because of papal iniquities and the corruption in the church, " 'the rod of punishment of the wrath of God' that had been raised up to chastise Christians for their infidelity to the spirit of the Bible."[19] Both had eventually to be defeated—spiritually and militarily.

Over the next decades, Protestant (that is, "protest") movements spread throughout central, eastern, and northern Europe, presenting their arguments in the vernacular languages, aided by the development of the printing press. They served as vehicles for protest against the Roman Church's authority and moral laxity and for the promotion of rising nationalism. Just as the Eastern Christian churches reflected linguistic differences as much as doctrinal ones, the development of the various Protestant churches in Europe now reflected linguistic and national distinctions.[20] The spread of these movements was aided by several factors: the rise of nationalism; the rise of a commercial middle class not dependent on feudal lands; the invention of printing and the spread of literacy in the vernacular, which made the rapid spread of ideas possible; and, finally, the continuing Ottoman threat to central Europe, which many construed as God's vengeance on a corrupt church.

The English Reformation was somewhat different and more openly political and national in its origins. The break with Rome was rooted in dynastic concerns rather than in doctrinal differences. Although doctrinal differences did emerge eventually, they were the product of a long evolutionary process. The English kings had long struggled against the papacy's authority. In the thirteenth and fourteenth centuries, Roger Bacon and William of Ockham, both Franciscans at Oxford, laid the theoretical foundation for opposition to papal authority as well as other issues that were to become important in Protestant reform. John Wycliffe in the fourteenth century translated the Bible into English. Finally, Henry VIII's break with the papacy in 1529 was precipitated by his desire to marry Anne Boleyn, for which he required an annulment of his marriage to Catherine of Aragon.

Henry had actually taken the pope's side in the dispute with Martin Luther, but things changed when the pope refused in 1527 to annul Henry's marriage to Catherine of Aragon because she had been unable to produce an heir. Two years later the king called together a meeting of Parliament to deal with the issue of the annulment, and this meeting brought together various strands of English opposition to the pope and the Catholic Church, both the nationalistic camp who favored the king over the pope and those who were influenced by Luther's reform movement. Finally, in 1532 Parliament recognized the authority of the English king over the church, and in 1534 the Acts of Supremacy established the king as head of the Church of England, a situation that continues to this day. Beginning in 1536, the monasteries in England were dissolved, bringing their wealth to the Crown and destroying the other main source of Roman Catholic power in England. But it took a century and a half, the beheading of a king, and a civil war before the Church of England was finally to become once and for all the established church. Meanwhile, a variety of Protestant sects arose in England, including the Puritans, who were to become the founders of the English colonies in America. Beginning in the early seventeenth century, the new colonies provided a safe haven for those religious dissenters who were persecuted in England—Puritans went to Massachusetts, Quakers to Pennsylvania, and Catholics to Maryland. But members of the Church of England settled in

Virginia, which, with New York, became the center of power and wealth in the new lands.

Calvinism began with Ulrich Zwingli, who was a contemporary of Martin Luther and, like Luther, was a Roman Catholic priest. Born in St. Gall in Switzerland in 1484, he was educated at the University of Basel and became a priest at the Great Minster Church in Zurich in 1518. There, he opposed the practice of indulgences two years after Luther had done so. In 1521, he convinced Zurich to reject an alliance with France, and from then on he took a leading political role, eventually persuading Zurich to declare war on the Roman Catholic cantons. Zwingli was killed in 1531 fighting for Zurich against the combined forces of the Roman Catholic cantons of Switzerland, but many of his ideas were espoused by John Calvin, the Geneva lawyer who was responsible for much of the development of the structure of Protestantism.

John Calvin was born Jean Cauvin in Noyon, France, in 1509, educated at the University of Paris, and received a law degree from the University of Orleans. At the time, the rector of the University of Paris, Nicholas Cop, was a Protestant, and it seems likely that Calvin came under his influence there. In 1534, Cop fled to Basel to escape persecution of Protestants in France, and Calvin joined him there a few months later. In 1536, Calvin went to Geneva, which was and is French speaking, to organize Protestant reforms there, but he and the city council disagreed, and in 1538 he went on to Strasbourg to minister to French Protestant refugees. Finally, in 1541, the Geneva city council accepted Calvin's proposals for reform, and he returned, remaining in Geneva until his death in 1564. Calvin's influence was based primarily on his preaching and his commentaries on the Bible. He shared Luther's belief in salvation through faith, predestination, and the sovereignty of God, all of which undermined the pope's authority. But he was a lawyer, not a priest, and his greatest contribution was in organization and governance.

Calvin's reforms were carried on to England and Scotland by John Knox, known today as the founder of the Presbyterian Church or the Church of Scotland. Knox, born in about 1510, was educated for the Catholic priesthood at the University of St. Andrews but came under the influence of Scottish reformers. In England, he served the king, but in 1554, when Mary Tudor, a Catholic, restored Catholicism in England, he fled to Geneva, where he came under Calvin's influence. In 1559, with the Protestant Queen Elizabeth on the English throne, Knox returned to Scotland, and in August 1560 the Scottish Parliament followed the English example, abolishing the pope's authority, banning the celebration of the Catholic mass, and establishing Protestantism

in Scotland. Thus, Knox is credited with the establishment not of the Anglican Church in Scotland, but of the Presbyterian Church, a reformed church
far closer in doctrine and organization to Calvin and the Protestant reformers on the Continent than was the Church of England. Like Calvin, Knox
became known as a great preacher, serving as a minister in both Frankfurt
and Geneva.

Rome's response to the Lutheran and Anglican challenges to papal authority took several forms. The first was the formation of new quasi-monastic
orders with the express purpose of bringing Protestants back to the Roman
Church and converting the heathen. Most notable among these orders was
the Society of Jesus, commonly called the "Jesuits," founded by the Basque
Ignatius of Loyola and six other students at the University of Paris in 1534.
They took vows of poverty and chastity and made known their intention to
do missionary work in Jerusalem or wherever the pope should send them.
In 1538, they traveled to Rome to seek the approval of Pope Paul III , which
they obtained in 1540. Ignatius, chosen as head of the new order, dispatched
his colleagues around Europe to create educational institutions. Training in
classical studies and theology and the conversion of non-Christians became
the Jesuits' primary missions, to which was added the stopping of the spread
of Protestantism. Like members of the mendicant orders, the Jesuits did not
live in closed communities governed by rule but were charged with ranging
widely throughout the world in pursuit of their mission and were directly
responsible to the pope. The order soon sent missionaries to India, Brazil,
and the Congo. Ignatius, however, was eager to go to Muslim areas,[21] having spent time with the Franciscans in Jerusalem as a young man. At the time
of his death in 1556, there were some thirty-five Jesuit colleges or secondary schools across Europe; by 1800, there were more than eight hundred
throughout the world.[22] In 1583, with the assistance of the French and Venetian ambassadors, the Jesuits opened a school in Constantinople.[23]

Other orders soon followed. In 1587, the Capuchins restarted missionary activity in the Middle East, first in Constantinople and then moving
east to the Armenians along the Persian frontier and south to the Copts in
Egypt.[24] The Lazarists, or the Congregation of the Priests of the Mission,
founded by Vincent de Paul, sent missionaries to North Africa and Mada-
gascar.[25] In 1604, following the treaty between France and the Ottoman Empire that granted Roman Catholic pilgrims and priests the right to visit the
Holy Places in Palestine, French clerics began to reside in Jerusalem. With
the expansion of the capitulations (agreements between the Ottomans and

other states) to cover the establishment of diplomatic missions, diplomatic status was also accorded the clergy who served the French consuls in Constantinople, Izmir, Sidon, Alexandria, and Aleppo. Priests could wear clerical garb openly and were under the protection of the French government, which enabled missionaries to move openly in the empire, and for most of the seventeenth century the Ottoman authorities ignored movement of Christians from one sect to another. Aleppo rather than Damascus became the headquarters of the Syrian mission because of its importance in trade and because it had a resident consul. In 1626, the Jesuits and the Capuchins arrived in Aleppo, followed by the Carmelites and the Franciscans.[26]

The second and specifically Vatican response to Luther and the other reform attempts was the Council of Trent. The idea of convening a church council to deal with the controversies raised by Luther and others was first proposed by Luther himself in 1520 and urged by Emperor Charles V as a way of countering the rising tide of the Reformation. However, it was not until 1537 that Pope Paul III actually issued a decree calling for the council, and it was only in 1545 that it was finally convened in Trent. Two years later it was moved to Bologna because of the plague, and in 1549 it was suspended. Recalled in 1551 by Pope Julius III (1550–1555), it was again suspended the following year. Its final sessions were held by Pope Pius IV (1559–1562) in 1562–1563. Participants in the Council of Trent were Roman Catholic and primarily Italian, though invitations were issued three times to Protestants to attend. The first two invitations, in 1551 and 1552, were addressed only to German Protestants, but the third, in 1562, was addressed to "each and all who are not in communion with us in matters of faith, from whatever kingdoms, nations, provinces, cities and places they come."[27]

The Council of Trent was the first church council to be exclusively Roman, lacking the participation of either the Eastern churches or the new Protestant churches. The purposes of Trent were to make plain the points of theological difference between the Roman Catholic Church and the rising Protestant churches, to standardize liturgical practices in the Roman Catholic Church,[28] and to reform the church in response to the criticisms that had been so influential in the Reformation. Thus, much of the discussion at Trent dealt with the relationship between faith and good works, a relationship that had come under attack from the Protestant concept of "the elect." This idea was a major factor in the Protestant churches' delay in embracing evangelical activity, for if one had to be one of the elect to be saved, there was little point in expending much energy in converting others. The council also addressed and tried to remedy the abuses attacked by Luther and the Protestants, in particular the sale of indulgences, the behavior of those in religious orders, and the education of the clergy. But in the end, far from effecting a reconciliation with Protestantism, the Council of Trent formalized the differences between Protestant and Catholic Christian doctrine, making reconciliation impossible.

The third response was the establishment of the Sacred Congregation for the Propagation of the Faith, known as the "Propaganda" (De Propaganda Fide), in 1622 by Pope Gregory XV . Missionaries had become embroiled in the growing western European religious schism as rulers competed for political hegemony in Europe. Rivalries between Venice, France, and the Habsburgs for papal support led to national competition for a presence in the Middle East instead of a concerted Catholic effort to bring Muslims to Christ and Eastern Christians to Rome. From the pope's perspective, centralization of the Catholic missionary enterprise under papal aegis through the creation of the Propaganda would provide uniformity and structure for Catholic goals and methods. Gregory XV centralized missions to spread Roman Catholicism in newly explored areas of the world. Fully conscious of European political realities emerging out of the Thirty Years War (1618–1648), the pope sent French missionaries to the Middle East, where the Portuguese had enjoyed historic jurisdiction. Catholics moved to bring lands lacking a resident bishop under their purview. A creed for "conversion" was standardized, emphasizing the pope's role as head of the church and fostering the enrollment of ethnic Greeks from the Middle East in the Greek College, which had been founded in Rome. Enrollment did not live up to expectations, though. Jesuits were called upon to undertake reform, and so a college under the auspices of the Propaganda subsequently opened in Rome, and a press was established to print liturgical and religious books. The first class consisted of "convert" Georgians, Persians, Nestorians, Jacobites, Melkites, and Copts.[29]

In 1626, seven members of the Capuchin order, an offshoot of the Franciscans that had placed itself under the direction of the Propaganda, sailed for Constantinople and Aleppo. During the decades that followed, they set up missions throughout the Middle East, going as far as Arabia and Persia, where they were granted permission to open schools during the reign of Shah Abbas. Catholic missionaries worked among the Maronites, Greek Orthodox, Armenians, and Jacobites.[30]

The vigorous Catholic response to the Protestant Reformation was thus led by a series of energetic popes who centralized authority and standardized church doctrine. But Protestant dissent and the Catholic reaction to it during the sixteenth and seventeenth centuries coincided with the process of European state building and dynastic control that had been evolving since the end of the Crusades. By the mid-seventeenth century, a hundred years after Martin Luther launched what became the Reformation, the combustion of religion and politics led to a series of religious civil wars in France and the religious–political wars on the Continent—the Thirty Years War, which resulted in the establishment of the European state system, solidifying a new religious and political map of Europe.

In France, the strong monarchy that emerged under Louis XIII and Louis XIV fostered Catholic interests as it expanded French economic and political hegemony in Europe and abroad. In the Middle East, the French had already made economic inroads in the Ottoman Empire and replaced Venice as protector of Catholics there. In 1569, as part of their diplomatic cooperation against the Habsburgs, the Ottomans and the French (Suleiman I and Francis I) entered into a series of economic agreements known as "capitulations" (*imtiyazat*) that allowed French merchants to trade in the Ottoman Empire subject to minimal tariff and with little government interference. Their employees were not subject to the *jizya* (head tax) or any of the regulations pertaining to minorities. As trade became more complicated, trading companies formed by merchants were backed by their countries of origin, which were willing to exert pressure on the Ottoman government on their own and their local protégés' behalf. Cardinals Richelieu and Mazarin, political advisers to the Bourbon monarchs Louis XIII and Louis XIV, expanded the capitulations to insist upon the inclusion of Catholic clergy to minister to Catholic merchants. Catholic clergy, and the establishment of French diplomatic representation in Constantinople in 1634 opened the door to a revival of Catholic missionary work in the Ottoman Empire that would work in tandem with French political interests.[31] In 1663, the French monarchy approved the formation of the Society of Foreign Missions of Paris (Société des missions étrangères de Paris), and France soon thereafter renewed its capitulations with the Ottoman Empire.[32] Jesuits, describing a decadent Ottoman Empire, looked to the End of Time. Writing about the sultan as the Antichrist, authors stressed France's historic role in Syria, which was now incorporated into the Holy Land, and evoked the memory of Louis IX as a key figure of the Crusades. They advocated that France zealously convert Syria and "send its light to the Oriental Church, plunged into the darkness of schism and heresy."[33]

The expulsion of the Jesuit order from French soil a century later did not impede competition for souls in the Middle East and church union. Pope Clement XIV's order to disband the Jesuits stranded the twenty-five members of the order working in Constantinople, the Greek islands, and Anatolia as well as the seventeen stationed in Syria and Egypt. Realizing that there was no secular authority available to transfer the expelled Jesuits' property to and that the Lazarists who replaced them in Constantinople, Izmir, 'Ayn Tura, and Aleppo were too few in number to take over all of their institutions, he urged the Jesuits to continue working not as Jesuits, but under such ambiguous titles as "temporary agents." Although royalist government representatives were replaced after the French Revolution in 1789, the French government made it clear to the Ottoman authorities that despite the regime's antireligious ideology, Paris would continue to maintain its protective role over Catholic missionaries. Throughout the revolutionary period and the Napoleonic Wars that followed, the French government continued to contest Catholic Habsburg claims over the protection of missionaries.[34]

By the end of the seventeenth century, then, there was a definitive shift in the relative societal, political, and economic momentum in Europe and the Ottoman Empire. The Ottomans, having been contained in the Balkans, no longer threatened Western and Central Europe militarily. The eighteenth century demonstrated the results of that shift as the Ottoman Empire stagnated, and European states began to impinge upon the empire more and more. The capitulations are the most dramatic evidence of that shift, but it can be seen also in the increase in the number of Europeans traveling to the Ottoman Empire as missionaries, traders, and even tourists. The stage was set for the military return of western Europe as well, and it occurred in 1798 with Napoleon's invasion of Egypt.

Throughout this period, however, Rome continued to make efforts to regain the allegiance of the Eastern churches. The Latin church had never been absent from the Middle East. Through its sponsorship of holy orders, in particular the Franciscans and the Dominicans, the Vatican had maintained a missionary presence after the Crusades in both the Middle East and Central Asia. Remnants of the Crusaders had survived, particularly on the Greek islands, and Rome had continued to send clergy to them, but in addition to these remnants there were the Eastern rite churches that had never accepted the decrees of the Council of Chalcedon in 451 and were known as "monophysites." These churches included the Coptic Church in Egypt, the Armenian Church, the Jacobites, the Nestorians, and the Maronites. The establishment of the Propaganda in the sixteenth century centralized these efforts, and the founding of the Society of Jesus (Jesuits) expanded them. Maronite and Greek colleges were established in Rome to train clergy for those churches.

At the Council of Florence in 1439, the papacy made a formal attempt at reestablishing union with the Egyptian Coptic Church. At that council, union was negotiated with several of the Eastern churches, including the patriarch of Constantinople, but, as noted earlier, these unions were generally cancelled as soon as the churches' representatives returned home. This was the case with the Copts. A delegation of Copts from Egypt and Ethiopia went to Florence, and in February 1442 a bull of union with Copts, Greeks, and Armenians was issued, and a joint mass held.[35] However, none of the representatives of the Eastern churches in Florence seemed to fully understand the meaning of union, and "the [Coptic] monks would recoil in horror whenever Western missionaries suggested they should accept the Council of Chalcedon."[36]

The Ottoman conquest of Constantinople and consolidation of power in the East put an end to the papacy's attempts to reestablish union with the Eastern churches for a hundred years until Pope Pius IV, following the approval of the Society of Jesus, assigned to the Jesuits the mission to the Copts. The mission set out in 1561. The patriarch of Alexandria again agreed to union with Rome, but without real understanding of the meaning of union to the papacy, so the union foundered.[37] Unlike the Maronites, who had a tradition of relationships with the West and reliance upon it dating back to the Crusades, the Copts did not look westward but instead maintained closer relations with the other churches that had rejected Chalcedon, the Jacobites and the Armenians. Throughout this period, the Franciscans maintained their presence in Egypt, making periodic attempts to reconcile the Egyptian church with Rome and even making the occasional individual convert from Coptic to Roman Christianity.

In 1594, a Coptic mission came to Rome, offering to submit to all the church councils, including Trent. There was talk of starting a Coptic college in Rome along the lines of the Maronite College, and by 1597 the Copts were requesting financial support from the pope. However, it became clear that this approach was entangled in disputes within the Coptic community, and following the death of Pope Clement VIII, the agreement of union was dissolved. Periodic attempts to achieve union between the two churches continued throughout the sixteenth century, led by the Franciscans, who opened a hospice and school in Cairo in 1687, but these attempts had no success. Neither the Jesuits nor the Franciscans had much success during the eighteenth century either, and their lack of impact is illustrated by the fact that few Egyptians visited Rome during this period, in contrast to the number of Armenians and even Ethiopians who went there.[38] At the end of this period, then, there was no Coptic Uniate Church, though individual Copts had thrown in their lot with the Franciscans. Only in 1829 were the Catholic Copts allowed to build their own churches, and in 1866 they were recognized by the Egyptian government. In 1893, they were officially separated from the Franciscans, and in 1895, when there were approximately five thousand Coptic Catholics in Egypt, Pope Leo XIII named the first Coptic Catholic patriarch.[39]

Relations between Armenians and the Latin church date from the time of the Crusades. The Armenian Kingdom of Cilicia was the last of the Crusader kingdoms in the Levant to be conquered by Muslims and thus remained a bastion of the Church of Rome until its conquest by the Mamluks in 1375. Like the other Eastern churches, the Armenian Apostolic Church sent a representative to the Council of Florence in 1439 and duly signed an agreement of union. But like the other agreements signed at the council, this one had no lasting effect, and the Armenian Church remained outside the Latin fold until the mid-eighteenth century. However, Armenians in Constantinople and the core areas of the Ottoman Empire had contact with the educational resources provided by the Jesuits and other Catholic orders. Although they were at a disadvantage within the empire because they lacked official corporate religious autonomy (millet standing) within the Ottoman system, by 1700 there were eight thousand Armenian Catholics in Constantinople alone.[40] By 1695, the Jesuits had established mission stations in Erzurum and Trebizond in Anatolia as well as in Persia.[41] In spite of periodic persecution, the Armenian Catholic Church continued to grow, claiming twenty thousand members in Constantinople in 1783.[42] Perhaps the most important and lasting Armenian Catholic influence was Mekhitar, an Armenian monk who went to Constantinople in 1700 and began to attract followers there. He joined the Catholic Church, but when he encountered opposition from the Armenian Church, he moved, with his followers, to the Morea, which was then Venetian territory. From there, the community moved on to the island of San Lazzaro in Venice in 1717 when conflict broke out between the Ottomans and the Venetians. The Mekhitarist monastery at San Lazzaro as well as a breakaway group that established itself in Vienna set up printing presses that became the catalyst for development of an Armenian literary language and the preservation of early manuscripts and works that survived only in Armenian.

In 1742, Pope Benedict XIV formally recognized the Armenian Catholic Church, with its patriarchate first at Sis and later at Antelias, near Beirut. Although the church was in communion with Rome, accepting the pope's authority, it continued to use an Armenian liturgy, as the Maronites continued to use an Arabic liturgy.

Just as Armenian Cilicia was a border state between Byzantium and the Arab kingdoms to the south and east, after the Mongols' retreat the Armenian homeland found itself on the shifting border between the Ottomans and the Safavids in the sixteenth and seventeenth centuries. When the region came under Safavid rule, many Armenians were forced to leave their homes and settle in Persian territory. They came from Julfa in present-day Nakhchivan (an Armenian enclave in Azerbaijan) and established residences outside of Isfahan in what would be called "New Julfa," creating a thriving community that exists to this day.

The evolution of the Melkite Uniate Church represents another paradigm for the relationship of Roman Catholic missionaries with an Eastern rite church. The Melkite Uniate Church used Arabic in its liturgy and was under the authority of the see of Antioch. It never relinquished its ties with the Orthodox Church of Constantinople. After the departure of the Crusaders in the fourteenth century, the Latin church maintained minimal contacts with the Melkites through the Franciscans, who had been designated "custodians of the Holy Land."[43] Following the Ottoman conquest of Constantinople in 1453, the Melkite Church was cut off from the patriarchate because Syria remained under Mamluk rule, and in the latter half of the sixteenth century, following the Council of Trent, the pope gave the Jesuits "'extraordinary missions'" to the Eastern churches. Their mission in Syria was, first, to solidify the relationship between the Maronites and the papacy and, second, to "initiate a full-scale missionary attack against the non-Uniate Churches of the East, to wit: the Melkite, Nestorian, Jacobite, and Armenian."[44] However, no Jesuit mission arrived in Syria until the 1620s. Meanwhile, the Greek College was founded in Rome in 1577, and the Maronite College was established in 1584 to train seminarians from the region and to make knowledge about these Eastern churches more accessible in the West.

Throughout the seventeenth century, the Orthodox Melkite Church hierarchy apparently did not regard the Latin missionaries as a threat to their authority, in part because the Latin missionaries behaved very much like

Melkite priests. They dressed the same way, often celebrated the same rites, and appear to have made no issue of their difference, but they gradually managed to lure away a significant portion of the Melkite clergy and secular elite. What the missionaries had to offer was increased security, derived from French protection codified in the capitulations of 1740, and material advantage, derived from their commercial ties to French merchants operating in Sidon and Aleppo in particular.[45] Catholics set up schools providing the "new" knowledge in mathematics, science, and Western languages. In 1706, the first printing press was established in Aleppo. Although it remained in operation for merely a decade—it was moved to Mt. Lebanon—it printed Bibles and religious materials.[46]

The Syrian Christians evolved from acting as interpreters and go-betweens (dragomans) for the French to becoming merchants in their own right, competing with the French. A Uniate patriarchate was established in Syria in 1724, and after that the French gave considerable preference to those Christians who adhered to the Uniate branch of the Melkite Church.[47] Interestingly, the English merchants operating in Syria at this period do not seem to have had much interest in attracting Syrian Christians to Protestantism.[48] By the end of the eighteenth century, although the Orthodox Melkite Church still represented a majority of Syrian Christians, it had lost much of its elite, including many of its clergy, to the Uniate branch, and the efforts of the patriarchate of Constantinople to reassert authority over the church caused increasing tension. By 1750, the overwhelming majority of Aleppo's Christians and many from Damascus were Catholic in one form or another. Although proselytizing in other parts of the empire, Catholics were apparently particularly successful in areas where there was a French diplomatic presence to back them up.[49] The Ottoman reforms of 1839 extended formal recognition to the Melkite Uniate Church.

Efforts to bring the Nestorians into the Vatican fold can be dated at least from the mid-sixteenth century, when in 1551, with the assistance of Roman Catholic Franciscan missionaries in Mosul, Hanna Sulaqa, a monk from the monastery of Rabban Hurmizd, was sent first to Jerusalem and then to Rome to be ordained as the first Chaldean Uniate patriarch.[50] Like so much in Assyrian history, this event had its origin in a family quarrel. In 1450, the Nestorian patriarch had enacted a law making the patriarchate hereditary. Because the patriarch had to be celibate, this law meant in practice that the patriarchate normally descended from uncle to nephew. However, when Simon Dinha succeeded his uncle as patriarch in 1551, some members of the

community opposed him, hence the approach to Rome. The Roman connection did not last—Sulaqa himself was assassinated in Diyarbekir soon after his return from Rome, and the two patriarchates shifted back and forth
several times between families and between Nestorian and Uniate until the
nineteenth century. A French Dominican mission arrived in Mosul in 1748,
but their activities were interrupted by the French Revolution, and it was not
until nearly a hundred years later that a French mission established a permanent and active presence. In 1838, Hanna Hurmizd was recognized by Rome
as the "patriarch of the Chaldeans" only after he agreed not to permit any of
his relatives to become bishops.[51] Rome then appointed a new Uniate patriarch who did not come from either of the warring families, and in 1844 this
patriarch received an imperial Ottoman decree recognizing him as patriarch
of the Chaldeans.

Jews living in the Middle East and North Africa, composing the other
non-Muslim minority to come into the sights of Christian missionary workers, numbered approximately one million by the end of the nineteenth century. Some were indigenous to the region before the Muslim conquests, such
as the Romaniote or Greek Jews of Asia Minor, the Judeo-Arabic-speaking
Jews of Yemen, Iraq, and Morocco, and the Judeo-Persian speakers of Iran.
These communities were enriched numerically and culturally by Spanish
Jews (Sephardim), exiled from Spain in 1492, who were allowed to reside in
Ottoman domains, and by European Jews (Ashkenazim) who found their
way into Islamic lands through exile or trade. By 1800 in the Western Mediterranean, Jews were the only significant non-Muslim minority; in lands
from Egypt east to Iran, they joined the Christians of various denominations
both as *dhimmi*s (non-Muslim subjects under Muslim law) and as Western
protégés—often competing for the same positions.[52]

Whereas Roman Catholic relations with the Christians of the Middle East
continued unbroken, it took some time for the various Protestant churches
to decide on their stance toward evangelization and missionary work. They
were far too occupied in the struggle to define themselves and to assert their
independence from Rome, both in the political and in the spiritual realm.
Their early interest in the Eastern Christian churches was founded on the
idea that these churches' rites, rituals, and beliefs might be far closer to those
of the earliest Christians than to those of the Roman Catholic Church that
they so opposed, an idea that the Roman Catholics tried to counter in their
efforts to establish relations with the Eastern churches. Thus, the Protestants

took a strong interest in the Eastern churches, but it was primarily an intellectual interest that took the form of collecting these churches' liturgical manuscripts, bringing them to Europe, and studying them intensively in an effort to support the reforms that they were urging on the church. Furthermore, the Calvinist doctrine of the elect served to discourage attempts to convert the heathen. When Protestant evangelism began to develop in the seventeenth century, it, like that of Spanish and Portuguese Catholics in the Age of Exploration, tended to follow the flag, though in the English colonies in North America and India, Anglican missionaries were by no means as integral to the conquest as the Franciscans and Jesuits were in South America and the American Southwest. But while these ecclesiastical contacts between West and East were continuing, the eighteenth century brought increasing contact on the more individual level, as Europeans, under the intellectual influence of the Enlightenment, sought to encounter the East in new ways. Scholars of the Middle East tend to date the modern period from Napoleon's invasion of Egypt in 1798. Specialists in missionary history regard the arrival of Pliny Fisk and Levi Parsons in Izmir in 1820, under the auspices of the American Board of Commissioners for Foreign Missions, as the starting point for the Christian missionary enterprise in the Middle East. Both are correct in some measure, but both ignore the long history of contact between what we now regard as West and East. So far in this volume we have tried to provide some of the context in which these seminal events occurred. Napoleon's invasion of Egypt, if we look forward, seems to mark the beginning of the European imperialist project in the Middle East, but if we look backward, it is simply another in the many French attempts to exert power and influence in the region dating back at least to the Crusades. The arrival of Protestant missionaries in the area brings a new piece to the religious mosaic. Until then, efforts to "convert" residents of the Ottoman and Persian empires were primarily Roman Catholic attempts to persuade members and especially the hierarchies of the Eastern Christian churches to accept the authority of the pope in Rome rather than the authority of their various patriarchs in Constantinople, Antioch, Echmiadzin, and Alexandria. Jerusalem continued to be of great emotional significance for everyone.

FOUR

The Great Awakening of the Protestants and the Anglicans

William Blake's famous lines written in 1804 tell us much about the development of the missionary impulse in Britain in the eighteenth century:

I will not cease from Mental Fight
Nor shall my Sword sleep in my hand:
Till we have built Jerusalem,
In England's green & pleasant Land.

As with the Crusades, there was an emphasis on conquest by the sword, on the centrality of Jerusalem, and now on the identification of England with Jerusalem—the millenarianism that marked the eighteenth and nineteenth centuries. Imperialism joined with the new ideas of the Enlightenment to inspire the Great Awakening in the mid-eighteenth century. Beginning with the preaching and writing of Reverend Jonathan Edwards in New England, the reform ideas spread to Britain, emphasizing the need to bring the whole world to Christianity. Revival movements on both sides of the Atlantic were directed toward what members saw as moribund church institutions. In the next three chapters, we consider the growth of foreign missions to the

Middle East from the United States and Europe from 1798 to 1914 in their political and intellectual context.

By the early eighteenth century, Calvin's ideas of election and predestination, which had been a deterrent to early missionary activity, were becoming less popular and being replaced by the view of Dutch theologian Jacob Arminius (1560–1609) that individual conversion, not predestination, determined salvation. This meant that faith could not only be shared, but spread abroad.[1] Several dissenting groups, all of which stressed personal religious experience, Christian fellowship, and individual interpretation of scripture, coalesced into what became known as "Pietism," a reform movement within late-seventeenth-century German Lutheranism based on the teachings and writings of Philipp Jakob Spener (1635–1705). Pietist institutions were founded in Halle, Germany. They included an orphanage and a university that trained missionaries. The movement gradually spread throughout central and northern Germany until Spener's death in 1705, when the movement declined. In 1727, however, Spener's godson Count Nicholas Ludwig von Zinzendorf revived the movement as the Moravian Church. Based on his estate at Herrnhut in Saxony, the Moravians developed the concept of the whole church as missionary church, and in the 1730s they began sending out missionaries to the West Indies, Greenland, Surinam, South Africa, the Gold Coast, and Ceylon.[2] The Moravians focused their attention on salvation of the individual soul, especially the "First Fruit"—the "most wretched heathen of them all" or "those whom nobody else would dare to approach."[3] Not limited to Moravians, Pietist influence extended to Puritans in New England, Presbyterians in Scotland, and the Methodists and Baptists in England.[4]

In addition to the theological shift, missionary activity was facilitated by the emergence of the British East India Company (founded in 1600) and the Dutch East India Company, which paid for chaplains to serve their staff. At first, the British, fearing interference with trade, did not allow for missionary work among the indigenous population, but the Dutch and the Danes did. In Denmark's effort to participate in the expanding globalization of trade, the Danish East India Company had been formed with royal support in 1616, and its first expedition landed in Ceylon in 1620. The Danes settled on the island of Tranquebar in the Bay of Bengal and established some trading stations on the mainland. By the middle of the seventeenth century, the small Danish colony was nearly forgotten but was re-formed by the Danish king Frederik IV in the early eighteenth century. Influenced by Pietism as well as by the English Society for Promoting Christian Knowledge (SPCK; founded in 1698) and the Society for the Propagation of the Gospel in Foreign Parts (founded in 1701), Frederik sent two Lutheran missionaries to convert the Indians to Christianity. Lacking Danish volunteers, the king turned instead to Halle, the Pietist institution in Germany, and the Royal Danish Halle Mission, called the "Tranquebar Mission," was formed. The Danish mission placed a special emphasis on the importance of language, founding the first printing press in India and printing the first Bible in Tamil.[5] The Danish mission is credited with providing a model as well as inspiration for subsequent Protestant global missionary efforts.[6] The British took charge of the mission in 1728.

As Britain extended its colonial reach, missionaries accompanied colonists and the functionaries of the trading companies who moved to the Americas and to India. The Society for the Propagation of the Gospel in Foreign Parts, established in London by royal charter and headed by the archbishop of Canterbury, was limited to British colonies, where it worked to fill parishes and foster religious teaching in the colonies. As such, it became part of the colonialist enterprise (as distinct from imperialism), and its activities were directed toward both colonists and "natives."[7] The issue of whether to include slaves in their work or not raised the same kind of objection that Crusaders of the twelfth century had faced: in the earlier case, it was a problem that slaves who converted to Christianity would then have to be freed; in the eighteenth century, the British colonists feared that conversion would make their slaves more difficult to control.[8]

The British colonies of North America had been founded by people seeking religious freedom from the control asserted by the established Anglican Church in England; and religious feeling was central to their development. The various colonies were settled by different religious groups—Massachusetts Bay Colony by Puritans, Virginia by Anglicans, Maryland by Roman Catholics, Pennsylvania by Quakers (Society of Friends), and so on. It was the New England Puritan and Scottish Calvinist traditions that gave rise to the First Great Awakening revival movement, its first act being to extend a call for missions to the local indigenous peoples and a later act, after the American War for Independence, to extend a call for foreign missions.

The movement described as the First Great Awakening emerged in the American colonies while they were still under British control and spread to Britain, inspired in no small degree by the writings of David Brainerd and Jonathan Edwards. David Brainerd was born in Haddam, Connecticut, in 1718, and died, probably of tuberculosis, at the home of Jonathan Edwards in Northampton, Massachusetts, in 1747. At the age of twenty-one, Brainerd had a religious experience that led him to devote his life to Christianity. He began preaching in 1742, and the following year he decided to dedicate himself to missionary work with the Native Americans. Supported by the Scottish SPCK, he worked first in western Massachusetts, near Stockbridge, and later in New Jersey and Pennsylvania. Brainerd's importance lies not so much in what he did, for he converted only a few, but in what he wrote and what was written about him, specifically in Jonathan Edwards's *An Account of the Life of the Late Rev. David Brainerd* (1749). Based on Brainerd's own journals and letters, the book had a tremendous impact both in America and in Britain. Brainerd demonstrated, at least to Edwards and his readers, that the simple act of preaching the gospel to non-Christians was so powerful that conversion would follow immediately.

Despite the tensions created by the American War for Independence, the religious revival that had begun with the work of Jonathan Edwards in colonial New England in the middle of the eighteenth century quickly spread to the home country. In Britain, it reflected social anxieties over industrialization and the existential fear of a populous, powerful, and revolutionary Roman Catholic France. This was also the period of the rebirth of millennial thinking that emerged in the wake of the French Revolution, when numerous evangelical millennialists predicted the imminent fall of the papal "anti-Christ" in Europe, to be followed by the Second Coming and Christ's Final Judgment.[9] Horrified by the events in Europe and the anticipated collapse of Catholic authority, the English aristocracy looked for solace and theological guidance to the Anglican Church but found only an apathetic established church that many considered not only utilitarian and formulaic, but neglectful in spreading the Gospel. The evangelical movements, in contrast, focused on individual religious revival or renewal and believed that Britain's providentially ordained colonial and commercial successes obligated it to undertake religious outreach to the unconverted.[10] Some also saw the suppression of the Jesuit order by the papacy in 1773, followed by the delinking of church and state in France by the revolutionary regime, as an opportune moment for Protestant intervention. Commercial networking and the intercontinental dissemination of information about newly discovered areas of the world generated even more interest in foreign missions. Many saw evangelicalism as "an ally both to help maintain the social order at home and to create outlets for the new religious zeal in missionary work abroad."[11]

Echoing the call of their American colleagues, British evangelicals emphasized the need for and the fact of redemption in Christ as preparation for his Second Coming, or the millennium. They highlighted the value of lay involvement and the possibility of creating new initiatives for evangelism and religiously motivated social action—such as the Abolitionist movement and labor reform—and proclaimed the worth of every soul. In reaction to Enlightenment rationalism, people returned to religious piety, Bible reading at home, and the establishment of countless voluntary religious associations. At the same time and often through the efforts of these same people—such as, for example, Captain Cook and others who voyaged to the South Seas and beyond—missions were launched to carry the Gospel to the farthest reaches of the planet,[12] just as the Spanish and Portuguese voyages to Asia and the Americas had launched Roman Catholic missions to those areas two hundred years earlier.

The nineteenth and early twentieth centuries were the high point of Protestant missionary activity throughout the world. The Industrial Revolution that began in England and spread to the United States and northern Europe empowered a Protestant middle class that sought to extend its influence and spread its religion, to which it attributed Protestant wealth and power. Protestant evangelism accompanied the imperial enterprises of Britain and Germany, taking advantage of the window of opportunity created by the weakness of the papacy, which controlled the Roman Catholic missionary enterprise. By 1830, that window began to close once France and the Vatican made their peace with each other, and the French, like the British and Germans, began to look toward empire building.

In the wake of the religious ferment generated by the Great Awakening and the networks and contacts built up for more than half a century, a number of new missionary societies appeared in England and Scotland during an era when religious association was a matter of individual choice: "The number of Dissenters, Nonconformists, and Methodists grew rapidly at the expense of the Established Church. With the weakening of the old 'Christendom' model of church/state unity, mission enthusiasts moved toward active evangelization as a way of getting people to join churches, rather than assuming they would remain in the tradition in which they were born."[13] Catholic missions were organized primarily by political entities—the Vatican and the kings of France, Spain, and Portugal—using as their tools monastic orders, in particular the Franciscans, Dominicans, and Jesuits. In contrast, Protestant missions were organized very differently in northern Europe, Britain, and America. In Protestant countries, evangelism was primarily the sphere of private individuals organized for the purpose, although frequently with at least quasi-governmental support. Thus, the central distinction between Catholic and Protestant remains: Catholic missions were state sponsored, whereas Protestant missions were organized by nonstate entities and individual initiative. Also, the Protestants, unlike the Catholics, sent married men and families abroad.[14]

The Great Awakening inspired the foundation of a number of new Protestant missionary societies. In 1792, the Particular Baptist Society for the Propagation of the Gospel Amongst the Heathen was founded by a self-educated shoemaker, William Carey . Drawing on the practical business models of the trading companies, the Baptist Missionary Society formed voluntary societies to recruit, fund-raise, and provide support for overseas missions. Other British societies included the London Missionary Society (1795), the Scottish (Edinburgh) and Glasgow Missionary Society (1796), the Anglican Church Missionary Society (CMS, 1799), the British and Foreign Bible Society (1804), and the Wesleyan Methodist Missionary Society (1817–1818). On the Continent, there were the Netherlands Missionary Society (1797), the German Bible Society (1814), the Basel School (1815) and the Basel Missionary Society (1822), as well as others in Denmark (1821), France (1822), Berlin (1824), Sweden (1835), and Norway (1842). In America, the American Board of Commissioners for Foreign Missions (ABCFM) was established in 1812. German Evangelicals and American Baptists (1814), Methodists, and Episcopalians (1821) also began to send missions abroad.[15]

From the beginning, Protestant missionary organizations in Britain, Germany, and the United States were linked through correspondence, publications, marriage, and the creation of missionary dynasties.[16] Some of these organizations were initially interdenominational, and many shared subscribers and information about practical matters. Anglicans subscribed to Baptist organizations and vice versa. In 1815, for example, the London Missionary Society listed among its foreign directors men from Basel, Berlin, Rotterdam, East Friesland, Denmark, Sweden, and the United States.[17] Charles Simeon at Cambridge University and the earl of Shaftesbury were supporters of the London Society for Promoting Christianity Amongst the Jews (also known as the London Jews Society) and members of the CMS, especially after the organization came under the jurisdiction of the Anglican Church. For a short time, even the Russians participated. After 1812, Czar Alexander I permitted British missionaries to operate in Poland and granted the Basel Mission to the Caucasus charters for schools, a seminary, a press, and churches; he also fostered extensive exploratory tours in Mesopotamia and Persia.[18] By the 1820s, however, opposition by the Orthodox clergy forced the expulsion of the Jesuits from Russia (1820), the elimination of freemasonry (1822), and the dismantling of the Bible Society School (1824).[19] In 1825, with Nicholas I's accession to the throne, the official orthodoxy that would become synonymous with the state was institutionalized in his conservative policy of "Autocracy, Orthodoxy, and Nationality," and the Protestant missions were closed.[20]

One problem all of these organizations faced was the recruitment of personnel. Lacking facilities to train missionaries, the English, like the Danes before them, initially turned to the Lutheran missionary training institutions that had been founded in the eighteenth century, such as Halle, the Berlin Missionary Seminary, and the Basel Mission Institute, founded by Christian Friedrich Spittler (1782–1867).[21] The German Christian Society (Deutsche Christentumsgesellschaft) provided a constant source of recruits for the newly emerging missionary societies[22] because even though the German societies had trained the missionaries, their churches ironically lacked the institutional structure required for providing mission stations. The British, with their growing empire, stepped in, producing what would become a fruitful synergy.[23] In 1815, ten of the seventeen CMS missionaries were German, but only three were ordained Englishmen. After that, though, the balance shifted rapidly. In 1817, of seventeen missionaries sent out, seven were English, and only four German.[24] By 1824, of the one hundred men the CMS sent overseas, one-third were from continental Europe. Although from 1824 to 1840 half were not of British origin, many had married English women. Between 1820 and 1850, the CMS recruited some one hundred missionaries educated at Basel.[25]

The Society for Missions to Africa and the East, later known as the CMS, worked in the Near East.[26] From the outset, the groups had four areas of endeavor: to abolish the slave trade; to overcome the hostility of the East India Company toward missionary work among Hindus and Muslims; to involve the Anglican Church in the missionary enterprise; and to proselytize among the Eastern churches. Only the latter two were relevant to the Middle East, though converting the Jews and regaining Jerusalem remained paramount. Most missions turned first to the Jews but, like the CMS, soon moved to "revitalize the Eastern Churches and equip them for active mission to Islam."[27]

The initial motivation for Protestant missions to the Middle East was the conversion of the Jews. Drawing on the Book of Revelation, some among the Calvinists and Puritans believed, as do many of today's Christian fundamentalists, that the "thousand-year reign" of Christ on earth could not begin until the Jewish people were restored to their homeland, ready to welcome Jesus as their messiah. This belief that the Jews would play a central role in Protestant eschatology had originated in the seventeenth century and, after having lain dormant in the eighteenth, reemerged at the beginning of the nineteenth among those premillennialists who believed that as the people of God the Jews had a unique past and were destined for an even more glorious future. Before that, however, Jews had to be dispersed throughout the world.[28] Interpreting the French Revolution and the subsequent advance of Napoleon's troops through Europe apocalyptically, British millennialists began to preach not only that the time was ripe for the onset of the millennium, but that man could move events along rather than await divine intervention. Napoleon's victories in Germany, Holland, and Italy, his expedition to Egypt and the Levant, his support for the Jews' return to the Holy Land, and his emancipation of French Jewry—all intensified interest in the Jews and their portended role in the unfolding eschatological process.[29]

The intellectual center of the evangelical movement was Holy Trinity Church, Cambridge, where cleric Charles Simeon mentored missionaries.[30] Using his position at Cambridge to expound upon Britain's special role as a bulwark against Rome in the millennial denouement that was certain to unfold in the wake of the French Revolution, Simeon emphasized the Jews' special role in the divine process, seeing signs in the politics of the era that Britain was the beneficiary of divine protection. Having been spared revolution in 1789 and 1830 (as it would be later, in 1848), Britain was seen to be the New Jerusalem, chosen to combat Rome, to send the light of the Gospel to the people living in darkness, and to bring the Jews into the Christian fold. "In converting the Jews to Christ," Simeon wrote and preached throughout England for nearly half a century, "we adopt the readiest and most certain way for the salvation of the whole world."[31] In other words, convert the Jews first, and the Gentile world will follow. It was in this context that such organizations as the London Missionary Society, the British and Foreign Bible Society (1804), and the London Jews Society (1809) were founded in England. By the end of the nineteenth century, there were more than twenty such organizations in England and Scotland alone.[32]

One figure instrumental in the London Jews Society was Joseph Frey, a Jewish convert who arrived in London in 1801.[33] Born Joseph Levi in Franconia, Frey received a traditional Jewish education and subsequently converted to Christianity in 1798. Once in London, he initially worked for the

London Missionary Society, becoming the first of many Ashkenazi converts to work among the Jewish immigrants, primarily from Germany, who were poor, spoke little English, and were unemployed. As would happen later, when active proselytization began in the Middle East, prohibitions against the missionaries were announced in the synagogues; and most of the Jews stopped visiting the missionaries and refused to send their children to the Free School. At that point, Frey and others, having received from the London Missionary Society little financial support for their work among the Jews, formed a new organization in 1809, the London Jews Society. Debate within the movement over whether the time was ripe for active conversion of the Jews—a debate that pitted those closer to the Anglican Church against the Dissenters—caused a split in the organization.

In 1815, the London Jews Society was rescued financially by those members who were closest to the Anglican Church. Under Simeon's leadership, they brought the society under the sole auspices of the Church of England, soon after which Frey resigned and went to America, where he embarked upon a second career.[34] The society, however, continued its work to bring indigent British Jews into the Christian fold. For the converted who had been cast out by their own people, the society provided employment: printing the society's journals, tracts, and copies of the New Testament in Hebrew. When rabbis pronounced a ban against reading the society's literature, Jews either tore it up or threw it back at the missionaries.[35] The society's efforts could hardly be considered cost effective or reflective of effort. According to its records, by 1859 only 829 Jews had been baptized, of whom only 367 were adults.[36] The society did, however, distribute a prodigious amount of literature.

Realizing that it was making little headway in England, the London Jews Society redirected its efforts "to the *state of the Jews abroad*."[37] It established missionary stations—that is, locations where a missionary lived partly or completely supported by the society on a more or less permanent basis. Stations were located in Berlin, Frankfurt, Amsterdam, Warsaw, and other European cities where there were large Jewish communities.[38] In 1812, connections with a Roman Catholic missionary from Malta who had been distributing tracts around the Mediterranean on behalf of the London Jews Society sparked interest in sending missions to the Middle East. Missionary Cleardo Naudi, a physician, suggested that members of the society be sent to the Jews in Jerusalem, Egypt, and Greece.[39] Protestants considered this an opportunity to supplant Latin missions and the Propaganda Fide during the Catholic eclipse. Moreover, using Malta as a base of operations gave them logistical support for missions throughout the Mediterranean and parts east. By the 1880s, the London Jews Society had set up missionary stations—which it was often later forced to abandon—in areas with significant Jewish communities: Smyrna (Izmir, 1829); Constantinople (1835); Tunis (1834); Morocco (1844); Algeria, Aleppo, and Baghdad (1845); Salonika (1847); Cairo (1847); Damascus (1870); Alexandria (1871); and Persia (1889).[40] Still in existence in the twentieth-first century, the London Jews Society changed its name to the Church's Ministry Among the Jewish People.

Malta had had a long history as a center of crusading Christianity. British territory since 1800, it served as a convenient commercial entrepôt as well as a Mediterranean base of missionary logistical operations, a place where both newcomers of all theological stripes (Catholic and Protestant) and seasoned travelers could meet and exchange practical information. Malta also had the benefit of an established a printing press, being able to print and stock the "Christian Scriptures in the liturgical languages of the Eastern churches and in Arabic, which could be streamlined into Ottoman territory by steady distribution."[41] For these reasons, the island became a launching pad for missionary activity in the Middle East.

Shortly after the end of the Napoleonic Wars, William Jowett, the first missionary sent by the CMS to the Mediterranean, sailed for Malta with the mission to disseminate "Christian truth among the Jews, Mahometans, and pagans, in particular those who border on the Mediterranean."[42] He was later joined by James Connor, who moved to Constantinople in 1816, and Christopher Burkhardt, of the Basel Mission, who would shortly make initial Protestant forays into the Holy Land. In his reports back to the London, Jowett, noting that the Eastern Christians were afflicted with "superstition" and "ignorance," suggested education as the best means for enabling them to become the vanguard in converting Muslims. In response, the CMS sent Basel-trained missionaries to Egypt, Smyrna, and Syria in 1825. Although these missions were short-lived,[43] Malta would serve as a place of refuge for missionaries during time of political turmoil or danger.

Napoleon's invasion of Egypt in 1798, a British military presence two years later, and the subsequent installation of an Albanian military officer, Muhammad Ali, as ruler diminished what little Ottoman authority remained there. Muhammad Ali and in particular his son Ibrahim Pasha created conditions in Egypt as well as in Palestine and Syria that were more favorable to missionary activity. Although Dr. Cleardo Naudi's letter to the CMS in 1811 had spurred the society to send William Jowett to examine the possibilities for missionary work in Egypt and the Levant, it was not until the mid-1820s, under Muhammad Ali's increased protection of Christians, that CMS missionaries were actually dispatched.[44] In 1825, five Basel-trained missionaries—William Kruse, Theodor Muller, Christian Kugler, John Lieder, and Samuel Gobat—were dispatched to Egypt.[45] Lieder would remain there for forty years, and Gobat moved on to become Anglican archbishop of Jerusalem. The London Jews Society also began to be active among the Egyptian Jews. The most important of the American Protestant missions, the United Presbyterians, would not arrive until 1854.

As would occur elsewhere, the goal of the CMS mission in Egypt shifted from conversion of the Jews and the Muslims to work with the local Christians—that is, the Copts. Lieder and his colleagues were charged with educating and "uplifting" the Coptic Church. William Kruse, one of the Basel CMS missionaries, started a boys' school in 1828, and his wife established a girls' school the following year, though the latter was suspended in 1830, when Mrs. Kruse became ill. It was revived in 1835 when a woman missionary, Alice Holliday, supported by the Ladies' Society for the Promotion of Female Education in the East, joined the Cairo mission and took charge of girls' education. She married John Lieder, and they continued the CMS missionary work in Egypt, even as support from London dried up. The schools were based on a Lancastrian model, whereby the older students undertook the teaching and training of the younger ones.[46] In 1845, Lieder reported that by then more than three hundred girls had acquired "sufficient literacy to grasp the Scriptures."[47] The teaching of literacy was central to all aspects of the mission because it made it possible for the Copts, even the women, to experience the scriptures directly rather than being dependent solely on priests and ritual. Efforts to reform the Coptic Church also centered on education, and so in 1840 the CMS Cairo Mission submitted to the Coptic patriarch a plan for the establishment of a seminary to train Coptic priests. It took three years before approval was obtained and instruction could begin. Although the students were chosen by the Coptic patriarch, "Lieder found their illiteracy in Arabic, Coptic, and English such that substantive instruction could begin only in 1845."[48] The seminary operated for only three years, but it inspired both secular government schools and the Copts to start their own educational institutions. Lieder himself remained in Egypt until his death in 1865, after which the mission languished until the British takeover of the Egyptian government in 1882.

Other members of the CMS and the London Jews Society went on to Jerusalem and were soon followed by representatives of the ABCFM, who had previously joined them in Malta. The London Jews Society engaged German-speaking Swiss pastor Melchior Tschoudy to visit Palestine, recommending that he learn Hebrew and Arabic, acquaint himself with the conditions of the Jews, and call upon the English consuls, who at that time were not part of the British government, but in the service of the Levant Company.[49] Tschoudy was soon followed by a second traveler. Joseph Wolff, a converted German Jew who had studied theology under Simeon at Cambridge, set off on a tour of the Middle East, where he visited Gibraltar, Malta, Alexandria, Cairo, Jaffa, Jerusalem, Beirut, Damascus, Aleppo, Mosul, Baghdad, and Basra. Along the way, he met with other missionaries, distributed a few copies of the New Testament, baptized a Jew here and there, and recorded his observations, later published in his book *Travels and Adventures of the Rev. Joseph Wolff* (1861). Testifying to the spirit of inquiry portrayed by the local Jews, Wolff encouraged the society to set up missions in Palestine and Syria. The reaction of the rabbis in Syria and Iraq was similar to that of the rabbis in England: the threat of excommunication of Jews who interacted with the missionaries.[50]

The end of the eighteenth century and the beginning of the nineteenth were also times of great intellectual and religious ferment in New England and the rest of the new United States. Furthermore, the country was engaged in pushing westward in what might be described as its own colonial enterprise, crossing the Appalachians to find new areas of settlement in the West. In this context, it is not surprising that among religiously oriented young men the idea of foreign missions would also take root.

The impetus for sending missionaries to the Near East (as the Middle East was generally called at least until World War I) was qualitatively different from that of the missionary enterprise elsewhere in the world (which may account for the Middle East missions being neglected in most missionary histories). Missions to the rest of the world—India, Africa, and the Far East—sought to convert the heathen. The peoples of the Near East could not be described as "heathen." They were not the naked or "noble savages" of the Enlightenment, at least not until the French Orientalist painters, not to mention authors Gertrude Bell and T. E. Lawrence, came along. Instead, as we have seen in the first chapters of this book, the people of the Middle East, Asia, and South Asia were an integral part of European history. The motivations for the missionary enterprise in the Near East were, like the Crusades, the regaining of the Holy Land and the millenarian conviction that conversion of the Jews and the defeat of the Antichrist (defined by Protestants as the pope and the Roman Catholic Church) were essential for the Second Coming. At a time when Britain was describing itself as the New Jerusalem, it became increasingly important to re-Christianize the old Jerusalem.

Other specifically American motivations were also at work here. America clearly regarded itself as a moral leader—that is, as a corrective to the moral excesses of the Old World. It saw itself as the city on the hill—the New Jerusalem. As such, it had a duty to carry its message to the world. However, before "liberty consonant with Christian belief could ever be established as a global phenomenon, the powerful Ottoman Empire and its Sultans"—who, to Protestants, were the contemporary manifestations of the ancient pharaohs—"would have to be converted or subdued."[51] But in order to carry out their mission, the New World American missionaries were ironically forced to rely on Old World British diplomatic support, the young United States not yet having diplomatic representation in the Middle East. The American missionaries' idealistic efforts gradually came to have another advantage as American commercial interests in the Ottoman Empire and elsewhere began to expand.[52]

The place of Williams College in missionary history was assured by the 1806 "Haystack meeting," led by Samuel Mills, a Willliams College student greatly influenced by Jonathan Edwards's followers, who were now called the "New Divinity" men. Williams College, founded in 1793 in the far northwestern corner of Massachusetts, was located near where David Brainerd had preached to the Native Americans fifty years earlier. The school drew its students largely from the surrounding area, a rough, hardscrabble region of small, isolated farm communities. Mills and four other students met to pray and discuss their religious beliefs in a grove of trees, but when their meeting was interrupted by a thunderstorm, they took refuge under a nearby haystack. Continuing their discussions in the haystack, they decided to devote their lives to foreign missions (rather than crossing the Appalachians to farm in Ohio), and thus the ABCFM was born. The organization was formalized in 1810, and three years later five ABCFM missionaries, accompanied by three wives, departed for India. At its founding, the ABCFM was primarily a New England Congregational movement, but it immediately began to form ties with Philadelphia and New York Presbyterians, and in 1826 the United Foreign Missionary Society, which included Presbyterian and Dutch Reformed representatives, merged with the ABCFM.[53]

In 1816, the Female Society of Boston and Its Vicinity for Promoting Christianity Among the Jews was organized to support the London Jews Society and to assist an ABCFM-sponsored Jewish school in Bombay. In 1818, the ABCFM decided to begin a mission to Palestine, and two young Andover graduates, Pliny Fisk and Levi Parsons, were designated for this task. After a year spent traveling around the country raising funds and founding "Palestine Societies" to support them, the two set off for Jerusalem in 1819,[54] taking with them a copy of Edwards's *The Life of Brainerd*. The ABCFM felt that Americans, unlike European Christians, had a special advantage in converting the Jews of the Holy Land because they were "the only Christian nation, which has never persecuted the descendents of Israel."[55] The young missionaries were to direct their attention also to Muslims, Roman Catholics, and members of the Eastern churches in addition to the Jews. Thus, the earliest ABCFM missionaries—including Fisk and Parsons in the Levant in the early 1820s and Harrison Gray Otis Dwight and Eli Smith in eastern Anatolia and Persia in the early 1830s—conducted exploratory missions to assess the possibilities for serious evangelical work.

Fisk and Parsons made their way toward Jerusalem via Malta, where the CMS had already established a presence and, most important, a printing press, and from there, after conversations with William Jowett of the CMS, they went to Smyrna, arriving in January 1820. Their instructions from the ABCFM included learning local languages, gathering information, and circulating tracts and Bibles. They were enjoined not to offend local custom and to teach in private.[56] At the end of the year, while Fisk remained in Smyrna as chaplain to the British Levant Company in the small but increasingly important Anglo-American commercial community there, Parsons went alone to Jerusalem.[57] His stay in Jerusalem was brief; in 1821, he returned to Smyrna, where he died the following year. He was replaced by Jonas King, who with Fisk and the celebrated Joseph Wolff toured Egypt on the way to Jerusalem. By then, Fisk was senior missionary and, on the advice of the British, realized that a permanent station in Jerusalem was not possible, so he instructed that William Goodell and Isaac Bird and their wives, who arrived at Malta in 1823, proceed to Beirut, which became the American base of operations. The Americans studied the local languages and established a mission, leasing the former Jesuit college at 'Ayn Tura until the Jesuits returned in 1831. They distributed Protestant Bibles and attempted to establish good relations with the Maronite Church.[58]

Relations with the Maronites soon soured. The Maronites, we should recall, were in communion with Rome and acknowledged the authority of the pope. They not surprisingly objected strongly to the distribution of these Bibles that did not include the Books of the Apocrypha. The Council of Trent had commanded that all who did not accept the Apocrypha be excommunicated, and in December 1823 the Maronite patriarch, concerned for his relations with the Vatican and the Roman Catholic missionaries, issued an anathema against the Protestants and ordered the burning of their Bibles.[59] The conversion to Protestantism and subsequent imprisonment and death of As'ad Shidyaq, a Syrian Greek Orthodox, who came to be called the "Martyr of Lebanon," exacerbated communal tension.[60] The Vatican supported the Maronite patriarch's actions, and in 1824 the Catholics of Aleppo obtained from the sultan in Istanbul a *firman* (royal decree) condemning books from "the land of the Franks," forbidding their importation, printing, and possession by Muslims.[61] Undeterred, by July 1824 the ABCFM missionaries had established a school for boys in Beirut and were taking both girls and boys from poor families into their homes for education.[62] Pliny Fisk died in Beirut in 1825.

The missionaries' work was hampered both by a lack of understanding of local politics and by political unrest that broke out with the Greek War of Independence. "The religious emissaries failed to understand that the individualistic, pietistic, disestablishmental, and optimistic style of the Great Awakening in the United States, which they brought with them was a threat to the communal, liturgical, inextricably political, and status quo system of the Near East churches."[63] Because Ottoman law mandated membership in specific religious communities designated by the authorities as recognized millets and did not permit voluntary, individual choice of faith, movement from religion to religion even by Christians from one Christian denomination to another was considered to create political instability and disruption of the conservative social order. The Americans found it difficult to conduct their work quietly— "Puritanism, by its eager commitment to a city built on a hill for all to see, required conflict with competing ideas."[64]

The Greek War of Independence that began in 1821 involved hostilities between Russia and Turkey that spilled over into British concerns about the viability of the Ottoman Empire and affected travel and communication in the region.[65] In March 1826, a Greek fleet attacked Beirut, and in retaliation the Muslims attacked local Christians. Missionary schools were closed. After the destruction of the Egyptian fleet that the Ottomans summoned to Navarino in 1827, Christians were suspected of treason. In the capital, Catholics were persecuted.[66] In Beirut, where plague and famine ensued, the British consul who had protected the missionaries fled, and the missionaries retreated to the safety of Malta in May 1828.

The ABCFM station in Smyrna also closed in 1828, not reopening until 1835. In May 1830, the Goodells went to open a mission station in Constantinople, and Isaac Bird returned to Beirut. The Americans regrouped, considering how to proceed. In 1827, the ABCFM had already decided to incorporate Palestine into a broader "western Asia" mission that included all of the eastern Mediterranean, while abandoning the conversion of the Jews to other missionary societies. Jerusalem, the board's original goal, remained unrealized. From the time of Fisk's visits in 1823, no ABCFM missionaries went to Jerusalem until it sent William McClure Thomson and his wife there in 1834.[67] Eliza Thomson died soon after, and her husband fled the city during the Egyptian attack on Jerusalem during their campaign to occupy Syria. Over the next several years, other ABCFM missionaries came, but no one stayed long, and in 1843 the mission in Jerusalem was abandoned to the Church of England.

Before the bombardment of Beirut by the British, the missionaries were warned of impending danger and closed their schools. An American naval ship then evacuated them to Cyprus. The ABCFM missionaries returned to Beirut in 1841 and prepared plans for expansion in both Beirut and Jerusalem, which they submitted to the board in Boston. In 1843, however, they were visited by Rufus Anderson, ABCFM's general-secretary, who expressed his doubts about the enterprise. Anderson basically opposed the missionaries' focus on education and insisted that they close the schools and concentrate instead on preaching and proselytizing. Without support from the Boston headquarters, the ABCFM mission was forced to abandon its schools as well as its plans to expand its work in Jerusalem and Palestine, leaving the field to other Protestant organizations and the Roman Catholics, who had reestablished their missions after 1830.

Despite all the ABCFM's efforts both in Boston and in the Levant, its early evangelical mission in Syria and Lebanon was essentially a failure, being continually interrupted by political events on the ground. In 1828, the missionaries retreated to Malta because of the Greek attack on Beirut. Ten years later they retreated again because of Maronite–Druze conflict in Lebanon. In 1848, following Rufus Anderson's visit, the mission was forced to abandon its educational efforts in favor of preaching and evangelization, leaving the field to other missions, both Roman Catholic and Protestant. In 1860, further internal strife, coupled with the disruption caused by the American Civil War at home, made it difficult for the mission to function at all. Finally, following Anderson's retirement as general-secretary, the mission was handed over to the Presbyterian Board in 1870. Nevertheless, the ABCFM mission was responsible for the most important surviving American educational institution, the Syrian Protestant College, later renamed the American University of Beirut.

The ABCFM's successes would come in Anatolia, the new focus of its activity. As a result of Dwight and Smith's reconnoitering, the ABCFM had established mission stations in Smyrna, Beirut, and Constantinople, and from the Constantinople station missionaries had been sent east to Brusa and Trebizond as well as to Urmia across the Persian frontier, where they were to work primarily with Armenians and Nestorians.

The ABCFM's history in Constantinople and Anatolia is quite different from its experience in Syria and Palestine. The British CMS had opened its Mediterranean Mission in Constantinople in 1819 but closed it two years later "because of political complications."[68] The Greek assault on Beirut in 1828 that sent William Goodell and his family to Malta led the ABCFM to establish a station in Constantinople in 1830. The Goodells were sent to work primarily with the Armenians—not, they said, to proselytize or to start a new church, but to improve the lot of Armenians, Greeks, and Turks through the founding of Lancastrian schools, as they had done in Egypt.[69] The Lancastrian method, which used the older children to teach the younger, enabled the missionaries to do more with less and eased the difficulties posed by the language barrier. By the end of 1831, Goodell claimed to have established four schools for Greek children, one in Constantinople and three in nearby villages; and by the end of 1832, that number had grown to more than twenty, with more than two thousand children.[70] These schools seemed to appeal especially to the relatively poor Greek community, but the Armenian community in Constantinople seemed less interested in Goodell's efforts, perhaps because the Armenians already had their own well-developed educational network, and the Armenian ecclesiastical hierarchy was very suspicious of the missionaries' efforts. The Armenian suspicions were echoed by the rabbis of Istanbul, who bitterly opposed the Western missionaries' efforts, and eventually by the Muslim authorities.

In 1839, many who had been friendly to the missionaries in Constantinople and Anatolia were imprisoned or exiled, and books were burned in the public squares.[71] But after the accession of the new sultan, the exiled missionaries returned, freer than ever to conduct their activities. Cyrus Hamlin, a different kind of missionary, arrived in Constantinople that same year. He was seemingly as concerned with the economic life of his target population as the spiritual. In 1840, Hamlin started an English-language school for boys at Bebek, which evolved into Bebek Seminary and finally, after the theological department was moved to Marsovan, into Robert College. But Rufus Anderson, in his 1843 visit, insisted on the primacy of teaching in the vernacular and emphasized the evangelical rather than civilizational mission.

The work of the Constantinople station as well as of those stations spreading eastward through Anatolia was primarily with the Armenian Christians—that is, members of the Armenian Apostolic Church under a patriarch recognized by the Ottoman authorities as the head of the Armenian millet. In 1846, the Armenian patriarch in Istanbul issued two bulls of excommunication, essentially cutting the missionaries off from any legal standing with the Ottomans. In response, a group of forty Armenians who had been close to the American Protestant missionaries organized the First Evangelical Armenian Church of Constantinople. By 1848, the church had a thousand members, all from the Armenian Apostolic Church and the Armenian millet in Istanbul. The following year, the Ottoman grand vizier issued a *firman* forbidding persecution of those Armenians who had joined the Protestants, and three years later, with the assistance of the British ambassador, Sir Stratford Canning, a *firman* from the sultan separated the Protestant millet from the Armenian Apostolic millet.[72]

From the time that the Constantinople station was established, the ABCFM extended its reach eastward through eastern Anatolia to Persia, where the British and the Basel Mission, which had established a mission in Tabriz in 1833, were already active; it also extended southeast into Mesopotamia. In 1830, Smith and Dwight were sent on an exploratory mission overland from Constantinople to northern Persia.[73] Their 2,400-mile journey took them through Asia Minor into the Caucasus and northwest Persia,[74] first to Erzurum, then through the heavily Armenian areas of northeast Anatolia to Tbilisi, the capital of Georgia, which had a large Armenian population and was under Russian control. After leaving Tbilisi, Smith was taken ill with cholera, and the two Americans took refuge with Swiss–German missionaries from Basel in the town of Shusha, where they remained for three months. Finally, they continued on to Tabriz, in northern Persia, where they found an English doctor and a British embassy. The journey had taken seven months. In the spring of 1831, Smith and Dwight visited Urmia, a town with a large Assyrian Nestorian population, and reported back to the ABCFM that it seemed to be a propitious site for a mission. The two returned to Constantinople in May 1831, just a year after their departure, and within two years the board sent Justin Perkins and his wife to establish a mission station in Urmia.[75] They were joined in 1835 by Asahel Grant, a physician, and his wife, Judith. In November 1835, the four Americans moved from Tabriz to Urmia, and in January 1836 they opened a school. Two more couples arrived from the United States in 1837, two single men in 1840, and in November that year Edward Breath, a printer, arrived with a printing press for the mission, which soon published versions of the Lord's Prayer and the Psalms in classical Syriac, the Nestorians' liturgical language.[76] Religious materials in modern Eastern Syriac were also printed. At this point, the Protestants were working with the Nestorian Church and its hierarchy and were in fact providing some cash subsidies to them. It was not until 1872 that a separate Protestant church was established among the Nestorians in Urmia.

Asahel Grant had come to believe that the Nestorians were one of the Lost Tribes of Israel and that the main body of the Nestorians lived not in Urmia, but in the Hakkari Mountains of Kurdistan. By 1839, he had persuaded his superiors on the ABCFM in Boston to allow him to undertake an exploratory trip in search of Nestorians in eastern Anatolia. In accordance with the board's instructions, he went first to Constantinople to meet a companion, Reverend Henry Augustus Homes. They then went to Diyarbekir and Mardin, where they were unable to find any Nestorians. At that point, Homes decided to return to Constantinople, but Grant pushed on to Mosul and then into the mountains, accompanied by two Persian Nestorians and a police officer provided by the Ottoman pasha in Mosul.[77] He reached the home of the Nestorian patriarch, Mar Shimun, where he stayed five weeks, returning to Urmia in time for Christmas in 1839. Grant returned to Urmia twice more before his death in Mosul in 1845.

The British had already begun contacting the Assyrians.[78] In the mid-1820s, Reverend Henry Leeves, the representative of the British and Foreign Bible Society in Constantinople, met a Chaldean bishop on his way back to Mesopotamia from a visit to Rome. He arranged to have Syriac Bibles taken to the Nestorian patriarch. About the same time, the peripatetic Joseph Wolff, whom we last encountered in Malta and the Holy Land with the early ABCFM missionaries Fisk and Parsons, also visited Persia. Though he was unable to reach the Nestorian patriarch in the mountains, he did take back manuscripts that enabled the Bible Society to print an edition of the Gospels in Eastern Syriac.[79] However, there was no attempt to engage the Assyrians directly until 1840, ten years after Smith and Dwight had journeyed to Urmia to explore the possibility of setting up a mission station. The catalyst for

British missionary activity was Colonel Francis Rawdon Chesney's Euphrates Expedition of 1835–1837. The British at this time were deeply engaged in the "Great Game" with Russia, attempting to halt Russian expansion from the Caucasus and Central Asia southward toward the Indian subcontinent and into eastern Anatolia and northwestern Persia, which lay on the land route to India. The Chesney expedition, which ultimately failed, was an attempt to demonstrate the practicality of a water route to India from the upper Euphrates. The Arabic interpreter for the expedition was Isa Rassam, a Chaldean Assyrian from Mosul.

Born in 1788, Rassam set off for Rome at the age of sixteen, intending to study for the priesthood. On his way, he visited an uncle in Cairo, who convinced him to go into business instead. While in Cairo, he came into contact with the British CMS, and in 1832 he accepted a position at the CMS printing press in Malta. In 1835, he married Matilda Badger, the sister of George Percy Badger, who was also working at the press at the time, and soon afterward he returned to Iraq as interpreter for the Euphrates Expedition. After the failure of the expedition in 1837, Rassam joined William Ainsworth, the scientist with the expedition, in an exploratory trip from Mosul north to Diyarbekir and finally back to England,[80] where Ainsworth sought support from the Royal Geographical Society for an exploration of the mountains of Kurdistan, with Rassam as interpreter. While in England, Rassam came under the influence of William Palmer of Magdalen College, Oxford, and met the archbishop of Canterbury. Under their influence, he rejected the low-church Anglicanism of the CMS in favor of the high-church Anglicanism that supported the SPCK. By January 1838, Ainsworth and Rassam had received support for their proposed expedition from both the Royal Geographical Society and the SPCK.[81]

The Royal Geographical Society charged Ainsworth and Rassam with exploring an area in a radius of 150 miles north of Mosul, tracing the course of the eastern Euphrates. The purpose was to "examine the hitherto inaccessible Jawar mountains, inhabited, it is said, by about 80,000 Nestorian Christians," with special attention to manuscripts in their monasteries; to collect artifacts and items of natural history; and "[t]o open a communication between the Church of England and the Nestorian Christians through the patriarch at Mosul."[82] In separate instructions, the SPCK sought information about the state of the Nestorian Church, its educational institutions, its liturgy, and its ecclesiastical structure. After many delays, Ainsworth and Rassam finally reached the Hakkari Mountains, where they spent only two weeks, traveling from Mosul through the mountains to Salmas in Persia and then returning to Mosul. They visited Mar Shimun only a month after the American Protestant Asahel Grant's second visit to the patriarch.

For the British, the Egyptian occupation of the Levant in 1831 presented an opportunity. The goals of the British mission societies working in Jerusalem were consonant with British Near Eastern policy, reflecting the congruence of British economic, religious, and strategic interests. The British were concerned about the stability of the Ottoman Empire—or, as it was increasingly being called during the nineteenth century, the "Sick Man of Europe"—in the wake of Russian penetrations in the Caucasus and the Black Sea, which threatened the route to British India and control of the strategic Dardanelles Straits. In 1798, Napoleon's Egyptian adventure had been a wake-up call for the security of British economic interests in the eastern Mediterranean; the Egyptian invasion of Syria that occurred in the aftermath of the Greek War of Independence threatened the Ottoman Empire directly.

Although subject to Ottoman authority, Muhammad Ali, who had become ruler of Egypt after the French retreat, authorized his son Ibrahim to fill the power vacuum created by the vacancy of the governorship at Acre. After all, the Egyptians had come to the aid of the Ottoman Empire both in Greece and in Arabia, where the Egyptians suppressed the Wahhabi revolt against Ottoman authority in 1803. Ibrahim's army moved up the Levantine coast through Syria to the Turkish border, to a point where the Ottomans felt threatened. What is important about the Egyptian occupation is that Ibrahim opened the region to Western economic and religious interests and fostered Christian participation in local government. By relaxing the discriminatory laws against non-Muslims and permitting the construction of churches and synagogues, the Egyptian interlude of the 1830s foreshadowed the Ottoman period of similar reform known as "the Tanzimat." The Egyptians were supported by the French, who occupied Algeria in 1830. In 1831, Jesuits returned to Syria, founding missions that would become influential in the 1860s. Italian influence was superseded by the French.[83]

While the London Jews Society worked against the obstinate refusal of "fallen Israel" to be converted, the missionaries also prayed for the overthrow of Ottoman rule in the region and clearly desired that the British government "protect" their work by influencing the Ottoman Sublime Porte (the empire's central government) to tolerate the conversion not only of Jews and Eastern Christians, but also of Muslims to Anglican Protestantism, an aim that was certainly problematical in the contexts of Anglo-Ottoman relations and the conflicts that arose between the missionaries' goals and the British government's goals.

These two interests unofficially coalesced during the 1830s and 1840s. From the outset, the London Jews Society had caught the imagination of important people active in the Church of England and in British politics. In addition to Charles Simeon of Cambridge, the archbishop of Canterbury, and most of the bishops, other patrons and supporters of the London Jews Society included the duke of Kent, the abolitionist William Wilberforce, and Ashley Cooper, the seventh earl of Shaftesbury, president of the society from 1848 until his death in 1885. Shaftesbury's mother-in-law was married to Lord Palmerston, the foreign secretary who forged British policy regarding the Ottoman Empire during the mid-nineteenth century.

In the context of Palmerston's Middle East foreign policy, Lord Shaftesbury's religious views resonated with British political and commercial policy.[84] Shaftesbury and the London Jews Society sought to repatriate the Jews in Palestine and to establish an Anglican church in Jerusalem.[85] Palmerston wanted to establish a British consulate in Jerusalem and believed the British had a role as protector of Jews and future converts to Protestantism.[86]

The British had been quick to exploit Muhammad Ali's policy. They requested permission to build a Protestant church in Cairo,[87] and they sent out feelers concerning the Church of Scotland's desire to establish a mission to Palestine.[88] But these endeavors paled in comparison with the concrete gains they achieved in the wake of the Egyptian crisis. When the Turks, under economic stress produced by a military modernization program, came under military threat from the Egyptians' approaching the capital, the British provided economic and diplomatic support. As a result, they were able to negotiate the Balta Liman economic agreement that opened the Ottoman Empire to British commerce and assisted in the push for minority rights under Ottoman law. Embodied in the Tanzimat from 1839 through 1876, these rights eradicated non-Muslims' *dhimmi* status and opened the way for Christian proselytization in the Middle East. In addition, Palmerston's defense of the Jews in the Damascus Affair of 1840 (a blood libel that accused Jews of Damascus of killing a Catholic priest) against French Catholic accusations provided Britain with a non-Muslim minority in the religious competition.[89] The French supported Roman Catholic interests; the Russians supported Eastern Orthodox interests; and now the British had Jewish clients who could be used when Near Eastern diplomatic maneuvering involved European support of non-Muslim religious minorities. Last and most significant, in the course of negotiating the Egyptian retreat from Syria, Britain achieved diplomatic and religious representation in the Holy Land: a British consulate would be established in Jerusalem; a Protestant bishop and a church would follow. The British were now positioned to check both Russian and French advances in the Middle East.[90]

By 1841, British strategic interests and the religious convictions of Prussian king Frederick William IV resulted in the establishment of a joint Anglo-Prussian archbishopric in Jerusalem, worked out with the Ottoman authorities. Although the new archbishop did not as yet have a physical church, he traveled to Jerusalem in September to carry out his mission.[91] The Anglo-Prussian agreement stipulated that a British clergyman was to serve as the first bishop; his successor would be Prussian. The position was first offered to Alexander McCaul, one of the early missionaries of the London Jews Society and professor of Hebrew at Kings College in London, but he declined, suggesting that the post would more appropriately be occupied by "a descendant of Abraham." So the church decided to send a Hebrew Christian "to lead fallen Israel to Christian truth."[92] The new bishop was Michael Solomon Alexander, a Jewish convert from Posen who worked for the London Jews Society as a missionary. He served as Anglican bishop in Jerusalem until his death in 1845.[93]

From the outset, the Anglican mission in Jerusalem reflected the British government's ambivalence about mixing mission and politics. Although Alexander was transported to Palestine on a British warship, he was cautioned that his mission was to be low key and directed only to Jews.[94] During his short tenure, the Anglican bishop laid the groundwork for the preaching, education, apprenticeship, and medical programs that would become hallmarks of Protestant work in the Holy Land. His lobbying the British government to pressure the Ottomans to permit the establishment of an Anglican church in Jerusalem led to unease among German Protestants and aroused suspicions among the Russian Orthodox and German and French Catholics about British intentions. Evangelical groups could work in concert so long as they were nonconfessional bodies unconnected with the state and distributed the Gospel but not prayer books. Lutherans initially "took for granted the widespread feeling in German Evangelical circles that the British Empire was divinely called to spread the gospel to a pre-eminent degree and appropriated this mission to the Church of England." By the 1840s, however, the CMS was not in close cooperation with continental Protestants: "'High Church' Lutherans ostracized their Evangelical brethren for associating with Anglican heretics"; and "Anglican elements, both inside and outside the Evangelical party were going behind the CMS to undermine the connection, sometimes in collaboration with dissenters and Scottish Presbyterians."[95] In 1845, the Orthodox patriarch also established residence in Jerusalem.

German Catholics had become interested in the Holy Land during the reign of Ludwig I of Bavaria, whose realm, the third-largest province in post-Napoleonic Germany, had a large Catholic population. In 1838, after his son Duke Maximilian Joseph returned from a pilgrimage to the Holy Land, where he was invested as a "Knight of the Holy Sepulchre" and begirded with the sword of the Crusader Godfrey of Bouillon, Ludwig established the Ludwig Missionary Society—the first society in Germany to raise funds on behalf of Palestine. Established as a branch of an older society that had been founded in Lyon in 1822, the organization supported pilgrimages and the dissemination of Christianity in Palestine. Under the king's leadership, it provided steady funding for the Franciscans in their capacity as "guardians of the Holy Sepulchre."[96] In 1843, following the example of his royal colleague Protestant Frederick Wilhelm IV, Ludwig spearheaded a major fund-raising drive for the Franciscans.[97] Two years later Pope Pius IX appointed a Latin patriarch of Jerusalem.

By 1840, American Protestant missionary organizations had turned their primary attention away from the Jews and toward the Eastern Christians, leaving missions to the Jews to the British. Jerusalem continued to attract seekers and settlers awaiting the End of Time, some of whom should be carefully distinguished from missionaries who sought to evangelize. One group was the American Church of Jesus Christ of the Latter Day Saints (Mormons), founded by Joseph Smith (1805–1844). Mormonism claimed that it and not the existing churches represented an authentic Christianity that focused on "the gathering," the millennium, and the "restoration of all things."[98] To the Mormons, the truth had been distorted or neglected by the churches, and a true church of saints needed to be established on prophetical-ly designated and sanctified territory. This implied two covenant communi-ties: the Jews ingathered from Babylon and restored to the land of the Bible and the Mormons as the chosen people in America. In 1841, Joseph Smith sent a member of the Mormon leadership, Orson Hyde, to reconnoiter the Holy Land. Upon his arrival in Jerusalem, Hyde quickly realized that his competition—American and British missionaries—were already ensconced in Jerusalem, and there would be minimal opportunity for Mormon mission-ary work in preparation for the Jews' imminent return. Therefore, the land had to be reconsecrated. The Jews were told that their "iniquity" was "pardoned" (that is, they had paid more than double for their sins), that the Day of the Lord was near, and that "the Gentiles" should assist Jewish people in the restoration. In anticipation of the prophesied events, Hyde consecrated and dedicated areas on the Temple Mount and the Mount of Olives.[99]

The first half of the nineteenth century thus saw the arrival of several small Protestant missions from northern Europe and America throughout the Near East, none of which was very effective in evangelizing either Muslims or members of the Eastern Christian churches. Although they were at first welcomed by indigenous Christians, the hierarchies of the Eastern churches soon perceived the danger the missionaries posed to their own authority and thus joined with the Ottomans and often the pope to limit their influence. It was not until the promulgation of Ottoman reform legislation between 1839 and 1858 that the Protestants would be able to broaden their activities.

FIVE

Missionaries and European Diplomatic Competition

Russian assertion of the role of protector of Eastern Christians in the mid-nineteenth century, a claim that had lain in abeyance since the Treaty of Kuchuk Kainarji, complicated an already tense situation within the Greek Orthodox community in Jerusalem.[1] Although the Greek Orthodox community was one of the three major Christian communities in the city (Catholics and Armenians were the other two), it had no powerful and active foreign protector like the French in the case of the Catholics (or Latins, as they were called) and the British for the Protestants.[2] Despite Russian assertions after Kuchuk Kainarji, the Ottomans played off Greeks and Catholics as each community vied for custody of the Holy Sites until the situation came to a head during the nineteenth century.[3] For example, the Ottomans gave the Catholics permission to repair damage from the 1808 fire at the Church of the Holy Sepulchre and allowed the restoration of the Latin Patriarchate of Jerusalem in 1847 (it had moved to Cyprus following the fall of Acre and the Crusader kingdom in 1291)[4] as well as the establishment of the Anglo-Prussian bishopric in 1841—all of which moved the Greeks to action. As imperial subjects, the Greek Orthodox community was able to purchase land, and in the 1840s it began to rebuild some of its convents and to open schools.

The Greek Orthodox Church also revived the Greek Orthodox patriarch-ate of Jerusalem, signifying the growing importance of the community but also revealing underlying institutional weaknesses that both Protestant and Catholic missionaries were quick to exploit.[5] By the nineteenth century, the Greek clergy were split between local Arab Orthodox, who occupied lower-level positions, and a small group of Greek monks and priests from the Greek islands who had authority in the church's upper levels. Competition between Greek and local Arab clergy for leadership of the Orthodox Church in Jeru-salem erupted during the Greek War of Independence (1821–1832). When the position became vacant in 1847, Russian participation in the election compli-cated an already tense situation. The Russians not only had to confront the reality of local politics within a Greek church that wanted to be independent and free to determine its own policy, but also criticism by the church officials back home over Greek neglect of the increasing numbers of Russian pilgrims traveling to the Holy Land. Having no local community in Jerusalem ex-cept for a few priests who ministered to these growing numbers of pilgrims,[6] nobles and peasants making the journey to Jerusalem by land and water, on foot, and even on their knees, Russia depended on support by communities in Russia and an annual contribution from Russian soldiers and sailors to sustain this religious and emotional connection. Pilgrims from Russia, both Christian and Muslim, were also used as a source of political leverage: in 1846, the government granted free passports to those who traveled to visit the Holy Sites.[7]

Concern over Latin usurpation of Orthodox rights in Jerusalem and the arrival of the Protestant missionaries in the Holy Land moved the czarist government to act to preserve the integrity of the Orthodox community. The Russian consulate in Beirut was given jurisdiction over Russian interests in Jerusalem, and in 1842 Czar Nicholas I authorized a fact-finding mission to the Holy Land in order to ascertain why the Protestants in particular were making headway with Orthodox Christians.[8] Porfiri Uspanski's reports mir-rored the views that the Protestants were sending back to England telling of misspent monies, dilapidated churches, and disputes between Greek and Arab clergy in the districts of Jerusalem and Antioch, whereas the "well-oiled Catholic and Protestant missionary machines were making inroads with the children of the Orthodox community."[9] For a decade, Uspanski lobbied St. Petersburg for a permanent Orthodox religious presence in Jerusalem, the establishment of educational institutions, and the amelioration of Greek–Arab relations within the church. The immediate result—likely due more to Russian politics than to religion—was plans for the establishment of a Russian ecclesiastical mission in Jerusalem. The establishment of educational institutions designed to counter Catholic and Protestant missions and to improve the lot of the Orthodox had to wait until the end of the Crimean War (1853–1856), which many Russians regarded as part of a religious crusade to take possession of the Holy Places.[10]

Not to be outmaneuvered, the French reasserted themselves as administrators of the Holy Sites in Jerusalem, a claim that France had confirmed in the context of the 1740 renewal of the capitulations, combined with a romantic nostalgia for the medieval Crusades that reemerged after the Napoleonic Wars. Just as the Russians faced political issues both in the Middle East and at home, the French had to contend with how domestic politics played out in relations with the Catholic Church at home and in support for religious mission abroad.

Events in Europe culminating in the French Revolution, the Napoleonic Wars, and Concordat of 1801 between Napoleon and the Vatican had impeded Catholic missionary work in the Middle East. By the mid-eighteenth century, the Vatican replaced Jesuits with Lazarists in Lebanon; Jesuits were expelled from most European Catholic countries; and in 1774, the Society of Jesus was suppressed by Rome. Despite its reestablishment under Pope Pius VII in 1814, by the 1820s less than five hundred members could be mobilized. In the Ottoman Empire, a few Lazarists still worked in Lebanon, as did Dominicans, who maintained the parish of Saint-Pierre-de-Galata under their care in Istanbul.[11] The only significant number of monastic houses was in Jerusalem—the Order of the Holy Land that was founded at the end of the Crusades to safeguard the Christian Holy Sites. There, the Franciscans tended an Arab flock, but almost all of the members of the order were either Italian or Spanish.[12]

With the restoration of the monarchy after their defeat in the Napoleonic Wars, the French worked to restore their national image. The publication of Joseph François Michaud's history of the Crusades (serialized from 1812 to 1822) at a time when France was in the process of occupying Algeria linked heralded medieval exploits with the new imperialist venture. In a commentary to a later edition, Michaud, a monarchist who believed that crusading enriched all the European nations engaged in it, compared France's mission in Algeria to that of Louis IX's thirteenth-century expedition to Tunis, noting that "the conquest of Algiers in 1830 and our recent expeditions in Africa are nothing other than Crusades."[13] In a similar vein, King Louis Philippe commemorated France's participation in the heroic effort at Versailles. In the newly redecorated palace, he devoted a special room to this epochal period in French history. Paintings such as Eugene Delacroix's 1840 *Entry of the Crusaders Into Constantinople on the Fourth Crusade* graced its walls, as did the coats-of-arms of families that had participated in the Crusades. Members of the French nobility—that is, those who had survived the revolution—competed for representation to the point that some who were not included when the room opened in 1840 produced documents, often forged, to prove that their forbears had been on the mission to Jerusalem or accompanied St. Louis to North Africa.[14] At the same time, however, Louis Philippe was reluctant to send missionaries to Algeria for fear of provoking sectarian tensions.[15]

In France, the government moved to reduce Catholic prominence in French education. From 1828 to 1850, Jesuits were banned from teaching in France for fear that they would prepare French youth for religious orders instead of educating them as free, independent citizens of the country.[16] In the absence of a state educational system, however, Catholics still controlled the schools. Their graduates did in fact support missionary work, and many entered orders that were actively seeking recruits because of increasing demand for Catholic missionary schools in the Middle East. During the 1830s, the French government provided funding for the work of the Lazarists and their college at 'Ayn Tura in Lebanon. At odds with the small Jesuit mission that had returned to Lebanon in 1831, the French government viewed the Lazarists as more Gallican. During the 1830s, the Lazarists supported the French-backed Egyptian regime in Syria, unlike the Jesuits, who supported the Ottomans.[17] Because of the Jesuits' support for the Turks, the superior of the French Jesuit mission in Syria was forced to leave; Father Ryallo dismantled the mission and settled in Malta in 1841. As late as 1847, Rome sent the Sisters of Saint-Joseph of the Apparition to assist the Latin missionaries still in Beirut, but pressure from the French government forced them to move to Jerusalem. Despite this opposition, between 1831 and 1864 the Jesuits established six residences in Ottoman Syria.[18]

France also needed a supply of educators to staff the French schools that were being established to compete with the Italian, American, and British schools sprouting up throughout the Middle East. Demand for French education was due in part to the increasing business connections between the French metropole and its economic periphery: the Maronite silk producers of Mount Lebanon traded with the city of Lyon, as did businessmen in the new centers of commerce that emerged with the French occupation of Algeria in

1830 and Tunisia in 1881. These commercial connections strengthened French relations with the Christian minorities of the Middle East and North Africa, who wanted French-language instruction for their children. [19]

The French also supported Catholic schools in the Middle East to counter the Protestant threat. During the mid-nineteenth century, France, despite its secular governments, was undergoing a Catholic revival much like the Protestant Second Great Awakening in Britain and America, a revival that translated into the proliferation of Catholic schools in France to strengthen the faith and lay interest in missionary work. The fact that Lyon not only was commercially connected to the Middle East but was also the seat of the Propagation de la Foi (1822), the lay society that funneled monies to the missionary orders abroad and to the seat of the reconstituted French Jesuit mission (1843) at Ghazir on Mount Lebanon, drew the French Catholic connection to the Middle East even closer.[20]

The establishment of Jesuit missionary schools in Syria and of the French consulate in Jerusalem (1843)—so that, as Prime Minister François Guizot wrote to his ambassador in Rome, the French diplomat would be "protecting the Catholic religion, those who profess it, and their institutions" and "extending as much as possible the action and effects of a patronage of which France will always take the glory"[21]—can be seen in the context of French reaction to British/Protestant ascendancy in the Middle East and specifically in Jerusalem. However, the ascension of Pope Pius IX to the papal throne in June 1846 and the creation of a Latin bishopric for the "prestige of Catholicism and the needs of the Palestinian mission" but under the authority of the Propaganda Fide created diplomatic problems for the French much like those the Russians had to deal with in Jerusalem. In 1847, the Latin patriarchate in Jerusalem was restored, but differences of opinion ensued between the Franciscans and the patriarch, the missionary Joseph (Guiseppe) Valerga, a Genoese, whom they saw as serving the interests of France.[22] In 1862, Pius IX set up a special department within the Propaganda to care for the interests of the Uniate churches in the Middle East.

After 1848, the resurgence of religious fervor in France led to increased mission work as French Catholics preached religion instead of revolution. Educating Catholics in France and sending missionaries abroad, "France distinguished herself as the *pays missionaire* par excellence." Pilgrims were encouraged to visit the Holy Land, whose borders were expanded to include all of the places where the people of Israel had lived: Jordan—where Mount Nebo and Moab were located—was added to the heartland of Palestine,

Syria, and Egypt.[23] The Jesuits founded the Catholic Press and organized indigenous women's congregations to teach in schools.[24]

French missionary expansionism became even more evident after 1852, when the newly inaugurated French emperor, Napoleon III —Bonaparte's nephew Louis Napoleon, who had been elected French president of the Second Republic in the wake of the 1848 uprisings—proclaimed the Second Empire and France's quest for imperial glory. As the run-up to the Crimean War reminded the French of the Treaty of Kuchuk Kainarji and of the capitulations, followed by a flurry of diplomatic activity in European capitals and troop movements along the Black Sea, the French king even flirted with the idea of establishing Catholic missions in Turkey. Instead of Turkey, however, he looked to Jerusalem, dispatching the Orientalist Catholic cleric Eugène Boré, who had studied Persian in Tabriz in 1838, to investigate the situation of the Holy Sites in Jerusalem. He and Bishop Valerga garnered the support of the French ambassador in Istanbul and his colleagues from Austria, Belgium, Spain, and Sardinia to convince the sultan to restore the Holy Sites to Latin control. The Russians warned against changes in the status quo, and when they were ignored, they mobilized troops in Moldavia and Wallachia, leading to the Crimean War.[25]

Although the Crimean War (1854–1856) was not fought in the Middle East, it had profound repercussions in the region. Napoleon III's plans for missions in eastern Turkey were never implemented, but during the Crimean War the French did create an important missionary institution that was clearly identified with France. The Oeuvres des écoles d'Orient (1855) was seen by its intellectual lay founders to be a vehicle to be used to spearhead the Catholic missionary enterprise in the Middle East. They believed not only that the Middle East was ripe for conversion because of the historic changes unleashed by the Crimean War, but that because the sultan was indebted to his Christian allies for their support during the war, the Ottomans would now allow missionaries to operate inside the empire. In this new world, France would take a leadership position because of its historic position as *fille ainée* of the Roman Catholic Church in Rome and because of the historic role it had played during the Crusades.[26] Like the Protestant volunteer organizations, the Oeuvres des écoles d'Orient depended on support at home: by 1863, more than two hundred thousand subscribers worked to raise money to support missionaries in the Middle East. One of the organization's first leaders was Father Charles-Martial-Allemand Lavigerie, whose experiences fundraising for and dispersing monies through the society for victims of the 1860

Druze–Maronite war in Lebanon would forge his ideology of mission in the service of France. The society was instrumental in founding French schools, hospitals, and shelters from Cairo to Constantinople.[27]

The Treaty of Berlin (1856) signed at the end of the Crimean War preserved the territorial and political integrity of the Ottoman Empire and neutralized the Black Sea. In the East, however, the Great Game continued under Nicholas's successor, Alexander II, who extended Russian reach in Central Asia past the ill-defined borders of the Caucasus, Iran, and Afghanistan to the Caspian Sea and Bukhara, where the imperial competition continued.[28] Nevertheless, the Turks were welcomed into the European family of nations, and, with Ottoman national sovereignty ensured by the major powers, it was thought that the "Sick Man of Europe" would be on the mend because of the prohibition of foreign intervention into its domestic affairs.

In the Ottoman heartland, as European powers and reform-minded Turkish bureaucrats pressed for more administrative changes in line with the Tanzimat reforms promulgated beginning in 1839, the government in Istanbul conferred citizenship on all, Muslim, Christian, and Jew (*hatt-i humayun*) in 1856 and with it military conscription on all residents of the empire. Not only was the historic dominant/subordinate Muslim/non-Muslim relationship ended with the abolishment of the *jizya* tax and the historic discriminatory practices, but non-Muslims could pay (*bedel askari*) to avoid military service. They were also permitted to purchase land and build new houses of worship. Furthermore, the Ottoman Empire officially allowed Christian missionary activity. Muslim reaction to Christian jubilation at the creation of millet status for Melkite Catholics in 1849 portended what was to come. The flamboyant expression of Catholic joy in a triumphant procession in Aleppo's streets, "replete with large crosses and the discharging of firearms in celebration," led to violence against Christian churches, shops, and homes in the city in 1850. The Ottoman authorities suppressed the rioters and restored order.[29]

Sectarian tensions that had bubbled beneath the surface of Christian–Muslim relations since the opening up of the Middle East to the West in the 1830s erupted again in a conflagration between Druze and Maronites on Mount Lebanon in 1860. Where Muslims and local elites felt threatened by the economic and social dislocation brought about by the Ottoman administrative reorganization and the institution of a secular political order, Christians saw "ethnic cleansing" and a sectarian struggle.[30] The Druze attacked and killed some twenty-two thousand Christians. With the help of the French fleet and troops in Beirut, the Ottomans restored order, but the French intervention resulted in the establishment in 1861 of a French-supported and protected semiautonomous region of Mount Lebanon under a non-Lebanese Christian governor, but effectively under Maronite control, which lasted until 1914. The fact that the "missionaries aligned themselves behind the avenging power of European (and even Catholic European) 'Christendom' was telling."[31]

For the Jesuits, along with the French consul and the rescue committees aiding the Christian refugees who fled the mountains during the Maronite–Druze conflict, the year 1860 was a turning point. Not only did they receive reparations from the Ottoman government for missions damaged during the unrest, but the French government granted scholarships to the Jesuit seminary at Ghazir, which after 1848 began to teach in French instead of Italian. After 1860, just as France actively took upon itself the role of protectors of Christians, so the Jesuits saw themselves as frontline troops in the "pacific crusade" to create a new world order in the Middle East. Interpreting a declining Ottoman Empire as decadent Islam, they saw an opportunity to bring all the Christian churches under the authority of Rome and to combat Protestantism at home and abroad. The Protestant threat was clearly stated in a description written in 1858 by Father Billotet about a village in Syria:

> They [Christians] are humiliated, abandoned, defenceless and without protection; the apostles of Protestantism offer them the support of the English consul, a Protestant minister himself, that of the Prussian Consul, no less than his colleague. America if need be and Holland are at their service. They are poor and lacked everything, the Biblist promises them help. They live in ignorance and are not educated, one will procure them teachers, schools, and books. How to resist such attractive promises? The predicant is therefore admitted in villages cleverly starts dogmatizing, takes the names of the adepts, they sign up in huge numbers and the work of the apostasy begins. Soon one counts by the hundreds the number of families giving up their fathers' faith, and today how many villages are entirely corrupted, moaning under the yoke of heresy.[32]

By the late 1870s, the Jesuits had established some five hundred schools in the Middle East. In response to the success of the Syrian Protestant College, in 1875 they moved their base of operations in Lebanon from Ghazir to Beirut and followed with the establishment of the University of Saint-Joseph. The Dominicans, Capuchins, and Franciscans were represented in Istanbul, and there were Latin missionaries in every major city in Turkey. By the 1880s, members of Catholic orders staffed hospitals, orphanages, asylums, and the more than thirty Catholic schools. In 1904, there were 3,397 Catholic missionaries in the Ottoman Empire; of these, 2,308 were French. The language of instruction in most of the missionary schools was French, and by 1860 Lazarist schools and missions had been established in Persia.[33] The avowedly secular French governments actively supported Catholic mission activity in the Middle East.

In Jerusalem, Anglican mission work continued unabated. Bishop Michael Alexander's work solely with the Jewish communities was contested by the CMS. His successor, Samuel Gobat (served 1846–1879), was less interested in converting Jews than with bringing Arab Christians and eventually Muslims to Protestantism. A French-speaking Swiss who had worked for the CMS editing missionary materials in Malta and as a missionary in Ethiopia, Gobat spoke Arabic and had traveled through Palestine, Mount Lebanon, and Egypt before taking up his post. Whether Gobat deliberately changed policy or not by focusing on Eastern Christians rather than on Jews, soon after his arrival in Jerusalem, he began to set up English schools not only in Jerusalem but throughout the Holy Land that were open to Jews and Arab Christians alike, an initiative much like that of the American Protestants near Beirut.[34] This shift in policy, which was opposed by the London Jews Society, initiated the rift between the Anglican bishop and the CMS that would result in an official split between the CMS and the London Jews Society during his tenure in Jerusalem. The CMS would work toward the indigenization of the Anglican Church in Palestine; the London Jews Society would continue evangelization.

In addition, Gobat's invitation to the CMS to set up an official mission in Jerusalem alienated the Catholic and Orthodox communities, especially after the Ottoman designation of a Protestant millet in 1850 that was to have equal status with the other religious communities in the Ottoman Empire.[35] In 1851, the CMS established a Palestine mission. Recognizing that northern Syria in the area of Mount Lebanon was American missionary territory, the CMS sent missions to southern Syria and to areas on both sides of the Jordan River, specifically to work among Eastern Christians. It also began to incorporate Henry Venn's administrative philosophy advocating the development of indigenous churches and evangelizing Muslims.[36]

Bishop Gobat also came into direct confrontation with the new British consul in Jerusalem, James Finn, who, although sympathetic to the missionary work—his father-in-law was Alexander McCaul and his wife, Elizabeth, was an active proselytizer for the London Jews Society—questioned the bishop's advocacy of the German Templer Society (Tempelgesellschaft), which set up agricultural settlements in and around Haifa, Jaffa, and Jerusalem, and his promotion of German missionary personnel without sensitivity to British interests.[37] In response to a request by Gobat, Theodor Fliedner, spiritual rector of Motherhouse of Deaconesses in Kaiserswerth on the Rhine sent deaconesses to Jerusalem to set up a German hospital and a girls' school for the Arab population. The ground floor of the Deaconesses' House on Mount Zion served as Protestant hospice for German pilgrims in the Holy Land.[38] In 1856–1857, Fliedner founded a hospital in Alexandria, Egypt.[39]

Most of the missionaries who followed Gobat to work in Palestine were Germans who received their missionary training at Basel under Christian Spittler. In 1852, Friedrich Adolf Strauss founded the Jerusalem Society to support the missionary, health, welfare, and educational projects undertaken by the Anglo-Prussian bishopric among Protestant Arabs in Jerusalem, Hebron, Haifa, and Jaffa. He had traveled to the Holy Land after his ordination and noted how little the customs of the people had changed over the millennia; he saw the "distressing fulfillment of the prophecies . . . and was touched by the truth of God's word." He questioned "how the present religious situation developed, and what our fellow-believers should do so that God's word, now receded into the shadows or totally lost, shall be proclaimed in those places where it was once revealed."[40] He hoped that his travel account *Sinai and Golgotha, Journey to the Orient* (1847) would generate pilgrimage to the Holy Land. He also set up a house of pious brethren (*Brüderhaus*) in Jerusalem for men who would be both workmen and missionaries—their Christian way of life serving as an example. One of the craftsmen sent to Jerusalem was Johann Ludwig Schneller, who later headed the Syrian Orphanage (c. 1855) and established the Schneller orphanage and training school at Bir Salem near Ramle.[41]

For his part, Finn, the British consul, sought to provide diplomatic protection for the increasing number of British tourists and Christian pilgrims as well as stateless Jews who were arriving as Jaffa became a port of call for the new steamship lines that began to ply the Levantine coast. He also established the Jerusalem Literary Society, which fostered study of the biblical Holy Land and looked to future agricultural development. These interests coalesced with those of his wife, Elizabeth, who preached the Gospel, founded agricultural settlements, schools, and clinics, and turned potential converts over to Bishop Gobat to be baptized.[42] Both Finn and Gobat complained about each other's work to London. In the end, Finn resigned and was transferred; Gobat died sixteen years later.

During the short term of Gobat's successor, Bishop Joseph Barclay, the Jerusalem Protestant community had become divided into German, Arabic, and Hebrew–English congregations. The joint bishopric was dissolved shortly after his death. At first reluctant to maintain the Anglican bishopric in Jerusalem, the archbishop of Canterbury was encouraged by Greek Orthodox support for a Protestant presence in the city to counter the Latins. The bishopric would continue to function but with somewhat altered goals: it would supervise English churches and schools in the Middle East; provide episcopal oversight of the "preaching of the Gospel to Jews, Arabs, and other non-Christian inhabitants of those countries"; and develop further relationships with Eastern Christians. Although the Anglican Church could encourage religious inquiry, its role would not be to convert members of other churches. Upon taking office, the new bishop, George Francis Popham Blyth took the bishopric further away from its original evangelical roots. Not only was the bishopric moving away from proselytizing among Jews—only 432 Jews had been converted by the London Jews Society[43]—but Blyth established good relations with the Greek Orthodox Church and planned the construction of an Anglican collegiate church, separate from Christ Church, a proposal that was opposed by both the London Jews Society and the CMS. Finished in 1910, St. George's in East Jerusalem became the representative institution for Anglicans working in and visiting the Holy Land, an international embassy of Anglicanism and the vehicle for Anglican–Orthodox ecumenism. The London Jews Society and its supporters continued its work among Jews with their schools, hospitals, and outreach programs. CMS focused on mission work with its schools, hospitals, and churches and drew upon native Christians. By the end of the 1880s, it had some fifty schools, compared with three London Jews Society schools.[44] By the turn of twentieth century, both Hebrew Christians and Arab Anglicans developed their own associations independent of the London Jews Society and the CMS, such as the Palestine Native Church Council, which became the voice of Arab Anglicans.[45]

Following the promulgation of the *hatt-i humayun* in 1856, the CMS decided the time was right to open missions in other areas of the Middle East. In Constantinople, a new mission was headed by Karl Gottlieb Pfander, who had attended the Basel Seminary and then gone to Tbilisi with other Basel missionaries. They were expelled following the Russian conquest of Georgia in 1839 and went to India, where they joined the CMS. In 1858, Pfander went on to Constantinople, where the Society for the Propagation of the Gospel in Foreign Parts and the American Congregationalists (ABCFM) and Methodists were already working. The mission was not to last long, however. Six years later, in 1864, the CMS, Society for the Propagation of the Gospel, and Bible Society missions were attacked and closed by the Ottoman police, and without the support of the British ambassador at the Porte (Lord Stratford de Redcliffe, who had negotiated the *hatt-i humayun* and was a staunch supporter of missions), who had returned to England, British missionary activity in the Ottoman capital came to an end.[46]

As long as American missionaries in Persia and to a considerable degree in the Ottoman Empire as well could not call upon their own diplomatic representatives for assistance in times of trouble, they also could not be accused of furthering their governments' imperial aims. British missionary societies were far more entangled with their government's political agendas than were the American societies, particularly because British imperial interests came to regard the Middle East as having greater importance. British imperial policy in the mid-nineteenth century was dominated by the increasing importance of India and of the routes to India. The Ottoman and Persian empires sat astride these routes, and what was perceived as their dysfunctionality was of increasing concern to the expanding imperial powers of Britain and Russia.

By midcentury, with the understanding that the goal of converting Muslims would be shelved for the time being and with the millennial enthusiasm for the conversion of the Jews of the Holy Land waning, American and British Protestants staked out their own spheres of missionary interest in areas where there were significant Eastern Christian populations. The ABCFM worked in Anatolia and until 1870 in Syria and Lebanon. Presbyterians took over from the ABCFM in 1870 in Persia, Syria, and Lebanon. The Presbyterians also worked in Egypt, where they encountered British missionaries (English and Scottish) who worked within the context of British imperial interests. "The mixed background of Anglicans (high and low parties, rational orthodoxy, evangelical piety, liturgical revival, etc) produced a varying, sometimes conflicting opinion as to the correct relation with Orthodox churches."[47]

In eastern Anatolia, soon after Asahel Grant's second visit to the Nestorian patriarch in 1841, the patriarch was also visited by William Ainsworth's expedition, sponsored jointly by the British Royal Geographical Society and the SPCK. Ainsworth's sponsorship reflected his dual objective—to scout out possible routes for a railroad through eastern Anatolia and to establish a relationship between the Nestorian Church and the Church of England. As a result of the Ainsworth expedition in 1839–1840, the archbishop of Canterbury sent George Badger with letters of introduction to the patriarch in 1842.

Meanwhile, in April 1841 a Nestorian archbishop requested aid from the English church, noting that Rome had already made some offers to the Nestorians. The Nestorians were particularly eager to receive aid to protect them against the Kurds.[48] In December of that year, the SPCK agreed to grant five hundred pounds "for the purpose of promoting the objects of the Society in Mesopotamia and Kurdistan."[49] By April 1842, a mission consisting of George Percy Badger and J. P. Fletcher was on its way.

George Percy Badger was to become the greatest English advocate of a mission to the Nestorians, and the eventual establishment of the Archbishop of Canterbury's Mission to the Assyrian Church[50] is undoubtedly due to the fact that Badger kept the idea before the British public for forty years. Born in 1815, the son of an army sergeant, Badger had grown up in Malta and had worked there for the CMS and the ABCFM printing press first in Malta and then in Beirut. He, like Isa Rassam, had a somewhat checkered religious history, beginning as a low-church Anglican with the CMS, becoming a Methodist, and finally by the late 1830s becoming attracted to the high Anglican church and seeking ordination in England.[51] By the time he and Fletcher set out on their mission, Badger's mother and sister, who was Rassam's wife, were living in Mosul.

Following his arrival in Mosul in January 1843, to arrange for the establishment of schools, Badger visited the Nestorian patriarch, Mar Shimun, who was in Ashitha "primarily to rally the villagers for an attack on a Kurdish chief."[52] By this time, of course, Asahel Grant had established relations with the Mar Shimun on behalf of American missions and had set up schools in the mountains. Badger acknowledged that he "did not fail to acquaint the patriarch how far we are removed in doctrine and discipline, from the American Independent missionaries . . . [and that] it would be injudicious, and would by no means satisfy us to have schools among his people by the side of theirs."[53] The Mar Shimun's price for allowing the schools was British assistance against the Kurds, and in March 1843 Badger wrote to the British ambassador in Constantinople, Sir Stratford Canning, to endorse the patriarch's desire to be confirmed by the Ottoman government as the exclusive civil ruler of Hakkari, subject only to the sultan and independent of all Kurdish chiefs.

Iraq as we know it today was not regarded as a single missionary field. The North, including the Mosul area and Kurdistan, was considered part of Ottoman Anatolia, and missions in that region addressed primarily the Armenians and Assyrians, whereas the South was treated as part of Arabia and the

Gulf when missions there were developed in the latter part of the nineteenth century. The Basel Mission, from its base in the Caucasus, where it worked with the Armenians, opened a school for Armenians in Baghdad in 1830.

The ABCFM had a missionary station in Mosul, also as part of its work with Armenians, but it abandoned that station before 1850. In 1849, the British consul in Mosul contacted the CMS in London with a request that the society begin work among the Nestorians. This request was followed by a similar appeal directly from the Chaldeans.[54] The fact that the Chaldeans appealed to the British in spite of their own ties with the Vatican shows how much of the motivation for such relations was the desire for European protection among minority Christian communities. Roman Catholic orders had a long history of relations with the Christians in eastern Anatolia and northern Mesopotamia, establishing a Uniate church called "Chaldean" among the Assyrians as early as the mid-sixteenth century. This Chaldean patriarchate was revived in 1830 with the appointment of a patriarch of Babylon based in Mosul, where Italian Dominicans were also active, and Carmelites were established in Baghdad. Both orders were transferred from the Italian to the French church in the 1850s.[55]

Unlike the European missionaries, American missionaries lacked significant government support. They had neither the protection of U.S. diplomatic representation nor the support of government policy. American Protestant missionary activity seems to have diminished during the 1850s and 1860s for a number of reasons. The domestic conflicts over slavery that resulted in the American Civil War in 1861 affected support for overseas missions, and the war itself dried up financing for the missions. Furthermore, divisions within the missionary movement over how to proceed and what priorities to pursue made it difficult to expand, although these divisions also resulted in the establishment, in the midst of the war, of the two longest-lasting missionary legacies, Robert College in Istanbul and the Syrian Protestant College. The end of the Civil War, the completion of the Ottoman reforms that permitted the establishment of independent Protestant churches and conferred equality on all Ottoman citizens, and the economic boom in both Europe and America that promoted fund-raising for missionary causes—all combined to create an explosion of Protestant missionary activity.

In Egypt, Said Pasha had allowed the formation of an American Presbyterian mission in 1854. Sparked by a chance visit to Egypt in 1852 by Dr. J. G. Paulding of the Associate Reformed Presbyterian Mission in Damascus, interest in this new field for work was followed up back home in Pennsylvania, where the United Presbyterian Church of North America authorized the establishment of an Egyptian mission. Initially led by veterans from Damascus—James Barnett and Gulian Lansing—the mission was joined by Thomas McCague, Andrew Watson, and Scottish missionary John Hogg. By 1897, with a staff of almost fifty, many schools and institutions, and the establishment of an autonomous evangelical church whose members spread the Gospel, the Americans became the most prominent Protestant organization in the country.[56]

Soon after their arrival in Egypt, the Americans abandoned their initial resolve to bring all to the faith and focused their work primarily on the Copts, whom they saw as needing moral uplifting. Like the Catholics and the Anglicans, the American Presbyterians viewed the indigenous Egyptian Christians as a "degraded" and backward community that had assimilated much of the oriental culture of their Muslim neighbors, but also at the same time as religiously apathetic and heroic in the fact that they had survived despite centuries of isolation and persecution at the hands of the Muslim majority. In their endeavor, the Presbyterians joined the three-way competition for the Copts' souls.

Unlike the CMS, which worked primarily with urban Copts and focused on formal schooling to raise the educational level of the Coptic Church, but not on turning Copts into Anglicans, the American Presbyterians had little interest in reforming the Coptic Church and its hierarchy. Instead, they worked with individuals and took a grassroots approach, pursuing the Calvinist goal of advancing intelligent Bible reading as the means for advancing religious truth. Using the Nile as a highway, the Presbyterians outfitted a Nile River boat with living quarters, conference room, and bookstore and sent it off—the first of many boats that plied the 750 miles between Alexandria and Aswan, linking preachers and peddlers of religious books and tracts with villagers along the river. Traveling by sail or tow downstream to Aswan, the "American riverboat missionaries" then floated upstream, stopping at points along the route, where they would enthusiastically sell Bibles and tracts that had been translated into Arabic to Copts who were eager to read scripture in a language they could understand. Then they established schools and churches, using Arabic as the linguistic medium of instruction and members of the new congregations to run the churches and spread the word.[57]

The American arrival in Egypt coincided with increased Catholic missionary activity in the Middle East due in part both to the renewed papal interest in union of the Eastern churches with Rome and, in Egypt, to the large numbers of Europeans arriving in the country because of diplomatic and commercial interests. Although official Catholic overtures by Pope Pius IX to the Coptic Church were rebuffed, Coptic converts to Roman Catholicism did form a Uniate church, most of whose members worshiped in private houses. In addition, the centuries' long presence of Jesuits and Franciscans in Egypt was augmented by the arrival of priests, nuns, and laypeople from many French, Italian, Maltese, Syrian, Austrian, Polish, and various other organizations. One source records that between 1844 and 1943 twenty-three separate Catholic women's organizations came to Egypt and operated schools there.[58] Although Catholics focused most of their energy in Cairo and Alexandria, their presence in the villages of upper Egypt challenged Protestant efforts in rural areas. By 1865, the Americans had established a base of operations at Assiut in Upper Egypt.

In the meantime, however, other Western churches arrived. The Franciscans began charity work in 1859, and in 1879 the Jesuits returned, establishing schools to provide Christian alternatives to the Protestants. In 1895, the Patriarchate of Alexandria was established. On the Protestant side, the United Presbyterian Church of North America, in association with the Reformed Church, established what became known as the "American Mission" in 1854 and by 1875 had mission stations from Alexandria to Assiut with a total of six hundred members. The American Mission was particularly active in setting up an education system, culminating in a college in Assiut. It also founded hospitals and by the end of the century had established an Egyptian church on the Presbyterian structural model.[59] Other European churches established their presence in Egypt on a smaller scale, particularly toward the end of the century.

This increasing Western missionary activity was especially evident in Anatolia, where Protestant schools flourished; in Egypt, where the establishment of British influence removed obstacles from missionary activity; and in Persia, where Roman Catholics had been present since the beginning of the seventeenth century, Anglicans and Presbyterians established a presence in the 1840s, and the archbishop of Canterbury established his own mission to the Nestorian Church of the East in 1884.

Education was central to the ABCFM mission in Anatolia, as it was to the CMS in Egypt. Missionaries saw no point in converting the illiterate to Protestantism, a faith that stressed the importance of a personal relationship with God through scripture. Furthermore, women's education was a priority. Just as the earliest ABCFM missionaries had been educated at Williams and Amherst colleges and Andover Seminary, the first women missionaries (those who were not wives of male missionaries) were educated particularly at Mount Holyoke College, only a few miles over the mountain from Amherst. Mount Holyoke, the first college for women in America, was founded by Mary Lyon in 1839. From the earliest days, the idea of mission was important, and a significant number of Mount Holyoke graduates and faculty served in Anatolia, in Persia, and in other foreign mission fields.

In the late 1840s and 1850s, as the Armenian Church hierarchy's opposition to Protestant missionary activity increased, it led to the establishment of the Protestant Armenian Evangelical Church and to the recognition by the Ottoman authorities of a Protestant millet. Armenian Protestant churches began to be organized throughout Anatolia.[60] Where a church was organized, a school was usually established as well—and often two schools, one for boys and another for girls. These churches and schools spread throughout the Armenian communities in Anatolia, often but not always with the assistance and guidance of American missionaries and American funding.

In 1860, the ABCFM mission structure in Anatolia was divided into three sectors: the Western Turkey Mission, extending from Constantinople east to Trebizond and from Smyrna east to Caesarea (Kayseri); the Central Turkey Mission, centered on the Cilician Plain and including Tarsus, Adana, Marash, Aintab, Hadjin, Zeitoon, and east to Urfa and Adiaman; and the Eastern Turkey Mission, including Harput, Malatya, Diyarbekir, Mardin, Bitlis, Van, and Erzurum.[61] The primary schools established in the outlying villages and in the main towns were usually the responsibility of the local Protestant churches, and the teachers were the local product of the higher-level mission schools. The success of the educational enterprise is indicated by the fact that by 1872 it was estimated that 85 percent of the Protestants in Anatolia were literate.[62] By 1909, there were 144 schools with 8,126 students in the Western Turkey Mission, 103 schools with 7,357 students in the Central Turkey Mission, and 90 schools with 4,531 students in the Eastern Turkey Mission. The language of instruction varied from place to place and included Armenian, Turkish, and even Arabic.[63]

In 1843, Justin Perkins, who had been working with the Nestorians in Persia, made a trip home to the United States to raise money for the Urmia mission and to recruit a female teacher to start a school for girls alongside his already-functioning boys' school. He visited Mount Holyoke College, and during his visit he succeeded in exciting the interest of Fidelia Fiske—a niece of Pliny Fisk, one of the first two ABCFM missionaries to the Near East—

who went to Urmia to start the girls' school. A bishop of the Nestorian Church, Mar Yohanan, had learned English from Asahel Grant's wife, Judith, and become interested in the education of women. He had visited Mount Holyoke with Justin Perkins and took his own two daughters to be the first students at the new girls' school, the Female Seminary.[64] Although the Mar Shimun forced the girls to leave the school in 1844, they soon returned. A particularly important aspect of the Female Seminary was the emphasis it placed on continuing contact between the students in Urmia and those at Mount Holyoke. Correspondence flowed in both directions, and emotional ties were established. Fidelia Fiske herself returned to Massachusetts in 1858 and died in 1864 at the age of forty-eight. Many other Mount Holyoke graduates went to teach in Urmia, and the school there survived until 1933, when it was closed by the Iranian government.

Meanwhile, Grant had convinced the ABCFM to establish a new mission at Mosul, and early in 1841 two missionary couples left Boston for Smyrna. Grant again left Urmia for the mountains, spending time with the Mar Shimun in July on his way to Mosul to meet the new missionaries. One of the American missionaries died on the way across the desert from Aleppo, and his wife was taken ill, only to die just after reaching Mosul. The party was met in Mosul by Mr. and Mrs. Rassam, the British vice consul and his wife. In fact, Rassam was a Nestorian, and his wife, the former Matilda Badger, was the sister of Reverend George Badger, the Anglican who was to be the most enthusiastic supporter of the establishment of an Anglican mission to the Nestorians.

Grant eventually reached Mosul, where he spent the winter with the new American missionaries setting up a school for Jacobite Christians. In June 1842, he returned to Urmia and this time was successful in getting permission to establish a mission station among the Nestorians at Ashitha, in the mountains a few miles north of Amadia near the present Iraq–Turkish border.[65] His siting of this mission station, which he began to build in the summer of 1842, on an isolated hilltop proved unfortunate. Grant again spent the winter of 1842–1843 in Mosul, returning to Ashitha in April 1843 but abandoning it in July because of the Kurdish uprising.

Grant and Thomas Laurie were in Ashitha in April 1843, working on their new house on the hill, when they found themselves in the middle of a two-pronged Kurdish attack from east and west to annihilate the Nestorians, which had "the acquiescence of the Turkish authorities." Grant "was becoming unpopular, not only as a friend of the Nestorians, but also as a literate

foreign observer who might live to tell the tale of what was about to happen."
He left Ashitha for Mosul on July 7, 1843. "Once the slaughter had begun,
the Nestorians, split among themselves and confused by the Anglican–Con-
gregationalist rivalry fostered by Badger, offered no effective resistance."[66]

The Kurdish leader Badr Khan's attacks were disastrous for the Nestorians. Ten thousand people, perhaps one-fifth of the Nestorian population in
the mountains, were killed, and many women and children were taken captive. In addition to the killings, the attacks drove many from their mountain homes to the plains near Mosul, creating a serious refugee problem
that was partially solved by the employment of the Nestorians as workers
in archaeologist Paolo Emilio Botta's excavations, where they formed a labor force that did not raise the difficulties that the employment of Arabs
did with the local authorities.[67] They were subsequently hired by Austen
Henry Layard as well to work on the excavation of Assyrian ruins.[68] Grant's
mission was never completed—the house on the hilltop was occupied by a
Turkish garrison, and Grant himself died in 1845. The Mosul mission was
abandoned in 1844, though it was reopened as a mission to the Nestorians
in 1849.[69]

The ABCFM had established eight missions in the Middle East in its first
fifty years, from 1820 to 1870: to Palestine, Syria, Greece as well as to the Armenians (Turkey–Armenia), the Nestorians, the Assyrians (eastern Turkey–
Iraq), the Jews, and the Muslims. However, by the end of the nineteenth century only the mission to the Armenians in Anatolia was still active. The Greek
mission had gradually ended as Greek independence and the Greek Orthodox Church created difficulties for the Protestant churches and schools. The
Palestine mission had been handed over to British missionaries by the 1840s.
The Syria–Lebanon mission was transferred to American Presbyterians in
1870, as was the mission to the Nestorian Assyrians in Urmia. The mission to
the Jews was closed in the 1850s, and missions to the Muslims were always a
minor footnote to other missions once the missionaries discovered that conversion of the Muslims was virtually impossible. Only the Armenians in Anatolia remained. The goal had originally been to stimulate Eastern churches to
reform, but by 1842, faced with opposition from those churches' ecclesiastic
hierarchies, Rufus Anderson reported the situation to the ABCFM, and it
responded with the decision to form local evangelical churches.[70] This strategy was similar to that of the Roman Catholics, who established a structure
of Uniate churches parallel to the linguistically and ethnically based Eastern
churches. The Anglican Church, however, continued to hold to the policy of

reforming the Nestorian Church rather than accepting its members as Anglicans. The reason for doing so was, of course, partly political in an attempt to assure that the Nestorians would not come to consider that they had a right to British protection, a powerful incentive for Eastern Christians to affiliate themselves with the Western missionary enterprises.

After half a century of organization and hard work, Protestant missionary organizations that began with such religious fervor at the beginning of the nineteenth century were reporting limited success. At home, challenges to biblical authority and faith from rationalism on one side and from ritualism and Rome on the other engendered less enthusiasm for foreign missions. CMS members despaired at the condition of Eastern Christianity, but missions to the Eastern Christians continued.[71] Although few Jews converted, restoration of Jews to Jerusalem remained a focus of some Protestant groups as countries scrambled for representation in the Holy City. A diplomatic presence in Jerusalem was viewed as an assertion of imperial and national legitimacy. By 1860, most Europeans were represented in the Holy Land: Prussia (1842), France (1843), Sardinia (1843), the United States (1844), and Austria (1849) had consulates in Jerusalem, and the Russians remained in Beirut and Jaffa. Established to protect nationals resident in the Holy Land, these diplomatic missions were called upon even more to assist the increasing number of pilgrims, tourists, scholars, and archaeologists who were visiting the Middle East for business and religious experience. Numerous organized and independent Christian groups became interested in the Holy Land and a number of them—Scots, Danes, Germans—sought to establish missions there. Scottish Presbyterians sought to proselytize, and members of the German Templer movement purchased land and settled in to await the End of Time.

At the same time, there was a sense on the part of many British Protestants not only that missions generated a poor return for investment, but that the Crimean War and the Sepoy Mutiny (1857) in India had presented what became lost opportunities. After all, a missionary appeal noted in 1860, "[w]hen the God of nations saw how ardently England engaged in the Crimean War for the defense of the territorial integrity of Turkey, whilst she made not the faintest effort for the conversion of either Turk or the Sepoy, He inflicted chastisement upon us which we should do well to consider. The Mohammedans have given us bitter cause lastingly to remember not only their existence, but also the great work we have to do among them."[72]

Had Britain, the Protestants wondered, lost its providential role in the world? "Protestantism is on trial before Catholic nations, and Christianity is put to the proof before Mahomedans and Hindoos." How, asked one evangelical minister, would Britain's Protestant Empire perform in this trial?[73]

The effects of the Crimean War, the Opium Wars—even though they led to missions in China and India—and the death in 1861 of Prince Albert of Britain, patron of the Livingstone missionary expedition to Africa, affected the British missionary enterprise. Economic problems caused by industrialization in Scotland, Wales, and rural England led to crises of faith that affected middle-class Britons and intellectuals who were being exposed both to academic approaches to the Bible and later to the challenge of Darwinism. Protestants also faced Presbyterian disunity, conflicts between high Anglicans and evangelicals that threatened the unity of the Anglican Church and the tensions between Nonconformity and the Church of England. All of these factors led to the "drift of . . . mainstream missionary thinking away from commerce and Christianity."[74] But instead of seeing the decline of Protestant evangelism, the last quarter of the nineteenth century—the heyday of European competition for colonies and worldwide influence and a period of unprecedented economic expansion—was also to prove the high point of Protestant evangelical activity.

SIX

The Imperialist Moment

From the Congress of Berlin to World War I

After 1870, Italy and Germany, at that time new countries on the European map, flexed their national muscles by looking for colonies in Asia and Africa. Imperial France, which had been humiliated by defeat in the Franco-Prussian War (1870), was now challenged by a Germany seeking diplomatic predominance in the Ottoman Empire and North Africa. Russia continued the Great Game in Central Asia. In 1877, while Britain was occupied in Afghanistan, Russia repudiated the Treaty of Paris, which had guaranteed the neutrality of the Black Sea. The Eastern Crisis that followed led once again to war between the Ottoman Empire and Russia, this time precipitated by a rebellion in Bulgaria. German diplomatic leadership ended the crisis at the Congress of Berlin in 1878, bringing Germany into the Middle East.

Although German imperial and Protestant ventures operated primarily in sub-Saharan Africa, Kaiser Wilhelm II also continued his predecessors' interest in Jerusalem. Previous German attempts to purchase and refurbish the medieval Muristan—the Church of the Order of St. John under Protestant auspices near the Church of the Holy Sepulchre—had been unsuccessful. But after the dissolution of the joint Anglo-Prussian Anglican bishopric in 1886, the kaiser reorganized the German parish and founded the Protestant

Jerusalem Fund (Jerusalem-Stiftung) in 1889. By 1893, he had approved plans for the Lutheran Church of the Redeemer, which he soon afterward placed under the administration of the Jerusalem Fund.[1]

By then, Germany had taken a cultural position linked to its national identity. The synergy and double ordination that had been possible for German and British Protestants early in the nineteenth century became more difficult, an Oath of Allegiance causing the loss of citizenship. As the *volkish* ideology took hold in Germany, some Christian groups advocated mission, with Germans taking the lead and promoting German culture along with Christianity. The idea had already been broached by Friedrich Strauss, founder of the Jerusalem Society, in the 1840s, when he noticed that most of the Protestants in Jerusalem spoke German and at least half of the Jewish population understood German: "May it not be the most natural way, the way given by the Lord himself, if the German people in particular undertook the task of mission there where God had prepared the way by diffusion of the German language? May we not praise the grace of God who has chosen for us the Land of Promise, even the most holy places of the earth? . . . It is evident that God has assigned to the German church the leadership of missionary activity in the Orient."[2]

By the 1880s, the Moravians, who supported the idea of a Protestant Reich, adopted the idea that the founding of the German Empire was a step on the path of salvation and synthesized nationalism and pietism into a *volk*-oriented mission where German Protestants would take the lead and promote German culture.[3]

German Catholics also became more nationalistic. Until the mid-1880s, they had contributed to Catholic organizations operating in the Middle East, but without considering the national origin of these institutions, most of which were French. Germans had participated in pilgrimages under the auspices of the French Committee for Pilgrimages to the Holy Land, and they had supported the Franciscans' missionary work in Jerusalem. They had awarded substantial funding to the Jesuit seminary in Lebanon and to the Order of St. Joseph of the Apparition and its institutions in Palestine, Cyprus, and Lebanon; and they had sent contributions to aid Christians hurt during the massacres of 1860. These activities in connection to non-German organizations were due in part to the fact that not only was there no German state until 1870, but during the new kingdom's early years of existence it was engaged in a religious–ideological struggle between Protestants and Catholics and an ideological conflict over the relationship between religion and state. As the *kulturkampf* subsided, and relations between Catholics and the state were normalized, Catholics began to "integrate themselves into German colonial policy and expand their representation in various foreign lands."[4]

German incursions into the Middle East did not occur without opposition by the French.[5] In 1875, the German Catholic Franciscan Ladislaus Schneider purchased plots of land in Jerusalem and in Qubeibeh, a village northwest of Jerusalem identified as the biblical Emmaus, intending to establish hospices and agricultural colonies there. Opposing the move, the French Franciscans had Schneider transferred to Alexandria. Soon after that, however, German Catholics, under the patronage of the archbishop of Cologne, established the Society of the Holy Sepulchre for the Promotion of Catholic Interests in the Holy Land. This new organization supported missionary work, sent detailed reports back to Germany about Christians in the Middle East, and contributed to the support of institutions in Syria, Palestine, Egypt, Asia Minor, and the Balkans. As contributions from Germany increased, Catholics, under the initiative of Father Schneider and Wilhelm Leopold Janssen, a Catholic activist from Aachen, formed the Palestine Society of Catholics in Germany in 1885 with the goal of bolstering the German Catholic presence in the Holy Land. In 1895, it merged with the Society for the Promotion of Catholic Interests in the Holy Land and, especially after Kaiser Wilhelm's visit to Jerusalem in 1898, began to acquire land and build institutions to offset French predominance.[6]

The German kaiser, who in his youth had ties to the Benedictines, combined pietism with a Hohenzollern medieval conception of the divine mission of German emperors, asserting his own self-image as Constantine the Great in furthering German imperial goals.[7] His visit to the Middle East in 1898, although designed to enhance Ottoman–German relations, was couched in Christian religious symbolism. Dressed in a white costume evocative of the Teutonic knights and with a golden eagle atop his helmet, Wilhelm rode into Jerusalem through a breach in the walls that had been prepared specially for his entourage. He was attended by a "host of knightly figures arrayed in the insignia and slowing mantles of the (military) order of St. John," which had both a Catholic and a Protestant branch, his visit evoking German emperor Frederick II, who had visited more than six centuries earlier during the Crusades. After dedicating a German Catholic abbey and a hospice on the Mount of Olives, among other institutions in the Holy Land, Wilhelm proceeded to Damascus, where he laid a wreath on the tomb of Saladin, which he subsequently paid to restore because the Muslim hero, as the kaiser noted, had been "a knight without fear or blame (*sans peur et sans reproche*) and had often had to teach his adversaries the true nature of 'chivalry.'"[8] After this visit, German relations with the Turks improved, but the kaiser failed to receive papal acquiescence to his challenge to French hegemony over Catholic interests in the region.

The French retained their dominant position in the Middle East and North Africa despite the incongruity of an avowedly secular French Third Republic that supported Catholic missionary work abroad. The preponderance of Catholic missionaries in the Ottoman Empire who were French and Roman Catholic missionary schools where the language of instruction was French illustrated a pragmatic convergence of goals that linked French politics in the assertion of France's protection of Latin Catholics with the work of French missionaries in the Middle East, explicitly seeking to re-create the Crusades.[9]

Ever fearful of being expelled from France, the Jesuits aligned themselves with those French interests that coincided with their own.[10] Journals such as *Missions Catholiques*, *Oeuvre de la Propagation de la Foi*, and *Oeuvre des Écoles d'Orient* publicized Catholic work in the Holy Land, where Notre Dame de France was established in Jerusalem and missionaries expelled from France found sanctuary. The Franciscans sought to retain their monopoly over Catholic schools in Jerusalem, but other groups soon entered. Supported by France, Lavigerie's White Fathers founded a seminary for Uniate Melkites; other groups with France's support included the Fathers of Sion, Dominicans, Assumptionists, Trappists, Benedictines, Carmelites, and Lazarists. The large number of missionaries in Jerusalem under French protection reflected France's attempts to buttress its imperial interests in the region. Although the Germans sought to stave off French predominance, until the last quarter of the nineteenth century the Franciscans sought to assimilate all converts to the Latin rite. By 1914, Roman Catholics in the Holy Land were represented by numerous orders and had built schools, orphanages, and agricultural enterprises on both sides of the Jordan River.[11]

In the spirit of pragmatic realpolitik, politicians of the Third Republic could advocate anticlericalism at home, but, according to the popular dictum, "anticlericalism is not an export," they still supported the missionaries abroad. They knew that the missionaries were protected by the capitulations and that the French government did not have to finance their work. Furthermore, the significant Maronite constituency in Lebanon could, if it allied with the missionaries, impede Anglo-American missionary incursions. In addition, the Uniate churches and the Catholic missions emphasized French links with the Crusades "that appealed in cultural, linguistic, and martial terms to both the nationalist and the imperialist."[12] In North Africa, the policy of support for French missionary work was put to use in Algeria and Tunisia by Cardinal Charles-Martial-Allemand Lavigerie (1825–1892), some of whose best friends were those very anticlericals in Paris.[13]

Lavigerie, a persuasive and strong-willed visionary who was also an advocate of French imperial interests, taught briefly at the University of Paris after his ordination and became the director of French schools in the Middle East. In 1856, he accepted leadership of the society Oeuvres des écoles d'Orient, and he worked in Syria just after the massacre of Christians there in 1860, an experience that left him decidedly anti-Muslim. Returning to France, he became bishop of Nancy, but soon thereafter, expressing an interest in working abroad, he was appointed archbishop of Algiers (1866). His advocacy of Catholic missionary work in North Africa, however, put him into conflict with the governor there, Patrice MacMahon (later president of France), but when cholera, famine, locusts, and drought struck Algeria in 1868, Lavigerie received permission to open orphanages and relief missions.[14]

In the same year, his appointment as apostolic delegate to the Sahara and the Sudan freed Lavigerie from French jurisdiction and enabled him to found the Society of Missionaries, also known as the "White Fathers." Although it began in Algeria, its work extended to Tunisia, Jerusalem, and sub-Saharan Africa, where it came into conflict with the Jesuits. An order of White Sisters was founded soon after. In the wake of the Franco-Prussian War in 1870, political instability in France, anticlerical sentiments, and Muslim uprisings against French rule in Algeria the next year led the European settlers in Algeria to organize for the purpose of representing their own interests in Paris. At that point, Lavigerie turned his sights to Tunisia for the purpose of reestablishing a French presence where Italians had been ministering to Catholic needs.

On land ceded by the bey of Tunis in a secret agreement to the French, Lavigerie was permitted to build a memorial chapel at Carthage—Saint Louis de Carthage—honoring the medieval Crusader and French king Louis IX. The chapel, staffed by the White Fathers, was a step in Lavigerie's program to resurrect a Christian empire in North Africa, to abolish slavery, to bring sub-Saharan Africans to Catholicism, and to establish a foothold in Jerusalem so that the White Fathers could bring Orthodox Christians to Rome. Four years later he moved the headquarters of the Mission of Algiers to Tunis, and he lobbied for a French protectorate in Tunisia—Carthage, after all, had been the home of St. Augustine.[15] In 1878, Pope Leo XIII agreed to give Lavigerie custody of the Church of St. Anne of Jerusalem, where the White Fathers established a seminary to train Orthodox Melkites in the White Fathers' own rite.

Lavigerie's methodology prepared the White Fathers and White Sisters for the "new style of Crusade." The White Fathers wore a modified Arab dress in order to adapt to their cultural milieu. There initially were to be no baptisms or preaching that might offend or threaten local leaders. Once the missionaries cultivated goodwill through the mission of charity—teaching, medical care, alms to the needy—they would be allowed to discuss religion with individual inquirers, but no conversion would be permitted until after four years of instruction. Lavigerie feared that hasty conversion could lead to apostasy. After achieving a critical mass of converts, the missionaries would be able to establish a mission and proceed to evangelize. To the cardinal, "charity"—education, medical care, and funds for the needy—was central for inspiring and winning respect of the North Africans. It was also the means for reconciling people to French rule and preparing them for conversion.[16]

When after the Treaty of Bardo France occupied Tunisia in 1881, an Italian newspaper remarked that "Cardinal [he would not become cardinal until 1882] Lavigerie renders to French influence in the Mediterranean greater service than an army corps."[17] As archbishop of Carthage, Lavigerie set up schools, clinics, and missions with the goal of resurrecting a Christian empire in North Africa. Lavigerie understood the difficulty of converting Arab and Berber Muslims to Christianity, but he believed that in the competition with Christianity for souls, Islam, which he viewed as vicious and full of vice, was making "redoubtable advances among the African population" and therefore had to be combated by force.[18] He considered the Protestants hardly a threat to anyone. During the 1830s and 1840s, missions of the London Jews Society were established in Morocco, and later, in the 1890s, French Methodists, Swedish Lutherans, and Baptists got involved in Algeria, but these groups had made little headway.[19] The goal was to make the Middle East Catholic, and here Lavigerie's plan was compatible with the French imperial mission. Together, the soldiers of France and the Catholic missionaries would transform the Middle East and North Africa:

> Certainly, one need not be a priest, but only a man to wish the transformation of the poor, fallen races of North Africa. . . . But ordinary preaching, personal proselytizing is powerless before the blind prejudices and implacable passions engaged in this resistance of barbarity. On the contrary, it is detrimental until Providence itself has made the preparation.
>
> The only true and effective preaching, in this moment, is the action of events which change the political situation of these regions. Without

knowing it, without willing it, *our governors and our soldiers are thus the agents of this new mission. They are the force, and force, for the Muslims, is God himself.* . . . While they strip the natives of their power, of their arms, of their secular traditions, we priests seek to calm and reclaim their embittered hearts by the exercise of devotion and charity. . . . No doubt what we thus obtain is not hasty and imprudent conversions, which would only be preparations for apostasy; it is a more durable work, a certain preparation, without jolts and dangers, for the transformation of the African world.

Thus the seed is sown. The work of centuries will make it ripen.

For us, who will not see the fruit, our reward is in the witness that we thus serve the cause of humanity, of France, and of God. [20]

French control over Algeria, Tunisia, and, to a lesser extent, Morocco, however, did not result in Muslim conversion to Christianity. Nevertheless, at the time of Lavigerie's death in 1892, several thousand French priests and nuns from a number of orders were ministering throughout the empire, opening schools and operating hospitals.[21]

Lavigerie's support of the republic and the movement he founded that was supported by the Roman Catholic Church, monarchists, conservatives, politicians, military officers, and missionaries helped ease anticlericalist regulations in France during the 1890s.[22] During the period of Catholic revival in France, when miracles, prophecies, and visions were surprisingly common (people spent their savings seeking supernatural cures, and thousands of visitors descended upon Lourdes every year), monarchists and conservatives feared the political Left. Businessmen, alarmed at the growth of unionism during the economic depression of the 1880s, supported economic protectionism at home. At the same time, they advocated expansion of the French Empire not only for increased markets abroad, but also to "provide a safety valve for a society in turmoil, and jobs for unemployed aristocrats, idle soldiers, and exiled missionaries."[23]

French relations with the Catholic Church deteriorated at the turn of the twentieth century, however, during the clerical–secularist battles that pitted the Right against the Left, contributing to the formal separation of church and state in 1905. Germany and Italy moved to encroach on French missionary territory in the Middle East and North Africa. In addition, the anticlerical 1901 Laws of Association that outlawed religious orders in France only increased the numbers of French nationals serving in the empire, but at the same time, by banning missionary recruitment on French soil, these laws resulted in a drastic reduction in the number of men and women actually preparing for missionary service. In 1907, the Vatican expressed concern about the viability of the traditional French claim to be the protector of the Catholics in the Ottoman Empire. French Catholics feared that French missions would decline and even disappear: in 1902, there were 304 French novices in the Sisters of Charity, but in 1914 the number was 216. The number of Sisters of Saint Joseph of the Apparition dropped from 80 in 1900 to 24 in 1914.[24]

In 1898, Pope Leo XIII, thwarting the German challenge to French protection of Catholics, reiterated France's "noble mission which has been consecrated not only by secular practice but also by international treaties as were recognized by Our Congregation of Propaganda and by its declaration of May 1888."[25] Three years later, although the pope remained silent when Germany and Italy challenged French hegemony over the Church of the Holy Sepulchre in Jerusalem, he established seminaries in Rome to train clergy of the Uniate churches and created Les Amis de la Syrie et du Levant to strengthen French influence by assisting Roman Catholic missionaries.[26]

With the 1904 break in diplomatic relations between France and the Vatican and the ensuing formal separation of church and state the following year, French missionaries came directly under the authority of the Vatican.[27] The rupture was opposed by the ministers of finance and public instruction, and the foreign minister immediately wrote to French representatives in Constantinople and Cairo that France still asserted its rights over French-protected institutions.[28] In the wake of the German challenge to French hegemony in North Africa in 1905, the French, in return for dominance in Morocco, acquiesced in the demand that individuals be permitted to choose their own consular protection, though they began regretting their decision after an incident involving two Catholic orders with predominantly Italian membership. Although these missionaries were officially French protégés, they turned to Italy and not to France for help. Then, five years later, Italian missionaries became active in Syria, with plans for a hospital and intending to transfer Syrian Capuchins and Carmelites to Italian rather than French protection. This effort led the French Quai d'Orsay (Ministry of Foreign Affairs), concerned about the decline of French manpower, to advocate recruiting missionaries on French soil in order to combat Italian missionary work in the Levant.[29]

Italians also moved on the educational front, prompting another French response. When Italian schools appeared in Turkey, Syria, and Morocco, they were intruding into a cultural sphere that by then had incorporated the *mission laïque*, a secularist approach to the spread of French culture. With the objective of replacing Catholic education and promoting French civilization, the *mission laïque* schools were comparable to those of the Alliance Israélite Universelle, founded some forty years earlier, which combined French education with Jewish studies and vocational and professional training. The French secular counterpart promoted French culture along with local languages and culture and instruction in practical subjects.[30] The problem was that in 1901 there were only seven French lay schools in the Ottoman Empire, with a total enrollment of 718 students. Despite the objections to missionary education at home, French education abroad was still in the hands of missionaries, who taught some 70,000 students in Catholic schools. "Don't oblige me . . . to sacrifice these 300 schools which need our aid and which lead by the hand the 80,000 who attend them, who are speaking French at this moment, who are impregnated with French ideas, who are growing up in the shadow of the French flag," pleaded the foreign minister at a Chamber of Deputies debate in 1904 as he and his supporters advocated funding for French missionary schools.[31] From 1904 to 1914, the French government's position remained the same, and funding for missionary schools abroad increased. Just before World War I, various foreign ministers sought a reassessment of the anticlerical laws, but the war changed everything.

Religious revivals not only in France but in Britain and America led a great variety of people to become engaged with the Middle East, or the Holy Land, in numerous ways. The mainstream churches' missionary enterprises were only the most visible. Some organizations, such as the Salvation Army and the Young Men's Christian Association (YMCA), were concerned primarily with social welfare, and others, such as the American Colony and the German Templer Society, were explicitly millenarian.

In the United States, evangelists from the North emerged from the Civil War believing it to be an apocalyptic struggle that identified Americans as a nation with that "kingdom of God among men which is righteousness and peace and joy in the Holy Ghost." Mission enthusiasts prepared to take conversion to Christ worldwide.[32] The 1870s were characterized by noonday prayer meetings attended by the poor and the college educated alike, evocative of Jonathan Edwards's First Great Awakening more than a century earlier.

Dwight Moody was emblematic of the American approach to evangelism that came to combine pietism and good works. A shoe salesman from Chicago, Moody worked with the YMCA, served with the Christian Commission during the American Civil War, and became a professional evangelist a few years after the end of the war. Teaching the "three R's—ruin by sin, redemption by Christ, and regeneration by the Holy Spirit," whose power would equip the believer for service to the church through evangelism and missions, Moody traveled throughout the United States and Britain, delivering his new evangelism, a mixture of middle-class respectability, premillennialism, and holiness teaching.[33] His style and the movement he founded were acceptable to a post–Civil War America that considered itself a Protestant country without an established church. Focused on individualism and denominational decentralization, evangelical movements were built around individual leaders and agencies, many of which were extraecclesiastical and dedicated to specific causes and independent fundraising.

Examples of these organizations included the YMCA and the Student Volunteer Movement. A British import, the YMCA was founded in 1844 as a religious response to the problem of urbanization. Its flexible methodology for the diffusion of religious knowledge, which incorporated prayer services with discussion and reading groups and, most notably, physical education, gave the YMCA the sobriquet *muscular Christianity*. In the United States, the evangelical movement became more diversified as it linked with colleges and universities promoting leadership training and educational and social work for youth in Sofia, Athens, Salonika, Constantinople, Beirut, and Jerusalem. In 1886, the first YMCAs were organized at the Syrian Protestant College and Robert College;[34] and in 1890, the YMCA work began in Jerusalem. Americans did not begin participating until 1919.[35] For its part, the Student Volunteer Movement, formed in 1886, galvanized the "missionary enthusiasm of thousands of collegians in America and England for 'the evangelization of the world in this generation,'"[36] a phrase that became the motto for the 1910 World Missionary Conference in Edinburgh, which was largely organized by the Student Volunteer Movement.

Britain, too, was undergoing a religious revival. Heavily influenced by Dwight Moody and the American Revival movement, with its emotional tent meetings, Britain hosted a number of American laymen and laywomen who preached in cities, farms, and seaside villages, many of which were undergoing economic distress. Emphasizing lay preaching, emotion, individual conversion, and holiness teaching, the movement brought many working-class people back to Christianity.

Another spurt of revivalism occurred in 1873, when some English evangelical Nonconformists invited Moody to preach in Britain. Moody's revivalist meetings coincided with the annual conferences of Christian workers held at Mildmay Park in north London and, beginning in 1875, with the interdenominational conferences held at Keswick in the English Lake District. The movement generated by Keswick led to the establishment in 1877 of the evangelical Cambridge Inter-Collegiate Christian Union and a major training college for clergymen and for missionaries. With less emphasis on the organization and a focus on the individual missionary, moral character, and zeal for the Gospel, nearly two hundred missionaries were sent to mission fields throughout the British colonies between 1881 and 1889.[37]

Even more "muscular" was the Salvation Army, the Christian mission founded in London in 1865 by William and Catherine Booth. Although the Booths were freelance evangelists, they did not envision their enterprise as an independent movement. However, when their converts were rejected by other churches, the mission became a place of worship and by 1878 had evolved into the Salvation Army. The movement arrived in the United States in 1880 and by the end of the century had spread throughout Europe and the English-speaking world. The combination of military trappings, evangelism, and social work made the Salvation Army distinct[38] and, along with Lavigerie's attempt to re-create the Crusades in Africa, gave real meaning to one of the most popular missionary hymns, "Onward, Christian Soldiers," as seen in the refrain:

> Onward, Christian soldiers, marching as to war,
> with the cross of Jesus going on before.
> Christ, the royal Master, leads against the foe;
> forward into battle see his banners go![39]

In Britain, news of the 1875 massacre of Christians in the Balkans created a public reaction against the British policy of keeping the Ottoman Empire intact. After all, it was inferred, if the Ottomans needed European support to stop the hemorrhaging of Balkan territory to Christian powers, then the teetering "Islam" was ready for evangelizing. Missions to Muslims had always been talked about, but because of government opposition and heavy penalties to religious proselytizers, British Protestants preferred using the backdoor approach through India to confronting the Ottoman Empire, Persia, or North African regimes directly.[40] Individuals such as Mary Louise Whately, daughter of an Anglican bishop, visited Egypt and decided to use her own funds to work there, remaining until her death in 1889. Even though she was supported by the Society for Promoting Female Education in the East, she was an exception.[41] At a CMS prayer meeting in 1881, the vicar of Fareham told his audience that Muslim power was waning and "that its time for practicing and prospering against the Prince of princes is now coming to an end":

> And many of you, probably, consider that the drying up of the River Euphrates predicted in the sixteenth chapter of Revelation, the effect of which is to be "the kings of the East," or the Eastern kingdoms, finding their way to Christ, is now fulfilling in the exsiccation and absorption of the Mohammedan power as a political and ruling power—that power which certainly has been the most impregnable obstacle to the spread of the Gospel among Eastern kingdoms. Certainly it is a sign of the times that the Crescent is waning before the Cross, that though Mohammadenism as a religion is not worn out, Mohammedan nations have come under the power or the influence of Christian rulers. Surely, then, the conversion of Mohammedans should be a special subject at missionary conferences.[42]

General Charles "Chinese" Gordon's martyrdom at Khartoum in 1885 and Lord Herbert Kitchener's subsequent victory at Omdurman in 1898 in the Sudan during the Mahdist uprising against British rule spoke to the continued Islamic challenge. Gordon specifically became a symbol of the highest form of heroism, one that appealed "to the faith missions' emphasis on commitment and sacrifice."[43]

Increased European involvement in the Middle East and North Africa was accompanied by a major push for missionary work in the region. Britain's purchase of shares of the Suez Canal in 1875 and the economic and political crises that followed in Egypt led to British occupation of Egypt in 1882, just after France had occupied Tunisia the previous year. With the territorial and sea-lane connections between Suez and India taking a prominent place in newly clarified British imperial goals, a British presence in Egypt and the Persian Gulf became more important. Once the British moved into Egypt, the CMS reentered and strengthened its Palestine program,[44] founding hospitals and schools and working among Copts and Muslims.[45] Major-General F. T. Haig of the CMS Parent Committee remarked that "the days of the Maohammedan Antichrist are numbered. The disintegration of the Turkish Empire proceeds apace."[46] Over the next twenty years, Britain divided the Persian Gulf into British and Ottoman spheres of influence, negotiating agreements with local rulers from Muscat to Bahrein. As British interests moved to the Arabian Peninsula and the Persian Gulf, the CMS and, with support from the Free Church of Scotland, the Cambridge Semitic scholar and evangelical Ion Keith-Falconer adopted Aden as a "jumping-off point" for the interior and worked from Muscat.[47]

Christianity had come to parts of Arabia, in particular Yemen and the trading cities of the Hijaz, in the earliest centuries of its history but had completely disappeared from Arabia by early sixteenth century, when Portuguese traders arrived in the Gulf. The Portuguese remained a presence in Oman for 150 years as part of their Indian trade, converting some of the population by force, but to little lasting effect. By the early nineteenth century, Britain had supplanted Portugal as the primary Western power in India, and the British, like the Portuguese before them, began to establish islands of control along the route to India. In 1839, Britain annexed the port of Aden, at the tip of the Arabian Peninsula, as a coaling station for their ships bound for India, and early in the twentieth century it delineated a protectorate in the hinterland. However, missionary work, particularly among the local population, would not become part of the British endeavor until the end of the nineteenth century, when Protestant missionaries began to explore Arabia as a mission field.

In 1886, Ion Keith-Falconer established a mission station at Aden under the auspices of the Free Church of Scotland to provide medical services to the local population. Although Keith-Falconer died of malaria within a year, he had been joined by a Glasgow doctor, B. Stewart Cowen. Soon thereafter a group of three young men, including Samuel Zwemer and James Cantine, met with John Lansing, professor of Old Testament at the Dutch Reformed Church Seminary in New Brunswick, New Jersey. They asked the church's Board of Foreign Missions to send them as missionaries to Arabic-speaking areas such as Arabia, but the church declined, citing financial difficulties. Undeterred, the young men pursued the idea on their own, and with Lansing's moral support and fund-raising assistance, the Arabian Mission was incorporated in 1891. General Haig, who had visited the gulf on behalf of the CMS in 1886, suggested to the young Americans that Oman, Bahrein, and Najd might be particularly propitious places to consider for a mission, but they instead began their work in 1891 in Basra, an important starting point for the pilgrimage to Mecca, establishing a medical station there soon afterward.[48] Zwemer had been a member of the Student Volunteer Movement and had studied Arabic at the New Brunswick seminary. Convinced that he had a religious calling, he began his prolific career in missionary work and writing in Arabia, the birthplace of Islam.[49] A station was set up the following year in Bahrein, where there had actually been a Christian bishopric in the third century, and another in Muscat, Oman, in 1893. Late that year the Reformed

Church accepted the Arabian Mission as part of its own efforts, thus making it eligible for donations from the church.

The entire Gulf coast gradually came under British protection, from Aden north to the Ottoman border at Basra. This protection initially provided some security for the American missionaries. Although the Arabian Mission's ultimate goal was to convert Muslims to Christianity, in practice it focused on providing medical care to the local population, though the missionaries used this care as a way to make contact, distribute Bibles, and spread the Gospel. In contrast to the situation elsewhere in the Middle East, there was no local Christian presence available for conversion to Protestantism. The mission's medical personnel traveled throughout the Gulf until World War I, when the conflict between the British and the Ottoman Empire made it impossible for work to continue. After World War I, with the defeat of the Ottoman Empire and the establishment of British control in Iraq as well as its reinforcement in the Gulf, the mission developed close ties with the sheikhly elite of the Gulf states, which made increased travel and activity possible. This activity was based at the Mason Memorial Hospital in Bahrein, founded in 1900.[50] American access to the area became limited in the 1930s, however. With the increased interest in the Gulf and the development of its oil resources, the British grew more and more suspicious of American activities, and they installed their own medical facilities in the region. The Anglican Church began to operate in the area, establishing a hospital in 1960 in the Buraimi oasis in Abu Dhabi.

In Arabia, then, the focus of missionary activity, both British and American (the Roman Catholics seem not to have entered this field except to minister to European residents there), was the provision of medical services as a way of becoming involved with the local population. The emphasis on education present in the rest of the region was lacking, probably because of the nature of the local population. Although this emphasis primarily on providing services existed in other mission fields, it can be seen as a sign of a shift in missionary thinking from an evangelical focus on conversion, whether to Christianity or specifically to Protestantism, to a focus on providing for the material needs of the local population, regardless of their religious affiliation.

During this period, missionary activity also expanded in Persia. Like the Armenians in Anatolia and the Maronites in Lebanon, one of the main goals of the Nestorians in Persia was to procure a measure of international protection because of their status as both an ethnic and a religious minority.

In late 1867 or early 1868, a letter written by Christian Rassam, translated by George Badger, and signed by fifty-three Assyrian bishops, priests, deacons, and *maleks* (tribal leaders) was delivered to the archbishop of Canterbury. This letter described in flowery Victorian detail the current state of the Nestorians as captive between "the Eastern Mohammed" and "the Western Mohammed—that is, the Pope," in a state of "spiritual ignorance" because of the "deplorable decay of learning" among them, and in an "isolated and forlorn condition." It asked the archbishop to "send spiritual labourers to us from your Church."[51] The fact that it was signed by tribal leaders as well as by members of the church hierarchy is significant. At the same time, the Mar Shimun himself wrote a considerably shorter and less flowery letter to the Russian czar, also requesting assistance, but being quite specific in naming the Kurds as the Nestorians' primary oppressors. The letter also describes the Nestorians as living "in the mountains of Kurdistan."[52]

Although the CMS had begun work in Isfahan in 1869, it was not until 1876 that an Anglican exploratory mission arrived to investigate the possibility of setting up a mission to the Nestorians. This mission, under Edward Cutts of London, arrived in Kochanes via Aleppo and Diyarbekir in July 1876 and stayed for three weeks, holding discussions with the Mar Shimun. They then went on to Urmia, where they met with the American Protestant missionaries who were there.

This mission was charged with encouraging the Nestorians to retain their three ecclesiastical orders—bishop, priest, deacon (in contrast to the Protestants); hold out against Rome; study scripture and reform the Nestorian liturgy (that is, to remove the Nestorian heresy); be peaceable subjects of the civil powers; and "report what steps should be taken in England to keep up communication with them [the Nestorians], to help them to maintain their position as a distinct Christian community, and to instruct them more perfectly."[53] The conflicts among the various Western missionary groups are very much in evidence here. The Anglican mission's goal was not convert Nestorians to Anglicanism, but to maintain the Nestorian Church, its episcopate, and its rituals because any hint that the goal was conversion jeopardized the raising of funds in Britain for the project. This approach contrasts with that taken by the Roman Catholic missions, which explicitly sought conversion to Catholicism, and with the Protestant missions, which, although at first they tried to reform the Nestorian Church, made it clear that reform of the church meant the abandoning of the doctrine, the hierarchy, and the rituals of the Church of the East.

Although the Cutts mission explicitly insisted that the Nestorians were subjects of the local powers, with no special relationship to Britain, its presence raised the hopes of the Mar Shimun that the Nestorians would soon receive British protection. Meanwhile, there were renewed difficulties with the Kurds. Like the Nestorians, the Kurds lived on both sides of the Ottoman–Persian border, and rumors that the Armenians might gain their own state and that the Nestorians might have British protection made the Kurds feel threatened. Although Constantinople apparently urged Sheikh Ubaydullah of Shamdinan to try to counterbalance the Christians' increased power, he distrusted the Ottomans, so he tried to establish good relations with the British and American missionaries. In October 1880, Ubaydullah, with a force of eight thousand men, including some Nestorians, crossed the border and occupied Mahabad in an attempt to persuade the Persian government to acknowledge his leadership of the Persian Kurds, as the Ottomans had done on the other side of the border. In the end, Ubaydullah withdrew to the Ottoman side of the border, where the British urged that he be punished. He was ordered to Constantinople and eventually exiled to Mecca.[54]

The first Anglican missionary sent to the Nestorians by the archbishop of Canterbury, an Austrian named Rudolf Wahl, arrived in November 1880 and set up his schools the following spring.[55] However, by 1885 it was clear that he had alienated everyone he came into contact with, and he was recalled. A year elapsed before two more missionaries could be sent out from England, though at this point the effort was dignified by the official title "The Archbishop's Mission to the Assyrian [Nestorian] Church."[56] One of the new missionaries, W. H. Browne, remained in Hakkari until his death in 1910; and his influence would live on in Surma, the aunt of the young Mar Shimun, after World War I.

The mission established itself first in Urmia, however, where Browne and his colleague, A. H. Maclean, set up schools for both children and Nestorian priests as well as a printing press. At the same time in Urmia, there were also American missionaries, J. H. Shedd and J. P. Cochran, as well as the Vincentians. Conflict seemed inevitable, and in 1887 Shedd tried to bring about a formal agreement in a "pan-Persian missionary conference" in Hamadan. Maclean, however, declined the invitation to attend, pointing out that the goals of the American and British missions were very different, though their target population might be the same.[57] The English missionaries began to open schools in outlying villages, but the Persian authorities periodically closed them, fearing the growing influence of England and potentially the opening of Russian missionary schools as well.

As the Anglican mission in Urmia became a success, attempts to extend its activities into the mountains were blocked by the Turkish authorities, who were convinced that the Mar Shimun's motives for wanting the British missionaries there were purely political.[58] However, in spite of official hostility, Browne went to Kochanes in late 1887 at the invitation of the Mar Shimun and remained there for twenty-three years. The Protestant missionaries continued to visit the Mar Shimun, and the Catholic priests also made trips into the mountains, but the only Westerner resident there was Browne.

In 1890, a group of Anglican women missionaries joined the men in Urmia, and by 1896, a dozen years after the official beginning of the Archbishop's Mission, it reached its height, with six Anglican clergy, five sisters, and two laymen. By then, in addition to the schools in Urmia itself, the mission was sponsoring 111 village schools. All of this activity was directed toward members of the Old Church (Protestant and Catholic schools directed toward their Assyrian clients also operated in Urmia). In addition to the schools, the missions also made grants to the local Nestorian clergy to assure continued allegiance.[59]

In 1896, yet another incident involving the Kurds took place. This time Mar Gauriel, a Nestorian bishop, and his companions were killed. Again, the Kurds of the region were acting with considerable independence from Constantinople. The murders were reported to Urmia and from there by the missionaries to the archbishop of Canterbury, who communicated with the British Foreign Office, which contacted British officials in Constantinople and Tehran. As a result, the Turks appointed a commissioner to investigate, but no case against the Kurds was proven, and no action was taken.[60] The important things to note here are the lines of communication and the impact that such communication undoubtedly had on the parties involved—both the Assyrian Nestorian leadership and the Ottoman government. These events also came on the heels of the massacres of Armenians in 1895–1896 in the same region. The fact that the Assyrian Nestorians were able, through the missionaries, to mobilize this kind of attention gave them an unrealistic sense of their own power vis-à-vis the secular government. Military power in the region ultimately belonged to the local authorities—Turk, Kurd, and Persian—and there was little hope that the British could do much more than talk. Following the murders, there were further attacks on Assyrians by Kurds, and many Assyrians fled their villages on the

Turkish side of the border to settle in the Urmia area and across the border in Russia.

Throughout the nineteenth century, the Russian Empire was pushing southward into the Near East, challenging the British for influence in Persia and challenging the Ottomans by reasserting its role as protector of Orthodox Christians throughout the Ottoman Empire and emphasizing within Russia itself its ecclesiastical presence in the Holy Land. Although there had always been some Russian pilgrimage to Jerusalem and the Christian Holy Sites, from the mid-nineteenth century on this pilgrim traffic burgeoned, financed by the Russian state and assisted by a growing network of Russian consulates throughout the Ottoman Empire. Sensitive to the fact of declining Orthodox numbers while the Catholic population in Jerusalem was rising, Russia was aware that without official standing in Syria the Russian Orthodox Church—as opposed to the Greek—"could not work openly as missionaries in a country they already recognized as Orthodox," nor could it compete with the French Catholics, who not only represented the universal Catholic Church but exercised authority over the Maronites.[61] Despite these obstacles and continuing religious and political competition with the Greeks in the face of rising pan-Slavic and religious sentiment in the homeland, Russia increased involvement in the Holy Land by opening a shipping line for pilgrims from Odessa to Jaffa and by purchasing land for chapels, hospices, schools, and a church. The creation of the Orthodox Palestine Society, which established schools and clinics, was an attempt to compete with the Catholics and the Protestants. In 1907, Czar Nicholas II would boast that the society, after twenty-five years of operation, owned a million rubles' worth of property, eight hostels for ten thousand pilgrims, a hospital and six clinics, and 101 schools with 10,400 pupils and had published 347 books on Palestine.[62] Interestingly, Russia's state sponsorship of pilgrimage to the Ottoman Empire was not limited to Christians but also included support of Muslims going to Mecca.

Czar Nicholas I's policy of "autocracy, Orthodoxy, and nationality" was played out in the Balkans and along Russia's expanding southern border. His predecessors' victories over the Ottomans in the Russo-Turkish wars culminated in Russia's press to dominate the Black Sea and to establish hegemony along the Caspian. Because Russian expansion into the Caucasus and eastward into Central Asia resulted in the inclusion of large Muslim populations into what had formerly been the Christian Russian Empire, the government came to see the advantages of encouraging Muslim pilgrimage from Russia to Mecca as a way of increasing Russian presence in the region. Throughout his reign, Nicholas fostered Christian missionary work along Russia's borders, but he was also faced with Muslim uprisings against Russian rule in the Caucasus.[63] Fears that the Russians had designs on India ignited British interest in Persia, Afghanistan, and Central Asia.

It was this challenge to Britain's land route to India that was the source of British diplomatic interest in the Kurdish and Assyrian areas. Urmia had been occupied by Russian troops in 1828, but they withdrew north of the Araks River following the signature of the Treaty of Turkmanchai in the same year. The treaty transferred the Yerevan khanate (present-day Armenia) to Russia. Georgia had already been incorporated into the Russian Empire in 1801. The presence of a Christian power directly to the north, in particular one that claimed a right of protection over Orthodox Christians in the Ottoman Empire, exerted a powerful attraction for the Nestorians. As we have seen, the Mar Shimun wrote to the Russian czar requesting protection and assistance in 1868, at the same time that some of his bishops sent a similar letter to Queen Victoria of Britain. Ten years later, in 1877–1878, Russia occupied much of eastern Anatolia during the Russo-Turkish War. In the Cyprus Convention, Britain promised to assist the Ottomans in maintaining the status quo with Russia, and, in order to implement this assistance, British military consuls were appointed to various towns in eastern Anatolia, including Van.[64] These consuls, however, were withdrawn within a few years.

Throughout this period, Nestorians, frequently in search of work, went back and forth across the Russian border, many remaining in villages around Yerevan in Armenia. The Russians could see the advantage of maintaining good relations with the Nestorians as a way of stirring up trouble in Kurdistan. British writers pointed out the possibility of Christian military support for Russia in case of further conflict with the Ottomans (who had been supported by Britain and France in the Crimean War with Russia).[65] Part of the British response to this perceived threat was to encourage Ottoman reforms that would provide greater protection for the Christians; the perception of the Russian threat also encouraged the Archbishop's Mission to the Assyrian Church, for the relationship between the archbishop of Canterbury and the Foreign Office was very close. In July 1886, *The Times* of London reported that a Russian newspaper had attributed Browne and Maclean's presence in Tiflis (Tbilisi) on their way to Urmia to "an attempt on the part of England to extend her political influence to the Nestorian Christians (who have hitherto enjoyed Russian protection)."[66]

Nestorian appeals to the Russian Orthodox Church can be documented from at least 1851.[67] As noted earlier, at the same time as the Nestorian bishops' letter was sent to Queen Victoria, the Mar Shimun appealed to the Russians. Mar Gauriel, who was killed by the Kurds in 1896, had discussed possible union with the Russian Orthodox Church in Tiflis in 1884. The Anglican Church was well aware of these overtures and had discussed them in their own contacts with the Russians. In 1897, however, these discussions took a more serious turn when the head of the church in Georgia was authorized to send a mission to Persia to investigate the possibility of union.[68] Within six months, the two priests sent from Yerevan had collected more than ten thousand Assyrian signatures on a document renouncing the tenets of the Old Church and seeking to join the Russian Orthodox Church.

Union was exactly what the Anglicans had also been working toward. The aim of the Archbishop's Mission to the Assyrian Church had always been to bring the Nestorians into doctrinal agreement with the rest of Christianity. Furthermore, it seemed appropriate to the Anglican missionaries for the Nestorians to become part of the Eastern Orthodox tradition—certainly they were opposed to the Nestorians joining with the Roman Catholics, but they were also adamant that the Nestorians should not become members of the Church of England. Therefore, when the Nestorians agreed to accept the beliefs of the Russian Church, the Anglican missionaries felt that their job was done, and they were fully prepared to withdraw from Urmia and their work with the Nestorians immediately.

In September 1898, a Russian mission arrived in Urmia and began to enroll members in the Orthodox Church. Each village church was taken over by the Russians and reconsecrated, and the villagers renounced their "heresy" individually. The Anglican missionaries, at the request of the Russians, continued to operate the village schools they had started until the fall of 1899, when they were handed over to the Russians. For their part, the Russians made no effort to extend their mission to Turkey, and the Mar Shimun made no attempt to maintain the Old Church in Persia. By 1903, the Russians were firmly established, running sixty local schools and a boarding school by 1905, a printing press, and newspapers in Russian and modern Syriac. The American Protestant mission remained in Urmia, as did the Roman Catholic, but the British Anglican mission essentially moved across the imperial border to Van, which had at least eighteen Assyrian villages as well as a Chaldean bishop and his diocese. Turkish forces as well as the Kurds were a presence on the Turkish–Persian border from 1903 onward, but their incursion into Persia was prevented by the Russian troops stationed in Urmia. The Russian presence in Urmia was legitimized in the Anglo-Russian Convention of 1907, which recognized a Russian sphere of influence in Azerbaijan, including Urmia.[69]

The Anglican missionaries, writing to the archbishop of Canterbury before their departure from Urmia, described the problems that had led to the end of the mission there as resulting from false and contradictory expectations on both sides. Whereas the British sought to "raise the spiritual condition of the [Old] Church," the Nestorians were interested primarily in political and financial support from the British government, but the political situation made it increasingly difficult for that help to be forthcoming.[70]

Russian success with the Nestorians in Urmia worried the French as well as the British, and the French government sent one of the Dominicans in Van to try to persuade the Mar Shimun to join the Catholic Church. When he declined, the French allied with a dissident member of the patriarch's family and began to enroll individual Nestorians as the Russians had done, attracting fifty thousand Nestorians and thirty thousand Armenians. The real persuasion lay in the French promises of money, rifles, and protection against the Kurds, and the Dominicans were reported to pay a sum of money to each convert.[71]

In 1910, the Anglican mission on the Ottoman side of the border decided to move from Van to Amadia in what is now Iraq, although there was no Nestorian Church there and in spite of opposition by the Kurds and the local Chaldean bishop.[72] Kurdish attacks on the Nestorians in Hakkari continued throughout this period, and many fled either to the Urmia area, where conditions for the Assyrians were as good or better than they had ever been,[73] or to Russia.[74]

The American Presbyterians, who had taken over the ABCFM mission in Urmia in 1870, not only continued the Urmia mission to the Assyrians but in 1873 expanded their activities to Tabriz, where they worked primarily with Armenians. They also expanded eastward and south to Hamadan, Tehran (where the American Presbyterian schools became the schools of choice for the Iranian elite), Meshed, and Kerman. The British CMS also established a center in Isfahan, gradually expanding through southern Iran and working primarily with Armenians.

There is no way in our limited space to do justice to the rich landscape of Western involvement in the Middle East at the end of the nineteenth century. The official church enterprises from the various European countries and the

United States were only the tip of the iceberg. In addition to those already mentioned, the American and British Bible Societies, the Christian Missionary Alliance, the Quakers, and the Seventh Day Adventists were also active. They coexisted with a plethora of other organizations that had more or less religious goals, both evangelical (that is, aimed at conversion or the saving of souls) and millennial. Private missionary groups, funded by individuals or local parishes, established themselves particularly in the Holy Land, though some of this activity can be seen in the founding and supporting of ABCFM schools and colleges in Anatolia.

Between 1820 and 1914, as the European countries steadily expanded their political and military presence in the Middle East and North Africa, the American Protestants also expanded their presence, and other Americans focused on commercial rather than political growth in the region. The Americans, however, did so under the protective umbrella of the European presence. The first American organization to establish a presence in the region was the ABCFM, which by the second half of the nineteenth century had concentrated its activities primarily in Anatolia. At the end of the nineteenth century, only the mission to the Armenians in Anatolia was still active. The ABCFM's Greek mission gradually ended as Greek independence and the Greek Orthodox Church created difficulties for the Protestant churches and schools. The Palestine mission had been handed over to British missionaries by the 1840s. The Syria–Lebanon mission was handed over to the Presbyterians in 1870, as was the mission to the Nestorian Assyrians in Urmia. The mission to the Jews was closed in the 1850s, and missions to the Muslims were always a minor footnote to other missions once the missionaries discovered that conversion of the Muslims was virtually impossible. Although one of the original goals of the missionary work was the reform of the Eastern Christian churches, by the end of the nineteenth century this goal had generally been abandoned in favor of the establishment of local Protestant churches.[75]

In the last decades of the nineteenth century, a series of international missionary conferences was held, both in parts of the mission field, such as India and Egypt, and in Europe and the United States. In Cairo, for example, delegates from twenty-nine Protestant missionary agencies met in 1906 to formulate a campaign to reach Muslims. Samuel Zwemer and others—including James Barton, the ABCFM's foreign secretary and missionary to the Ottoman Empire—looked forward to the twentieth century as an opportunity to reach Muslims through a variegated approach of evangelistic appeal, philanthropy, and education. Their call to the Student Volunteer Movement to spearhead this mission set a precedent for the conference in Edinburgh that followed. [76]

Only Protestants participated in the meetings that culminated in the 1910 World Missionary Conference. Organized by Joseph Oldham of the British Student Christian Movement, led by Lord Balfour of Burleigh, a former British cabinet minister, and taking as its goal "The Evangelization of the World in This Generation," the conference brought together twelve hundred representatives of Protestant denominations and missionary societies, mainly from North America and northern Europe. In their ten days of deliberations, the delegates considered the reports of eight commissions, which had been working over the previous two years. The titles of these commission reports provide a clear indication of the concerns of the Protestant missionary enterprise at the time: "Carrying the Gospel to all the Non-Christian World," "The Church in the Mission Field," "Education in Relation to the Christianization of National Life," "Missionary Message in Relation to the Non-Christian World," "The Preparation of Missionaries," "The Home Base of Missions," "Missions and Governments," and "Co-operation and the Promotion of Unity." Cooperation and the promotion of unity were to have the most resonance going forward. The conference established the Continuation Committee, which, under the leadership of the American Methodist John Mott, traveled to India, Southeast Asia, and the Far East to assess the work of the missionary movement. Although endeavors were interrupted by World War I, the committee formed the basis for the establishment in 1921 of the International Missionary Council, the precursor of the World Council of Churches. The Edinburgh conference provided the framework for the future of the Protestant missionary enterprise. As Christian unity and inclusiveness became increasingly important, interaction among all Christian churches resulted in the increasing power of the ecumenical movement.[77] The conference also highlighted the second issue that would challenge the foreign missionary movement in the coming years: the concern that the West did not have all the answers and that more respect should be given to other religious traditions, a concern that was heightened by the events of World War I and gave rise ultimately to interfaith dialogue.

SEVEN

Achievements and Consequences

Intended and Unintended

B y the start of World War I in 1914, there was a significant Christian missionary presence in the Middle East. Whether working as institutional extensions of French, German, or Russian policy in the Middle East and North Africa or on an individual basis as most British and American Protestants did after a century of work, Catholics, Orthodox, and Protestants had purchased property and established churches and schools. By 1914, 75 percent of all Western Protestant enterprises in Anatolia and the Balkans (still part of the Ottoman Empire) were under the control of the ABCFM. Other ABCFM enterprises—in Syria, Persia, and Egypt—had been transferred to the Presbyterian Church, which had been active in the region since the mid-nineteenth century. In Anatolia, there were 150 ABCFM personnel in twenty stations as well as at least 1,000 local staff. Most of their work was with the Armenian population, and by this time the missionary-inspired Armenian Protestant Church had fifteen thousand members. In Syria, the Presbyterians had four stations with a foreign staff of 50 and a local staff of 200. Here too, a local Protestant church had been formed with a membership of perhaps three thousand. In Egypt, the American Protestants had about fifty schools in 1914.[1] Because by the end of World War I many of these institutions ceased to exist, it is useful to take stock of the missionary enterprise at its height, during the euphoria following the World Missionary Conference of 1910 in Edinburgh in the decade preceding the war.

In determining any outcomes assessment of the effort expended, however, it is important always to bear in mind not only the connection that the missionaries had with the peoples of the Middle East, but also the relationship between the missionaries and their home societies. To take just one example, the Protestant missionaries in the Middle East took as one of their main goals the education of women and girls and the improvement of their lot. This effort should be considered in light of the position of women in Europe and America and the role that the availability of missionary careers played in broadening the options available to women at the time. Some of the by-products of the missionary endeavor such as biblical archaeology and local nationalism must be viewed in the context of the contemporary European and American worldview.

The obvious place to begin is with the issue of conversion, but, unlike other areas of the world of missionary work, proselytization in the Middle East was exceedingly complex. It might seem self-evident that the goal of the missionary enterprise is conversion of members of one religion to another. In the Middle East, then, one would assume that the goal of the Protestant missionaries after they arrived in the early nineteenth century was to convert Muslims and Jews to Christianity, and, indeed, that was their original aim. However, Muslim opposition and the enforcement of regulations against apostasy as well as Jewish disinterest quickly forced the missionaries largely to abandon that goal and to substitute for it the attempt to "improve" the state of the Eastern Christian churches or, if that failed (as it did), to establish new Protestant churches that paralleled the ethnic–linguistic structure of the Eastern churches to serve their converts. The Vatican had adopted this strategy centuries earlier, establishing Uniate churches parallel to the Eastern churches, with ecclesiastical hierarchies that accepted the suzerainty of Rome. These churches were often small, had controversial leadership, and were not recognized as legitimate autonomous millets.[2] The low success rate in outright conversion, however, led to other methods of spreading the Word—through witness (living a Christian life) and education.

Education was a central part of all the various missionary enterprises. For Protestants, literacy—the ability to read the Bible for oneself—was a matter of theology. To read the Bible in one's own language was a cornerstone of Protestantism, essential for the development of one's personal relationship to God, and this belief led to translations of the Bible into local vernaculars.

Two consequences of translation into Armenian or Syriac or Arabic were the creation of literary languages that became vehicles for modern literature and political thought as well as the establishment of printing presses that enabled dissemination of the new literature.

For the Roman Catholics, access to God came more through participation in the liturgy than through a personal interpretation of the Gospels. Thus, the education of priests was a way to establish and preserve Vatican control, although even for Protestants boys' education was strongly directed toward the training of ministers and teachers. But by the end of the nineteenth century, both groups realized that although conversion remained a primary objective, the lure of modern education was the key to attracting local youth. Modernize them, the Protestants advocated—make them a living advertisement for Protestantism—and conversion would surely follow. Better the indirect route than overt proselytization that would alienate the Muslim authorities.

At first because of trade and later because Egyptian and Ottoman legal reform movements opened the Middle East to the West, Catholics and Protestants offered more than reading and writing. French Catholic schools provided a broader curriculum that stressed foreign languages such as French, Italian, and Greek as well as arithmetic, history, geography, and bookkeeping. These subjects were of interest to parents who wanted jobs for their sons in the ever-growing commercial firms dotting the Middle East as Western economic penetration increased. As the Jesuit educational mission in the Levant grew quickly, due in part to the development of two indigenous religious orders that were devoted to teaching—the Marianettes and the Xaveriens—both Catholics and Protestants also understood the allure of the professions and established medical schools in Lebanon: the Catholic Saint-Joseph and the Syrian Protestant College.

Whereas American institutions such as the Syrian Protestant College and Robert College as well as some of the Anatolian colleges were never under the direct control of churches or missionary organizations, the Catholics, with their explicit links to the French government, adopted teaching methods and curricula that would be less likely to offend the French and Ottoman authorities. They stressed "regeneration"—morality and modernity through education—and, like the Protestants, their educational institutions transmitted bourgeois civic culture to the "orientals" much like the French education provided to the poor and to the colonies. The Protestant CMS in Egypt similarly sought to uplift the indigenous Copts whose ancestors had produced the progenitors of European culture, but who, in the Protestants' view, by the nineteenth century had already passed the torch of progress to Europe. Using the Bible as their guide and European methods of schooling and social control, John Lieder and his followers sought to restore the "rationality," "morality," and "order" they believed the Copts' ancestors had pioneered.[3]

Teaching and curriculum were adapted to local conditions: parents were not interested in the study of dead languages, so Catholics in Lebanon stressed French instead of Latin. Like the Americans, they cast a wider net, opting for larger classroom attendance rather than focusing on outright conversion. It was better that the Jesuits teach Orthodox Christians, Muslims, and Jews than let the Protestants get them.[4] In addition to languages and practical subjects, schools taught a liberal arts curriculum that incorporated history and Western thought.

By the end of the nineteenth century, Western religious schools found themselves competing with Western secular schools established in the Ottoman Empire by the governments of Russia, Germany, Italy, and France. Like the schools of the Alliance Israélite Universelle, which attempted to reinforce Jewish religious identity in the context of French culture, the French *mission laïque* and the various European schools established in the Middle East recruited students to propagate Western secularism.[5] In Egypt after 1882, the British created an English–French educational school system designed to train small numbers of the Egyptian elite to staff the colonial bureaucracy.[6] American schools, having already undergone both the crisis of language instruction and the Darwin controversy, emerged with English as the language of instruction at the Syrian Protestant College, the disassociation of the college with the missionary movement, and reliance less on locals than on instructors imported from America. With the shift from religious evangelism and its emphasis on the Bible and on the millennium in religious time to secular education with its need to look to the present, Americans fostered technical education and modernization.[7] Science and technology were equated with Western dominance, but Howard Bliss, the president of Syrian Protestant College, also sought to inculcate Western social ideals and morals, advocating civic ideas and public service, obedience to the laws of the land and the college, stressing American values of a benevolent international power.[8]

As noted earlier, improvement in the status of women was an important goal of the Protestant missionaries, although it did not particularly excite the Catholics, and in the mission field it was closely linked to education. Islam, with its veiling and seclusion of women, customs that the local Christian population also commonly observed, presented a particularly visible target for Protestant women missionaries. The early Protestant missionaries, especially the Americans, were encouraged and even required to be married, and marriages often took place only days before the missionary couple departed for the mission field. These missionary wives would, upon their arrival, often take local girls into their homes and start tiny, home-based girls' schools. These schools gradually grew into more formal institutions, often parallel to the boys' schools started by the missionary husbands. The missionary movement in Britain and the United States in particular coincided with the women's movement and with the "Christian home" movement—the two actually promoting somewhat opposing views of the role of women in society. Whereas the women's suffrage movement focused more on women's rights outside the home, the "Christian home" movement emphasized women's maternal role, their responsibility to support their husbands and to share in their work, and their importance in maintaining an orderly home. Advocacy of these middle-class values as well as the growth of the spirit of self-sacrifice and service that came about with the development of entrepreneurial capitalism emerging from the Industrial Revolution led hundreds of thousands of Protestant European and American women to volunteer, hand out leaflets, donate money, subscribe to magazines, and engage in charitable and philanthropic activity. Those who engaged in missionary work transmitted the belief that their views of hygiene, childrearing, sexual practices, gender relations, and household arrangements were the norm.[9] As early as 1819, the ABCFM charged missionary wives with spreading the gospel of "conjugal fidelity and domestic attachment, parental care and filial obedience," to "educate the rising generation [and] to ameliorate the condition of the female sex." By the 1830s, the Christian Home had become a mission agency in its own right. Elizabeth Dwight, noting that the mother had the obligation to raise her children as a witness to the world, wrote from Constantinople that "the heathen want not only ministers of the word, but *pious, well-educated families* . . . to be the living, bright examples of the doctrines of Christianity." The wife, therefore, carried on missionary work that was just as important as the ordained husband.[10]

Of particular importance in the recruitment and training of women Protestant missionaries was Mount Holyoke College in South Hadley, Massachusetts. Its founder, Mary Lyon, came from a background similar to that of the men who founded the ABCFM. Like them, she was from a small, isolated, rural town in Massachusetts and had been deeply influenced by the Second Great Awakening. Her influence is readily apparent in the career of Fidelia Fiske, the niece of Pliny Fisk, who was one of the first two missionaries the ABCFM sent to the Middle East in 1820 and who died in Palestine in 1825. She attended Mount Holyoke, where she came under the charismatic spell of Mary Lyon and was recruited by Justin Perkins in 1843 to start a girls' school in Persia.[11]

The Fiske Female Seminary in Urmia was a conscious emulation of Mount Holyoke in its curriculum and values. Although it focused on Bible study, it also taught history, geography, grammar, arithmetic, chemistry, physiology, and astronomy.[12] This education marked a major change for a community in which only the priests had heretofore been literate. The aim of this education, however, was not to promote the independence of women, but rather to encourage them to be good wives and mothers and to establish proper home life. The impact of Mount Holyoke women extended throughout the missionary world. By 1859, sixty Mount Holyoke alumnae worked for the ABCFM throughout the world, and 20 percent of all ABCFM women in 1889 were its graduates.[13]

An altogether different example of women's education was established in Constantinople. The Home School, later the American College for Girls, was founded in 1871 by the ABCFM's Women's Board of Missions and became essentially the women's counterpart of Robert College. Unlike Robert, however, the American College for Girls was supported directly by the ABCFM until 1908. Education for girls was ubiquitous throughout the missionary stations of Anatolia, but it was generally at the elementary school level. The American College was entirely different. For one thing, it was located in the imperial capital and therefore drew from a more diverse and urban population, though the students primarily tended to be Christian. For another, however, it also drew students from Muslim families who were attracted by the possibilities of Westernization and modernization for their daughters. In 1908, the college severed its ties with the ABCFM, though it retained its explicitly Christian orientation, particularly in its fund-raising activities in the United States. In Constantinople, particularly in the wake of the 1908 Young Turk revolution, it presented a more secular aspect. Even to its American supporters, its "civilizing" mission became more important than proselytizing.[14] The college successfully navigated the transition from a missionary institution appealing mainly to Christians of the empire to one providing a Western education for Turkish women. By the end of World War I, it had lost most of its Christian clientele because the Ottoman Empire lost not only its Greek and Armenian populations in Anatolia, but also its Balkan territories, which had provided significant numbers of girls to the American College. Instead, the college increasingly attracted members of the Turkish elite, a situation replicated by Presbyterian schools in Iran.

The ABCFM had divided its operations in the Ottoman Empire into four mission administration areas: European, Western, Central, and Eastern Turkey. To a great extent, its activities in Anatolia were in education, and they had a major, though controversial, impact on the Christian population there. The methods of sponsorship, governance, and financing of these institutions were extremely varied and complex, ranging from direct supervision and financing from the Boston headquarters to private American support and local Armenian support. A description of some of these schools provides a picture of the ABCFM's impact on the Christian society that to a great extent would disappear from Anatolia by the end of World War I.

Marsovan became an educational center for western Turkey. The Mission Boarding School for Girls, founded by William Goodell and his wife in 1845, moved there in 1865, and its first principal was a Mount Holyoke graduate, Ann Eliza Fritcher. Anatolia College was founded there in 1886. Another Mount Holyoke graduate, Laura Farnum, started a girls' school in Bardizag, near the Gulf of Izmit, in 1872. A boys' school started there in 1879 later became Bithynia High School. The Protestant schools were not the only ones in Bardizag, for there were also Armenian Apostolic and Armenian Catholic schools in the town. In 1884, Laura Farnum was invited to move the girls' school to Adabazar, a larger and wealthier town about seventy-five miles east of Istanbul, where the school's expenses would be met by the local Armenian Protestant community.[15] The towns where the boys' and girls' high schools were located were at the center of large areas, with primary schools in the surrounding villages. For example, the area around Bursa had nine Armenian Protestant congregations, each of which supported its own elementary school. The Girls Boarding School in Bursa, supported by the Women's Board of the Pacific, an affiliate of the ABCFM, was founded in 1876. A girls boarding school founded in Izmir in 1878 became the American Collegiate Institute and is still operating. The boys' school started in the following year became International College. Greek Protestant schools were also started in Izmir. A network of schools and churches also developed over an area of forty-five thousand square miles around Kayseri,[16] and by 1909 there were forty-four schools with two thousand students. Girls' and boys' high schools were started in Talas in 1889 but were closed in 1917. In Sivas, a boys' teachers college was founded, and in 1914 it moved to a new, expanded campus. The following year, however, all the Armenians in the area were deported to Syria.

The Central Turkey Mission centered on Aintab, Marash, and Urfa. The first Armenian Evangelical Church in Aintab was built in 1855, and girls' and boys' schools were opened. Four years later a girls' training school was opened, which was steadily expanded until a large new building was built in 1885. That building was still being used in 1980 as a nurses' residence for the United Board hospital in what is now Gaziantep. A similar story can be seen in Marash, where there were three Armenian Evangelical churches as well as boys' and girls' schools. The high schools moved to Hadjin in 1879, where there was also an Armenian Apostolic boys' school. Because there was no education in the area beyond the high school level, graduates went on to study in Izmir and Istanbul and even at Oberlin College in the United States.[17] Theological education was not neglected; a theological seminary was established at Central Turkey College in Aintab, and St. Paul's Institute in Tarsus was opened in 1891.

Harput was the center of ABCFM activity in eastern Turkey. A network of so-called "common schools" was established in the surrounding villages, offering primary education and supported by the local congregations. The Armenian Apostolic Church also opened schools in the area. In 1859, the theological seminary that had been opened in Tokat moved to Harput, and two years later a female seminary was established in large part to educate the wives of the students at the theological seminary. By 1866–1867 in Harput and its outstations, 1,129 boys, 573 girls, and 855 adults were being taught in the mission schools. At the same time, Armenian Apostolic and Armenian Catholic schools in the area had a total of 3,764 boys, 609 girls, and 607 adults in their classes.[18] Although Protestants were clearly in the minority in the region's Armenian population, the difference in the ratio of boys to girls in the Protestant schools is notable, illustrating the American Protestant emphasis on girls' education.

After 1866, schools were opened in Malatya and Bitlis, near Lake Van. In 1870, two sisters, Charlotte Ely and Mary Ely, 1861 graduates of Mount Holyoke, opened the Mount Holyoke Girls Seminary for Kurdistan in Bitlis. The school survived until 1895, when it was closed because of the massacres and deportations of Armenians, and the American missionary in charge, George Perkins Knapp, was exiled "on charges of having helped to incite the Armenians to rebellion."[19] Another 1861 Mount Holyoke graduate, Olive Parmalee, founded the Mardin Girls School, the only Arabic-language secondary school in Turkey, to serve the Arabic-speaking Assyrian population in the area. The Armenian Evangelical Union also started twelve schools in a dozen Kurdish-speaking villages, but they all were destroyed in the 1895 massacres.

In Van itself, the Armenian Apostolic Church had started common primary schools by the 1850s. In 1878, another Mount Holyoke graduate founded a girls' seminary, and by 1915 Van, with an Armenian population of thirty thousand, had a mission compound consisting of a church, six school buildings, a lace school, a hospital, a dispensary, and four missionary residences. In May 1915, however, the Russian army, including an Armenian volunteer force and led by Armenian generals, arrived in Van, but a few months later the Turkish army returned, and the Armenian and foreign population fled. Many of these Armenians became refugees in Russia and provided the leadership for the Soviet Republic of Armenia ten years later, and the American missionaries returned home through St. Petersburg.[20]

In the 1880s and 1890s, seven American colleges were founded in Anatolia, all of which had some connection with the ABCFM. The differences between them reflect the variety of American missionary-related activities going on in the region at the time. In 1870, the Armenian Evangelical Union, the organization of Protestant churches that had begun to be established in the late 1840s, met in Urfa and petitioned the ABCFM for a college. The ABCFM accepted the plan the following year, and in 1874 the Central Turkey College was incorporated in Massachusetts. It opened the following year on a campus in Aintab for which the land had been donated by a local Turk, and the language of instruction was Turkish. An associate girls' college was opened in Marash in 1880. A medical department was started in 1876 but closed a decade later. The college came under suspicion of supporting Armenian nationalists by the mid-1890s, and the Armenians of Aintab suffered from the massacres of 1895 and 1909. Finally, in September 1915 the college faculty were exiled to Deir ez-Zor in the Syrian desert, and the buildings were occupied by the Turkish military. When British troops arrived in Aintab in December 1918, they, too, occupied the college buildings, though the college managed to reopen in 1921. However, the French, who by then controlled Cilicia, withdrew from Aintab in December 1921, and most of the Armenian population followed them to Syria soon afterward. The Central Turkey College ultimately moved to Aleppo, where it still exists as Aleppo College.

By 1877 in Harput and its vicinity, there were twenty-two Protestant churches, eighty-three primary schools with 2,469 students, four intermediate schools, boys' and girls' secondary schools, and a theological seminary. In 1878, Armenia College in Harput was incorporated in Massachusetts. Harput had become something of an educational center, with a small French Catholic secondary school for Armenians nearby, a German secondary school for Armenian orphans after the 1895 massacres, as well as an official Ottoman government high school for Muslims. Armenia College, whose name was changed at Ottoman insistence in 1888 to "Euphrates College," was from the beginning coeducational at the lower levels. In 1898, it had a total of 1,051 students at all levels, though by 1913 enrollment fell to 606. Many of its graduates went on to the Syrian Protestant College to study medicine or pharmacology.

Bebek Seminary had been founded by Cyrus Hamlin in the 1840s and later moved to Marsovan. In 1886, Anatolia College was founded on the basis of the seminary and was incorporated in Massachusetts in 1894. Because of its location, Anatolia College always had a greater proportion of Greeks in both its faculty and its student body than did several of the other colleges, and this factor was to affect its future. By 1913, its faculty included 10 Americans, 11 Armenians, and 9 Greeks, and its student body was composed of 200 Greeks, 160 Armenians, 40 Russians, and 25 Turks.[21] The college closed in 1916 when its buildings were taken over by the Turkish army and reopened in 1919. However, it closed again in 1921 when the Kemalist army took over, expelled the foreign faculty, and executed three Greek faculty members. The college reopened in Thessaloniki following the expulsion of its Greek constituency from Anatolia, and it continues to operate there.

The town of Tarsus carries great significance for Christians as the traditional birthplace of St. Paul. In 1868, Elliott Fitch Shepard, a wealthy New York lawyer who had married a daughter of William Vanderbilt and who was an ardent Calvinist and member of the Fifth Avenue Presbyterian Church, visited Tarsus on a tour of the Middle East. After his return to New York, he was approached by Harutune Jenanyan, an Armenian graduate of Central Turkey College, a student at the Union Theological Seminary in New York, and a member of the Fifth Avenue Presbyterian Church, with a proposal to start a college in Tarsus. This project was completely separate from the ABCFM, though it clearly supported the same general purposes.[22] St. Paul's Institute in Tarsus opened in the fall of 1888. Meanwhile, because the American Civil War had cut off supplies of cotton to Europe, both the French and the British sought alternative sources. The British turned to Egypt, and the French to Cilicia, where they opened a railway from Adana to Mersin passing through Tarsus in 1887. The Jesuits opened a college in Tarsus, and the Presbyterians of New York saw St. Paul's Institute as a way to save Tarsus from the Papists and the social evils brought by the French railway.[23] Shepard died in 1893, leaving an endowment of $100,000 to St. Paul's, equivalent to at least $1 million today, a gift that enabled it to survive to the present day.[24] Following World War I, the French occupied Tarsus, then withdrew in 1921. St. Paul's closed for a year, then reopened as Tarsus American Koleji under ABCFM's control.

The Apostolic Institute in Konya was, like St. Paul's, completely separate from the ABCFM, but, unlike St. Paul's, it lacked a wealthy patron. It also lacked a network of so-called common schools, the primary schools that acted as feeders to the other colleges. It was founded by Harutune Jenanyan after his break with St. Paul's, and, following the 1895 massacres, he established several orphanages that fed students to the college. He also raised funds in the United States, setting up an independent board in New York chaired by the pastor of Marble Collegiate Church. The Apostolic Institute closed in 1915 following the deportation of Armenians from Konya, then reopened after the war, but when Allied troops left in 1921, it closed permanently. The ABCFM took over the college's buildings to use them as an orphanage in order to assert American ownership of them, and it gradually paid out the funds remaining as relief.

Smyrna (today Izmir) was the site of the earliest Protestant missionary activity in Anatolia but never developed a significant Protestant community. Nevertheless, the ABCFM felt that it was important to have a presence there, and a boys' school was started in 1880 to complement a girls' school that was already functioning. In 1903, the combined institution was incorporated in Massachusetts as International College, providing a four-year preparatory course and four years of college instruction. Most of the students were Greek, and the language of instruction was English. In 1922, the Greeks were forced out of Smyrna by the Kemalist army, but International College continued until 1934, with mostly Turkish students and without ABCFM support. It then moved to Beirut, where it became the preparatory department for the American University of Beirut.[25]

Of the seven American colleges founded in Anatolia, then, two ceased to exist, and four moved to Greece, Syria, or Lebanon. Only the one in Tarsus continues to operate. The large system of Protestant primary schools also ceased to exist because its target population disappeared, and Turkish law prohibited foreigners from teaching at the primary level.[26]

The missionaries' work did not go unnoticed. The Eastern church hierarchies responded in various ways to the missionaries' arrival. The reaction of the Maronite hierarchy in Lebanon to the earliest American missionaries in the 1820s, for example, was initially positive but then turned negative.[27] The reaction of the Armenian hierarchy in Constantinople also shifted from positive to negative and by 1850 had become so negative as to force the establishment of the Armenian Protestant Church. In the case of the Copts, however, the arrival of the CMS missionary John Lieder seems to have had a direct and positive effect on the local church with the election of a new patriarch, Cyril IV, in 1854. "Upon his accession, Cyril mounted a campaign of 'reform' that spoke to all the concerns evangelicals had raised, and employed all the techniques evangelicals had endorsed in their writings."[28] He encouraged the education and literacy of the Coptic priesthood, a perennial criticism offered by the missionaries, who promoted the importance of the ability to read biblical texts, and he imported a printing press from Austria with the aim of creating printed versions of Coptic manuscripts. Perhaps most important, he established what came to be called the "Great Coptic School" in Cairo in 1855. Like the missionary schools, it taught languages, including English, French, and Italian, as well as secular subjects such as history, mathematics, and science.[29] The education gained by Coptic laymen at the school proved invaluable not only in the reform of the church, but in the Copts' greater ability to enter into public life, particularly under the British administration later in the century.

Eastern Christians, Roman Catholics, and Muslims were also active in expanding educational resources for their members. How much this activity can be directly attributed to the Protestant example is debatable because all these communities had educational institutions before the Protestants arrived.

In the Jewish community, as rabbinic opposition mounted not only to Christian proselytizing but to attendance of Jews at missionary schools, a group of European Jews based in Paris founded the Alliance Israélite Universelle in 1860 with the goal of providing modern secular education to Jews in Islamic lands and the Balkans. There had been attempts to provide Western Jewish schools since the 1840s, but these schools were short-lived. Beginning with the opening of the first school in Morocco in 1862, the Alliance Israélite Universelle established during its first decade of operation schools in the Balkans, Palestine, Iraq, Morocco, Syria, and Turkey. By the end of the century, schools in Egypt, Iran, Lebanon, Libya, and Tunisia had been added. By World War I, the organization had built a network of more than 180 schools for boys and girls, teaching some forty-three thousand students. The schools taught a French curriculum with some Judaic subjects, trained alumni to return to their home towns to teach, and, like the French *mission laïque* that followed, had a profound impact on the people of the Middle East, with even Muslim elites sending their children to the schools.[30]

All these schools and the work of missionaries served as vanguards of modernization and Westernization. They became exemplars of modern technologies in many areas—agriculture, printing, and medicine—and promulgators, through both formal education and example, of modern Western habits of thought. Missionaries were instrumental in introducing not only printing and medicine, but also new farming methods and technology that contributed to commerce and transportation. Millenarian groups, whose energies were directed to the land, fostered agricultural colonies, where they introduced wind-powered flour mills, European-built mechanized oil presses, and hydraulic cotton bales. Europeans imported water pumps from England and America and installed them in Jerusalem, Jaffa, Haifa, and Nablus. New farming methods and crops using seeds and tools from the United States were introduced. Instead of using local materials in the construction of churches, schools, and hospitals, Europeans imported lumber, nails, and tempered steel roof tiles from Marseilles and used European construction techniques.[31] The German Templers established the first machine factory in Palestine, promoted tourism, and engaged in viticulture. They were instrumental in bringing carriage traffic to Palestine and began adapting roads to wheeled traffic.[32]

Missionary education is also credited with contributing to the emergence of local nationalisms, including Arab, Armenian, and Assyrian, as opposed to a specific religious identity or identification with the imperial power, though it should be noted that Kurdish nationalism emerged at the same period without much missionary input. In this regard, modern literary languages that became vehicles for the transmission of Western political ideologies and the construction of ethnicity fostered by the study of pre-Islamic Middle Eastern cultures were key factors. The role that missionaries played in the development of the Assyrian literary language, Armenian nationalism, and Arab ethnicity provides cases in point.

In the case of the Assyrians, missionaries were important in the development of a common literary language and a modern Nestorian literature. The importance of printing and "print capitalism" in the development of national identity has been well documented,[33] and we have seen that all of the missionary groups attached great importance to it as well. Their goal, however, was not to create national identity among their target populations. Indeed, they were very aware of the danger of creating separatist identities. Their aim in setting up printing presses as soon as possible in their missionary effort was rather to print primarily biblical texts, liturgies, and religious tracts. The American Protestants were particularly anxious to print these materials in the vernacular so that they could be readily understood by the people on whom the mission focused. The Roman Catholics did not share this goal, and printing was not as central a part of their mission as it was for others. The Anglicans were concerned about preserving the ancient rites of the Assyrian Nestorian Church, so their presses printed in both the liturgical and the vernacular languages. The printing presses were also important for the production of teaching materials, and therefore works in English, French, and Russian were also produced.

As the Assyrians began to move toward a secular national identity, the missionary printing enterprises had a mixed effect, however. Printing codifies language, and the languages spoken by the various missionary groups and by Assyrians and Chaldeans in Persia and the Ottoman Empire were different. These differences in linguistic usage and in alphabet were codified when they were set in type by the missionary presses, and efforts to standardize the written language continue to this day. Although that effort to standardize the written language was beneficial for the development of nationalism and nationalist communication, it also had the effect of eliminating the regional diversity that existed before the mid-nineteenth century. Just as the missionary enterprise fragmented the Assyrian community along European and Western Christian lines, the missionary printing presses also fragmented the community.

Working at a time when nationalism emerged as the operative political ideology in the West, Western missionaries were seen to be complicit in the development of local nationalism in the Middle East. The first decade of the new century saw the transformation of both Middle Eastern empires into constitutional monarchies. This reflected the rise of nationalism in the region, a phenomenon that had begun with the Greek War of Independence in the 1820s and continued through Bulgarian struggle for independence from the Ottomans and the Balkan wars of 1912–1913. Western missionaries were thought to be involved in the nationalist movements, in particular the rise of

Armenian and Arab nationalism. In both cases, the curriculum and textbooks of the missionary schools as well as the values they represented were blamed (or given credit, depending on one's point of view). In eastern Anatolia in the last years of the nineteenth century, the missionary schools were thought to be hotbeds of anti-Ottoman agitation, and the local Turks accused missionaries of aiding Armenian nationalists.

Perhaps the most controversial and contentious role ascribed to the missionaries in the development of national identity and nationalism concerned the Armenians. Since the time of the Roman Empire, the Armenian people had been a border population straddling empires, populating much of the border between the Roman and then Byzantine empires and Persia. With the replacement of the Byzantine Empire by the Ottoman Empire, Armenians continued to play the same frontier role, though their population in eastern Anatolia was intermingled with the Kurds, also a cross-border population. The literary and linguistic groundwork for Armenian national feeling was laid in the early eighteenth century by a Roman Catholic monk known as "Mekhitar." As noted in chapter 3, he established a monastery on the island of San Lazzaro in Venice, where he and his monks devoted themselves to the study of early fourth and fifth century Armenian religious manuscripts. The Mekhitarist monks established a printing press in San Lazzaro and another at their house in Vienna and are credited with the preservation and translation of much Armenian literature.

The Russian push into the Caucasus in the late eighteenth century opened a new frontier for the Armenians, and the Armenian population in Russia increased with each Russian conquest of Turkish territory—in 1778, in 1822, and in 1878. Each time, like the Assyrians of Persia, Armenians were either absorbed into Russia or fled across the new border to join their Christian coreligionists. By 1896, there were an estimated eight hundred thousand Armenians in Russia, two million in Anatolia, and perhaps another seven hundred thousand in the cities of western Turkey, and a nationalist movement had begun to develop in the Caucasus.

The first Armenian nationalist party, the Hnchags, was founded in 1887 in Geneva, Switzerland, by Armenian Russian intellectuals, espousing an ideology and methodology similar to that of other Russian and European movements of the period.[34] By the early 1890s, Armenian intellectuals in Europe "had established paramilitary nationalist–socialist committees in Eastern Europe and Turkey for the purpose of setting up an autonomous and eventually independent Armenian socialist republic in Eastern Turkey."[35] Like similar socialist movements in Russia and eastern Europe at the time, including Labor Zionism, this movement was completely secular and as such was opposed by the Armenian ecclesiastic hierarchy, which feared the Ottoman response that was not long in coming. The Hnchag movement was also, however, opposed by the American missionaries in the region. Cyrus Hamlin, the founder of Robert College in Constantinople, saw the movement as a "deliberate plot to foment revolution and massacres of innocent Armenians—and to secure Western intervention in Turkey."[36]

The Hnchags soon set up cells in the Ottoman Empire—in Erzurum, Trebizond, Kharpert, Smyrna, Aintab, and Aleppo. In 1890, they organized demonstrations against the Ottoman government and in favor of Armenian independence in Erzurum and Constantinople, and Sultan Abdul Hamid II responded by organizing Kurdish troops and using them for attacks on Armenian villages along the Russian frontier. The disturbances spread to Kharpert the following year, where there was an American missionary presence at Anatolia College, and some professors were arrested. Twenty thousand Armenians fled to Russia in 1892 and 1893, and in 1894 massacres of the Armenians in eastern Anatolia began in response to continuing Hnchag demonstrations and revolt. In August 1894, a Hnchag rebellion in Sasun in eastern Turkey resulted in the massacre of ten to twenty thousand Armenians, and the next year the violence spread to Constantinople, where perhaps a hundred were killed. As the violence spread throughout the Armenian towns of eastern Anatolia, the American missionaries fled, and their property was damaged. An estimated one hundred thousand Armenians were killed between 1894 and 1896, half a million were made homeless, and sixty thousand more fled to Russia. Others fled to the United States, Syria, Palestine, Egypt, Bulgaria, and Greece.[37]

The following year the revolutionary initiative shifted from the Hnchag Party to the Tashnag Party, an explicitly Marxist party founded in Tbilisi in 1890 with the objective of gaining Armenian autonomy within the Ottoman Empire rather than complete independence. Tashnag guerrilla activity began in Van in 1896, and in August of that year, in the most audacious act yet, the Tashnags seized the Ottoman Imperial Bank in Constantinople. Five to seven thousand Armenians in the capital were killed in the aftermath. Violence continued, both in the East and in the capital, but the focus of missionary activity turned to relief and reconstruction efforts.

The rise of Armenian nationalism, then, can be seen as emanating primarily from European and Russian sources rather than from American missionaries, though clearly the Americans' educational efforts, especially in eastern Anatolia, had opened an intellectual space for these new ideas. Both the missionaries and the Armenian Apostolic Church opposed the nationalist independence and autonomy movements, though individual missionaries were surely sympathetic to them and may have lent their assistance. However, the response to the violence presages the shift in missionary focus that was to come during and after World War I twenty years later. American missionaries began relief efforts in 1895, with contributions by John D. Rockefeller and others, and Clara Barton and the Red Cross went to Turkey the following year to deliver aid. Orphanages were opened and reconstruction supplies were provided. Relief was also provided by the Armenian General and Benevolent Union, founded in Cairo in 1908. By 1914, the union had fifty-nine chapters in Turkey as well as chapters in Europe and the United States.[38]

The role missionaries played in the development of the Arab renaissance or "awakening" also remains controversial. [39] Although many historians today reject missionary influence on Arab nationalism, there is an understanding that both Protestants and Catholics working in the Levant had a considerable impact on the creation of the "idea of Syria." For Muslims, the territorial and geographical dimensions of Muslim Syria, or *bilad al-sham*, had been part of local culture since the Islamic conquest. In the Ottoman Empire, Syria comprised the provinces of Aleppo, Sidon, and Damascus. For missionaries, it was the northern extension of the Holy Land. As early as 1833, Eli Smith wrote that "[Syria is the] general name for the country that lies along the whole breadth of the eastern end of the Mediterranean sea, extending inland to the deserts of Arabia, and having the territories of Egypt on the south, and the river Euphrates with the mountains of Cilicia on the north. . . . The southern part of it is Palestine, the ancient land of promise. On the north of it, beyond the Euphrates, is Mesopotamia."[40]

Both Protestants and Catholics saw the Middle East as the land of the Bible and connected the region's pre-Islamic past to the Christian peoples of the area. But as many missionaries wrote the history of the region, they projected the idea of a pre-Islamic Syria that linked the ancient classical and Arab worlds. The Presbyterians associated the Copts in Egypt with the Pharaohs and the earliest Christians, so they saw their task as educating local Christians about their historic link with the glories of ancient Phoenicia. "There will yet be a new Phoenicia, a new Syria, better cultivated, better governed, with a wider diffusion of Christian truth," wrote Henry Jessup of the Syrian Protestant College.[41]

The creation of a modern literary Arabic language led to the writing of histories, the formation of literary societies, and the publishing of periodicals that propagated the idea of a Syrian identity that included both Christians and Muslims. Such Greek Orthodox and Armenian Protestant converts as As'ad Khayyat and Gregory Wortabet as well as Christian literati such as Butrus al-Bustani wrote about a Syrian identity.

At the same time, Jesuit scholars in the neighboring University of Saint-Joseph cultivated ties with the Maronites, continuing the French Catholic association of Syria with the Holy Land and the French Crusader past.[42] By the turn of the twentieth century, the Oriental Faculty of the University of Saint-Joseph offered courses in classical Semitic languages, local ancient history, epigraphy, archaeology, and geography. Its scholars taught and published books about Syria and Lebanon that traced a straight historical trajectory from the region's pre-Islamic past to its multicultural present. These studies by renowned Orientalists such as Henri Lammens, Louis Jalabert, Louis Cheikho, Sebastian and Louis Ronzavelle, and others became key texts used in the dissemination of separatist Lebanese and Syrian identities.[43] Scholars focused on the role of Lebanon as a religious sanctuary for oppressed Christians and stressed Lebanon's Phoenician past and its close association with France. Their works and those of their Maronite acolytes were instrumental in the Franco-Maronite alliance that resulted in the creation of Lebanon in the twentieth century.

In North Africa, Cardinal Lavigerie linked the indigenous Berbers to the ancient inhabitants of North Africa in his campaign to restore Christianity to North Africa. Reflecting views of nineteenth-century sociologists that Berbers and Arabs came from different ethnic stock, Lavigerie and the White Fathers perpetrated the "Kabyle myth," according to which the Berbers were not only sedentary and more culturally gifted, but, like Sicilians and Iberians, also more closely connected to North Africa's Christian, European past. Just as the French military spearheaded the reintegration of North Africa into the Western world, its missionaries would reestablish St. Augustine's church at Carthage in a region that had once been overwhelmingly Christian. Like missionaries in Lebanon, they examined the Berber language and Berber Islamic practice for remnants of Christianity and used archaeology to bolster the pre-Islamic Christian connection. Missionaries studied monuments and ancient topography, excavated church ruins, collected artifacts, and built museums to house them.[44] These links to the pre-Islamic Christian world rose in tandem with the opening of the Middle East to the West and revived interest first in ancient Egypt and then in the land of the Bible. The discovery of the Rosetta Stone by Napoleon's soldiers paved the way for the expansion of knowledge about ancient Egypt, and Jean-François Champollion's decipherment of Egyptian hieroglyphics led to the development of Egyptology and interest in all things Egyptian.[45]

This activity had its parallels in Mesopotamia (Iraq) and Persia (Iran). Under the sponsorship of the British Museum, scholar-diplomats surveyed Babylon, Basra, and ancient Assyrian Nineveh. In Persia, Georg Friedrich Grotefend and Sir Henry Creswicke Rawlinson worked on Old Persian and deciphered cuneiform. This could not have been accomplished without the transcriptions by Karsten Niebuhr at Persepolis or Rawlinson's own painstaking copy of the inscriptions on the Behistun Rock. Cracking the cuneiform code extended human history to prebiblical eras at a time when Europeans took interest in their Greek and Near Eastern roots. The concept of biblical lands was expanded to incorporate areas from Egypt to Mesopotamia. This was duly noted by the German kaiser, Wilhelm II, during his trip to the Middle East in 1898 when he sponsored excavations at Byblos.

In the case of the Assyrians, archaeology proved critical to the development of a national identity. At the beginning of the nineteenth century, the group we now refer to as "Assyrians" were the remnants of the ancient Nestorian Church of the East as well as of the parallel Uniate Catholic Church, the Chaldeans. They were scattered primarily in small agrarian villages in the mountainous area of eastern Anatolia and what is now northern Iraq, home also to a large Kurdish population, and on the plain surrounding Urmia in northwestern Persia. Anglican missionaries began to work in the region in the 1830s, and Americans were active in Urmia by 1840.

Christianity served as the first and most important pillar of Assyrian identity as it existed in the Ottoman and Persian empires and as it evolved under the impact of the West in the nineteenth and twentieth centuries. The second pillar upon which this identity was built was ancient Assyria, as revealed in the excavations of Nineveh and other Assyrian cities around Mosul. Christian identity was upheld, reinforced, and enhanced by the Western missionaries and their promise of protection against the Muslims. "Assyrian" identity was created on the basis of European archaeological discoveries, for there was no historical memory or textual evidence within the Nestorian community prior to these discoveries. Instead, the conventional wisdom is the (almost certainly apocryphal) story that Austen Henry Layard looked at the reliefs he was finding and at his workmen and exclaimed that because the two looked alike, these must be the Assyrians come to life.[46] However, the story does date from the time of Layard's excavations. When Layard's young assistant, Hormuzd Rassam, arrived in England with Layard, he introduced himself in British society as a descendent of the ancient Assyrians and even as the forty-fourth cousin of Nebuchadnezzar, though it was reported that the president of Magdalen College, Oxford, felt that this connection was not necessarily something to be proud of.[47]

In 1840, there was no such profession as archaeologist, nor was there much knowledge of the great art of the Assyrian Empire. Archaeology, the search for and study of ancient material culture, was conducted by amateurs—travelers, adventurers, diplomats, and schoolmasters—and was in a real sense a product of the romantic period. Indeed, if a wealthy Englishman's estate did not have a "romantic ruin," he might very well have his architect construct one. Furthermore, although today we draw a clear distinction between archaeology and religion—between archaeologists and missionaries—in the nineteenth century the two were closely intertwined, particularly in Middle Eastern archaeology. European archaeologists working in the Middle East were trying to validate biblical history, and their finds became the subject of heated debates in the press as well as in intellectual and religious circles.

Assyria was known from the Old Testament and from ancient Greek texts, which told different stories. The early excavators were Paolo Emilio Botta, who was appointed French consul in Mosul in 1841 for the explicit purpose of excavating Nineveh, and Austen Henry Layard, who first saw the Assyrian mounds in 1842 and returned to excavate them in 1845 under the auspices of Sir Stratford Canning, British ambassador to Constantinople.[48] The purpose of the excavations was to reify the stories of the Old Testament.

In the case of Assyrian archaeology, religion and archaeology were intertwined in their personnel as well. Hormuzd Rassam, Layard's assistant and successor, was the younger brother of Christian Rassam, the British vice consul in Mosul who was married to Matilda Badger, sister of George Badger, missionary and the greatest English advocate of missions to the Assyrians. Layard hired Hormuzd to supervise the Nestorian workers at the sites, and Hormuzd returned to England with Layard. The discoveries were to provide the second foundation for Assyrian identity as it evolved in the twentieth century. The link to religion and the Bible would be broken, and "Assyrian" would become the name that could be used in a secular, nationalist context to bridge the gaps created by religious differences.

European and American travelers followed in Napoleon's footsteps, encouraged by the French and then English military presence in the region that offered protection for tourists and by the new steamship lines that provided easy connections between Europe and the Middle East. The "Grand Tour" that began with sites in Greece and Italy soon added the ancient and biblical Middle East to itineraries in Europe and the classical world. Designed to impart culture and refinement, the tour also provided exposure to more distant lands and encouraged further exploration. Interest in the region was further stimulated by the work of artists such as David Roberts, who produced drawings that could be converted to easily disseminated lithographs. But there was a real distinction between European and American "Orientalist" art. Europeans, notably the French, tended to be more overtly imperialist and demeaning toward the local population, whereas American artists responded more to the need for biblical links, stimulated by the missionaries working in the region.[49]

The use of the name "Holy Land" in travel literature spawned an interest in travel to the region and involvement with it on a variety of levels. The Middle East was a special place for Christians, both Protestant and Roman Catholic. Catholic pilgrimage to Jerusalem and the Holy Land had continued unbroken since before the Crusades, as had Catholic ecclesiastical involvement with the region.[50] Pilgrimage was less important in the Protestant world, and interest in the Bible as text was of greater importance. It was this interest that stimulated travel as well as archaeology, which in its earliest phase in the Middle East was an effort to document on the ground the stories in the Bible. As late as 1907, *Cook's Handbook for Palestine and Syria* (the guidebook published by Thomas Cook & Son, the large British travel company) was authored by Reverend J. E. Hanauer, clearly an Anglican clergyman, and its focus is on visiting sites with biblical connections. In an effort to encourage business, Thomas Cook donated money to various missionary groups.

For Christians after the Crusades, the Holy Land had become a transcendental perception instead of a physical place. Shifting gears once again as travel to the region became easier and more popular in the nineteenth century, Christians faced a different geographical reality. As French Catholics identified Stations of the Cross and encouraged pilgrimage, Protestant tourists, students, artists, and dilettantes explored, mapped, illustrated, and depicted nineteenth-century facts in biblical terms, seeing in the local Bedouin, for example, vestiges of ancient Israelites. At the same time, Christian scholars identified biblical sites and explored the Sea of Galilee, the Jordan River, and the Dead Sea. Edward Robinson, one of the most important students of the region, laid the foundations for the historical study of Palestine. Discoverer of the Herodian fortress of Masada, Robinson also identified the arch on the Western Wall in Jerusalem, which still bears his name.

Societies such as the Palestine Exploration Fund were founded in London, the United States, Germany, and Russia to foster study of the Holy Land. Precise maps of Jerusalem by Charles Wilson and Charles Warren led not only to serious archaeological study, but also to paintings and illustrations that found ready audiences in Europe and America that bought the postcards and travelers accounts produced for a burgeoning market interested in the Holy Land. Physical reconstructions of the Holy City could be seen on the shores of Lake Erie, and, with the advent of photography, traveling slide shows and parlor tours brought the region—both real and imagined— into Americans' living rooms.[51] Not to be outdone, during the 1890s the Dominicans established the École biblique et archaeologique.

Travel to the Holy Land and the renewal of agricultural settlement in Palestine were closely connected with spread of millenialism in Europe and the United States. Early archaeological efforts were directed toward "proving" the historical accuracy of the Bible, and increased European presence in the region made tourism as well as pilgrimage a popular activity.[52] Millenarian thinking, encouraged by the increasing reification of the Bible in the Holy Land, was an important motivation for the Protestant missionary enterprise of the nineteenth century, but in addition to stimulating religious activity, it also was a factor in increasing interest in "the land of the Bible."

Although Catholic and Orthodox settlers came and remained within the framework of established churches and did not establish communal settlements, many Protestants were millennial disciples. Traveling to the Holy Land either as members of pietistic movements or as individuals, these Protestants did not wish to control or subdue Palestine; rather, they saw the Holy Land as they imagined it from reading the Bible. Although with ease of travel Christians could now reach the physical Jerusalem, they retained a post-Crusades transcendental view of the city and its residents as if the Holy Land were suspended in biblical time, and the Bedouin were Old Testament Hebrews. In *Innocents Abroad*, Mark Twain noted that the Presbyterian travelers

found a Presbyterian Palestine, and they had already made up their minds to find no other, though possibly they did not know it, being blinded by their zeal. Others were Baptists, seeking Baptist evidences and a Baptist Palestine. Others were Catholics, Methodists, Episcopalians, seeking evidences endorsing their several creeds and a Catholic, a Methodist, an Episcopalian Palestine. Honest as these men's intentions may have been, they were full of partialities and prejudices, they entered the country with their verdicts already prepared, and they could no more write dispassionately and impartially about it than they could about their own wives and children.[53]

The postcards these tourists sent back and the talks to neighbors they gave when they returned perpetuated a Holy Land mania for the past that was much like the "Egyptomania" that gripped European travelers to Egypt.

A number of groups established a permanent presence. The German Templer movement established colonies in Haifa, Jaffa, Jerusalem, and the Galilee. The Swedish Church of the New Jerusalem (Swedenborgians), founded by Emmanuel Swedenborg, established settlements in Jaffa and near Tyre in Lebanon. In 1841, the Mormon Church sent Orson Hyde to Jerusalem to dedicate the Holy Land for the return of the Jews.

Perhaps one of the most unusual communities was founded by Anna and Horatio G. Spafford, who settled in Jerusalem in 1881 after considerable trial and misfortune befell the family. On the way to the Holy Land, four of their daughters drowned in a shipwreck, and then soon after that their young son died of scarlet fever. Bereft, Spafford developed heterodox views about death and the afterlife that put him at odds with the Presbyterian Church, to which he had belonged. Once settled in Jerusalem, the Spaffords, who were later joined by Swedish Protestants, established a communal lifestyle that they believed to be similar to that lived by the early Christians and provided food and employment to the poor of Jerusalem. After the death of Horatio Spafford, his widow, Anna, led the group known as the "American Colony," but group cohesion did not survive. After her death in 1923, her daughter, Bertha Spafford Vester, maintained the property as the American Colony Hotel, which became an important gathering place for Arab literati and Western travelers and officials.[54]

The Ottoman authorities responded to the growing Western missionary presence swiftly and decisively, despite the promulgation of the Tanzimat, which the missionaries saw as an opening for conversion of Muslims. In the 1860s, the revelation that CMS missionaries had baptized a dozen Turks led the authorities to imprison the Turkish Christians, close CMS assembly halls, confiscate Bibles and Bible Society publications, and, despite consular protest, evict missionaries from their homes. The Turkish government informed the British government that conversions from Islam would not be permitted, and the CMS mission in Istanbul was virtually shut down. The situation led one missionary who remained to write home that "[p]roselytizing efforts offend both the religious and the political sensibilities of the Mussulmans. . . . An European missionary could not visit in Muhamadan houses without rousing suspicion. No church for the public Christian service of Turks would have any chance of being authorized by the government. No missionary school for Muhammadan youths would be tolerated."[55]

Muslim reaction to Christian missionary work developed during the reign Abdul Hamid II. Coming to power at the end of the Tanzimat period in 1878, the sultan had to deal with the implementation of the freedom-of-religion edicts that allowed Christian missionary activity. But he also understood freedom of religion as the empire's right to defend its religion, Islam, against missionary activity, which the Ottomans saw as a direct attack on Islam: "After bemoaning the fact that 365 Muslims were living under the Christian yoke," an Ottoman pamphleteer wrote at the end of the nineteenth century that "[the defence of these millions of Muslim brethren] must be primarily carried out by the intellectuals of the Islamic world. There should be no doubt that the main aim of the missionary movement today is the destruction of our religion and social morals. For this reason it is imperative that the intellectuals of Islam should persevere in their religious struggle against the united forces of the missionary high command."[56] To that end, the Ottoman authorities implemented a number of measures designed to combat what they saw as the missionary menace and to strengthen Sunni orthodoxy within the empire.[57]

Measures were taken to strengthen the faith of the Bedouin of Syria, whom the Ottomans regarded as lax in observance, and to bring religious schismatics such as the Kizilbash of Sivas in Anatolia,[58] the Yezidis of northern Iraq, the Zaydis of Yemen, and the Nusayris in Syria back to the Islamic Ottoman fold by convincing their leaders of the benefits of Hanafi orthodoxy and the positive rewards of becoming soldiers in the sultan's army. When the carrot failed, the stick was used. The authorities in Istanbul sent in troops, but force sparked rebellion among the Yezidis, which in turn led to rethinking of the situation and taking a page out of the missionaries' book.

The Ottoman authorities bureaucratized the conversion process by sending only authorized preachers trained in Istanbul to rural areas instead of freelance preachers. In Christian areas, witnesses, including members of the convert's family, had to be present at formal conversions of Christians to Islam in order to verify that the conversion was voluntary so that the priest would remove the new Muslim's name from his list so as to rebut the charge that Muslims kidnapped young boys and girls to forcibly convert them to Islam. The conversion issue was particularly significant in central Anatolia—an Armenian area—where it became central to the Armenian massacres in 1894–1895.[59]

With the Western powers' attention focused on the Armenian issue, conversions of Christians to Islam and the arrest and deportation of the missionary George Knapp from the Bitlis Boys Academy sparked reactions in the American press, which the Ottoman legation in Washington monitored and reported back to Istanbul. Articles from the Ottoman press that criticized the missionaries for meddling in the internal affairs of the Ottoman Empire were translated and transmitted, but at the same time the Turks had to rebut accusations that deporting missionaries was official Ottoman policy. Unlike for the Catholics and the Anglicans, there was no Protestant institution with which to liaise, so the authorities used tactics of surveilling missionary activities and easing their movement out of areas of conflict.[60]

The most significant Ottoman effort to counter missionary activity was the establishment of modern schools that mirrored the Christian schools in their effort to create a literate middle class.[61] In 1905, the governor of Beirut wrote that the only way for the Ottomans to "ensure that Muslim children are saved from the harmful clutches of the Jesuits and Protestants [in this city] is for there to be established a network of modern schools capable of competing with them."[62] By that time, there were more than two hundred American schools in the empire competing with the Catholic, Anglican, and Jewish schools for the hearts and minds of Ottoman children.

At the same time, Ottoman authorities were loath to provoke a confrontation with the Western powers. They may have perceived the CMS, whose missionaries were working with the Druze and the Bedouin, as an espionage front for the British, but rather than come down hard, they used enforcement of Ottoman law to hinder the construction and certification of missions and schools. Petitions to the government were denied, as was certification for nonstate schools, a situation that forced the administrations of the American University of Beirut and the University of Saint-Joseph medical colleges to have their graduates certified twice—once by the West and then by an Ottoman licensing exam in Istanbul. The Imperial School of Medicine in Istanbul decided later that the examination of medical students would be either in Turkish or in French; English or Arabic was not acceptable. What the Turks were doing was merely following European practice—"Turkey is playing the same game [as the European powers]," wrote a CMS representative. "She feels that her dominion is honeycombed by foreign institutions, that the State Religion is threatened, and she follows the same example, and I do not see by what treaty rights we can expect to maintain our position. Let us imagine a Mahometan Potentate sending missionaries to England, and opening schools denouncing Christianity in London: I doubt if we should bear it silently."[63]

Throughout chapters 4 to 7, we have drawn linkages between political events, the rise of imperialist interest in the Middle East, and the growth of the missionary enterprise. These links become more obvious and important in the early twentieth century, culminating in World War I, the collapse of the Ottoman and Persian empires, and the redrawing of political boundaries in the aftermath of the war. The rise of nationalism had a major impact on missionary activity in the region.

A major charge against the missionaries has been that they, the educational opportunities they afforded, and the encouragement they gave to separatist movements resulted in large-scale emigration of Christians from the Middle East to Europe and America, with the result that today the region is considered part of the Muslim world, and the presence of Christians has been forgotten. As we review the areas of impact of the missionary enterprise in the Middle East in the nineteenth century, the centrality of education and the expansion of literacy become clear. Not only did the missionaries start schools at the primary through university levels, but these schools ultimately promoted the status of women, the establishment of national or subnational identities, and the rise of nationalism. This emphasis on education and literacy is peculiarly Protestant, for reasons we described earlier, but the enthusiastic reception of these schools led both Roman Catholics and Muslims to redouble their efforts in the field.

In assessing the impact of the missionaries prior to World War I, we have focused primarily on institutions rather than on individuals, but it arguably was the individuals who had the most impact and influence. Two can be singled out here for their impact on the relations between the West and the Middle East in the coming decades.

The first is the Reformed Church missionary in Basra, John Van Ess. Born the son of Dutch immigrants in 1879, Van Ess graduated from the Princeton Theological Seminary, specializing in Semitic languages, and went to Mesopotamia with the Arabian Mission of the Reformed Church of America in 1902. The Arabian Mission was known particularly for its medical work in the emirates and Oman, but Van Ess was primarily an educator. His knowledge of Arabic made him immediately useful as a translator and interpreter for both Ottoman and British officials. In 1911, he married a fellow missionary, Dorothy Firman, a 1906 graduate of Mount Holyoke College who had joined the mission in 1909. In 1912, he started a school for boys in Basra, which attracted the sons of the local sheikhs right away, and in the same year his wife opened a school for girls. In 1914, Van Ess was appointed temporary American consul in Basra, a post he held until July 1915, when he returned to the United States.[64] In his diplomatic capacity, he informed the British commander in 1914 that Basra was undefended, thus allowing the British forces to take the city. Van Ess then assisted the British in establishing a police force and education system in Basra. Although he went to the United States on leave in 1915, he returned to Basra the following year.

The Van Esses' linguistic skills, their familiarity with the villages of southern Iraq, and their close ties with the Shiʿi sheikhs of the region formed the basis of their long-lasting relationship with Gertrude Bell and the British authorities. Bell's biographer notes, "Almost from the moment the British occupied Basrah, he [Van Ess] had been providing them with information and supplying them with Arab agents behind the Turkish lines."[65] However, when the British proposed installing Faisal or Abdullah as king in Iraq after the war, Van Ess, on the basis of his knowledge of the tribes, made his objections known forcefully to Bell. He insisted that the Shiʿi sheikhs would not accept a Sunni, Sharifian ruler, and his advice was confirmed in 1920 when the sheikhs launched a serious revolt against British authority. Despite their disagreements, Bell and the Van Esses remained close friends until her death.

The Boys' School of High Hope, as the Van Esses' school in Basra was called, reached its height of influence in the late 1920s and early 1930s, when the majority of its students were Muslim and its graduates found positions in the government, the professions, and the oil industry.[66] By the end of the 1930s, however, as nationalistic and anti-British feeling intensified in Iraq, influential Muslims no longer sent their sons to be educated there, preferring to send them to the state schools. Instead, the mission school attracted mainly the sons of the poor. Van Ess himself continued to have influence with the U.S. government and in the United States through his writing. His *Spoken Arabic of Iraq* became the standard text. John Van Ess died in 1949, but his wife, Dorothy, continued to write and speak publicly until her death in 1975.

Another Princeton graduate and missionary was also to have a singular impact on the political scene in which he found himself. Howard Baskerville, son and grandson of Presbyterian ministers, graduated from Princeton in 1907, majoring in religion. Just before his graduation, he contacted the Presbyterian Board of Foreign Missions and eventually accepted a position teaching at the mission-run American Memorial School in Tabriz in northern Persia.[67] He arrived in Tabriz in September 1907. The school had a mixed enrollment—80 Muslim students and 135 Christian, Armenian, and Assyrian students. Like Van Ess's school in Basra, the Presbyterian school attracted the sons of the local Muslim elite. This period was one of great political upheaval in Persia. In 1906, a constitutional movement had forced the Qajar shah to establish a parliament, or *majlis*, which proceeded to write a constitution along Western liberal lines. The following year, however, Russia and Britain, without Persian participation, signed the Treaty of St. Petersburg, dividing Persia into Russian and British spheres of influence. Tabriz fell in the Russian sphere.

The shah died on January 1, 1907, and was succeeded by his son, who suspended the *majlis* and launched a coup against the new constitutional government. Tabriz became the center of opposition to the new shah, led by Sattar Khan, and the city came under siege by the royalist forces, aided by Russian-trained troops. Baskerville, who had studied "constitutional government" under Woodrow Wilson at Princeton, lectured on the subject to Armenian students and offered to organize a student force of 150 to aid Sattar Khan. The American consul in Tabriz, William E. Doty, attempted to stop Baskerville, warning him against interfering in Persia's internal affairs, and he "was furious to learn that Baskerville had been making use of the library at the American consulate, doing research in the *Encyclopaedia Britannica* on how to make grenades."[68] By April 1909, after a ten-month siege, Tabriz had nearly run out of food and medicine. In mid-April, Baskerville and a British journalist volunteered to slip out of the city and search for food in the surrounding area. Their first attempt failed, and they tried again to find a way out of the city a few days later. As Baskerville and a few of his students made their way through the walls, he was shot and killed by a sniper on April 20, 1909.

Howard Baskerville was buried in the Armenian Christian cemetery in Tabriz at the age of twenty-four, but his death had its effect. Publicity about it spurred action by the British and the Russians to get the shah to allow representatives into the city, thus breaking the siege and encouraging opposition to the shah, who was deposed later that year. "When the Persian parliament finally reconvened that November, one of its first acts was a speech of tribute to Baskerville."[69] He has become a legend and a martyr in Iran, although the American Presbyterian community in Tabriz at the time was apparently rather relieved to be rid of their young activist. The American consul, William Doty, who was the first to hold the Tabriz post and had been sent there primarily to protect the fifty or so American missionaries, may also have been somewhat relieved to have a thorn in his side removed. In 2003, a bust of Baskerville was erected in front of Constitution House in Tabriz, the site of Sattar Khan's home. He is still remembered in Iran.

In the end, Western missionaries' greatest impact in the Middle East may have been at the individual and personal level. Both John Van Ess and Howard Baskerville played roles in the political development of the countries in which they lived, in part because they straddled the two cultures—East and West—and both, like the missionaries in Anatolia who were supporters of the Armenian nationalist movement, identified with the people of the region. Even Van Ess, who clearly assisted the imperial power, supported local ambitions against the outsiders, whether British or Arab. The missionaries lived and worked among the people of rural areas, small towns, and villages and at a different social and economic level than diplomats in the capital. Thus, they had access to different sources of information that often proved useful to government representatives and were able to have an impact well beyond their immediate sphere.

EIGHT

World War I

Nationalism, Independence, and the Fate of the Missionary Enterprise

The Protestant missionary movement reached its height in the World Missionary Conference held in Edinburgh in 1910. After a century of increasing activity around the world, coupled with the economic, political, and military dominance of western Europe and the United States, countries from which the missionaries came, they had every reason to expect continued expansion and success. How could they have guessed that within a decade, particularly in the Middle East, the entire structure would lie in ruins? Yet the signs of impending disaster were there.

The 1908 Young Turk rebellion by the Committee for Union and Progress set in motion a course of events that would lead to the demise of the Ottoman Empire and result in significant territorial and demographic changes that would affect the Middle East for the rest of the twentieth century. Drawing upon widespread discontent produced by bad harvests, tax inequities, military defeat, and economic hardships, the reform-minded military officers, who were based in Salonika, also garnered support from mutinous Ottoman troops in the Balkans. In 1909, Abdul Hamid II was replaced by his brother, Mehmed V, and it seemed that an era of reform and liberalism was under way. During the next four years, the Constitution, which had been suspended since the Russo-Turkish War in 1877, was restored; elections were held; and administrative reforms were instituted. Peoples of the empire enjoyed the freedoms of a modern civil society.

Despite the reforms, however, the Ottoman Empire continued to lose territory in the Balkans and North Africa. In the space of three years, Bulgaria declared its independence, Austria annexed Bosnia-Herzegovina, Albania rebelled against Ottoman rule, and Italy occupied the last Turkish provinces in North Africa—Tripoli and Benghazi. Sensing weakness, the rest of the Christian Balkans went to war against the Ottoman Empire in 1912 and 1913. By the end of the Balkan Wars, the empire had lost all of its European possessions and, as a result, for the first time ruled over a population that was predominantly Muslim. The military humiliation, accompanied by inflation and shortages of food and other commodities, led a contingent of the military wing of the Committee for Union and Progress, who feared that concessions to the Europeans were in the offing, to put into power a triumvirate—Enver, Talat, and Cemal—military officers would rule the empire until the end of World War I.

Persia, too, underwent economic and political change. While the Qajar Empire was collapsing in the late nineteenth century, the Russian Empire continued its push south into northwest Persia, a region contiguous with the areas of eastern Anatolia, where the Russians had made a series of territorial gains in the late eighteenth and nineteenth centuries. The object of Russian expansion in the north and British imperial designs in the south, Persia looked to other European powers and the United States for economic and military assistance. By the end of the nineteenth century, rulers of the Iranian Qajar dynasty had sought Russian military assistance and awarded economic concessions to European businessmen in order to raise money to pay for reform and to support an increasingly luxurious lifestyle. While the European advisers, new Western schools, and foreign travel by Iranian officials to Russia, India, and the Caucasus exposed them to the political ideologies engaging intellectuals to the north and west of their borders, at the same time control of their economy by foreigners led to local opposition. The replacement of cheap imports for locally produced goods and the intensification of cash-crop farming of tobacco over subsistence agriculture resulted in unemployment and low wages. Muslim clergy and local businessmen opposed the awarding of tax collection and construction contracts to non-Muslims. In 1890, a coalition of religious leaders and businessmen organized a successful boycott of tobacco, causing the government to annul the tobacco concession granted to a British firm. In 1903, there were riots against the government and minorities after the shah awarded economic concessions to Russia and the collection of customs duties to a Belgium firm. Two years later, encouraged by Japan's defeat of European Russia, religious leaders and businessmen, joined by artisans and westernized intellectuals, pressured the shah for a constitution. His successor, Muhammad Ali Shah, who came to the throne in 1907 and was kept in power by the Russians and the support of conservative Shi'ite clergy, opposed the Constituent Assembly and was deposed the following year.

Meanwhile, in light of the growing German threat demonstrated by the Berlin to Baghdad Railway concession and increased trade in the region, Russia and Britain came to an agreement over their differences regarding Persia, Tibet, and Afghanistan and in 1907 signed the Anglo-Russian Convention, which effectively divided Iran into three zones in which the major powers asserted their own spheres of influence. Beginning at the Caucasus, northern and central Iran—including Urmia, Tehran, Isfahan, and most of the country's major cities—came under Russian influence. The British controlled the Southeast, and the area in between, where oil was later found, was the neutral zone. With the capital under Russian control and without British objection, the shah ruled, but he was unable to prevent the decentralization of the country. Tribal disorder ensued, and taxes were not collected despite American financial advice. When in 1914 oil became a major factor in British foreign policy,[1] the country was effectively divided into zones of Russian and British influence.

The relationship between Germany and the Ottoman Empire, which dated back at least to 1898 when the kaiser visited the Holy Land, had deepened through the first decade of the twentieth century, leading up to events in the summer of 1914. Sultan Abdul Hamid II had already turned to Germany as a counterweight to Britain. He engaged Germans to train and equip his armed forces; he also granted permits to German companies for the construction of both the Hijaz Railway to carry pilgrims to Mecca and the Berlin to Baghdad Railway, which, had it been completed all the way to Basra as planned, would have enabled the Germans to circumvent the Suez Canal on the way to their East African colonies, thus challenging the British route to India.

With the outbreak of war in August 1914, the Middle East became a major battleground for the conflicting powers. On November 5, 1914, the Ottoman Empire entered the war on the side of Germany. The next day Britain declared war on the Ottomans and sent a British force from India to protect Persian oil installations. The British also established a bridgehead at Basra in

Mesopotamia, and the Russian threat loomed to the north. In December, the Turks, under the leadership of Enver Pasha, one member of the ruling military triumvirate, moved into northeastern Anatolia to engage the Russians, where, despite their initial superiority in numbers, they were defeated at Sarikamish in early January 15, losing all but fifteen thousand men of their army of ninety thousand.[2] At the same time, the British thwarted Cemal Pasha's advance on the Suez Canal, and the Turks retreated back through Palestine to Syria with remnants of their army. The Turkish strategy of engaging the Russians in northeastern Turkey and the Caucasus and the British at the Suez Canal created a war zone throughout most of Anatolia and the Arab provinces, a situation that placed large numbers of missionaries and eastern Christians in harm's way.

For four years, people in the Middle East lived a nightmare of war, massacres, deportations, economic privation, famine, and disease, as survivors later described it, but even in 1914 the "unprecedented horror" was foreshadowed by the British representative in Aleppo, who wrote:

> [T]he calling out of reserves of all classes up to the age of 45 years produced general misery and distress. Authorities made no secret that they merely aimed at wringing exemption money from such of the Christians as could pay, and did not need them as soldiers. The payment of this money has fallen terribly hard on almost all those who have managed to effect[,] it there being hardly any gold in circulation and the authorities insisting on payment in hard cash. Thus merchants and shopkeepers whose resources are paralysed by the moratorium and whose merchandise is requisitioned by the military commission have to scrape together beg or borrow sufficient cash to pay exemption money for themselves, their sons or their employees, meanwhile what is left of their merchandise lies in depot or even at the custom house with no possibility of sale or withdrawal the customs, nevertheless exacting the ordering cadre housing dues. Taxes are levied continually and even with armed force. Venality is as strong as ever, and certain food commodities requisitioned by the authorities are being sold in the Moslem quarters at less than half the original price. Even horses requisitioned are being dispersed the same way. If the Military requisition continues much longer and the moratorium is prolonged for another two months there will be famine and general bankruptcy and ruin. The country is being devoured by human locusts.[3]

The toll on lives and property affected the region for generations.

At the outset, the Ottomans conscripted all young men, including Christians and Jews, mobilizing an army of more than a million, but as the initial euphoria of war dissipated, desertions began. Militarily ill equipped and loathe to dig ditches under Muslim subalterns, many Christians and Jews in Iraq and Syria fled to areas under British control. In other areas, such as Persia, local disturbances took the lives of missionaries, and mobs sacked mission stations in Tabriz and the Presbyterian hospital.[4]

British and French institutions and personnel, with their countries at war with the Turks, found themselves in a precarious situation. As early as September 1914, the British Foreign Office advised CMS and London Jews Society missionaries to leave Jerusalem for Egypt, where they were soon joined by the Anglican bishop. The Turks ordered French Catholic clergymen to leave, but through contacts in Istanbul the clergy managed to suspend the expulsion order temporarily. As foreign consuls left, Catholic interests were overseen by neutral Spain, and the deportation of French Catholics from Jerusalem to Italy placed German and Austrian Catholics suddenly in charge of institutions where once the French held sway.[5]

Some Catholic clergymen remained to interpret or provide intelligence to the British and the French about terrain and local conditions, information that assisted in the Anglo-French expulsion of the Turks. In North Africa, the White Fathers served as military chaplains and hospital workers and cared for wounded soldiers.[6] At the same time, the French were fearful of the Muslim call for jihad and decried the de-Christianization of Jerusalem, which evoked for them Saladin's reconquest of the Holy City in 1187.[7]

Financial support dwindled as the Turks abrogated the capitulations, disrupting European banking and commercial channels and cutting off the flow of funds that supported missions, schools, and hospitals. Missions and personnel also lost legal and diplomatic protection as foreign consuls were deported. Orphanages, hospitals, and schools were commandeered to be used as Turkish hospitals and billets or were turned into Muslim schools. When Cemal Pasha arrived to take command in Jerusalem, he made the Augusta Victoria Hospital his headquarters.

The German government and the American representatives stepped in where they could, but their protests to the Ottoman authorities met with uneven results. The United States, which did not declare war on the Ottoman Empire, hoped that members of the Young Turk elite who had attended American schools would temper their policies and practice religious toleration. Americans also looked to their own commercial interests. By the first decade of the twentieth century, even before direct American political involvement in the region, the Ottoman Empire had become a major trading partner with the United States, sending tobacco, figs, and more than fifty tons of licorice for candy and chewing gum, though perhaps the more important factor was the amount of American missionary investment in schools and hospitals, particularly in Anatolia. President Woodrow Wilson had advised the Turks to stay out of the war because Allied ships dominated the Mediterranean and could easily invade Turkish coastal cities from Smyrna to Jaffa.[8]

Even after entering the war against Germany in 1917, America did not declare war on the Ottoman Empire, so Americans were still in a position to assist coreligionists. Until the U.S. consul in Jerusalem, Dr. Otis Glazebrook,[9] left in May 1917, he helped the Catholic and Anglican clergy. After he left, the Spanish consul, Conde de Ballobar, oversaw American interests. The Vesters at the American Colony in Jerusalem hid clergymen and safeguarded the Anglican Cathedral's silver crosses, chalices, vestments, and carpets and stored valuables, including property deeds belonging to the French Dominicans, the École biblique et archaeologique, the Sisters of St. Joseph, and Notre Dame de France.[10]

In some places, the Turkish government modified its position and allowed missionary work to continue. When Robert College found itself inundated with students because British and French schools were closed, Talat Pasha assisted with food and fuel.[11] In the Turkish interior, however, Christians, in particular Armenians, found themselves at risk, in part because of their foreign connections both with Americans and with Russia.

The war took its toll on missionary staff. Only some 20 percent of the Protestant missionaries remained in the Middle East, and, of these, many died of cholera, typhus, and typhoid. When German missions were cut off by the Allied advance, some of the missionaries worked with the American and British societies that picked up the slack. By 1916,

> six missions had been abandoned and only half the board's missionaries were at their posts and assisting with local relief. Some of the rest were on furlough, several had died during epidemics, while others carried on relief work in southern Russia or Syria. . . . At the close of the war, schools and churches with few exceptions had been broken up; the Turkish government occupied most hospitals, equipment and furnishings being scattered or carried off. Only 36 missionaries remained and some 200 of the former 1200 native workers were still alive.[12]

Most of the native workers were Armenians, who suffered the same fate as the rest of the Armenian community in eastern Anatolia. But with more than 50 percent of twenty- to thirty-year-old men enlisting in the Allied armies, Protestant mission societies found themselves short of ordained ministers to send into the field. Wartime conditions also hampered mission work. There were limited travel facilities because fewer steamship lines sailed to the Middle East, and stringent conditions were placed on issuing passports, causing some of the paperwork to be rerouted through the United States. Nevertheless, missionaries stayed in the Middle East to render service and relief work.

The devastation resulting from the war left the future of missionary work dire indeed, but it also provided the impetus for change. Missionaries had always been involved in the amelioration of living conditions. They provided education and medical services and encouraged economic development through training in agriculture and other skills. The massacres of Armenians in Anatolia in 1894 and 1895 had brought the missionaries into the area of disaster relief as they established orphanages and generally did all they could to help those who were homeless. World War I forced the missionary institutions to shift their activities even more from evangelism to relief and assistance, the activities we now generally ascribe to nongovernmental organizations.

From the standpoint of the missionary enterprise, three wartime episodes stand out: the humanitarian disaster of the Armenian massacres and deportations from Anatolia beginning in 1915, which were followed after the war by massacres of the Greek Christian population and eventually by the League of Nations–sponsored population exchange between Greece and Turkey; the famine in Syria during the war and the missionary response; and the attacks on the missionary institutions in Urmia in 1917.

The Ottoman leadership, in particular Enver Pasha, who had led the Turkish army against the Russians, held Russian–Armenian forces responsible for their disastrous defeat at Sarikamish in late 1914. This assignment of blame, coupled with the German call to jihad, led the Turks to regard the Armenians as a fifth column inside the empire, and in April 1915 Enver led an attack on the heavily Armenian city of Van, where there was also a strong ABCFM missionary presence.[13] The Armenians, under the leadership of the Tashnag Party, held out for weeks, until May, when the approach of Russian–Armenian forces caused the Turks to lift the siege and flee. The Russians retreated to Tbilisi in August, but the incident confirmed the Turks' view of the Armenian population. On April 24, 1915, a date still memorialized by Armenian communities throughout the world, the Turks rounded up and killed the Armenian intellectual leadership in Constantinople. In May, massacres and deportations began both in southern Anatolia and along the Russian frontier in northwestern Anatolia, apparently ordered by the Young Turk government and in many cases carried out by Kurdish irregulars. The massacres began in the heavily Armenian area of Cilicia, just north of Syria, and spread throughout eastern Anatolia. The missionaries found themselves on the front lines of the disaster because the Armenians had been their primary clients, and they were therefore able to document the disaster in numerous firsthand reports that were widely disseminated in the United States and Europe. As early as April 24, 1915, U.S. ambassador Henry Morgenthau began to query Turkish leaders about the Armenians, but his continued entreaties had no effect. By that summer, Morgenthau was appealing regularly to Washington to intervene, in part because of his concern for the missionaries, and he continued to raise the issue with the Turks.[14] However, the massacres and deportations continued, and by early 1916 one-third to one-half of the Turkish Armenian population of perhaps two million had perished. Half a million Armenians fled Anatolia, an estimated 300,000 to the Caucasus and 150,000 to Syria, where the Ottoman commander Cemal Pasha seems to have provided some protection.[15] Those Armenians who fled to Syria found themselves in a country still under Ottoman control and ravaged by famine and the privations of war. Although those who fled to Russia were no longer under Ottoman control, they soon found themselves caught up in the Russian Revolution.

The famine in the Arab provinces of the Ottoman Empire during World War I is one of the great untold stories of the war, overshadowed, particularly in Europe and America, by the massacres and deportations of Armenians that were taking place at the same time. Syria, Lebanon, and Palestine were affected not only by Ottoman military conscription that left few men to work the farms, but by a disastrous combination of an inadequate supply strategy, rapacious grain merchants, and callous military officers who commandeered anything that could be used for the war. The famine that resulted from bad harvests and a plague of locusts that descended on the Levant in 1915–1916 was exacerbated by the British blockade of the Levantine coast that cut off supplies and by the huge influx of Armenian refugees from Anatolia. Although the Armenian humanitarian crisis received considerable attention in America and in Europe, the famine in the Arab provinces remained a hidden disaster, despite causing the deaths of perhaps hundreds of thousands of Syrians and Lebanese.[16] In Palestine, American relief efforts were supervised by Dr. Glazebrook; the American Colony ran a soup kitchen; and in Lebanon and Syria the Syrian Protestant College became a center for aid and assistance. Food, money, and materiel were sent by the American Committee for Armenian and Syrian Relief as well as by American Jewish organizations.

Despite his draconian rule, Cemal Pasha allowed food and supplies to reach the Syrian Protestant College and permitted American institutions to provide humanitarian assistance at a time when food was scarce and the cost of supplies, labor, and transportation had swelled. The college remained open throughout the war, closing for only two weeks in 1917.[17] The United States still remained neutral, and Turkish and American diplomats remained at their posts, despite calls from American interests in the Middle East to send ships and troops. Former New York City College president John H. Finley, head of the wartime Red Cross in Palestine, urged America not only to send the Red Cross, but "that which Christ said he came to bring—a sword . . . [and] make common cause with the forces of justice against the demons of cruelty."[18] President Wilson, who did not want American troops fighting in the Middle East, stood firm against members of his cabinet who wanted America in the war against the Turks, especially as reports of atrocities against the Armenians reached the press. Humanitarian aid was dispatched, and businessmen continued to operate. Not wanting to alienate a major noncombatant power, the Turks apologized to the missionaries and permitted the use of American English after having forbade its use, as an enemy language, at the beginning of the war.[19]

The Nestorians in northern Persia also faced difficulties during the war. The Kurdish invasion of the plain of Urmia in October 1914 was followed in December by the Turkish offensive against Russia in the Caucasus. At this point in the war, the Russians and British were allies against the Turks, who were allied with the Germans, and the United States was still neutral. The British missionaries were therefore evacuated first to Tabriz and then through Russia to England. As neutrals, the Americans remained in Urmia. In January 1915, the Kurds and Turks took Urmia, causing the Russians to withdraw to the north. During the previous autumn, many Nestorians had fled from Turkey to the Urmia area, some taking refuge in the mission, and, with the Russian withdrawal, some ten thousand more fled north, following the Russian troops. At the same time, three thousand Nestorians from surrounding villages took shelter in the French Catholic mission in Urmia and seventeen thousand in the American mission.[20] In May 1915, the Russians, following their defeat of the Turks at Sarikamish, reoccupied Urmia. In July, they withdrew again, followed by thousands of Christians, but as the tide of war turned again against the Turks, the Russians returned and strengthened their forces in the area through 1916. In the winter of 1916, the Russians launched an offensive against Turkey, taking much of eastern Anatolia, including Van, going as far south as Ruwanduz (now in Iraq), and cutting off the Turkish forces in Persia.[21] In March 1917, however, the Russian Revolution took place in Moscow, and the Russians withdrew from Urmia.

When the Russians strengthened their forces in the Urmia area in 1916, they recruited the Nestorian refugees from Hakkari, the mountainous region of eastern Anatolia, and under the leadership of Agha Patrus this group acted as advance scouts as the Russians prepared to invade eastern Anatolia. The Nestorians' familiarity with the mountains made them an invaluable resource. After the Russians evacuated Urmia in the summer of 1917, the Russian-trained Christians, both Armenian and Nestorian, assisted by two hundred White Russian soldiers who had remained behind, were able to keep the Turks from taking the city. English and French officers were sent from Tiflis (Tbilisi) to assist them.[22] However, with the Russians otherwise occupied, the Turks had gradually regained much of the territory of eastern Anatolia in spite of Armenian efforts to hold it. The alliance between the local Christians and the Russians as well as the influx of Nestorian and Armenian refugees from Turkey into Urmia aroused anger among the local Persian Muslim population as well as among the Kurds, and in February 1918 they attacked the Christian quarter of Urmia. This attack was followed three weeks later by a Kurdish warlord's assassination of the Mar Shimun and his escort. The Hakkari refugees in Persia then took their revenge on the Muslim villages. These events and reciprocal massacres were followed immediately by the fall of Van and the arrival in Urmia of twenty thousand Armenian refugees pursued by Turkish troops.[23]

The withdrawal of the Russians from northern Persia in 1917 heightened British concerns about the security of the land route to India as well as of the oil fields of Baku. A British force under the command of Major General Lionel Charles Dunsterville began to move northward through Persia toward the Caucasus, where he planned to use Armenian and Georgian forces to divert the Turkish army from activity in Iraq and the Middle East. By this time, a large British force was in Iraq, gradually working its way north toward an eventual occupation of the entire country. By May 1918, Dunsterville, based in Hamadan, where he commanded a force of two hundred British soldiers and twelve hundred Cossacks, was trying to link up with the Nestorian and

Armenian forces in Urmia in an effort to keep the Turks from taking Tabriz.[24] The Nestorian fighting force left to meet the British, who had moved north to Bijur. But both sides were delayed, and the British retreated to Hamadan, and the Nestorians, under Agha Patrus, went back toward Urmia. In the meantime, the civilian population, left largely undefended in Urmia and under attack by the Turks, fled the town in a state of panic, taking with them their livestock and all their belongings.

The flight south from Urmia to Hamadan became the central event in the Assyrians' developing national narrative. Thousands of refugees died on the way. Those who survived were taken by the British to Iraq, where they were resettled temporarily in the Baquba refugee camp outside Baghdad. For the next fifteen years, the British attempt to find a new home for the Assyrians was complicated by the drawing of the northern boundary of Iraq, which cut through the Assyrian region, separating Mosul and Amadia, and their hinterlands from the Hakkari Mountains in Turkey, which had been the homeland of many of the refugees in Baquba. These efforts were also affected by the efforts of the League of Nations to provide self-determination for all the minorities of the former Ottoman Empire as well as by the rise of Iraqi nationalism and the struggle for independence from Britain. At the same time, the Assyrians were further handicapped by a leadership crisis of their own. Mar Benjamin Shimun, who had been assassinated in 1918, was succeeded by his ill brother, who himself died two years later, to be succeeded in turn by his eleven-year-old nephew. The most influential member of the patriarchal family was a woman, Surma, Benjamin's sister, who as a young girl had lived in the household of the Anglican missionary William H. Browne (and had nearly married him). Surma, however, went to London in 1919, leaving the community leaderless and subject to fragmentation.[25]

Throughout the 1920s, the British and the League of Nations searched for solutions to the Assyrian refugee problem. This problem was exacerbated after the final resolution of the Turkish boundary question that set the Iraqi–Turkish border north of Amadia but south of Hakkari, thus separating many of the refugees from their homelands. The problem was in part resolved when many of the Assyrians from Persia gradually returned there and those whose home villages lay within Iraq returned to those villages.

Humanitarian, political, and religious considerations converged during the war. Loath to engage in politics before World War I, American missionaries found themselves engaged in politics during and after the war. The issues concerning the Middle East that had occupied them were whether the United States should go to war with Turkey and the nature of postwar settlements.

The meeting of the minds between the Protestant missionary constituency and President Woodrow Wilson can scarcely be overstated, though the intertwining of Protestantism, the evangelical missionary movement, and politics in the United States is a very complex issue. Wilson's father and grandfather were Presbyterian ministers. Wilson himself, before becoming president of the United States, had been president of Princeton University, a school with strong Presbyterian ties, whose board of trustees was chaired by industrialist Cleveland H. Dodge. Dodge's family was strongly identified with the Syrian Protestant College, and he served also as chairman of the board of Robert College in Constantinople. Wilson, confident that American ideals were righteous and that he personally was destined to promote freedom and democracy in the world, advocated an activist foreign policy that fostered self-determination for the minority populations of the Middle East and elsewhere.[26] Although he sympathized with the people of the Middle East who suffered during the war, he initially sided with American Protestant missionary interests, which moved to protect personnel and property in the region and opposed sending American troops there. Missionary institutions in Anatolia and in Syria—in Anatolia the ABCFM had more than 150 staff members and dozens of schools educating more than twenty-five thousand students—were in the cross-fire of the fighting on all fronts.[27] Furthermore, by the beginning of the war American Protestants owned more than $20 million worth of property in the region. As human suffering and institutional destruction increased, American Protestants used their family connections with industrialists and politicians at home to lobby in favor of humanitarian aid but against direct American military involvement in the Ottoman Empire. James Barton, the ABCFM's foreign secretary, and other American missionaries underscored their neutrality in the conflict. Others stressed that theirs were local institutions in close relationship with the indigenous population, in contrast to the British, French, and German missionary institutions, which had imperial connections. Because of the American policy, U.S. diplomatic personnel and missionaries were able to continue to operate in Turkey throughout the war.

By World War I, members of the Bliss family of the Syrian Protestant College and the Dodge family of Robert College in Constantinople had formed dynastic connections as members of the two families intermarried.[28] When Howard Bliss succeeded his father, Daniel, as president of the Syrian Protestant College in 1902, he could draw upon the support of Cleveland H. Dodge, who had gone to Princeton with Woodrow Wilson and remained close friends with him. These connections were evident throughout Wilson's presidency. Dodge's philanthropic support for Christian causes and institutions in the Middle East led to his direct involvement in Syrian and Armenian relief during the war and reinforced his belief that the future of the Middle East lay in a federated Turkish empire under American or British protection. Although President Wilson's subsequent political statements about self-determination clearly represented his own views, it was said that they also reflected the president's association with Dodge.[29] Later encapsulated in his Fourteen Points, Wilson's views were contradictory; inconsistencies had to be worked out.

The most effective and long-lasting American missionary response to the disasters brought upon the Near East by World War I was clearly not political, but humanitarian: the establishment of Near East Relief, which continues to this day under the name "Near East Foundation," though it has never been affiliated with any religious group. The organization had its beginning in a cable from U.S. ambassador Henry Morgenthau to the Department of State in September 1915, "urging the formation of a committee to raise funds and provide ways and means for saving some of the Armenians."[30] By then, two relief funds had already been set up in the Near East: the Syrian–Palestine Relief Fund, established in December 1914 by Talcott Williams, dean of the Columbia University School of Journalism, and Stanley White, Syrian secretary of the Presbyterian Board of Foreign Missions; and the Persian War Relief Fund, established in March 1915, also by the Presbyterian board. When contributions to the latter fund began to decline in the summer of 1915, Robert Speer, general-secretary of the Presbyterian board, appealed to the Rockefeller Foundation for assistance, and it was under the auspices of that foundation that the various American relief organizations active in the Near East came together.[31]

On September 3, 1915, Ambassador Morgenthau suggested in a cable that the Department of State urge Charles Crane and Cleveland Dodge to form a committee for raising funds to resettle the Armenians in California, Oregon, and Washington. On September 16, Dodge convened a meeting at his office in lower Manhattan (he was vice president of the Phelps-Dodge Corporation), attended by Charles Crane, vice president of the Constantinople College for Women and a friend of President Wilson; D. Stuart Dodge, Cleveland's uncle and a member of the board of the Syrian Protestant College; James Barton of the ABCFM; and representatives of the missionary boards of the Presbyterian, Reformed, and Methodist churches, the American Bible Society, the Federal Council of Churches, the YMCA, and the Jewish Emergency Relief Commission. By November, the group had been joined by James Cardinal Gibbons and Philip Rhinelander, Episcopal bishop of New York.[32] At its second meeting, the group adopted the name "Committee on Armenian Atrocities," but in November the Persia War Relief Fund, the Syria–Palestine Committee, and the Committee on Armenian Atrocities merged, and the name was changed to "American Committee for Armenian and Syrian Relief."[33]

By November 1, 1915, nearly $95,000—almost a million dollars in today's currency—had been raised and sent to the region, most of it to Ambassador Morgenthau in Constantinople, but some also to Persia. Within two years, by September 1917, more than $4 million had been raised and sent to the Near East—$1.7 million to Constantinople, $1 million to Tbilisi, $700,000 to Tabriz, $642,000 to Beirut, and smaller amounts to Baghdad, Cairo, Jerusalem, and Tehran.[34] In October 1917 and again in November 1918, President Wilson himself urged the American people to contribute to the American Committee for Relief in the Near East (the American Committee's new name) or to the American Red Cross for relief efforts in the Near East. By the time the war came to an end, the organization had changed to the new name and had applied for an official Act of Incorporation from the U.S. Congress. Its stated goal was "to provide relief and to assist in the repatriation, rehabilitation, and reestablishment of the suffering and dependent people of the Near East and adjacent areas."[35] This charge is notable for its assumption that the refugees who had fled Anatolia would be repatriated and their homes reestablished, perhaps under an American or European mandate. Mustafa Kemal's establishment of a nationalist Turkish state precluded this outcome, however.

With the end of the war and the defeat of the Ottoman Empire, the map of the Middle East would be redrawn. Missionaries, throwing themselves into discussions about the future of the region, lobbied for direct American involvement in the postwar reconfiguration of the region. In order to keep the French on the periphery and the Soviet Union out of the Middle East altogether, the British approved of an American presence in eastern Anatolia.[36] However, any U.S. involvement in Syria would conflict with the secret British and French agendas that had given control of southeastern Turkey, northern Iraq, Syria, and Lebanon to France and the area of today's Jordan, southern Iraq (or Mesopotamia), and a small area around Haifa to Britain. Jerusalem was to come under international administration. While negotiating with the French, Britain was also corresponding with the Sharif of Mecca about establishing an independent Arab state, which Arabs would later see as their due for their revolt against the Turks. In 1917, the British issued the Balfour Declaration, promising a home for the Jews in Palestine. These various British and French agreements for the postwar Middle East clearly contradicted arrangements the powers had with each other and clashed with Wilson's anti-imperialist and pro-independence policies—inconsistencies that the 1919 Paris peace conference was set to address. The mandate system that emerged from the deliberations was a compromise—Armenia, Syria, Mesopotamia, Palestine, and Arabia were to be newly created nations on the verge of independence, supervised by the major powers overseen by a League of Nations. No thought, however, was given about how these mandates would be apportioned or whether the local population wanted them. It was suggested that the United States be given the mandates of eastern Anatolia—considered to be Armenia—and Syria. However, this scenario was complicated by the fact that by the end of the war the area to be designated the Armenian mandate no longer contained many Armenians. For several years after the war, many held onto the hope that the Armenians would be able to return, but Mustafa Kemal's campaign in eastern Anatolia that ultimately created a new Turkish state prevented such a solution.

Anxious to restake their claim to Syria, French troops arrived in Beirut in 1918, only to find a destitute population. In response, missionaries, who had served the French military in various capacities, returned to provide relief for the war victims and to reestablish a French presence in the face of British and Arab nationalist competition. During that first year there, they distributed fifteen thousand tons of foodstuffs costing twenty million francs.[37]

For Howard Bliss, who by World War I had become an advocate of Arab Syrian nationalism, Wilson's views about self-determination and America's mission as a force for promoting democracy in the world—espoused in the "Fourteen Points" speech he delivered to a joint session of Congress on January 8, 1918—dovetailed with the ideals that American Protestants had been teaching for half a century. After all, American educational institutions pioneered the kind of modernization that was designed to foster development and the capacity for self-determination.

In preparation for the armistice talks, an informal study group had already been established to reconcile Wilson's conflicting ideas about a postwar Middle East. In 1918, "the Inquiry," a secret task force, was set up in the New York Public Library. Consisting of more than one hundred scholars, the group included a strong missionary representation; James Barton had William H. Hall, professor at the Syrian Protestant College and secretary of the American Committee for Armenian and Syrian Relief, appointed. Although Barton favored an American protectorate of a free Armenia, he advocated a federated Ottoman Empire, fearing the deleterious effect on minorities of a balkanized Middle East. In his plan, a Western nation would safeguard the Christians of Georgia, Armenia, Syria (including Lebanon and Mesopotamia), a Jewish area around Jerusalem, Turkish Anatolia, and a Greek enclave around Smyrna. Constantinople would be advised by an international commission.[38]

By 1919, the ABCFM–American political connection did not go unnoticed. The Protestant community had conflicting emotions about religious involvement in politics. At one point, Barton was advised not to advocate openly for Armenian freedom. In May, three missionaries were disciplined by the ABCFM's Executive Committee for their activities in support of Albanian and Bulgarian interests. Humanitarian relief to the thousands of Christians caught in the Turkish maelstrom was one thing, but to use the American Committee for Relief in the Near East to request an American mandate in Turkey was regarded as "cultural and religious imperialism."[39]

Almost immediately after the war, the American government was assailed by foreign and domestic lobbyists, all of whom considered their interests to be legitimate in the context of the various proposals on the table in Paris. Arabs—supported at the peace conference in 1919 by Emir Faisal of Syria, who had led the pro-British Arab Revolt; by T. E. Lawrence, dressed in his flowing white robes; as well as by Armenians, Greeks, and Turks, not to mention those in favor of the Zionist project in Palestine—looked to self-determination. The British did not accept the Persian delegation that came to Versailles. At home in the United States, Jewish sponsors and opponents of Zionism, missionary advocates and opponents of a Jewish home in Palestine, and American supporters of a free Syria that included a Palestine safeguarded by the United States—all produced testimonies supporting their respective views. What better solution could there be, they thought, than an independent Syria under the guardianship of a mandatory power, preferably the United States, supervised by the League of Nations? The 1919 Paris peace conference provided an opportunity for the missionaries to present their case.[40] At this juncture, Cleveland Dodge asked Howard Bliss, the president of the Syrian Protestant College, to address the conference; Bliss, perhaps more than anyone else, was instrumental in persuading President Wilson to send a fact-finding mission to the Middle East.[41]

Emir Faisal had suggested the idea of a commission of inquiry to determine the future of the Arab provinces when he arrived in Paris in January 1919. The commission's intent was "to visit Syria and Palestine and ascertain the wishes of the population by an exhaustive investigation on the spot."[42] The proposal was supported by Wilson, accepted by Prime Minister David Lloyd George of Britain, but opposed by Georges Clemenceau of France; nevertheless, the Council of Four at Versailles approved it on March 25, 1919. Britain appointed two commissioners, Sir Henry McMahon and Commander D. G. Hogarth, though they ultimately did not participate; France made no appointments to the commission; and President Wilson appointed two close friends, both of whom had Protestant connections. What became known as the King–Crane Commission has occupied a controversial place in the historiography of the modern Middle East, even though its results were in fact inconsequential.[43] Both Dr. Henry Churchill King and Charles Crane were active in American politics and as trustees of Near East Relief had participated in humanitarian projects directed to the Middle East during the war. King, another close friend of President Wilson, was president of Oberlin College as well as a Congregational minister, a former YMCA official who had traveled extensively to the Holy Land, and a "promoter of Christian internationalism."[44] Charles Crane, heir to a plumbing supply fortune, was an autodidact supporter of czarist Russia. In addition to contributing to Wilson's presidential campaign, he was a major donor to Protestant causes and institutions, the Dodge Relief Committee and Robert College among them. Other members of the commission included Albert Lybyer, who had taught at Robert College, and William Yale, observer for the American State Department and resident agent for the Standard Oil Company. All but two of the nine-man team had connections to the Protestant enterprises in the Middle East.[45]

What began as an international commission became an American one as both the British and the French at first demurred but then finally refused to participate. The commission's work was delayed for three months as the Allies' attention was diverted by the Greek invasion of Smyrna (Izmir) in May 1919. Once the commission got under way, from June 10 through July 21, the group traveled more than a thousand miles to nearly forty cities in Syria, Palestine, and Turkey, but not to Mesopotamia. The commissioners spoke with European officials, local notables, and American relief workers aiding Armenians; conducted hundreds of informal interviews; and received more than eighteen hundred petitions. The commission's findings were based on data culled without any formal methodology in what the group thought would provide a composite picture of popular attitudes. However, the sample was not proportional and was heavily weighted toward Christian representation.[46]

The King–Crane Commission submitted its report to the U.S. delegation at the peace conference in late August 1919. It supported the establishment of a mandate for Syria, including Palestine, and one for Iraq. The Syrian mandate would preserve the unity of Syria but provide for Lebanese autonomy, and Iraq was to remain one integrated country. Both states were to be structured as constitutional monarchies, with Faisal as king in Syria, and the monarch in Iraq to be chosen by a plebiscite. As for the mandatory power, the commission preferred the United States or, failing that, Britain, but on no account France. Finally, the commissioners stated that although they had begun with a bias in favor of the Zionists in Palestine, they had concluded, after seeing the situation on the ground, that they should "recommend a limitation of Zionist ambitions."[47] As a result, only the Syrian Arabs were pleased, for the King–Crane Commission concluded that the peoples of the Middle East— aside from the Jews and the Maronites, who preferred British and French rule, respectively—almost unanimously wanted an American mandate over a united Syria, which included Palestine without a Jewish homeland.

As for Anatolia, James Barton in Constantinople urged guarantees for an integral Armenia. Worried about the fate of Armenian refugees, he and other Protestants endorsed an American mandate in Anatolia, whereas at the same time representatives of non-Muslim ethnic groups favored either Greek sovereignty in Smyrna or Assyrian and Kurdish independence in some parts of eastern Turkey. With the situation in Armenia deteriorating and fearing that relief and repatriation would be neglected, Cleveland Dodge and the American Committee for the Independence of Armenia lobbied for a second inquiry mission to deal specifically with Armenia. Led by General James G. Harbord, the chief of staff under General John J. Pershing, the committee was composed primarily of military officers, who interviewed representatives of groups in Turkey and the Caucasus.[48] None of the King–Crane recommendations would be acted upon. In fact, the commission's report was not even published until December 1922.

The Americans never ratified the Treaty of Versailles, leaving the British and the French to sort out wartime agreements. For their part, the Allies were more concerned with the Arab areas of the Middle East than with Anatolia. The British, acceding to domestic pressure over the cost of keeping so many troops in Asia Minor, began to withdraw. Even with American refusal to occupy any mandate, the French refused the offer of occupation over Armenia or Constantinople but did send troops to Cilicia and Syria. There was little possibility at this juncture for an independent Armenia in Anatolia because most of the Armenian population there had been killed or fled, although an independent Republic of Armenia was established to the east in 1918 and survived until December 1920, when it was incorporated into the Soviet Union. Meanwhile, the British acquiesced when the Italians, citing wartime agreements, and the Greeks, looking to a "Greater Greece" (that would include Greek-populated areas around Aidin and Bursa in the Anatolian interior), sent troops to Smyrna. Soon after the Greek forces entered the city, however, shots were fired. Pandemonium, looting, and killing ensued, leaving between three and four hundred Turks and one hundred Greeks dead. While the diplomats dithered, Atatürk (Mustafa Kemal) reorganized Turkish forces and in what became known as the "National Pact" moved to establish an independent Turkey, whose borders would not be decided at Versailles or San Remo, but on the ground in Anatolia.

In April 1920, the San Remo Conference of the Supreme Allied Council decided that mandates for Syria and Lebanon should go to France and those for Iraq and Palestine should be given to Great Britain. The postwar settlements of the fate of the Ottoman and Persian empires moved from regional politics into the realm of European geopolitics. As word of the Allies' decisions regarding the fate of Turkey spread, more Turks joined Atatürk and the nationalists. However, the Treaty of Sèvres, signed in August 1920, supported Greek nationalist aspirations and recognized the independence of the Republic of Armenia. Turkey was to be divided into French, Italian, and Greek spheres of influence; the Greeks were awarded part of Thrace; and Britain controlled the Straits. The Turks were not required to pay reparations, but they did have to underwrite the cost of foreign occupation; their finances would be under international control; and restrictions on arms and the strength of their armed forces were imposed.

In effect, the British in the 1920s were trying to impose nineteenth-century power politics to resolve the post–World War I "Eastern Question." Their unilateral imposition of terms at Sèvres, however, led to a Turkish nationalist offensive against British and Greek troops that lasted until a Turkish victory in 1922. The result was a massacre of Greeks in Smyrna, followed by a League of Nations–sponsored population exchange between Greece and Turkey. The withdrawal of French troops from Cilicia, ratified by the Treaty of Lausanne in 1923, left most of Anatolia in Turkish hands. Only the southeastern border of the new state of Turkey and the associated problems of the Kurds and oil remained to be settled. The border was finally demarcated in 1925 after negotiations between Turkey and Great Britain, which resulted in the incorporation of oil-rich Mosul into the British Mandate for Iraq.[49]

The Sèvres Treaty never came into effect. Mustafa Kemal's success in conquering territory in Anatolia created a new Turkish state with which the Allied powers had to contend. In 1922, according to the ABCFM, American investment in Turkey amounted to $100 million, a sum greater than that invested by all of the Lausanne peace conference participants put together.[50] Nevertheless, the United States, which had not declared war on the Ottoman Empire, was not a participant at Lausanne, though it did send three observers, who sat in on the meetings of the three commissions at the conference. The United States was particularly concerned about the rights of Americans in Turkey and the protection of Christians. The Lausanne Treaty was signed on August 6, 1923. Two issues were resolved outside the treaty: the exchange of population between Greece and Turkey, which was handled in a separate agreement between the two governments and administered by the League of Nations; and the demarcation of the northern boundary of Iraq. When Great Britain and Turkey failed to reach agreement on the boundary, the Council of the League of Nations awarded Mosul to Iraq in December 1925. Turkey accepted the decision in June 1926.

By the fall of 1924, conference participants had ratified the Lausanne Treaty, but the United States had not. A campaign was mounted to gain Senate ratification, led by Allen Dulles, chief of the Near East Division of the Department of State, and supported by James Barton of the ABCFM as well as Near East Relief, Robert College, the Near East Colleges Association, and even the U.S. Chamber of Commerce, representing American business interests in Turkey. Not surprisingly, the Armenian American community opposed ratification. On January 18, 1927, the Senate rejected the treaty.

By the mid-1920s, the British and the French controlled the Middle East and North Africa either as colonies, protectorates, or mandates. Though nominally independent, Egypt was to a great extent governed by the British, and Morocco by the French. Nevertheless, strong nationalist movements in both countries mitigated the extent of their control. British influence remained strong in Persia in spite of the military nationalist government of Reza Shah Pahlavi (1925–1941), and by World War II the British and the Russians had again divided the country. Rising nationalism everywhere had a profound effect on Western missionary activity in the region.

NINE

Setting the Agenda

From Conversion to Witness—and Back

B y 1925, the political map of the Middle East had totally changed from its configuration a decade earlier. The Ottoman Empire, having lost World War I, had been dismembered and become the Republic of Turkey, no longer a multinational, multiconfessional empire. Persia, which had been effectively divided into zones of Russian and Persian influence during the war, had acquired a new monarch, Reza Shah Pahlavi, and would soon acquire a new name, "Iran." The Russian threat from the north had diminished as the newly established Soviet Union turned inward. British influence, however, increased as the British established League of Nations–sanctioned mandates over Iraq and Palestine, including Trans-Jordan, both formerly part of the Ottoman Empire, and continued their control of Egypt. France took mandatory control over Syria and Lebanon. The demographics had also changed as much of the Armenian and Greek population of Anatolia that had formed the target population for the missionaries had been killed or had fled Anatolia or returned to Greece in the population exchange of 1925. All these changes had profound effects on the missionary enterprise, as did changes in Europe and America.

For many decades, the Ottoman and Persian governments had tried to regulate the missionary schools, but although laws were passed, enforcement was spotty. In the Ottoman Empire, the Law on Education of 1858 had required the licensing of all non-Muslim schools and their adherence to the rules of the Ministry of Education. In 1869, a new Law on Education tried to impose Ottoman authority by requiring local authorities to approve textbooks and curricula, and this law was tightened in 1880. In 1894, Turkish teachers, paid by the Ottoman government, were to be assigned to non-Muslim schools to teach Turkish.[1] The new Turkish government abolished the capitulations, and although it had pledged guarantees for Allied philanthropic, religious, and educational institutions, the political uncertainty during the early days of the new republic created difficulties in planning for the future. In 1922, of 110 missionaries listed on rosters, there were 84 American missionaries actually working in Turkey. The rest worked for Near East Relief or were assigned to nearby areas in the Caucasus, Syria, the Aegean Islands, and Greece. Thirteen mission stations operated at Istanbul, Brusa, Izmir, Merzifon, Harput, Tarsus, Adana, Gazientep (Aintab), and Marash. Completely dependent on the sufferance of the Turkish government, the missionaries were also pressed by zealous Turkish nationalists on one side and Muslims on the other, both of whom opposed any Christian proselytizing. They operated to the letter of the law, taking religion out of the classroom and demonstrating virtue by "living the life" and providing example for potential converts to follow. Nonetheless, Muslim critics found this approach an insidious method for the entrapment of children by agents of American imperialism.[2]

The end of the war also left a chaotic Persia that, although officially neutral during the war, had been sympathetic to the Germans and the Ottomans, neither of whom had imperial territorial claims. Sliced into Russian and British zones of influence, Persia was the target of Russian, German, and Ottoman military operations and the victim of war, famine, and disease, especially in the Kurdish and Christian areas of Urmia. At Versailles, the British refused to allow the Persian delegation to be seated and in an attempt to create a virtual protectorate over the country proceeded to take control of Persia's military and finances, even over the objections of the Iranian Constituent Assembly, France, and the United States. As the Russian civil war spilled over into northern Persia and local rebellions broke out along the Caspian and in Azerbaijan, the British sought the support of the central Persian government and local Arab tribes who resided near the oil fields. British concern about India, oil, and Bolshevism dominated their attempts to control Iran. When Reza Khan, a military officer from the Cossack Brigade overthrew the monarchy in 1921, the British acquiesced as the new government annulled capitulations granted to Russia (now the Soviet Union), suppressed rebellions in the rest of Persia, and granted the Anglo-Persian Oil Company a monopoly of Persian oil.

Throughout much of the nineteenth century, there had been tension, particularly in the Protestant missionary enterprise, between evangelical efforts to convert Muslims, Jews, and Eastern Christians to Protestantism and the view that modernization—of ideas and lifestyle—must precede true conversion. This has been referred to as the "Christ–culture dialectic," and it underlay the conflict between a focus on evangelistic preaching and conversion, on the one hand, and on education and economic development, on the other. Rufus Anderson, the longtime general-secretary of the ABCFM, personified this conflict, placing the emphasis firmly on conversion to Christianity, not to Western civilization, a position that was reflected in his insistence on teaching in local rather than Western languages. His retirement in 1870 moved this focus of the debate just as Western imperialism was reaching its zenith. From 1870 through the end of World War I, the "civilizing" camp was in the ascendancy, particularly in the American Protestant missionary movement. (Europeans were always less enthusiastic about this focus, regarding it as Anglo-American activism in contrast to the European pietist tradition.) An ever-increasing and varied group of "missionary"—or perhaps, more accurately, Christian—organizations sent workers to every corner of the globe, including the Middle East. No longer was proselytization paramount, though it continued to be important. Instead, education, medical services, and the social services provided by such organizations as the YMCA took precedence, though their Christian orientation was unmistakable.

This view represented the postmillennial position held by the mainline churches, according to which efforts should be directed toward establishing Christ's kingdom on earth in preparation for the Second Coming, whereas the premillennials, who were gradually gaining strength, held that the Second Coming would provide the occasion for mass conversion to Christianity. The two camps also differed on the meaning of the so-called Great Commission, "Go ye into all the world and preach the Gospel," the importance of which the more liberal postmillennials subordinated to their attitude toward the validity of other religions. Both agreed, however, that Western civilization was best.[3] The premillennial position reached the height of its influence in the 1910 Edinburgh World Missionary Conference, the slogan of which was "The Evangelization of the World in This Generation," but the conference was primarily an Anglo-American affair, with one thousand of its twelve hundred delegates coming from English-speaking countries. Despite the emphasis on evangelism, the legacy of the conference was to be the ecumenical movement. Although the statistical high point for American mainline Protestant missions would not be reached until the late 1920s, Edinburgh "would come to seem in retrospect a singular moment of success and untroubled enthusiasm."[4]

Since its founding in 1888, the Student Volunteer Movement had been the major vehicle for missionary recruitment in the United States and Britain, adopting the "watchword" used later by the Edinburgh conference. The university students inspired by the Student Volunteer Movement went abroad under the auspices of their own church missionary societies and particularly on behalf of the YMCA. Although the movement initially regarded the British Empire as "providential"—that is, provided by God for the evangelization of the world—by 1910 this view was beginning to be questioned as concerns with racism and rising nationalism began to be heard.[5] World War I and its aftermath reinforced these concerns and the growing tension between the demand for resources for foreign missions and domestic social needs. The number of missionaries in the field peaked in the 1920s, but recruitment was down, and, finally, the Student Volunteer Movement, at its quadrennial convention in 1928, "abandoned the older conception of evangelization of the heathen world by Anglo-Saxon Protestants implicit in the famous watchword in favor of a broader view of Christian world missions,"[6] a view that continues to dominate the thinking of the mainline churches today.

In the Middle East, the Armenian massacres that had occurred periodically in the last quarter of the nineteenth century and into the first quarter of the twentieth, creating refugees and orphans who needed care, encouraged this shift of focus toward humanitarian assistance. World War I and its aftermath intensified this need, particularly in the Christian populations that had formed the primary audience for the Western missionaries. The most important and immediate response to this need was the establishment of Near East Relief, an organization that began during the war and brought together many of the mainline religious groups in the United States that had been active in the Middle East—Protestant, Catholic, and Jewish—providing a single fund-raising and administrative organization that was able to tap U.S. government and corporate resources and mount nationwide campaigns. Its personnel were largely the missionaries who had worked in Anatolia before and during the war and either stayed on or returned to assist with the relief effort, and they knew the area firsthand. By early 1920, Near East Relief had divided its efforts administratively into four regions: Constantinople, the Caucasus (Georgia and Armenia), Syria (including Lebanon and Palestine), and Persia. The goal was still repatriation of the Christians, in particular Armenians, to Anatolia, though that goal faded after Mustafa Kemal's victory at Izmir in 1922. Near East Relief took over such major facilities as the former German orphanage in Jerusalem, the largest bakery in Constantinople, which had provided bread to Turkish and German troops during the war, and the czarist barracks in Alexandropol (now Gyumri), which became an orphanage for Armenian children. By early 1921, the organization had a field staff of 270,[7] many of whom were former missionaries. But by late 1923, donor fatigue had set in, and Near East Relief limited its interests to caring for women and children. Large orphanages were established, and there was a focus on training for self-sufficiency. The missionary presence diminished, and the civilizational side of the debate won out.

With the rise of Kemalist secular Turkish nationalism, there was no future for Western missionary activity in Turkey, though in 1922 the ABCFM still occupied thirteen mission stations there.[8] With the abolition of the capitulations, no longer could the missionaries "consider themselves privileged advocates of a justice guaranteed from without."[9] Some of the educational institutions survived and still do, serving primarily Turkish Muslim students and abiding by Turkish educational requirements, but without any Christian identification. ABCFM activity in Anatolia was further limited by the financial constraints of the Great Depression in the 1930s, but in 1939 it still operated a hospital in Gazientep, Tarsus College for boys, the American Collegiate Institute for girls near Izmir (Smyrna), the American Academy for Girls in Scutari, and a boys' trade school at Kayseri.[10] The independent colleges, including Robert College and Istanbul College for Women, which had always insisted on their lack of affiliation with religious bodies in spite of their clearly Christian orientation, fared better than the more overtly religious schools. Both adapted more easily to the secularization of Turkey and made themselves useful to the new Turkish government, particularly in technical areas.[11] The ABCFM, Robert College, the Istanbul College for Women, the Near East Colleges Association (which included several of the former missionary schools in Anatolia that had moved to Greece), the YMCA and its counterpart for women, the YWCA, as well as American business groups gradually came to support the new Turkish government,[12] and in 1927 the United States reestablished full diplomatic relations with Turkey despite the Senate's failure to ratify the Lausanne Treaty. In 1934, a claims commission set up under the Lausanne Treaty awarded $192,000 to the ABCFM for its losses in Anatolia during World War I.[13]

The establishment of League of Nations mandates in Syria, Lebanon, Palestine, and Iraq eased the path for Western missionary presence in those countries. Within three years after the end of the war, the Presbyterian mission had all of its prewar institutions up and running, though considerable resources were still being devoted to refugee relief. There were three schools for boys, at Sidon, Tripoli, and Aleppo; three more for girls, at Beirut, Sidon, and Tripoli; and many village schools that received mission support, though they were not actually run by the mission, but by local evangelical churches. Missionaries were giving more attention not only to education but also to economic development at the village level, medical services, and assistance to orphans.[14] A new attitude toward the local Christian churches was also evident, culminating in the 1930s in Near East Relief's transfer of its large orphanage at Antelias, near Beirut, to the Armenian Church for its use as a seminary to train a new priesthood to replace the Armenian religious establishment in Anatolia that had been decimated by the war. But this increased acceptance of the Eastern churches by the missionaries was a response also to a new emphasis within the Western Protestant churches on ecumenism, which was an outgrowth of the 1910 Edinburgh conference.

Other Protestant missionary societies became active in Syria and Lebanon during the interwar period—the Seventh Day Adventists, the Evangelical Church of God, the Bible Lands, Gospel Mission, and the Christian and Missionary Alliance—as well as other missions from England, Ireland, Scotland, France, and Denmark. But most important were the French Catholics, operating now with the support of the French mandatory government. The Catholics had a long history of activity in Syria and Lebanon, including their close relationship with the Maronite Church, and they had a network of Catholic schools, capped by the University of Saint-Joseph in Beirut. With few soldiers in the Middle East—most of the French forces remained in Europe—and in dire financial straits, the French government was only too pleased to draw on the funds and expertise of Catholic missionaries, who were eager to reclaim the institutions taken over by the Turks during the war.[15]

Catholic and Protestant apprehension over the future of mission and Christian institutions in the Holy Land was alleviated in 1922 with League of Nations approval for the establishment of the British Mandate for Palestine. Catholic concerns that the Balfour Declaration would lead to a privileged Jewish position in Jerusalem that would compromise Catholic rights in the Holy City receded as the British held to the status quo and maintained Ottoman policy. Throughout the 1930s and 1940s, the Vatican moved to replace the French as the representative of Catholic jurisdiction over the Holy Sites institutions.[16] Although the Church of England had a major presence, anchored by the Anglican Cathedral in Jerusalem, it and the Presbyterian Church had been redirecting their focus since the establishment of a Protestant presence in the Holy Land almost a century earlier. The Anglican Church and the CMS continued to work with the Arab communities, as did the Presbyterians; the London Jews Society, seeing in the Balfour Declaration a step toward the restoration of the Jewish presence in the Holy Land, continued its evangelizing of the Jews.[17]

Palestine, being the true Holy Land, was flooded with missionaries and other religious workers. The mainline American churches had not been particularly active in Palestine before the war, leaving that field to the British, but now other American Christian organizations—including the Southern Baptists, the Assemblies of God, the Church of the Nazarene, the Christian and Missionary Alliance, the Society of Friends (Quakers), and the YMCA—became active, and in general they deferred to British authority.[18] German institutions, such as the large German orphanage in Palestine, were taken over by other religious organizations. During the 1920s, more than thirty Protestant missionary societies from different countries, in addition to Catholic and Orthodox missions, were active in Palestine.[19]

The League of Nations approved the British Mandate for Iraq in September 1924, and the northern border with Turkey was delineated the following year. Before the war, the British CMS had taken over the missions in Mosul that had been run by the ABCFM and the American Presbyterians, but these missions were abandoned after the war.[20] In 1924, as the mandate came into force, a joint American mission was established, bringing together the Presbyterian Church in the USA, the Dutch Reformed Church, and the Reformed Church in the United States (German) and setting up mission stations in Mosul, Dohuk, Hilla, Kirkuk, and Baghdad. An American-run boys' school was established in Baghdad, though it was taken over by the Dutch Reformed Church in 1933. The most important Protestant mission in Iraq, however, was the Dutch Reformed Mission, which had been headquartered in Kuwait since the beginning of the century. Its Iraqi presence was originally based in Basra, under John Van Ess and his wife, but moved to Baghdad in 1920.[21] The most influential missionary institution in Iraq, however, was Baghdad College, founded by American Jesuits in 1932.

In 1931, at the urging of the Chaldean patriarch of Baghdad, Pope Pius XI asked the Jesuits to set up schools in Baghdad, and the following year four American Jesuits arrived and established a high school for boys under the control of the New England province of the Jesuits. Although the impetus for the school had come from the Christian community, and Christian boys were the first students, it soon attracted Muslims as well. Unlike many other Westerners, the Jesuits remained in Baghdad throughout World War II, and the school became the school of choice for the elite of Baghdad, even enrolling the prime minister's sons. Until the Jewish exodus to Israel in 1951, the school also had many Jewish students, just as the Alliance Israélite Universelle network of Jewish schools had Muslim students. By the 1950s, the student population of Baghdad College was divided evenly between Muslims and Christians, and in 1956 the Jesuits opened another college, al-Hikma. In 1967, however, the U.S. embassy in Baghdad was closed because of the Arab–Israel War of 1967. The following year, a Ba'athist coup in Baghdad led to the nationalization of all private schools, Muslim and Christian. The Jesuits at al-Hikma were forced out of Iraq in November 1968, and in August 1969 Baghdad College was also taken over, and its Jesuit faculty deported. The school continued, after a fashion, and both of Saddam Hussein's sons attended. More important, the influence of the Jesuit college ultimately survived the Saddam regime. In 2005, the *New York Times* reported that the three leading candidates for prime minister, all Shi'is, were graduates of Baghdad College.[22]

From the 1890s on, the primary Western missionary presence in the Arabian Peninsula had been the American Dutch Reformed Church medical mission, with stations in Bahrain, Muscat, and Kuwait. They had opened a hospital in Kuwait in 1914 and a women's hospital there in 1927. The Muscat station included a school and a hospital that opened in 1934,[23] and the missionaries also provided some medical services to the royal family of Saudi Arabia. Scottish missionaries were active in Yemen. The interwar period saw the beginnings of tremendous change in the peninsula and in the gulf with the discovery of oil. The British had longstanding relationships with the sheikhs of the gulf and with Aden, at the tip of Yemen, and they continued to control the sheikhs' dealings with the outside world. At the same time, Americans began to establish a special relationship with the Saudis, although the Wahhabi rulers of Saudi Arabia did not permit any Western religious personnel to be active in the kingdom.

In Iran, the Urmia station was rebuilt after World War I, and missionaries returned, optimistic that the new government would allow the resumption of missionary activity. Schools were built, and with new road construction Christians were able to travel to and from remote areas. But by the mid-1920s the new government first curtailed and eventually made it impossible for schools and other institutions to operate. The government passed laws forbidding foreigners from engaging in a propaganda war against Muslims—an anti-Communist edict, but it could be applied to Christians—and school curricula had to be brought into line with the new nationalist curriculum. In August 1932, Iranian subjects were forbidden to attend elementary school classes in mission schools, which in turn dried up the pool of potential secondary school students, and medical-licensing regulations limited the number of missionary physicians. The next year the government closed the missionary station at Urmia. The Protestant response was to create the Evangelical Church of Persia, organized in 1934 under Persian leadership, and by 1935 missionary work, including education, had been handed over to the local churches and native personnel.[24] In 1936, the Lutheran Orient Mission to the Kurds in Mahabad, begun in 1910, was shut down, and in 1940 the Iranian government took over all the Presbyterian schools, paying the missionary board compensation of $1.2 million.

The Presbyterians and Anglicans started other notable mission schools and hospitals in Iran, including hospitals in Hamadan and Meshed and schools in Isfahan, Shiraz, and Tehran. Alborz College, like Baghdad College a high school–level institution, educated much of the Iranian leadership as well as the expatriate community. Alborz had been founded in 1873 as an elementary school but was gradually expanded into a secondary school under Dr. Samuel Jordan, who led it from 1899 to 1940. In 1940, it was placed under Persian direction, though it continued to be known as the "American College of Tehran."[25]

In general, missionary activity during the interwar period and beyond was notable for the founding of institutions of higher education and medical facilities, which were more acceptable to the new nationalist governments than were primary and secondary schools. This activity was possible for several reasons. In the Middle East, British and French control opened a space in which the missions could operate. At the same time, the development of national education networks increased the number of students who sought higher education. We have already mentioned the founding of Baghdad College and the impact it has had on Iraqi life. Perhaps the most important institution to be founded in this period was the American University in Cairo, which opened in the fall of 1920. Like Robert College in Istanbul and the

American University of Beirut, which had changed its name from "Syrian Protestant College" in 1920, the American University in Cairo avoided any direct missionary connection, although its first president, Dr. Charles Watson, had resigned from the United Presbyterian Board to take the post. The university was also unusual in that more than half of the first applicants were Muslim, far more than was the case at other mission schools.[26]

There was local Muslim reaction to the missionary-founded schools. After the capitulations were abolished,[27] the rector of al-Azhar Mosque in Cairo, despairing at Egyptian intellectuals' previous ineffectual responses against missionary and social service incursions in Egypt, established a committee to respond to missionary works. To the members of the committee, modernist Sheikh Rashid Rida's warnings about the missionary danger to Muslims conflicted with his acquiescence to Muslim attendance in secular schools such as the American University of Beirut until there were compatible Muslim institutions.[28] But by 1930 there were some 450 missionaries in Egypt with a native staff of about 1,500, and an American missionary, Samuel Zwemer, who had begun his career with the Reformed Church mission in the Gulf, came to Egypt to devote himself to the conversion of Muslims and entered al-Azhar on two occasions to hand out tracts to Muslim students. The reaction by al-Azhar clerics was followed by debate and an attack on missions by the Egyptian liberal and nationalist press, antimissionary poems, and letters to the government opposing outright proselytization by staff members in mission schools and hospitals. Missionaries were accused of using hypnotism, bribery, and jobs, handing out candy to children, adopting babies, and attacking the Prophet Muhammad. Graduates of the American University in Cairo accused the university of working hand in glove with the imperialist powers. In response, the Corps of al-Azhar High 'Ulema met and issued a manifesto in which it not only warned Muslims about tricks and deception in missionary schools and hospitals and began an antimission fund-raising campaign but also demanded that the Egyptian government take measures to "eradicate" the evil—"to protect the religion, to preserve the people and safeguard children from the 'claws' of missionaries."[29] To the Muslim Brotherhood and anti-imperialist nationalists, this statement was not enough. They viewed the missionaries as neo-Crusaders and sought complete local control over education.[30]

For many Protestant missionaries going back to Rufus Anderson, the goal of the missionary movement was not to recruit new members to the American (or English or European churches, but instead to have their "converts" establish indigenous churches. Once these churches were established, the mission could and should withdraw, committing its resources elsewhere.[31] Thus, an Armenian Protestant Church had been founded in Constantinople in 1848 in response to opposition to the mission by the Armenian Gregorian Church. Similarly, the Presbyterian mission in Egypt had formed the Evangelical Church in Egypt, which in 1865 had sixty-seven members and by the 1950s could claim twenty-seven thousand members, almost all of whom were Copts.[32] The Evangelical Church of Persia was established in 1934. This resistance to recruitment into the missionary churches was expressed especially forcefully by the Anglicans, who in their work with the Nestorians in eastern Anatolia and western Iran struggled to explain that to become Christian was not to become English or to acquire any of the rights and protections of the English.

The idea of indigenization was a problem only for the Protestants, of course. Roman Catholic missionaries had never questioned that their goal was to recruit members to the worldwide Catholic Church obedient to the pope. During the heyday of both imperialism and foreign missions following Rufus Anderson's retirement in 1870, the idea of establishing indigenous churches and handing over control to a missionary-trained local hierarchy became much less popular, especially among American missionary establishments, but after World War I it again gathered strength as resources for foreign missions dwindled and as political independence led to increased resistance to foreign institutions. Several factors contributed to this change. Although the 1910 Edinburgh World Missionary Conference was regarded as the high point to foreign missions, the signs of change were already evident. There was an increasing awareness of the Eurocentrism that was often at the core of missionary activity as the missionaries' mission became Western civilization, customs, and values at least as much as religious faith. Missionaries themselves became more aware of the strengths of the cultures in which they found themselves working and less secure in the idea of supplanting these cultures with Western values. This awareness was particularly strong in the Middle East, where in comparison to Africa there already existed a high literary culture and a large indigenous Christian population. Added to this ideological shift was the disruption caused by World War I. The violence of the conflict among Christian powers led Christians to question the innate superiority of European culture even as it limited the recruitment of missionary staff and the availability of resources. Again, this was particularly true for the Middle East, which was engulfed militarily in the war. Missionaries were forced to leave the region, and missionary institutions were closed. Finally, after the war, financial resources were diverted to domestic needs rather than sent abroad, and churches in Europe and the United States became more cognizant of the needs and deficiencies of their own societies. This shift in funding was followed by the financial constraints caused by the Great Depression beginning in 1929.

In 1932, a volume entitled *Re-Thinking Missions* was published. Written by Harvard professor William Ernest Hocking , it was essentially the report of a commission established and funded by John D. Rockefeller Jr. that sent researchers to India, Burma, China, and Japan to evaluate American Protestant foreign missions and make recommendations for the future. The commission represented the major missionary churches in the United States: Northern Baptist, Congregational, Methodist, Presbyterian (both branches), Episcopal, and Reformed Church. Although the commission did not directly address missions in the Middle East, its conclusions were enormously influential throughout the missionary field, pointing the way forward toward an ecumenical approach to the enterprise. The report summarized the new mainline Protestant thinking about foreign missions. It is time, the report said, to prepare for the transition from foreign missionaries who were necessarily temporary to indigenous churches that would have a permanent presence in their countries,[33] with the role of the foreign mission being to assist the indigenous churches. At the same time, there was a recognition that resources hitherto devoted to foreign missions were needed at home, particularly in a time of economic depression. The corollary to this recognition was, of course, the ecumenical movement that had been gathering steam since the Edinburgh conference and that provided the framework for relations between the European and American churches, on the one hand, and not only the new, now indigenous Protestant churches, but also the original Eastern churches, on the other.

The most visible evidence of the ecumenical movement is the World Council of Churches, finally established in 1948 though it had been agreed to in 1937 as a merger of organizations that had grown out of the Edinburgh conference. Today it includes 157 member churches and nearly 200 affiliates in more than 120 countries—Protestants, Anglicans, Orthodox, and even some Pentecostals.[34] The Roman Catholic Church works closely with the World Council and sends representatives to its meetings. One of its regional subcouncils is the Middle East Council of Churches, which includes not only the Orthodox and Armenian churches, but also the Uniate churches, the Anglicans, and the Evangelical churches started by the missionaries.

By 1939, the mainline churches that had formed the backbone of the Protestant foreign missionary enterprise since the early nineteenth century were retreating from the field, concentrating instead on supporting the indigenous Eastern churches as well as the local Protestant churches that had been formed under their patronage. Rufus Anderson's goal of replacing the missionary enterprise with indigenous churches was realized as the mainline churches in Europe and America became less and less able to support a large missionary presence both financially and ideologically. Instead, the Protestant churches that had come into existence gradually since the early 1850s ran their own schools and churches, essentially establishing the same kind of structure as the Roman Catholic Church had in setting up Uniate branches of the Eastern churches since the sixteenth century. Resources for foreign missions diminished, both because of financial demands at home and because of ideological shifts that interpreted foreign missions as racist attempts to impose Western values. Particularly after World War II, the resources that had been devoted to education, health, and economic assistance were increasingly funneled through governmental organizations such as the U.S. Agency for International Development (USAID) and NGOs, including what came to be called faith-based NGOs. At the same time, however, other missionary-oriented organizations were establishing a presence in the region, particularly in the Holy Land.

World War II had much the same impact on the Western missionary enterprise in the Middle East as had World War I. Resources for foreign missions dried up or were unavailable, and the missionaries went home. But this time they did not come back. Once again the political map of the region was utterly changed. The old empires that had been replaced by states under European control were now replaced by independent states. A nationalist Turkish state was firmly entrenched in Anatolia; by the end of 1946, both the British and the Russians had withdrawn from Iran; France relinquished its control over Syria and Lebanon in 1947; and Britain withdrew from Palestine in late 1947. Iraq and Egypt were nominally independent, though both had a significant British presence, but nationalism was increasingly powerful, and by the mid-1950s the British had withdrawn. Most important, of course, was the establishment of the new State of Israel in part of what had been the British Mandate for Palestine.

The withdrawal of the European powers and the protection they had afforded the missionaries also contributed to the eroding of the Western missions. In Egypt, for example, the immediate postwar years saw greater restrictions by the Egyptian government on the mission schools, restrictions that now were imposed on both Protestants and Catholics equally.[35] The antimissionary movement of the 1930s spurred changes in the curriculum at the American University in Cairo, moving it toward secularism and an emphasis on "social ethics" without specific connection to any religion. Following the Nasserist takeover in 1954, for the first time no prayers were said at the university's opening convocation in 1956. "The history of AUC thus reflects the transition of American Christian missions toward forms of social engagement that became associated, in the second half of the twentieth century, with nongovernmental organizations (NGOs)."[36]

The Suez invasion by Britain and France in 1956 ended their missionary efforts in Egypt. The Egyptian government nationalized all Roman Catholic schools not run directly by the Vatican—that is, the French Catholic schools—and deported all British subjects. The CMS, the British and Foreign Bible Society, and the Nile Mission Press were closed, and their bank accounts frozen. Seventy American missionaries remained, mostly in Assiut and Cairo, but their days were numbered.[37] Seeing what had happened to the British, the American Mission (the mission of the United Presbyterian Church of North America in association with the Reformed Church) began to transfer its assets, including its schools, to the Egyptian Evangelical Church, which became independent in 1957 and soon changed its name to the "Coptic Evangelical Church."[38] By this time, the American Mission had 196 churches and 26,663 members.[39] The paternalism of former years became fraternalism as both the American and Egyptian churches were equal members of the World Council of Churches. The American Presbyterian Board of Foreign Missions became the Commission on Ecumenical Mission and Relations.[40] However, American support for Israel finally made the position of the American Mission in Egypt untenable as anti-American feeling intensified. At its annual meeting in 1966–1967, the American Mission determined to dissolve, and on June 5, 1967, the Israeli preemptive strike on Egypt prompted the American embassy in Cairo to evacuate all Americans from the country,[41] although a few members of the mission staff returned later to work for the Evangelical Church. More than a hundred years of American missionary activity in Egypt had come to an end.

Since the late 1930s, mainline Protestant missionaries had made clear their support for the Palestinian Arabs and against Western support for the Zionist movement and the establishment of the State of Israel. Staff members at the American University of Beirut were well aware of Arab attitudes because of contact with their students' families throughout the Middle East.[42] In 1938, the American consul-general in Jerusalem had warned Washington "that the Christian clergy and missionaries agreed with the Arabs about the threat of 'Jewish domination' from continued Jewish immigration."[43] Once the State of Israel was established, creating a massive refugee problem, particularly in the countries bordering Israel, the missionaries worked with the United Nations Relief and Works Agency, the agency charged with caring for the Palestinian refugees. The lead organization in the agency was the American Friends Service Committee, a Quaker (Society of Friends) relief organization, but other mission-related organizations also took part. The American Mission in Egypt also began to make other connections to enhance its social service work, receiving a Ford Foundation grant in 1952 to assist its dairy cattle project in Assiut. By the 1960s, the Egyptian Evangelical Church was taking part in projects with such secular organizations as CARE and the United Nations Educational, Scientific, and Cultural Organization.[44] This increasingly became the pattern: the faith-based organization would receive funding from a secular organization to carry on social, economic-development, and relief work.

The British decision to place the issue of the future of Palestine in the hands of the United Nations had profound implications for missions in the Holy Land. For Catholics and mainline Protestants, practical concerns over the future of both their institutions and the indigenous Christian communities overrode the theological implications related to the dispersion and return of Jews to Palestine. Despite pressure from Catholic missionaries working in the Middle East and from indigenous Catholic communities in the region that supported the establishment of an Arab state in Palestine, throughout the 1947–1948 deliberations at the United Nations the Vatican's primary concern was the safeguarding of the Holy Sites in Jerusalem. To that end, Catholics favored internationalization of Jerusalem under United Nations' auspices. After the establishment of the State of Israel, however, Catholic fears that the Jewish state would eliminate Christian influences from Jerusalem were quickly allayed, though in the aftermath of the Arab–Israel War of 1948, the Roman Catholic Church found its institutions located in Jewish Israel and most of its population living in Jordan either as residents of the West Bank or as refugees fleeing from Israeli-controlled territory. Of ten thousand Latins living in Jerusalem and neighboring towns in 1948, only three thousand remained in the 1970s. Issues concerning the Holy Sites and support for the return of Palestinian refugees so that the Holy Places would not become "lifeless museum pieces" remained Catholic concerns.[45]

For Anglicans, the 1948 war led to a split in Jerusalem between the indigenous Anglican Church centered at St. George's Cathedral and the Church's Ministry Among the Jewish People, successor to the London Jews Society, which continued its ministry at Christ Church, the oldest Anglican church in Jerusalem. Like the Catholics of Jerusalem, the Anglicans found themselves operating in Jordanian East Jerusalem and serving a dwindling population, even though many of the church properties were located in Israel. In addition to developing emergency facilities for refugees and in response to indigenization of the church community, the diocese moved away from its original mission-centered philosophy and began transferring significant responsibility to local Palestinian Christians. In 1957, a Palestinian bishop was appointed, and in 1962 a theological college opened. After the Israeli occupation of the West Bank in June 1967, the Anglican diocese was reorganized to deal with the challenge of urban and professional emigration and the Israeli occupation. Identifying with the Palestinian national cause, the Arab Anglican bishops have deepened links with the Latin, Armenian, and Greek communities and a number of the Evangelical Middle East churches. The creation of the Middle East Council of Churches is a manifestation of evolving Arab Christian interfaith dialogue.[46] In addition, by the 1990s a Palestinian liberation theology emerged in the Anglican Church with the publication of Na'im Ateek's book *Justice and Only Justice: A Palestinian Theology of Liberation*;[47] in the context of Palestinian nationalism, this theology has moved toward the abandonment of the use of the Old Testament because of the possibility of its conflation with Judaism.

Catholics responded to the influx of Jews to Israel in the wake of the European Holocaust with the establishment the Oeuvre de Saint-Jacques l'Apôtre to work with the children of mixed marriages, Jewish converts and the descendents of converts, Catholic spouses, and non-Jewish refugees or immigrants. Backed by the prefect of the Sacred Congregation for the Oriental Churches, the organization set out to work with Hebrew-speaking Israelis to "implant the Church within the Jewish people in such a way that Jews who become Christians should be able to preserve their national character, in much the same way that members of any other people or nation are able or invited to do so."[48]

Premillennial American evangelical and Pentecostal Protestants saw in the creation of the State of Israel a "sign of the times" in the unfolding of the eschatological plan. Whereas before World War II British missionaries were dominant, a combination of factors—religious belief, the Israeli gov-

ernment's decision to maintain the status quo in religious matters, and economic hardship during the early years of the new state—led to a flood of
varied missionary activity in the Holy Land after the war. The influx of destitute refugees from postwar Europe and Jews from Middle Eastern countries
provided candidates for conversion. Representatives of established churches
and many individual missionaries went to Israel, which during the 1950s and
1960s became the most evangelized country on earth. It is estimated that several hundred missionaries of various denominations operated among a Jewish population of some 630,000 in 1948 and more than two million by 1967.
Charles Kalisky, the Jerusalem representative of the American Board of Missions to the Jews,[49] wrote that "in the city of New York alone the number of
Jews is three times the entire population of the State of Israel. Yet the number of missionaries working among the Jews in New York is no more, and
possibly less, than the total number working in the city of Jerusalem alone."[50]

Whereas the mainline churches viewed the 1967 war as a crisis, the evangelical churches saw it in millennial terms as yet more evidence of the unfolding of history and so supported the new political state of affairs. The mainline
churches' activities were increasingly channeled into their relief and economic-development activities, particularly as the American government became
more willing to fund "faith-based" NGOs. Although the mainline denominations' Web sites continue to emphasize, for American consumption, their
efforts at proselytization, in fact most proselytizing is done by the evangelical and Pentecostal groups. However, proselytizing by foreigners is illegal in
most of the Middle East, so it is carried on by local converts or in a somewhat
sub rosa fashion by Westerners whose primary activity is nonreligious.

The issue of religious freedom had been a concern of Western missionaries in the Middle East ever since the Ottoman reforms of the mid-nineteenth century, but it did not emerge as an important U.S. foreign policy
issue until the 1990s. A conference sponsored by Freedom House in 1996
led to the "Statement of Conscience of the National Association of Evangelicals Concerning Worldwide Religious Persecution," which put the problem
of religious persecution in the national spotlight. Various Christian groups,
including the Southern Baptist Convention, the Lutheran-Missouri Synod,
the Christian Coalition, the United States Catholic Conference, the Episcopal Church, the Salvation Army, the National Association of Evangelicals,
as well as groups representing Jews, Baha'is, and Tibetan Buddhists lobbied
for American legislative action to secure religious liberty across the globe. In
response, the Clinton administration created the State Department Advisory

Committee on Religious Freedom, and congressional hearings followed. In May 1997, a bill was introduced in the U.S. Congress to set up an office to monitor religious persecution and to impose sanctions against countries engaged in a pattern of religious persecution.

Proponents of the legislation, primarily conservative Christian and evangelical groups, were concerned with relieving the persecution of coreligionists in China, Vietnam, and the Sudan and with fostering global religious freedom. Some businessmen and political conservatives, however, questioned the impact that possible sanctions would have on globalization and free trade. Despite their concerns and the Clinton administration's opposition to the bill for its focus on "single-issue" policy that could disrupt established diplomatic process, the bill was passed and signed into law as the International Religious Freedom Act of 1998 (IRFA).[51]

Under IRFA, the Office of International Religious Freedom was established in the State Department. Headed by an ambassador-at-large for international religious freedom, the office is charged to "promote freedom of religion and conscience throughout the world as a fundamental human right and as a source of stability for all countries; assist newly formed democracies in implementing freedom of religion and conscience; assist religious human rights NGOs in promoting religious freedom; and identify and denounce regimes that are severe persecutors of their citizens or others on the basis of religious belief."[52] To that end, the office monitors religious persecution worldwide, prepares annual reports detailing such acts that are particularly severe violations of religious freedom—such as torture, degrading treatment or punishment, prolonged detention without charges—and participates in congressional hearings about international religious freedom. It also works to address problems by devising diplomatic and conflict-resolution strategies to foster and implement reconciliation programs between parties involved in religious disputes.

Critics of IRFA contend that in addition to its single-issue focus, the promotion of an American model of religious toleration is one that does not just work to improve human rights but also supports Christian missionary work in countries where religious proselytization is viewed as a violation of their religious freedom. Although there are laws against missionary work in most Middle Eastern countries, IRFA reports the presence of Christian missionaries in most of them, and because of IRFA American missionaries abroad are "increasingly aware that they can report difficulties they encounter, whether in obtaining visas or distributing literature, to appropriate U.S. embassies or the Department of State in Washington and they are increasingly likely to receive helpful responses."[53]

It would not be accurate to conclude that the mainline Protestant churches have abandoned foreign missions. Indeed, the Presbyterian Church Web site heralded 2009 as a "'turnaround year'—the year that our church renewed its commitment to sending out mission workers."[54] However, the strategies by which missions are conducted have changed dramatically. Rather than establishing mission stations with Western staff, as was the pattern in the nineteenth century, Protestant churches today emphasize partnership with local organizations, so that the American church partially or fully supports financially the staff needed by the local organization. The location of continued activity tends to follow the historical connections of each denomination: the United Church of Christ (formerly the Congregational Church) is active in Turkey, the Presbyterians in Egypt, and the Episcopalians in Jerusalem. Partnership was particularly easy for the Episcopal Church because its affiliation with the Anglican Communion with the Church of England and the Anglican churches of the former British Empire made partners readily available.

The situation in Turkey is especially interesting. In effect, the ABCFM never left, and it managed to maintain several of its institutions. Global Ministries, the umbrella organization of the United Church of Christ and the Disciples of Christ, supports three staff members in Turkey, two as co-general-secretaries of the ABCFM in Istanbul and the third as a teacher and dean at Uskudar American Academy in Istanbul.[55] But it is the Friends of the American Board Schools in Turkey (FABSIT) Foundation that "is the contemporary, secular heir of the American Board of Commissioners for Foreign Missions,"[56] which originally founded the schools. In 1968, Turkish law was changed to require Turkish owners for all institutions, and the Health and Education Foundation was established to meet this requirement. The foundation now manages three schools (the American Collegiate Institute in Izmir, Tarsus American College in Tarsus, and the Uskudar American Academy) as well as the Gazientep American Hospital.[57] The ABCFM teacher at Uskudar describes her role as a "Ministry of Presence."[58] Through FABSIT, Uskudar received $400,000 from USAID in 2009 to support and upgrade its library and media center, another example of the growing synergy between aid organizations and what had been missionary institutions.

Lebanon continues to be a center of Christian activity in the region, but now both Catholic and Protestant religious and benevolent activity is carried on by the local Christian churches rather than by Western churches. The key

Protestant organization is the Near East School of Theology in Beirut, an interdenominational seminary established in 1932 to train ministers for the evangelical churches of the region that American and European Protestant missionaries had founded in the nineteenth century. Although the Presbyterians saw 2009 as a "turnaround year," Egypt does not appear to be an area of focus for them. Instead, Presbyterian World Mission has singled out Central and Latin America, Africa, and Taiwan as areas of particular interest.[59] Global Ministries supports two staff members in Egypt, both in refugee work and jointly appointed with the Evangelical Lutheran Church.[60] Episcopalians partner with their Anglican colleagues, supporting St. Luke's Anglican Hospital in Nablus, where the American church pays for the medical director, and al-Ahli Arab Hospital in Gaza. Partners for many of these quasi-missionary activities include the Arab Group for Christian–Muslim Dialogue, the Middle East Council of Churches, the Union of Armenian Evangelical Churches in the Near East, and the World Student Christian Association.

Although the mainline Protestant churches have by and large chosen not to try to expand their activities in the Middle East but rather to work through the institutions and structures that already exist, the real expansion worldwide has taken place in the evangelical and Pentecostal community. Although the mainline churches largely abandoned the watchword of the 1910 Edinburgh conference—"the evangelization of the world in this generation"—the evangelical churches reaffirmed the Great Commission of Jesus with which we began this volume: "Go therefore and make disciples of all nations." In contrast to the mainline Protestants, these groups have often supported Zionism and the State of Israel as a way station on the path to the Second Coming. They have also tapped into another tradition drawn from earliest Christianity—the Pauline tradition of the tent maker. Paul, a tent maker from Tarsus, used his skill as a means of support while he traveled throughout Greece and Asia Minor to spread the Gospel on his mission of conversion. Today's evangelical missionaries have borrowed the same language and technique.

Like the mainline churches, the evangelicals do not set up mission stations from which to establish schools or clinics or new churches. Instead, they bring skills that are needed by the society and conduct their ministries from within. A look at the Assemblies of God Web site, for example, gives us an idea of how this works. Assemblies of God is a relatively moderate evangelical church, but foreign missions clearly remain central for its members.[61] A variety of mission possibilities is offered, from full-time careers to short-term assignments. A career missionary is expected to have a college degree and successful pastoral experience in the United States. But the list of "opportunities" available is particularly instructive: the mission includes beekeepers and other agricultural workers, English teachers, computer technicians and Web masters, medical personnel, and even a football player-coach. In the Eurasia area, which includes the Middle East and Central Asia, the locations of all positions is listed as "sensitive": in other areas of the world, the specific country of the opportunity is given, but in Eurasia, much of which is primarily Muslim, the church does not indicate publicly where its missionaries will go.

By the 1950s, the Middle East was increasingly regarded as "the Muslim world," with the exception of Israel, and religious pluralism was less and less acceptable to the region's governments. In his book *Caravan: The Story of the Middle East*, published in 1951, the anthropologist Carleton Coon described the region as a mosaic,[62] but that description has become less and less accurate, at least with respect to religion. The Christian populations of the region have been diminishing since their destruction in Anatolia during and after World War I, and that trend accelerated after World War II. The Arab–Israeli conflict has resulted in considerable Palestinian Christian emigration, for that population is relatively well educated and urban. The same occurred during the Lebanese civil war, as Lebanese Christians found it relatively easy to immigrate to Europe and America. The identification of Christians with the West, intensified by their links to the missionaries, became increasingly suspect throughout the region. In 2003, when the United States invaded Iraq, many missionary groups looked forward eagerly to the potential for increased activity in Iraq because of U.S. control. Instead, the invasion and political upheavals throughout the region have accelerated the further decimation of the ancient Christian communities there. The Middle East has become more than ever the Muslim world.

Introduction

1. See Mark A. Noll, *America's God: From Jonathan Edwards to Abraham Lincoln* (New York: Oxford University Press, 2002); Mark A. Noll, *The Rise of Evangelicalism: The Age of Edwards, Whitefield, and the Wesleys* (Downers Grove, Ill.: InterVarsity Press, 2003); and the series "A History of Evangelicalism" published by InterVarsity Press.

2. See, for example, Ellen Fleischmann, "Evangelization or Education: American Protestant Missionaries, the American Board, and the Girls and Women of Syria (1830–1910)," in Heleen Murre-van den Berg, ed., *New Faith in Ancient Lands: Western Missions in the Middle East in the Nineteenth and Early Twentieth Centuries*, 263–280 (Leiden: Brill, 2006); Ellen Fleischmann, "The Impact of American Protestant Missions in Lebanon on the Construction of Female Identity, c. 1860–1950," *Islam and Christian–Muslim Relations* 13 (2002): 411–426; Carolyn McCue Goffman, "Masking the Mission: Cultural Conversion in the American College for Girls," in Eleanor H. Tejirian and Reeva Spector Simon, eds., *Altruism and Imperialism: Western Cultural and Religious Missions in the Middle East*, 88–119 (New York: Middle East Institute, Columbia University, 2002); Nancy L. Stockdale, "Biblical Motherhood: English Women and Empire in Palestine, 1848–1948," *Women's History Review* 15 (2006): 561–569; Nancy L. Stockdale, "An Imperialist Failure: English Missionary Women and Palestinian Orphan Girls in Nazareth, 1864–1899," in Martin Tamcke and Michael

Marten, eds., *Christian Witness Between Continuity and New Beginnings: Modern Historical Missions in the Middle East*, 213–232 (Berlin: Lit, 2006).

3. Eleanor A. Doumato, "An Extra Legible Illustration of the Christian Faith: Medicine, Medical Ethics, and Missionaries in the Arabian Gulf," in Tejirian and Simon, eds., *Altruism and Imperialism*, 167–182, also published in *Islam and Christian–Muslim Relations* 13 (2002): 377–390; Dana L. Robert, "The 'Christian Home' as a Cornerstone of Anglo-Missionary Thought and Practice," in Dana L. Robert, ed., *Converting Colonialism: Visions and Realities in Mission History, 1706–1914*, 134–165 (Grand Rapids, Mich.: Eerdmans, 2008); Dana L. Robert, "Mount Holyoke Women and the Dutch Reformed Missionary Movement,1874–1904," *Missionalia* 21 (1993): 103–123; and Paul D. Sedra, "John Lieder and His Mission in Egypt: The Evangelical Ethos at Work Among Nineteenth Century Copts," *Journal of Religious History* 28 (2004): 219–239.

4. See Walter Russell Mead, *Special Providence American Foreign Policy and How It Changed the World* (New York: Routledge), 2002; Ussama Makdisi, *Artillery of Heaven: American Missionaries and the Failed Conversion of the Middle East* (Ithaca, N.Y.: Cornell University Press, 2008).

5. For example, Haim Goren, "The German Catholic 'Holy Sepulchre Society': Activities in Palestine," in Yehoshua Ben-Arieh and Moshe Davis, eds., *Jerusalem in the Mind of the Western World 1800–1948*, 155–172, With Eyes Toward Zion V (Westport, Conn.: Praeger, 1997); Ruth Kark, "The Contribution of Nineteenth Century Protestant Missionary Societies to Historical Geography," *Imago Mundi* 45 (1993): 112–119; Ruth Kark, "The Impact of Early Missionary Enterprises on Landscape and Identity Formation in Palestine, 1820–1914," *Islam and Christian–Muslim Relations* 15 (2004): 209–235; and the series "With Eyes Toward Zion" published by Praeger.

6. See Brian Stanley, *The Bible and the Flag: Protestant Missions and British Imperialism in the Nineteenth and Twentieth Centuries* (Leicester, U.K.: Apollos, 1990); Andrew Porter, *Religion Versus Empire? British Protestant Missionaries and Overseas Expansion, 1700–1914* (Manchester, U.K.: Manchester University Press, 2004); Michael Marten, *Attempting to Bring the Gospel Home: Scottish Missions to Palestine, 1839–1917* (London: Tauris Academic Studies, 2006); as well as the products of such efforts as the North Atlantic Missiology Project, based at the University of Cambridge.

7. Bernard Heyberger and Chantal Verdeil, "Spirituality and Scholarship: The Holy Land in Jesuit Eyes (Seventeenth to Nineteenth Centuries)," in Murre-van den Berg, ed., *New Faith in Ancient Lands*, 19–41.

1. The Spread of Christianity

1. George Atiya, *A History of Eastern Christianity* (1967; Millwood, N.Y.: Kraus Reprint, 1991), 25–27.

2. Bruce Chilton, *Rabbi Paul: An Intellectual Biography* (New York: Doubleday, 2004), 39.

3. Ibid., 143.

4. Ibid., 175.

5. Robin Lane Fox, *Pagans and Christians* (New York: Knopf, 1987), 282, 314–317.

6. Jonathan P. Berkey, *The Formation of Islam: Religion and Society in the Near East, 600–1800* (New York: Cambridge University Press, 2003), 1–50.

7. Chilton, *Rabbi Paul*, xv.

8. Fox, *Pagans and Christians*, 271.

9. Shaye J. D. Cohen, "Conversion to Judaism in Historical Perspective: From Biblical Israel to Postbiblical Judaism," *Conservative Judaism* 36 (1983), 41.

10. Chilton, *Rabbi Paul*, 79.

11. Peter Brown, *The World of Late Antiquity, AD 150–750* (New York: W. W. Norton, 1989), 27–28.

12. On Constantine and Constantinople, see Judith Herrin, *Byzantium: The Surprising Life of a Medieval Empire* (Princeton, N.J.: Princeton University Press, 2008).

13. Stephen Neill, *A History of Christian Missions*, 2nd ed., revised by Owen Chadwick (New York: Penguin Books, 1986), 33–42; Kenneth Scott Latourette, *A History of the Expansion of Christianity*, 7 vols. (New York: Harper & Brothers, 1937–1945), 1:85–92.

14. Garth Fowdon, *Empire to Commonwealth: Consequences of Monotheism in Late Antiquity* (Princeton, N.J.: Princeton University Press, 1993), 88.

15. Pierre Maraval, "The Earliest Phase of Christian Pilgrimage in the Near East (Before the 7th Century)," *Dumbarton Oaks Papers* 56 (2002), 66–67.

16. Steven Runciman, "The Pilgrimages to Palestine Before 1091," in Kenneth M. Setton, ed., *A History of the Crusades*, 1:68–80 (Madison: University of Wisconsin Press, 1969).

17. Ramsay MacMullen, "Two Types of Conversion to Early Christianity," *Vigilae Christianae* 37 (1983): 174–192; Morton Smith, "Pauline Worship as Seen by Pagans," *Harvard Theological Review* 73 (1980): 241–249.

18. Quoted in Ramsay MacMullen, *Christianizing the Roman Empire (A.D. 100–400)* (New Haven, Conn.: Yale University Press, 1984), 2.

19. W. H. C. Frend, "Christianity in the Middle East: Survey Down to A.D. 1800," in A. J. Arberry, ed., *Religion in the Middle East: Three Religions in Concord and Conflict*, 2 vols. (New York: Cambridge University Press, 1969), 1:239–240.

20. Norman P. Tanner, *The Councils of the Church: A Short History* (New York: Crossroad, 2001), 14.

21. However, it would be an exaggeration to describe Edessa as a Christian town. There was a continuity of culture because paganism continued to be a strong presence, and pagan festivals were celebrated at least as late as the end of the fifth century (Hans Drijvers, "The Persistence of Pagan Cults and Practices in Christian Syria," in Nina G. Garsoian, Thomas F. Mathews, and Robert W. Thomson, eds., *East of Byzantium: Syria and Armenia in the Formative Period*, 35–43 [Washington, D.C.: Dumbarton Oaks, 1982]).

22. Latourette, *A History of the Expansion of Christianity*, 1:103

23. Krikor H. Maksoudian, "The Religion of Armenia," in Thomas F. Mathews and Roger S. Wieck, eds., *Treasures in Heaven* (New York: Pierpont Morgan Library, 1994), 24.

24. Ibid., 26.

25. Robert W. Thomson, "Mission, Conversion, and Christianization: The Armenian Example," *Harvard Ukrainian Studies* 12–13 (1988–1989), 45.

26. Brown, *The World of Late Antiquity*, 115.

27. On the Arab conquests, see Hugh Kennedy, *The Great Arab Conquests: How the Spread of Islam Changed the World We Live In* (Philadelphia: Da Capo Press, 2007); on the importance of the survival of the imperial capital, see Mark Whittow, *The Making of Byzantium, 600–1025* (Berkeley and Los Angeles: University of California Press, 1996), 162.

28. Berkey, *The Formation of Islam*, 1–50.

29. Richard W. Bulliet, *Conversion to Islam in the Medieval Period: An Essay in Quantitative History* (Cambridge, Mass.: Harvard University Press, 1979).

30. On conversion, see Georges C. Anawati, "Factors and Effects of Arabization and Islamization in Medieval Egypt and Syria," in Speros Vryonis Jr., ed., *Islam and Cultural Change in the Middle Ages*, 18–41 (Wiesbaden, Germany: Otto Harrasowitz, 1975); Sidney H. Griffith, "The View of Islam from the Monasteries of Palestine in the Early Abbasid Period: Theodore Abu Qurrah and the *Summa Theologiae Arabica*," *Islam and Christian–Muslim Relations* 7 (1996): 9–28.

31. Isidore of Seville, a contemporary of Muhammad, saw the world in apocalyptic terms (John V. Tolan, *Saracens: Islam in the Medieval European Imagination* [New York: Columbia University Press, 2002], 3–21).

32. Kennedy, *The Great Arab Conquests*, 346–350, 353–354.

33. Norman Daniel, *Islam and the West: The Making of an Image* (Oxford: Oneworld, 1993), 14–15; R. W. Southern, *Western Views of Islam in the Middle Ages* (Cambridge, Mass.: Harvard University Press, 1962), 1–33;

34. Daniel, *Islam and the West*, 16.

35. Atiya, *A History of Eastern Christianity*, 292.

36. Ibid., 272–273.

37. Ibid., 294, 262, 276.

38. Janet Abu Lughod, *Before European Hegemony: The World System A.D. 1250–1350* (New York: Oxford University Press), 1989.

39. John Howe, "The Nobility's Reform of the Medieval Church," *American Historical Review* 93 (1988): 317–339; Benjamin Z. Kedar, *Crusade and Mission: European Approaches Toward the Muslims* (Princeton, N.J.: Princeton University Press, 1984), 42–96.

40. See H. E. J. Cowdrey, "The Reform Papacy and the Origin of the Crusades," in H. E. J. Cowdrey, ed., *The Crusades and Latin Monasticism, 11th–12th Centuries*, 65–83 (Aldershot, U.K.: Ashgate, 1999).

41. The Great Schism took on greater significance in the church's mind in later centuries as the first explicit example of the fracturing of Christendom (the monophysite and Nestorian churches do not seem to have much importance). See, for example, Tanner, *The Councils of the Church*, 51.

2. The Latin West in the Middle East

1. In the thirteenth and fourteenth centuries, the papacy sent Dominicans and Franciscans to convert the peoples of the Silk Road—Central Asia and ultimately China.

2. H. E. J. Cowdrey, "The Reform Papacy and the Origin of the Crusades," in H. E. J. Cowdrey, *The Crusades and Latin Monasticism, 11th–12th Centuries* (Aldershot, U.K.: Ashgate, 1999), 65–66.

3. Steven Runciman, "The Pilgrimages to Palestine Before 1095," in Kenneth M. Setton, ed., *A History of the Crusades*, 1:68–78 (Madison: University of Wisconsin Press, 1969).

4. Jonathan Riley-Smith, *What Were the Crusades?* 3rd ed. (San Francisco: Ignatius Press, 2002), 14.

5. Christopher Tyerman, *Fighting for Christendom: Holy War and the Crusades* (New York: Oxford University Press, 2004).

6. Cowdrey, "The Reform Papacy," 70.

7. Tyerman, *Fighting for Christendom*, 157.

8. Norman Housley, "Jerusalem and the Development of the Crusade Idea, 1099–1128," in Benjamin Z. Kedar, ed., *The Horns of Hattin* (Jerusalem: Yad Izhak Ben Zvi, 1992), 28–29.

9. James H. Forse, "Armenians and the First Crusade," *Journal of Medieval History* 17 (1991): 13–22; Bernard Hamilton, *The Latin Church in the Crusader States: The Secular Church* (London: Varioram,1980), 188–211.

10. After 1181, the Maronite Church answered to the pope directly but retained its own patriarch and religious rites as well as the use of Arabic rather than Latin. Maronite representatives attended the Fourth Lateran Council and retained a link with the French royal family well into the eighteenth century, when union between the Maronite Church and the Catholic Church became official.

11. Hamilton, *The Latin Church in the Crusader States*, 208.

12. The chapel was a compromise to ensure that the Latins would not be accused of admitting heretics to the shrine but at the same time that the Jacobites would be able to participate in their own liturgy within church confines (ibid., 195).

13. Quoted in Aharon Ben-Ami, *Social Change in a Hostile Environment: The Crusaders' Kingdom of Jerusalem* (Princeton, N.J.: Princeton University Press, 1969), 61–62.

14. Benjamin Z. Kedar, *Crusade and Mission: European Approaches Toward the Muslims* (Princeton, N.J.: Princeton University Press, 1984), 48–52, 147–154; Denys Pringle, "Churches and Settlement in Crusader Palestine," in Peter Edbury and Jonathan Phillips, eds., *The Experience of Crusading*, 2:161–178 (Cambridge: Cambridge University Press, 2003).

15. Robert I. Burns, S.J., "Christian–Islamic Confrontation in the West: The Thirteenth-Century Dream of Conversion," *American Historical Review* 76 (1971), 1386.

16. Ibid., 1389.

17. Quoted in ibid., 1390.

18. Quoted in Kedar, *Crusade and Mission*, 61.

19. Tyerman, *Fighting for Christendom*, 563.

20. James M. Powell, "The Papacy and the Muslim Frontier," in James M. Powell, ed., *Muslims Under Latin Rule, 1100–1300* (Princeton, N.J.: Princeton University Press, 1990), 189–192.

21. Peter the Venerable was already writing about Islam as heresy (John V. Tolan, *Saracens: Islam in the Medieval European Imagination* [New York: Columbia University Press, 2002], 155). Note the policies of separation undertaken in Spain that would be implemented in the Fourth Lateran Council (David Nirenberg, *Communities of Violence: Persecution of Minorities in the Middle Ages* [Princeton, N.J.: Princeton University Press, 1996]; James Muldoon, "Tolerance and Intolerance in the Medieval Canon Lawyers," in Michael Gervers and James M. Powell, eds., *Tolerance and Intolerance: Social Conflict in the Age of the Crusades*, 117–123 [Syracuse, N.Y.: Syracuse University Press, 2001]).

22. Saladin expelled the Latins and gave control of the Church of the Holy Sepulchre to the Greeks.

23. James M. Powell, *Anatomy of a Crusade, 1213–1221* (Philadelphia: University of Pennsylvania Press, 1986), 18.

24. Kedar, *Crusade and Mission*, 114–116.

25. Innocent III's role in the Fourth Crusade is still debated, but he was pleased that the outcome meant the end of the schism (John Gilchrist, "The Lord's War as the Proving Ground of Faith: Pope Innocent III and the Propagation of Violence [1198–1216]," in Maya Shatzmiller, ed., *Crusaders and Muslims in Twelfth-Century Syria* [Leiden: Brill, 1993], 76).

26. Tyerman, *Fighting for Christendom*, 609, 611.

27. Gilchrist, "The Lord's War as the Proving Ground of Faith," 71–72.

28. Kenneth Scott Latourette, *A History of the Expansion of Christianity*, 7 vols. (New York: Harper & Brothers, 1937–1945), 2:193.

29. Jessalyn Bird, "Crusade and Conversion After the Fourth Lateran Council (1215): Oliver of Paderborn's and James of Vitry's Missions to Muslims Reconsidered," *Essays in Medieval Studies* 21 (2004), 24.

30. Kedar, *Crusade and Mission*, 131–132.

31. Burns, "Christian–Islamic Confrontation in the West."

32. Marshall W. Baldwin, "Missions to the East in the Thirteenth and Fourteenth Centuries," in Setton, ed., *A History of the Crusades*, 5:456.

33. Powell, *Anatomy of a Crusade*, 159. Francis was not opposed to crusade; he simply used a different strategy (Christoph T. Maier, *Preaching the Crusades: Mendicant Friars and the Cross in the Thirteenth Century* [Cambridge: Cambridge University Press, 1994], 8–16).

34. Baldwin, "Missions to the East," 5:456; Stephen Neill, *A History of Christian Missions*, 2nd ed., revised by Owen Chadwick (New York: Penguin Books, 1986), 99. On the influence of Joachim of Fiore on Franciscan thought, see David Burr, "Antichrist and Islam in Medieval Franciscan Exegesis," in John Victor Tolan, ed., *Medieval Christian Perceptions of Islam: A Book of Essays*, 131–152 (New York: Garland, 1996).

35. Kedar, *Crusade and Mission*, 138–139.

36. Quoted in Hamilton, *The Latin Church in the Crusader States*, 332.

37. Elizabeth Siberry, "Missionaries and Crusaders, 1095–1274: Opponents or Allies?" in W. J. Sheils, ed., *The Church and War: Papers Read at the Twenty-First Summer Meeting and the Twenty-Second Winter Meeting of the Ecclesiastical Society*, 103–110 (Oxford: Blackwell, 1983).

38. Ibid.; Maier, *Preaching the Crusades*, 8–16; Baldwin, "Missions to the East," 5:476.

39. James Muldoon, *Popes, Lawyers, and Infidels: The Church and the Non-Christian World, 1250–1550* (Philadelphia: University of Pennsylvania Press, 1979), 3–28; 45–48.

40. Kedar, *Crusade and Mission*, 119–121.

41. Bird, "Crusade and Conversion," 24–26; Tolan, *Saracens*, 209–212; Penny J. Cole, *The Preaching of the Crusades to the Holy Land, 1095–1270* (Cambridge: Medieval Academy of America, 1991), 112–116.

42. Baldwin, "Missions to the East," 5:460–462. See also E. Randolph Daniel, *The Franciscan Concept of Mission in the High Middle Ages* (Lexington: University Press of Kentucky, 1975), 67–75.

43. James of Vitry, quoted in Baldwin, "Missions to the East," 5:460.

44. Burns, "Christian–Islamic Confrontation in the West," 1396.

45. Kedar, *Crusade and Mission*, 116–129.

46. Baldwin, "Missions to the East," 5:456, 462.

47. On Prester John, see Charles F. Beckingham and Bernard Hamilton, eds., *Prester John, the Mongols, and the Ten Lost Tribes* (Aldershot, U.K.: Variorum, 1996); on rumors of the recovery of the Holy Land by the Mongol khan, see Sylvia Schein, "Gesta Dei per Mongolos 1300: The Genesis of a Non-Event," *English Historical Review* 94 (1979): 805–819.

48. Baldwin, "Missions to the East," 5:473; Neill, *A History of Christian Missions*, 103–104.

49. See Peter Jackson, "The Crisis in the Holy Land in 1260," *English Historical Review* 376 (1980): 481–513; and Peter Jackson, "Hulegu Khan the Christian: The Making of a Myth," in Peter Edbury and Jonathan Phillips, eds., *The Experience of Crusading*, 2:196–213 (Cambridge: Cambridge University Press, 2003).

50. J. Richard, "Le Début des relations entre la papauté et les Mongoles de Perse," *Journal Asiatique* 237 (1949): 291–297.

51. Baldwin, "Missions to the East," 5:495. On John of Monte Corvino, the establishment of Franciscan order in China, and the Latin bishopric in China, see Neill, *A History of Christian Missions*, 107–110.

52. Quoted in Kedar, *Crusade and Mission*, 156; see also Baldwin, "Missions to the East," 5:453–456.

53. On Llull, see Kedar, *Crusade and Mission*, 189–199.

54. Baldwin, "Missions to the East," 5:504–505.

55. Ibid., 5:490–496.

56. Ibid., 5:497.

57. John L. Boojamra, "Athanasios of Constantinople: A Study of Byzantine Reactions to Latin Infiltration," *Church History* 48 (1979): 27–48.

58. Michael Dols, *The Black Death in the Middle East* (Princeton, N.J.: Princeton University Press, 1977); Baldwin, "Missions to the East," 5:499.

59. Gerhard Weiss, "The Pilgrim as Tourist: Travels to the Holy Land as Reflected in the Published Accounts of German Pilgrims Between 1450 and 1550," in Marilyn J. Chiat and Kathryn L. Reyerson, eds., *The Medieval Mediterranean: Cross-Cultural Contacts*, 119–131 (St. Cloud, Minn.: North Star Press of St. Cloud, 1988).

60. Carol Delaney, "Columbus's Ultimate Goal: Jerusalem," *Comparative Studies in Society and History* 48 (2006): 260–292.

3. Disintegration, Revival, Reformation, and Counter-Reformation

1. As the papacy's political power waned after the thirteenth century, the missionary enterprise received support from the princes of Europe—the Holy Roman emperor, the French, and, by the sixteenth century, Spain and Portugal. In the Middle East and specifically in the Ottoman Empire, French support of the Vatican in the late medieval period (the "Avignon papacy") led directly to the capitulations negotiated with the Ottoman Sublime Porte (central government) in the seventeenth century and French protection of Christian minorities in the region.

2. John France, *The Crusades and the Expansion of Catholic Christendom 1000–1714* (London: Routledge, 2005), 300.

3. This migration of Christians from Ottoman territories left a commercial vacuum that the Ottoman authorities were quick to perceive. It is in this context that Sultan Bayezit II encouraged Jewish refugees from Spain (Sephardim) to settle in the Ottoman Empire. An educated minority population that brought linguistic, technological, and diplomatic skills honed in Muslim and Christian Spain, the immigrants settled in the Balkans, Anatolia, and as far east as Aleppo. They also came with commercial trade connections with their coreligionists throughout the Mediterranean that later extended to Amsterdam and the Americas.

4. France, *The Crusades*, 290–295. Ferdinand and Isabella's campaigns to seize the North African coast were seen as continuations of the Crusades, as were Portuguese expeditions around Africa into the Indian Ocean.

5. Linda Colley, *Captives* (New York: Pantheon, 2002).

6. Norman P. Tanner, *The Councils of the Church: A Short History* (New York: Crossroad, 2001), 70–73.

7. Quoted in Jonathan Riley-Smith, *The Crusades*, 2nd ed. (New Haven, Conn.: Yale University Press, 2005), 277.

8. Charles A. Frazee, *Catholics and Sultans: The Church and the Ottoman Empire, 1453–1923* (New York: Cambridge University Press, 1983), 19.

9. James Hankins, "Renaissance Crusaders: Humanist Crusade Literature in the Age of Mehmed II," *Dumbarton Oaks Papers* 49 (1995): 111–207.

10. Ibid., 113.

11. France, *The Crusades*, 314–315.

12. Muriel Atkin, "Russian Expansion in the Caucasus to 1813," in Michael Rywkin, ed., *Russian Colonial Expansion to 1917*, 139–187 (London: Mansell, 1988).

13. France, *The Crusades*, 239.

14. John Joseph, *The Modern Assyrians of the Middle East: Encounters with Western Christian Missions, Archaeologists, and Colonial Powers* (Leiden: Brill, 2000), 56.

15. Stephen Neill, *A History of Christian Missions*, 2nd ed., revised by Owen Chadwick (London: Penguin, 1986), 121.

16. By 1525, Spain held important port cities as Mers el-Kebir, Tripoli, and Oran came under Christian control and Algiers became a vassal city (France, *The Crusades*, 291–296). On Columbus's plan for a crusade to take Jerusalem, see A. Hamdani, "Columbus and the Recovery of Jerusalem," *Journal of the American Oriental Society* 99 (1979): 39–48.

17. Quoted in P. po-Chia Hsia, *The World of Catholic Renewal* (Cambridge: Cambridge University Press, 1998), 165, cited in France, *The Crusades*, 296.

18. France, *The Crusades*, 297.

19. Timothy Marr, *The Cultural Roots of American Islamicism* (New York: Cambridge University Press, 2006), 92; see also George W. Forell, "Luther and the War Against the Turks," *Church History* 14 (1945): 256–271.

20. When we come to consider the Protestant missionary enterprise beginning in the eighteenth century, we will see that the various Protestant churches tended to establish missions where their governments were exercising imperial or commercial influence or both. The exception is the American missionaries, whose sending churches originated, like the American population, in many countries in Europe.

21. Kenneth Scott Latourette, *A History of the Expansion of Christianity*, 7 vols. (New York: Harper & Brothers, 1937–1945), 3:22.

22. See John J. Callahan, S.J., "A Brief History of Jesuit Education," Cheverus High School, at http://www.cheverus.org/upload/images/docs/jesuits/Brief_History_of_Jesuit_Education__Callahan_f_632909075586888750.pdf, accessed December 24, 2010.

23. Frazee, *Catholics and Sultans*, 73.

24. Ibid., 72–77.

25. Latourette, *A History of the Expansion of Christianity*, 3:23

26. Bruce Masters, *Christians and Jews in the Ottoman Arab World: The Roots of Sectarianism* (New York: Cambridge University Press, 2001), 80–95.

27. Quoted in Tanner, *The Councils of the Church*, 82.

28. Frazee, *Catholics and Sultans*, 137–138.

29. Ibid., 88–92.

30. Joseph, *The Modern Assyrians of the Middle East*, 36; Yaha Armajani, "Christian Missions in Persia," in *Encyclopaedia Iranica* 5, available at http://www.iranica.com/newsite/articles/unicode/v5f5/v5f5a018.html, accessed December 24, 2010.

31. Masters, *Christians and Jews in the Ottoman Arab World*, 68–70; Frazee, *Catholics and Sultans*, 67–68. See also Palmira Brumett, *Ottoman Seapower and Levantine Diplomacy in the Age of Discovery* (Albany: State University of New York Press, 1994).

32. Joseph, *The Modern Assyrians of the Middle East*, 35.

33. Quoted in Bernard Heyberger and Chantal Verdeil, "Spirituality and Scholarship: The Holy Land in Jesuit Eyes (Seventeenth to Nineteenth Centuries)," in Heleen Murre-van den Berg, *New Faith in Ancient Lands: Western Missions in the Middle East in the Nineteenth and Early Twentieth Centuries* (Leiden: Brill, 2006), 35.

34. Frazee, *Catholics and Sultans*, 163–165.

35. Ibid., 53–54.

36. Ibid., 56.

37. Ibid., 61. The Coptic monks were officially separated from the Franciscans, and in 1895, when there were approximately five thousand Coptic Catholics in Egypt, Pope Leo XIII named the first Coptic Catholic patriarch.

38. Ibid., 90.

39. Ibid., 178.

40. Frazee, *Catholics and Sultans*, 178.

41. Ibid., 180.

42. Ibid., 185.

43. Robert M. Haddad, *Syrian Christians in Muslim Society: An Interpretation*, Princeton Studies on the Near East (Westport, Conn.: Greenwood Press, 1970), 18.

44. Ibid., 17.

45. Robert M. Haddad, "Conversion of Eastern Orthodox Christians to the Unia in the Seventeenth and Eighteenth Centuries," in Michael Gervers and Ramzi Jibran Bikhazi, eds., *Indigenous Christian Communities in Islamic Lands Eighth to Eighteenth Centuries*, 449–459, Papers in Mediaeval Studies no. 9 (Toronto: Pontifical Institute of Mediaeval Studies, 1990).

46. Bruce Masters, "Aleppo: The Ottoman Empire's Caravan City," in Edhem Eldem, Daniel Goffmann, and Bruce Masters, eds., *The Ottoman City Between East and West: Aleppo, Izmir, and Istanbul* (Cambridge: Cambridge University Press, 1999), 56; see also Abraham Marcus, *The Middle East on the Eve of Modernity: Aleppo in the Eighteenth Century* (New York: Columbia University Press, 1989).

47. Haddad, *Syrian Christians in Muslim Society*, 48.

48. Ibid., 39.

49. Masters, *Christians and Jews in the Ottoman Arab World*, 95.

50. Joseph, *The Modern Assyrians of the Middle East*, 30.

51. Ibid., 31.

52. Reeva Spector Simon, Michael Menachem Laskier, and Sara Reguer, eds., *The Jews of the Middle East and North Africa in Modern Times* (New York: Columbia University Press, 2003).

4. The Great Awakening of the Protestants and the Anglicans

1. Andrew Porter, *Religion Versus Empire? British Protestant Missionaries and Overseas Expansion, 1700–1914* (Manchester, U.K.: Manchester University Press, 2004), 32–33.

2. Lyle L. Vander Werff, *Christian Mission to Muslims—the Record: Anglican and Reformed Approaches in India and the Near East, 1800–1938* (South Pasadena, Calif.: William Carey Library, 1977), 19–20; Susan Thorne, *Congregational Missions and the Making of an Imperial Culture in Nineteenth-Century England* (Stanford, Calif.: Stanford University Press, 1999), 27–28.

3. Philipp Prein, "Mission to Arcadia: The Moravian Invention of an African Missionary Object as an Example of the Culture of German Nationalism and Colonialism," *German History* 16 (1998), 332.

4. William Carey (1761–1834), founder of the Baptist Missionary Society (1792), knew the work of the Puritans, Moravians, and Pietists in India. His "independents" were missionary movements that operated independently of state church support.

5. Daniel Jeyaraj, "Mission Reports from South India and Their Impact on the Western Mind: The Tranquebar Mission of the Eighteenth Century," in Dana L. Robert, ed., *Converting Colonialism: Visions and Realities in Mission History, 1706–1914* (Grand Rapids, Mich.: Eerdmans, 2008), 23.

6. Ibid., 28.

7. Porter, *Religion Versus Empire?*, 17–19; Thorne, *Congregational Missions*, 28.

8. Porter, *Religion Versus Empire?*, 25.

9. R. H. Martin, "United Conversionist Activities Among the Jews in Great Britain, 1795–1815: Pan-Evangelicalism and the London Society for Promoting Christianity Amongst the Jews," *Church History* 46 (1977), 438.

10. Clarke Garrett, *Respectable Folly: Millenarians and the French Revolution in France and England* (Baltimore: Johns Hopkins University Press, 1975), 17–30, 121–144.

11. A. L. Tibawi, *British Interests in Palestine, 1800–1901: A Study in Religious and Educational Enterprise* (London: Oxford University Press, 1961), 4. See also Porter, *Religion Versus Empire?*, 33–40, and V. Kiernan, "Evangelicalism and the French Revolution," *Past and Present* 1 (1952), 44–50.

12. C. Peter Williams, "British Religion and the Wider World: Mission and Empire, 1800–1940," in Sheridan Gilley and W. J. Sheils, eds., *A History of Religion in Britain: Practice and Belief from Pre-Roman Times to the Present* (Oxford: Blackwell, 1994), 383. Note the work of William Wilberforce in the Abolition movement and Ashley Cooper in factory reform. Both were supporters of the London Jews Society.

13. Dana L. Robert, "Introduction," in Robert, ed., *Converting Colonialism*, 9.

14. Ibid., 10.

15. Vander Werff, *Christian Mission to Muslims*, 25.

16. Porter, *Religion Versus Empire?*, 133.

17. Ibid., 117.

18. Vander Werff, *Christian Mission to Muslims*, 100.

19. Paul W. Werth, *The Margins of Orthodoxy: Missions, Governance, and Confessional Politics in Russia's Volga–Kama Region, 1827–1905* (Ithaca, N.Y.: Cornell University Press, 2002), 14.

20. In the context of religion and empire, beginning with Ivan IV, Russian czars began to attempt to convert non-Russians to Orthodoxy. The government's policy

was relaxed under the enlightened reign of Catherine the Great and then reinstituted under Nicholas I (Michael Khodarkovsky, "The Conversion of Non-Christians in Early Modern Russia," in Robert P. Geraci and Michael Khodarkovsky, eds., *Of Religion and Empire: Missions, Conversion, and Tolerance in Tsarist Russia*, 115–143 [Ithaca, N.Y.: Cornell University Press, 2001]).

21. Spittler also served as secretary-general of the German Christian Society (Deutsche Christentumsgesellschaft), an umbrella organization that had become a German-speaking center of international Protestant activism looking "for concrete and innovative ways of carrying out what they saw as the will of God in the face of the evil existing in the world" (Paul Jenkins, "The Church Missionary Society and the Basel Mission: An Early Experiment in Inter-European Cooperation," in Kevin Ward and Brian Stanley, eds., *The Church Mission Society and World Christianity, 1799–1999* [Grand Rapids, Mich.: Eerdmans, 2000], 50; Frank Foerster, "German Missions in the Holy Land," in Yehoshua Ben-Arieh and Moshe Davis, eds., *Jerusalem in the Mind of the Western World, 1800–1948*, With Eyes Toward Zion V [Westport, Conn.: Praeger, 1997], 185).

22. The Lutheran pastor C. F. A. Steinkopf was secretary of the German Christian Society from 1795 to 1801; from 1801 until his death in 1859, he served as chaplain of the Savoy Chapel congregation in London and foreign secretary of the British and Foreign Bible Society (Jenkins, "The Church Missionary Society and the Basel Mission," 52–53). On the international Protestant "network," see Erich Geldbach, "The German Protestant Network in the Holy Land," in Moshe Davis and Yehoshua Ben-Arieh, eds., *Western Societies and the Holy Land*, 151–169, With Eyes Toward Zion III (New York: Praeger, 1991); and Porter, *Religion Versus Empire*, 56.

23. Andrew F. Walls, *The Missionary Movement in Christian History: Studies in the Transmission of Faith* (Maryknoll, N.Y.: Orbis Books, 1996), 169.

24. Ibid., 170.

25. Jon Miller, *The Social Control of Religious Zeal: A Study of the Organizational Contradictions* (New Brunswick, N.J.: Rutgers University Press, 1994), 42, as cited in Paul D. Sedra, "John Lieder and His Mission in Egypt: The Evangelical Ethos at Work Among Nineteenth-Century Copts," *Journal of Religious History* 28 (2004), 224.

26. There had been isolated missionary forays into the Middle East. During the early eighteenth century, individual members of the Moravians, United Brethren, and Quakers tried to gain access to the Ottoman sultan in order to begin missionary work in the empire, but to no avail. There were also short-lived missions to Persia (Vander Werff, *Christian Mission to Muslims*, 100).

27. Kevin Ward, "'Taking Stock': The Church Missionary Society and Its Historians," in Ward and Stanley, eds., *The Church Mission Society and World Christianity*, 22.

28. The belief that 1666 was the year of the onset of the millennium was a factor in Oliver Cromwell's decision to readmit Jews to England in the seventeenth century.

29. Mel Scult, *Millennial Expectations and Jewish Liberties: A Study of the Efforts to Convert the Jews in Britain, up to the Mid–Nineteenth Century* (Leiden: Brill, 1978), 80–81.

30. Among Simeon's students was Henry Martyn, one of the earliest missionaries to the Middle East and translator of the Bible into Arabic, Persian, and Urdu (Porter, *Religion Versus Empire*, 212).

31. From Charles Simeon, *Discourses on Behalf of the Jews* (London, 1839), quoted in Michael Ragussis, *Figures of Conversion: "The Jewish Question" and English National Identity* (Durham, N.C.: Duke University Press, 1995), 5.

32. Scult, *Millennial Expectations and Jewish Liberties*, 90. The American counterpart to the London Jews Society was the American Society for Evangelizing the Jews (see Jonathan D. Sarna, "The Impact of Nineteenth-Century Christian Missions on American Jews," in Todd M. Endelman, ed., *Jewish Apostasy in the Modern World*, 232–254 [London: Holmes and Meier, 1987]).

33. Mel Scult, "English Missions to the Jews—Conversion in the Age of Emancipation," *Jewish Social Studies* 35 (1973): 3–17.

34. It is not entirely clear why Frey resigned; some say he was dismissed after a colorful career. On Frey, see Yaron Perry, *British Mission to the Jews in Nineteenth-Century Palestine* (London: Frank Cass, 2003), 15; on Frey's career in America, see George L. Bodin, "Joseph S. C. F. Frey, the Jews, and Early Nineteenth-Century Millenarianism," *Journal of the Early Republic* 1 (1981): 27–49.

35. Scult, "English Missions to the Jews," 7.

36. Robert Michael Smith, "The London Jews' Society and Patterns of Jewish Conversion in England, 1801–1859," *Jewish Social Studies* 43 (1981), 283.

37. From *The Jewish Expositor* (1819), as quoted in ibid., 290 n. 78, emphasis in original.

38. Note the negotiations with Czar Alexander I in 1817 to establish a colony of Jews in the Crimea (Scult, *Millennial Expectations and Jewish Liberties*, 107).

39. Tibawi, *British Interests in Palestine*, 6–7. Although it is not clear why Naudi was interested in promoting Protestant missions, A. L. Tibawi posits that "in the absence of Catholic missions, Protestant missions were a second best or he may have been an opportunist seeking personal advantages" (20). Whatever his motivations, Naudi and later his brother were well received in London.

40. Perry, *British Mission to the Jews*, 15.

41. Kenneth Cragg, "Being Made Disciples—the Middle East," in Ward and Stanley, eds., *The Church Missionary Society and World Christianity*, 122–123.

42. Jowett's assignment quoted in Tibawi, *British Interests in Palestine*, 21, from *Proceedings of the CMS* (1813–1815).

43. Sedra, "John Lieder and His Mission in Egypt," 224. In 1825, the CMS sent a group of continental Lutherans, including John Lieder, from the Basel Seminary to Egypt, their mission being to recall the Coptic Church "to a Biblical faith," but not convert its members to another church. Most missionaries left Egypt for other places, after which a new mission had to make a fresh start. John Lieder worked in Egypt until his death in 1865. See Jocelyn Murray, *Proclaim the Good News: A Short History of the Church Missionary Society* ([London: Hodder and Stoughton, 1985), 33.

44. A short-lived Moravian mission had existed in Egypt in the eighteenth century.

45. Sedra, "John Lieder and His Mission in Egypt," 224.

46. Ibid., 229–231.

47. Quoted in ibid., 231–232.

48. Ibid., 233. The CMS, which worked primarily with urban Copts, focused on formal schooling to raise the educational level of members of the Coptic Church, not to make Copts into Anglicans. John Lieder's training college for Coptic Orthodox priests probably had more to do with the Coptic revival under the Coptic pope Cyril IV (1854–1861). Nevertheless, an Egyptian Episcopal Church on the Anglican model was eventually formed.

49. The first Protestant missionary known to arrive in the Holy Land was Christopher Burkhardt of the Basel Missionary Society (Thomas Stransky, "Origins of Western Christian Missions in Jerusalem and the Holy Land," in Ben-Arieh and Davis, eds., *Jerusalem in the Mind of the Western World*, 137–154.

50. Tibawi, *British Interests in Palestine*, 6–8; 12; see also Reeva Spector Simon, "The Case of the Curse: The London Society for Promoting Christianity Amongst the Jews and the Jews of Baghdad," in Eleanor H. Tejirian and Reeva Spector Simon, eds., *Altruism and Imperialism: Western Cultural and Religious Missions in the Middle East*, 45–65 (New York: Middle East Institute, Columbia University, 2002).

51. Timothy Marr, *The Cultural Roots of American Islamicism* (New York: Cambridge University Press, 2006), 88–89.

52. Joseph L. Grabill, *Protestant Diplomacy and the Near East* (Minneapolis: University of Minnesota Press, 1971), 5.

53. "The Board's ultimate objective in the Near East and elsewhere was nothing less than the winning of all peoples to the kingdom of God" (Vander Werff, *Christian Mission to Muslims*, 103); nevertheless, it was understood early on that Muslims were off limits.

54. Clifton Jackson Phillips, *Protestant America and the Pagan World: The First Half Century of the American Board of Commissioners for Foreign Missions, 1810–1860* (Cambridge, Mass.: Harvard East Asian Monographs, 1969), 135.

55. S. E. Dwight's "Address to the Palestine Society," in R. S. Storrs, *A Sermon . . . at the Ordination of the Rev. Daniel Temple, and Rev. Isaac Bird* (Boston: n.p., 1822), 44, quoted in Phillips, *Protestant America and the Pagan World*, 135.

56. Grabill, *Protestant Diplomacy and the Near East*, 6.

57. Ibid., 7; Robert L. Daniel, *American Philanthropy in the Near East, 1820–1960* (Athens: Ohio State University Press, 1970), 19–20.

58. Ussama Makdisi, *Artillery of Heaven: American Missionaries and the Failed Conversion of the Middle East* (Ithaca, N.Y.: Cornell University Press, 2008), 87; A. L. Tibawi, *American Interests in Syria, 1800–1901: A Study of Educational, Literary, and Religious Work* (Oxford: Clarendon Press, 1966), 14–15.

59. Makdisi, *Artillery of Heaven*, 95–97.

60. Ibid.

61. Ibid., 99.

62. Ibid., 91.

63. Grabill, *Protestant Diplomacy and the Near East*, 7.

64. Ibid.

65. The Greek War of Independence marked the beginning of nearly a century-long process that transformed the Ottoman Empire from an empire that was fairly

evenly divided between Christians and Muslims to one that was predominantly Muslim. It also created a mood of philo-Hellenism in both England and the United States, resulting in the earliest examples of Christian philanthropic engagement with the Middle East. This philanthropic urge dovetailed with and encouraged the missionary enterprise that was developing in the region at the same time. The Greek struggle for independence seized Americans' imagination, opening new opportunities for evangelical work among the Greeks and other Eastern Christians. The AB-CFM sent young Greeks to study in the United States, and several graduated from Amherst and Yale. American sympathy for the Greek revolt spurred the first great American philanthropic effort in the region and in many ways can be seen as prefiguring the response to the Armenian massacres during and after World War I (Daniel, *American Philanthropy in the Near East*, 1–17; Phillips, *Protestant America and the Pagan World*, 139).

66. Charles A. Frazee, *Catholics and Sultans: The Church and the Ottoman Empire, 1453–1923* (New York: Cambridge University Press, 1983), 224.

67. David H. Finnie, *Pioneers East* (Cambridge, Mass.: Harvard University Press, 1967), 171; Tibawi, *American Interests in Syria*, 7.

68. Rev. Charles T. Riggs, "History of the Constantinople Station, 1831–1931," in American Board of Commissioners for Foreign Missions, Near East Mission, ed., *Centennial of the Constantinople Station* (Constantinople: The Mission, 1931), 54.

69. Ibid.

70. Frank Andrews Stone, *Academies for Anatolia: A Study of the Rationale, Program, and Impact of the Educational Institutions Sponsored by the American Board in Turkey: 1830–1980* (Lanham, Md.: University Press of America, 1984), 37.

71. Riggs, "History of the Constantinople Station," 55.

72. Ibid., 57.

73. Finnie, *Pioneers East*, 207.

74. Daniel, *American Philanthropy in the Near East*, 32. Smith and Dwight's book, *Missionary Researches in Armenia: Including a Journey Through Asia Minor, and Into Georgia and Persia* (London: George Wightman, 1834), became a travel classic.

75. Finnie, *Pioneers East*, 209–210.

76. Ibid., 219.

77. Ibid., 228–231.

78. Part of the Assyrian Church had established communion with the Roman Catholic Church in the mid–sixteenth century (see chapter 3). The Nestorians lived primarily on the plains surrounding Mosul and Diyarbekir and were henceforth referred to as "Chaldeans." The Nestorian Church, or the Church of the East, was centered in the Hakkari Mountains of eastern Anatolia and the plains surrounding Urmia in northern Persia.

79. J. F. Coakley, *The Church of the East and the Church of England* (Oxford: Clarendon Press, 1992), 18–19.

80. Ibid., 20–21.

81. Ibid., 25.

82. Quoted in ibid., 24.

83. Chantal Verdeil, "Between Rome and France, Intransigent and Anti-Protestant Jesuits in the Orient: The Beginning of the Jesuits' Mission of Syria, 1831–1864," in Martin Tamcke and Michael Marten, eds., *Christian Witness Between Continuity and New Beginnings: Modern Historical Missions in the Middle East* (Berlin: Lit, 2006), 23–24.

84. Edwin Hodder, *The Life and Work of the Seventh Earl of Shaftesbury, K. G.*, 3 vols. (London: Cassell, 1888), 1:310–315.

85. The story is related in detail in Tibawi, *British Interests in Palestine*, 37–57. Pertinent documents are published in Albert M. Hyamson, *The British Consulate in Jerusalem in Relation to the Jews of Palestine, 1838–1914*, 2 vols. (London: Jewish Historical Society of England and Edward Goldston, 1939).

86. Historians continue to debate the nature of missionary influence on Palmerston's policy. Tibawi advocates the position that his policy did have a missionary aspect, whereas Meir Verété maintains that political and commercial considerations held sway (Tibawi, *British Interests in Palestine*, 42; Meir Verété, "The Restoration of the Jews in English Protestant Thought," *Middle Eastern Studies* 8 [1972]: 3–50). The problem in the relationship with missionaries continued throughout the regime of Bishop Alexander.

87. Tibawi, *British Interests in Palestine*, 37.

88. Ibid., 67; see also Michael Marten, *Attempting to Bring the Gospel Home: Scottish Missions to Palestine, 1839–1917* (London: Tauris Academic Studies, 2006).

89. See Jonathan Frankel, *The Damascus Affair* (New York: Cambridge University Press, 1997).

90. French and Prussian consulates were established in 1843.

91. Although the British did not have permission to build a church, another London Jews Society missionary, the Dane John Nicholayson, who had been in Jerusalem since the 1820s, was already overseeing the construction of a chapel despite the fact that the building was illegal (Thomas Hummel, "Between Eastern and Western Christendom: The Anglican Presence in Jerusalem," in Anthony O'Mahony, ed., *The Christian Communities of Jerusalem and the Holy Land: Studies in History, Religion, and Politics* (Cardiff, U.K.: University of Wales Press, 2003), 149–152.

92. Tibawi, *British Interests in Palestine*, 50.

93. Endelman, *Radical Assimilation in English Jewish History*, 158–159.

94. Hyamson, *The British Consulate in Jerusalem*, 1:xxxvii–xxxviii, 46–47; Tibawi, *British Interests in Palestine*, 55–57.

95. John Pinnington, "Church Principles in the Early Years of the Church Missionary Society: The Problem of the 'German' Missionaries," *Journal of Theological Studies*, new series, 20 (1969), 528.

96. Martin Lückhoff, "Prussia and Jerusalem: Political and Religious Controversies Surrounding the Foundation of the Jerusalem Bishopric," in Ben-Arieh and Davis, eds., *Jerusalem in the Mind of the Western World*, 181.

97. Haim Goren, "The German Catholic 'Holy Sepulchre Society': Activities in Palestine," in Ben-Arieh and Davis, eds., *Jerusalem in the Mind of the Western World*, 156–157; Foerster, "German Missions in the Holy Land," 191.

98. Steven Epperson, "Dedicating and Consecrating the Land: Mormon Ritual Performance in Palestine," in Eli Lederhendler and Jonathan D. Sarna, eds., *America and Zion: Essays and Papers in Memory of Moshe Davis* (Detroit: Wayne State University Press, 2002), 92.

99. Ibid., 96–97. Consistent with other Protestant groups, by the end of the nineteenth century the Mormons recalibrated their theology to pursue conversion of the Jews.

5. Missionaries and European Diplomatic Competition

1. Issues in the Holy Land were only part of Russian interest in a revived Byzantine Empire, a Christian empire in the eastern Mediterranean. Plans were considered but not implemented at the end of the eighteenth century and beginning of the nineteenth century during the reigns of czars Catherine II and Paul I (Adam Knobler, "Holy Wars, Empires, and the Portability of the Past: The Modern Uses of Medieval Crusades," *Comparative Studies in Society and History* 48 [2006], 301–305, 308–309).

2. For centuries, Russia had claimed a special relationship with the Greek Church of Constantinople, regarding itself as the legitimate heir of the Byzantine Empire. It is this claim that was confirmed in the Treaty of Kuchuk Kainarji.

3. Anthony O'Mahony, "The Latins of the East: The Vatican, Jerusalem, and the Palestinian Christians," in Anthony O'Mahony, ed., *The Christian Communities of Jerusalem and the Holy Land: Studies in History, Religion, and Politics* (Cardiff, U.K.: University of Wales Press, 2003), 100.

4. The Vatican rejected the Franciscan monopoly over Catholic rights and established a Latin patriarchate backed by French diplomacy, illustrating French rather than Habsburg dominance (O'Mahony, "The Latins of the East," 100).

5. During the Crusades, the Greek Orthodox patriarch lived in Constantinople and returned to Jerusalem after the Mamluk conquest. During that time, the patriarch was chosen from local Orthodox Arab candidates. Under Ottoman rule (1517), the Greek patriarch who was placed in Jerusalem initiated the custom of nominating a Greek successor not living in Jerusalem but instead from Constantinople (Derek Hopwood, *The Russian Presence in Syria and Palestine 1843–1914: Church and Politics in the Near East* [Oxford: Clarendon Press, 1969], 20–21). The Greek patriarch represented all Christians in Jerusalem.

6. Yehoshua Ben-Arieh, "Patterns of Christian Activity and Dispersion in Nineteenth-Century Jerusalem," *Journal of Historical Geography* 2 (1976), 56–57.

7. Alex Carmel, "Russian Activity in Palestine in the Nineteenth Century," in Richard I. Cohen, ed., *Vision and Conflict in the Holy Land* (New York: St. Martin's Press, 1985), 48–49; see also Eileen M. Kane, "Pilgrims, Piety, and Politics: The Founding of the First Russian Ecclesiastical Mission in Jerusalem," in Martin Tamcke and Michael Marten, eds., *Christian Witness Between Continuity and New Beginnings: Modern Historical Missions in the Middle East* (Berlin: Lit, 2006), 178–179, 187.

8. The Russian consulate established in Jaffa in 1820 was moved to Beirut in 1839 so that Russia could better protect its pilgrims and provide a more effective voice in Constantinople.

9. Quoted is Carmel, "Russian Activity in Palestine," 57; the information regarding the controversial Russian emissary is from Theofanis George Stavrou, "Russian Interest in the Levant 1843–1848," *Middle East Journal* 17 (1963): 91–103; and Hopwood, *The Russian Presence in Syria and Palestine*, 33–45. See also Rachel Simon, "The Struggle Over the Christian Holy Places During the Ottoman Period," in Cohen, ed., *Vision and Conflict in the Holy Land*, 23–44.

10. Hopwood, *The Russian Presence in Syria and Palestine*, 47. See also Orlando Figes, *The Crimean War: A History* (New York: Metropolitan Books, 2010), 1–23.

11. In the Concordat of 1801, which Napoleon negotiated with Pope Pius VII, the place of the clergy and church property were regulated; France made a commitment to protect Catholic missionaries abroad. Napoleon reestablished the Lazarist seminary of St. Esprit and the Société des missions étrangères but ordered that they be merged and placed under the control of the archbishop of Paris and thus, by extension, the French state (J. P. Daughton, *An Empire Divided: Religion, Republicanism, and the Making of French Colonialism 1880–1914* [New York: Oxford University Press, 2006], 33–34).

12. Mathew Burrows, "'*Mission Civilisatrice*': French Cultural Policy in the Middle East, 1860–1914," *Historical Journal* 29 (1986), 112, 116. Note that the missionaries in Istanbul were also Italian.

13. Quoted in Jonathan Riley-Smith, "Islam and the Crusades in History and Imagination, 8 November 1898–11 September 2001," *Crusades* 2 (2003), 156.

14. Ibid. 155–156; Knobler, "Holy Wars, Empires, and the Portability of the Past," 293–325.

15. J. Dean O'Donnell Jr., *Lavigerie in Tunisia: The Interplay of Imperialist and Missionary* (Athens: University of Georgia Press, 1979), 4–5. From 1830 until the 1860s, the policy of the French governors of Algeria was separation rather than assimilation. France fostered colonial settlement in Algeria but religious and ethnic separation rather than religious proselytization among the Muslims in order to keep the peace. On French colonial policy, see Robert Aldrich, *Greater France: A History of French Overseas Expansion* (New York: Palgrave, 1996).

16. On the Jesuit conspiracy theory, see Geoffrey Cubitt, *The Jesuit Myth: Conspiracy Theory and Politics in Nineteenth-Century France* (Oxford: Clarendon Press, 1993).

17. In 1831, Fathers Planchet and Riccadonna accompanied Monsigneur Mazlum, a Greek Catholic Melkite staying at Rome, to Syria to become spiritual directors of a reopened Greek Catholic seminary on Mount Lebanon. The struggle between locals and the Jesuits for control of the church illustrated that Jesuits needed local support for their work (Chantal Verdeil, "Between Rome and France, Intransigent and Anti-Protestant Jesuits in the Orient: The Beginning of the Jesuits' Mission of Syria, 1831–1864," in Tamcke and Marten, eds., *Christian Witness Between Continuity and New Beginnings*, 24–26; Burrows, "'*Mission Civilisatrice*,'" 114–115; see also Ussama Makdisi, *The Culture of Sectarianism: Community, History, and Violence in Nineteenth Century*

Ottoman Lebanon [Berkeley and Los Angeles: University of California Press, 2000], 88–89).

18. Verdeil, "Between Rome and France," 23–27; Burrows, "*Mission Civilisatrice*," 114–115.

19. James J. Laffey, "The Roots of French Imperialism in the Nineteenth Century: The Case of Lyon," *French Historical Studies* 6 (1969): 78–92.

20. Ibid.

21. Quoted in Thomas Stransky, "Origins of Western Christian Missions in Jerusalem and the Holy Land," in Yehoshua Ben-Arieh and Moshe Davis, eds., *Jerusalem in the Mind of the Western World, 1800–1948*, With Eyes Toward Zion V (Westport, Conn.: Praeger, 1997), 148.

22. Stransky, "Origins of Western Christian Missions," 148–149. In 1291, the position of the Latin patriarch had died when Acre was taken by the Muslims. The title survived in Europe with a Latin titular prelate who had jurisdictional power until it was restored in 1847 (O'Mahony, "The Latins of the East," 99).

23. Burrows, "*Mission Civilisatrice*," 1170; see also Bernard Heyberger and Chantal Verdeil, "Spirituality and Scholarship: The Holy Land in Jesuit Eyes (Seventeenth to Nineteenth Centuries)," in Heleen Murre-van den Berg, ed., *New Faith in Ancient Lands: Western Missions in the Middle East in the Nineteenth and Early Twentieth Centuries* (Leiden: Brill, 2006), 22–23. Latin missions were established in Jordan after the Crimean War (Eugene L. Rogan, *Frontiers of the State in the Late Ottoman Empire: Transjordan 1850–1921* [Cambridge: Cambridge University Press, 1999], 124–125).

24. Elizabeth Thompson, "Neither Conspiracy nor Hypocrisy: The Jesuits and the French Mandate in Syria and Lebanon," in Eleanor H. Tejirian and Reeva Spector Simon, eds., *From Altruism to Imperialism: Western Cultural and Religious Missions in the Middle East* (New York: Middle East Institute, Columbia University, 2002), 73.

25. Charles A. Frazee, *Catholics and Sultans: The Church and the Ottoman Empire, 1453–1923* (New York: Cambridge University Press, 1983), 226–227, 306–307.

26. Burrows, "*Mission Civilisatrice*," 117–118.

27. O'Donnell, *Lavigerie in Tunisia*, 2.

28. Note the Anglo–Persian War of 1856–1857 while Russia was still occupied in the Crimea.

29. Bruce Masters, *Christians and Jews in the Ottoman Arab World: The Roots of Sectarianism* (New York: Cambridge University Press, 2001), 158. See also Bruce Masters, "The 1850 Events in Aleppo: An Aftershock of Syria's Incorporation in the Capitalist World System," *International Journal of Middle East Studies* 22 (1990): 3–20.

30. Ussama Makdisi, "Reclaiming the Land of the Bible: Missionaries, Secularism, and Evangelical Modernity," *American Historical Review* 102 (1997): 680–713. On the events of 1860, see Caesar E. Farah, *The Politics of Interventionism in Ottoman Lebanon 1830–1861* (London: Centre for Lebanese Studies in association with I. B. Tauris, 2000).

31. Makdisi, "Reclaiming the Land of the Bible," 704.

32. Quoted in Verdeil, "Between Rome and France," 30–31.

33. Burrows, "*'Mission Civilisatrice*,'" 116; Yaha Armajani, "Christian Missionaries in Persia," in *Encyclopaedia Iranica* 5, available at http://www.iranica.com/newsite/articles/unicode/v5f5/v5f5a018.html.

34. See Charlotte van der Leest, "The Protestant Bishopric of Jerusalem and the Missionary Activities in Nazareth: The Gobat Years, 1846–1879," in Tamcke and Marten, eds., *Christian Witness Between Continuity and New Beginnings*, 199–211.

35. Thomas Hummel, "Between Eastern and Western Christendom: The Anglican Presence in Jerusalem," in O'Mahony, ed., *The Christian Communities of Jerusalem and the Holy Land*, 153–154; A. L. Tibawi, *British Interests in Palestine 1800–1901: A Study in Religious and Educational Enterprise* (London: Oxford University Press, 1961), 104–105.

36. Rogan, *Frontiers of the State in the Late Ottoman Empire*, 127; Lyle L. Vander Werff, *Christian Mission to Muslims—the Record: Anglican and Reformed Approaches in India and the Near East, 1800–1938* (South Pasadena, Calif.: William Carey Library, 1977), 157; Andrew Porter, *Religion Versus Empire? British Protestant Missionaries and Overseas Expansion, 1700–1914* (Manchester, U.K.: Manchester University Press, 2004), 167–168. Son of the Reverend John Venn, who was a founder of the Clapham Sect, Henry Venn advocated the development of indigenous churches through what became known as his "three selves" formula—self-financing, self-governing, and self-propagating (C. Peter Williams, "The Church Missionary Society and the Indigenous Church in the Second Half of the Nineteenth Century: The Defense and Destruction of the Venn Ideals," in Dana L. Robert, ed., *Converting Colonialism: Visions and Realities in Mission History, 1700–1914*, 86–111 [Grand Rapids, Mich.: Eerdmans, 2008]).

37. Frank Foerster, "German Missionaries in the Holy Land," in Ben-Arieh and Davis, eds., *Jerusalem in the Mind of the Western World*, 183–194. An offshoot of the German pietist movement, the German Templer Society, organized in Wurttemberg, subscribed to the belief that true Christians should seek refuge in the East and await the Day of Judgment. The movement broke with the Evangelical Church when its leader, Christoph Hoffmann (1815–1885), despairing after 1848 that the existing church had failed, advocated that true believers—"the People of God" (*das Volk Gottes*)—would rescue mankind from the pervasive anti-Christian spirit. When at the end of the Crimean War it seemed that the Ottoman Empire was on the verge of collapse, Hoffmann deemed the time ripe for the "People of God" to take control of Palestine, whose heir, although it had been promised to the Jews, was Hoffman's group because the biblical Jews no longer existed. From 1868 to 1875, more than one-fourth of the movement—some 750 persons—settled in Palestine. Because of harsh conditions, lack of support back in Germany, and a lack of understanding of the theological differences that initiated the break with the Evangelical Church, the Templer movement changed its emphasis: it worked to improve the situation in the Holy Land and to provide a good example. The implementation of these goals led to the establishment of seven settlements in Palestine: Haifa and Jaffa (1869); Sarona (1871); Jerusalem (1878); Wilhelma (1902); Galilean Bethlehem (1906); Waldheim (1907). Based primarily in agricultural settlements, the Templers engaged in commerce, trade, industry, tourist promotion, and various free professions. They introduced modern farming methods, wheeled transportation, steam-operated flour mills, and hotels on a European stan-

dard. On the Templers, see Alex Carmel, "The German Settlers in Palestine and Their Relations with the Local Arab Population and the Jewish Community, 1868–1918," in Moshe Ma'oz, ed., *Studies on Palestine During the Ottoman Period*, 442–465 (Jerusalem: Magnes Press, 1975); and Alex Carmel, "The Political Significance of German Settlement in Palestine, 1868–1918," in Jehuda L. Wallach, ed., *Germany and the Middle East, 1835–1939*, International Symposium, April 1975, 45–71 (Tel Aviv: Institute of German History, 1975).

38. Foerster, "German Missionaries in the Holy Land," 188–189.

39. Kenneth Scott Latourette, *A History of the Expansion of Christianity*, 7 vols. (New York: Harper & Brothers, 1937–1945), 6:27; see also Uwe Kaminsky, "German 'Home Mission' Abroad: The *Orientarbeit* of the Deaconess Institution Kaiserwerth in the Ottoman Empire," in Murre-van den Berg, ed., *New Faith in Ancient Lands*, 191–209.

40. Quoted in Foerster, "German Missionaries in the Holy Land," 184–185.

41. Ruth Kark, Dietrich Denecke, and Haim Goren, "The Impact of Early German Missionary Enterprise in Palestine on the Modernization and Environmental and Technological Change, 1820–1914," in Tamcke and Marten, eds., *Christian Witness Between Continuity and New Beginnings*, 153.

42. Tibawi, *British Interests in Palestine*, 86–121. Thomas Hummel questions whether Gobat orchestrated or tolerated the policy to direct missionary work to Eastern Christians—contravening the British government's initial charge to Bishop Alexander (Hummel, "Between Eastern and Western Christendom"; see also Beth-Zion Lask Abrahams, "James Finn: Her Britannic Majesty's Consul at Jerusalem Between 1846 and 1863," *Transactions of the Jewish Historical Society of England* 27 (1982): 40–50.

43. Ruth Kark, "The Impact of Early Missionary Enterprises on Landscape and Identity Formation in Palestine, 1820–1914," *Islam and Christian–Muslim Relations* 15 (2004), 215.

44. Kark, Denecke, and Goren, "The Impact of Early German Missionary Enterprise in Palestine," 151. In 1884, Scottish missionaries proselytized among Jews in Tiberius (Michael Marten, "Imperialism and Evangelization: Scottish Missionary Methods in Late 19th and Early 20th Century Palestine," *Holy Land Studies* 6 [2006]: 155–186).

45. Hummel, "Between Eastern and Western Christendom," 156–160; Michael Marten, "Anglican and Presbyterian Presence and Theology in the Holy Land," *International Journal for the Study of the Christian Church* 5 (2005): 182–199.

46. From the British perspective, all Assyrians were Nestorians. Members of the Assyrian Uniate Church are referred to as Chaldeans.

47. Eugene Stock, *The History of the Church Missionary Society: Its Environment, Its Men, and Its Work*, 3 vols. (London: Church Missionary Society, 1899), 2:151–155.

48. Vander Werff, *Christian Mission to Muslims*, 100–102.

49. J. F. Coakley, *The Church of the East and the Church of England* (Oxford: Clarendon Press, 1992), 34.

50. Quoted in ibid.

51. Ibid., 35.

52. Ibid., 38.

53. Quoted in ibid., 39.

54. Stock, *The History of the Church Missionary Society*, 2:142.

55. Latourette, *A History of the Expansion of Christianity*, 6:54.

56. Heather J. Sharkey, *American Evangelicals in Egypt: Missionary Encounters in an Age of Empire* (Princeton, N.J.: Princeton University Press, 2008), 18.

57. Ibid., 27, 35; Vander Werff, *Christian Mission to Muslims*, 144–146.

58. Sharkey, *American Evangelicals in Egypt*, 32.

59. Latourette, *A History of the Expansion of Christianity*, 6:26.

60. The extent to which the organization of Armenian Protestant churches was a vehicle for the expression of dissent within the Armenian community is difficult to define. Certainly, several of the early Armenian Protestant ministers were Armenian priests whom the patriarch in Istanbul had sent into exile.

61. Frank Andrews Stone, *Academies for Anatolia: A Study of the Rationale, Program, and Impact of the Educational Institutions Sponsored by the American Board in Turkey, 1830–1980* (Lanham, Md.: University Press of America, 1984), 70.

62. Ibid., 72.

63. Ibid.

64. Amy Porterfield, *Mary Lyon and the Mount Holyoke Missionaries* (New York: Oxford University Press, 1997), 69–70.

65. David H. Finnie, *Pioneers East* (Cambridge, Mass.: Harvard University Press, 1967), 235.

66. Ibid., 238, 239.

67. Ibid., 235.

68. See also Sara D. Shields, *Mosul Before Iraq: Like Bees Making Five-Sided Cells* (Albany: State University of New York Press, 2000), 52–58.

69. Ibid., 239–241.

70. Vander Werff, *Christian Mission to Muslims*, 108.

71. Porter, *Religion Versus Empire?* 189, 217–218.

72. Quoted in Porter, *Religion Versus Empire?* 218–219. See also Brian Stanley, "Christian Responses to the Indian Mutiny of 1857," in W. J. Sheils, ed., *The Church and War: Papers Read at the Twenty-First Summer Meeting and the Twenty-Second Winter Meeting of the Ecclesiastical Society*, 277–289 (London: Blackwell, 1983); and Olive Anderson, "The Growth of Christian Militarism in Mid-Victorian Britain," *English Historical Review* 86 (1971): 46–72.

73. Quoted in Stewart J. Brown, *Providence and Empire 1815–1914: Religion, Politics, and Society in the United Kingdom 1815–1914* (New York: Longman, 2008), 206.

74. Andrew Porter, "'Commerce and Christianity': The Rise and Fall of a Nineteenth-Century Missionary Slogan," *Historical Journal* 28 (1985), 617.

6. The Imperialist Moment

1. The Church of the Redeemer is a faithful copy of the medieval church that is buried beneath it and known by the Persian name "Muristan"; it is one of three

churches in the complex built in the twelfth century by the Order of St. John during the Crusades; the complex included a hospital. See Thorsten Neubert-Preine, "The Founding of German Protestant Institutions in Jerusalem During the Reign of Kaiser Wilhelm II," in Haim Goren, ed., *Germany and the Middle East: Past, Present, and Future*, 27–33 (Jerusalem: Magnes Press, 2003).

2. Quoted in Frank Foerster, "German Missions in the Holy Land," in Yehoshua Ben-Arieh and Moshe Davis, eds., *Jerusalem in the Mind of the Western World, 1800–1948*, With Eyes Toward Zion V (Westport, Conn.: Praeger, 1997), 187–188.

3. Philipp Prein, "Mission to Arcadia: The Moravian Invention of an African Missionary Object as an Example of the Culture of German Nationalism and Colonialism," *German History* 16 (1998): 328–357.

4. Haim Goren, "The German Catholic 'Holy Sepulchre Society': Activities in Palestine," in Ben-Arieh and Davis, eds., *Jerusalem in the Mind of the Western World*, 155.

5. Kenneth Scott Latourette, *A History of the Expansion of Christianity*, 7 vols. (New York: Harper & Brothers, 1937–1945), 6:38. The Franciscans sought to retain their monopoly on schools in Jerusalem, and the French government began to support other French orders, such as Charles-Martial-Allemand Lavigerie's White Fathers Seminary for Melchites, Fathers of Sion, Dominicans, Assumptionists, Trappists, Benedictines, Carmelites, and Lazarists.

6. Goren, "The German Catholic 'Holy Sepulchre Society,'" 155–165.

7. Godehard Hoffmann, "Kaiser Wilhelm II und der Benediktinerorden," *Zeitschrift für Kirchengeschichte* 106, no. 3 (1995): 363–384.

8. Jonathan Riley-Smith, "Islam and the Crusades in History and Imagination, 8 November 1898–11 September 2001," *Crusades* 2 (2003), 151–152.

9. As noted in chapter 5, Mathew Burrows estimates that there were 3,397 Catholic missionaries in the Ottoman Empire in 1904, compared to only 11 Lazarists there in 1824; the majority were French (Mathew Burrows, "'Mission Civilizatrice': French Cultural Policy in the Middle East, 1860–1914," *Historical Journal* 29 [1986], 116).

10. Elizabeth Thompson, "Neither Conspiracy nor Hypocrisy: The Jesuits and the French Mandate in Syria and Lebanon," in Eleanor H. Tejirian and Reeva Spector Simon, eds., *From Altruism to Imperialism: Western Cultural and Religious Missions in the Middle East* (New York: Middle East Institute, Columbia University, 2002), 68–69.

11. Latourette, *A History of the Expansion of Christianity*, 6:38; Eugene L. Rogan, *Frontiers of the State in the Late Ottoman Empire: Transjordan 1850–1921* (Cambridge: Cambridge University Press, 1999), 122–159; J. P. Daughton, *An Empire Divided: Religion, Republicanism, and the Making of French Colonialism, 1880–1914* (New York: Oxford University Press, 2006), 52–55; Dominique Trimbur, "A French Presence in Palestine—Notre Dame de France," *Bulletin du Centre de Recherche Français de Jérusalem* 3 (1998): 117–140.

12. J. P. Spagnolo, "The Definition of a Style of Imperialism: The Internal Politics of French Educational Investment in Ottoman Beirut," *French Historical Studies* 8 (1974), 581.

13. These anticlericals included Jules Ferry and Léon Gambetta (J. Dean O'Donnell Jr., *Lavigerie in Tunisia: The Interplay of Imperialist and Missionary* [Athens: University of Georgia Press, 1979], 13; see also François Renault, *Cardinal Lavigerie: Churchman, Prophet, and Missionary*, trans. John O'Donohue [London: Athlone Press, 1994], and Bradley Rainbow Hale, "The Soul of Empire: The Society of Missionaries of Africa in Colonial Algeria, 1919–1939," Ph.D. diss., University of Connecticut, 2005).

14. O'Donnell, *Lavigerie in Tunisia*, 1–22.

15. Ibid., 12.

16. Ibid., 17–18. The recent film *Of Gods and Men* (2010) demonstrates Lavigerie's methodology.

17. Quoted in Robert Aldrich, *Greater France: A History of French Overseas Expansion* (New York: Palgrave, 1996), 129.

18. Quoted in O'Donnell, *Lavigerie in Tunisia*, 19–20.

19. Jean-Louis Miège, "Les Missions Protestantes au Maroc, 1875–1905," *Hespéris* 42 (1955): 153–186.

20. Quoted in O'Donnell, *Lavigerie in Tunisia*, 20–21, emphasis added by O'Donnell.

21. Aldrich, *Greater France*, 128–129.

22. Despite the outlawing of Jesuit schools and the exiling of Jesuits from France in 1880, the ban on religious schools in Lyon was not rigorously enforced.

23. Thompson, "Neither Conspiracy nor Hypocrisy," 70–71; on the Catholic revival in France and the popularity of the pilgrimage to Lourdes, see Eugen Weber, *From Peasants Into Frenchmen: The Modernization of Rural France, 1870–1914* (Stanford, Calif.: Stanford University Press, 1976), 370–371, 354.

24. Annette Renee Chapman-Adisho, "*Mission Civilisatrice* to Mandate: The French and Education in Syria and Lebanon," master's thesis, University of Louisville, 1998, 60–61.

25. Quoted in William Shorrock, "Anti-Clericalism and French Policy in the Ottoman Empire, 1900–1914," *European Studies Review* 4 (1974), 37.

26. Latourette, *A History of the Expansion of Christianity*, 6:8.

27. Thompson, "Neither Conspiracy nor Hypocrisy," 72.

28. Shorrock, "Anti-Clericalism and French Policy," 38–40.

29. Ibid., 48–49.

30. Randi Deguilhem, "Turning Syrians into Frenchmen: The Cultural Politics of a French Non-Governmental Organization in Mandate Syria (1920–1967)—the French Secular Mission Schools," *Islam and Christian–Muslim Civilization* 13 (2002), 452.

31. Quoted in Shorrock, "Anti-Clericalism and French Policy," 43; see also Burrows, "'*Mission Civilizatrice*,'" 132–133.

32. Quoted in George M. Marsden, *Fundamentalism and American Culture*, 2nd ed. (New York: Oxford University Press, 2006), 11.

33. Randall Balmer, *Encyclopedia of Evangelism* (Waco, Tex.: Baylor University Press, 2004), 467; see also Stewart J. Brown, *Providence and Empire 1815–1914: Religion, Politics, and Society in the United Kingdom 1815–1914* (New York: Longman, 2008), 278–

282, 381. According to Balmer, Moody's eschatology "drifted more and more toward premillennialism and away from social reclamation" (467).

34. Because the Hamidian regime of the Ottoman Empire regarded all youth organizations as seditious, YMCAs developed more easily after the Young Turks came to power in 1908.

35. Robert L. Daniel, *American Philanthropy in the Near East, 1820–1960* (Athens: Ohio State University Press, 1970),184–186; William J. Baker, "To Pray or to Play? The YMCA Question in the United Kingdom and the United States, 1850–1900," *International Journal of the History of Sport* 11 (1994): 42–62.

36. Marsden, *Fundamentalism and American Culture*, 35.

37. Brown, *Providence and Empire*, 283. Some revivalists took to uniforms and military bands. With the growing public support for military and imperial heroes in 1878, the Christian Society renamed itself the "Salvation Army" and declared war on "home heathenism" (ibid., 284).

38. Balmer, *Encyclopedia of Evangelism*, 597–598.

39. Lyrics by Sabine Baring-Gould and music by Arthur S. Sullivan, available at http://www.hymnsite.com/lyrics/umh575.sht.

40. Andrew Porter, *Religion Versus Empire? British Protestant Missionaries and Overseas Expansion, 1700–1914* (Manchester, U.K.: Manchester University Press, 2004), 220. A major conference to plan strategy on missions to "Mohammedans" was convened at CMS House in 1875.

41. Latourette, *A History of the Expansion of Christianity*, 6:24.

42. Rev. W. S. Dumergue, "C.M.S. Work Among the Mohammedans," *Church Missionary Intelligence* (January 1882), quoted in Porter, *Religion Versus Empire*, 215–216.

43. Porter, *Religion Versus Empire?*, 223.

44. Lyle L. Vander Werff, *Christian Missions to Muslims—the Record: Anglican and Reformed Approaches to India and the Near East, 1800–1938* (South Pasadena, Calif.: William Carey Library, 1977), 158–159.

45. Latourette, *A History of the Expansion of Christianity*, 6:24.

46. Quoted in Porter, *Religion Versus Empire?*, 222.

47. Ibid.; Stephen Neill, *A History of Christian Missions*, 2nd ed., revised by Owen Chadwick (New York: Penguin, 1986), 310–311.

48. Fatma al-Sayegh, "American Missionaries in the UAE Region in the Twentieth Century," *Middle Eastern Studies* 32 (1996), 124.

49. Thomas S. Kidd, *American Christians and Islam: Evangelical Culture and Muslims from the Colonial Period to the Age of Terrorism* (Princeton, N.J.: Princeton University Press, 2009), 59–61.

50. Al-Sayegh, "American Missionaries in the UAE Region," 128.

51. Quoted in J. F. Coakley, *The Church of the East and the Church of England* (Oxford: Clarendon Press, 1992), 56.

52. John Joseph, *The Modern Assyrians of the Middle East: Encounters with Western Christian Missions, Archaeologists, and Colonial Powers* (Leiden: Brill, 2000), 99.

53. Quoted in Coakley, *The Church of the East and the Church of England*, 69.

54. Joseph, *The Modern Assyrians of the Middle East*, 110–113.

55. Coakley, *The Church of the East and the Church of England*, 80–81.

56. Ibid., 100.

57. Ibid., 114.

58. Ibid., 123.

59. Ibid., 187–188.

60. Ibid, 213–214.

61. The number of Orthodox Christians in Palestine declined from 90 percent of the Christian population in 1840 to 67 percent in 1880, whereas during the same period the Catholic population rose from three thousand to thirteen thousand (Derek Hopwood, *The Russian Presence in Syria and Palestine, 1843–1914: Church and Politics in the Near East* [Oxford: Clarendon Press, 1969], 100, 210–211). See also Derek Hopwood, "'The Resurrection of Our Eastern Brethren' (Ignatiev): Russia and Orthodox Arab Nationalism in Jerusalem," in Moshe Ma'oz, ed., *Studies on Palestine During the Ottoman Period*, 394–407 (Jerusalem: Magnes Press, 1975); Alex Carmel, "Russian Activity in Palestine in the Nineteenth Century," in Richard I. Cohen, ed., *Vision and Conflict in the Holy Land*, 45–77 (New York: St. Martin's Press, 1985); and Yehoshua Ben-Arieh, "Patterns of Christian Activity and Dispersion in Nineteenth-Century Jerusalem." *Journal of Historical Geography* 2 (1976): 49–69.

62. Hopwood, *The Russian Presence in Syria and Palestine*, 117, 131.

63. On Russia's ambivalence about whether to tolerate or proselytize Muslims, see Daniel Brower, "Russian Roads to Mecca: Religious Tolerance and Muslim Pilgrimage in the Russian Empire," *Slavic Review* 55 (1996): 567–584.

64. Joseph, *The Modern Assyrians of the Middle East*, 103.

65. Ibid., 100–101.

66. Coakley, *The Church of the East and the Church of England*, 112.

67. Ibid., 219.

68. Ibid., 221.

69. Ibid., 231, 243, 279, 317.

70. Ibid., 319–320.

71. Ibid., 259, 264.

72. Ibid., 309.

73. Joseph, *The Modern Assyrians of the Middle East*, 129.

74. Coakley, *The Church of the East and the Church of England*, 318.

75. The Anglicans, for whom reform of the Eastern churches remained a primary goal, avoided establishing new churches. There was clearly a political aspect to this decision because the formation of new Anglican churches was thought to give the members the prospect of a "special relationship" with the British.

76. Kidd, *American Christians and Islam*, 58–64.

77. To celebrate the centennial of the 1910 conference in Edinburgh, the World Missionary Conference was convened again in Edinburgh in June 2010 with the motto "Witnessing to Christ Today." Eight commissions worked for several years on a variety of subjects. The new motto and topics concern the changes in the missionary

enterprise over the past century. Roman Catholics and representatives of the Eastern churches were included this time.

7. Achievements and Consequences—Intended and Unintended

1. John A. DeNovo, *American Interests and Policies in the Middle East 1900–1939* (Minneapolis: University of Minnesota Press, 1963), 96. In the Ottoman Empire, there were more than three thousand Catholic missionaries (Mathew Burrows, *"Mission Civilisatrice"*: French Cultural Policy in the Middle East, 1860–1914," *Historical Journal* 29 [1986], 116).

2. Charles A. Frazee, *Catholics and Sultans: The Church and the Ottoman Empire, 1453–1923* (New York: Cambridge University Press, 1983), 312–313.

3. Paul D. Sedra, "John Lieder and His Mission in Egypt: The Evangelical Ethos at Work Among Nineteenth Century Copts," *Journal of Religious History* 28 (2004), 226–227.

4. Samy F. Zaka, "Education and Civilization in the Third Republic: The University of Saint-Joseph, 1875–1914," Ph.D. diss., University of Notre Dame, 2006, 128–129.

5. Randi Deguilhem, "Turning Syrians into Frenchmen: The Cultural Politics of a French Non-Governmental Organization in Mandate Syria (1920–1967)—the French Secular Mission Schools," *Islam and Christian–Muslim Relations* 13 (2002), 451–452; Marta Petricioli, "Italian Schools in Egypt," *British Journal of Middle Eastern Studies* 24 (1997): 179–191; Aron Rodrigue, *French Jews, Turkish Jews: The Alliance Israélite Universelle and the Politics of Jewish Schooling in Turkey 1860–1925* (Bloomington: Indiana University Press, 1990), 75–76.

6. Vickie Langohr, "Colonial Education Systems and the Spread of Local Religious Movements: The Cases of British Egypt and Punjab," *Comparative Studies in Society and History* 47 (2005), 166.

7. Ussama Makdisi, "Reclaiming the Land of the Bible: Missionaries, Secularism, and Evangelical Modernity," *American Historical Review* 102 (1997): 680–713; A. L. Tibawi, "The Genesis and Early History of the Syrian Protestant College (Part II)," *Middle East Journal* 21 (1967): 199–212.

8. Michael Adas, *Machines as the Measure of Men: Science, Technology, and Ideologies of Western Dominance* (Ithaca, N.Y.: Cornell University Press, 1989); Fruma Zachs, "From the Mission to the Missionary: The Bliss Family and the Syrian Protestant College (1866–1920)," *Die Welt des Islams* 45 (2005), 277–278.

9. Dana L. Robert, "The 'Christian Home' as a Cornerstone of Anglo-Missionary Thought and Practice," in Dana L. Robert, ed., *Converting Colonialism: Visions and Realities in Mission History, 1706–1914* (Grand Rapids, Mich.: Eerdmans, 2008), 134–140.

10. Ibid., 143, 145–146.

11. Amanda Porterfield, *Mary Lyon and the Mount Holyoke Missionaries* (New York: Oxford University Press, 1997), 64.

12. Ibid., 70.

13. Ibid., 6.

14. Carolyn McCue Goffman, "Masking the Mission: Cultural Conversion in the American College for Girls," in Eleanor H. Tejirian and Reeva Spector Simon, eds., *Altruism and Imperialism: Western Cultural and Religious Missions in the Middle East* (New York: Middle East Institute, Columbia University, 2002), 91.

15. Frank Andrews Stone, *Academies for Anatolia: A Study of the Rationale, Program, and Impact of the Educational Institutions Sponsored by the American Board in Turkey, 1830–1980* (Lanham, Md.: University Press of America, 1984), 82–86.

16. Ibid., 90.

17. Ibid., 105.

18. Ibid., 116, 117, 119.

19. Ibid., 122.

20. Ibid., 127–129.

21. Ibid., 194.

22. Ibid., 207.

23. Ibid., 209.

24. Ibid., 215.

25. Ibid., 255.

26. Ibid., 256.

27. Ussama Makdisi, *Artillery of Heaven: American Missionaries and the Failed Conversion of the Middle East* (Ithaca, N.Y.: Cornell University Press, 2008).

28. Paul D. Sedra, "Modernity's Mission: Evangelical Efforts to Discipline the Nineteenth-Century Coptic Community," in Tejirian and Simon, eds., *Altruism and Imperialism*, 228.

29. Ibid., 229.

30. Rachel Simon, "Education," in Reeva Spector Simon, Michael Menachem Laskier, and Sara Reguer, eds., *The Jews of the Middle East and North Africa in Modern Times* (New York: Columbia University Press, 2003), 149–150; see also Michael M. Laskier, *The Alliance Israélite Universelle and the Jewish Communities of Morocco, 1862–1962* (Albany: State University of New York Press, 1983); Rodrigue, *French Jews, Turkish Jews*.

31. Ruth Kark, "The Impact of Early Missionary Enterprises on Landscape and Identity Formation in Palestine, 1820–1914," *Islam and Christian–Muslim Relations* 15 (2004), 219–221.

32. Alex Carmel, "The German Settlers in Palestine and Their Relations with the Local Arab Population and the Jewish Community, 1868–1918," in Moshe Ma'oz, ed., *Studies on Palestine During the Ottoman Period* (Jerusalem: Magnes Press, 1975), 445–446.

33. Benedict Anderson, *Imagined Communities: Reflections on the Origin and Spread of Nationalism* (London: Verso, 1983).

34. Geneva was also the center of the early Kurdish nationalist movement.

35. Robert Mirak, *Torn Between Two Lands: Armenians in America, 1890 to World War I* (Cambridge, Mass.: Harvard University Press, 1983), 183.

36. Ibid., 209.

37. Ibid., 219, 47.

38. Ibid., 176.

39. George Antonius attributes the beginning of Arab nationalism to the Arab literary societies that began in Syria in the 1840s. See George Antonius, *The Arab Awakening: The Story of the Arab National Movement* (Philadelphia: J. B. Lippincott, 1939); see also Albert Hourani, *Arabic Thought in the Liberal Age: 1798–1939* (New York: Oxford University Press, 1970).

40. Eli Smith, *Missionary Sermons and Addresses* (Boston, 1833), 147, quoted in Fruma Zachs, "Toward a Proto-Nationalist Concept of Syria? Revisiting the American Presbyterian Missionaries in the Nineteenth-Century Levant," *Die Welt des Islams* 41 (2001), 152.

41. Quoted in Zachs, "Toward a Proto-Nationalist Concept of Syria?" 155.

42. Asher Kaufman, *Reviving Phoenicia: In Search of Identity in Lebanon* (New York: I. B. Tauris, 2004), 21–54.

43. Ibid., 31; Rifaʿat Ali Abu El-Haj, "The Social Uses of the Past's Recent Arab Historiography of Ottoman Rule," *International Journal of Middle East Studies* 14 (1982): 185–201.

44. Bradley Rainbow Hale, "The Soul of Empire: The Society of Missionaries of Africa in Colonial Algeria, 1919–1939," Ph.D. diss., University of Connecticut, 2005, 66–91.

45. Timothy Mitchell, *Colonizing Egypt* (Berkeley and Los Angeles: University of California Press, 1991); Donald Malcolm Reid, *Whose Pharaohs? Archaeology, Museums, and Egyptian National Identity from Napoleon to World War I* (Berkeley and Los Angeles: University of California Press, 2002); James Stevens Curl, *Egyptomania: The Egyptian Revival—a Recurring Theme in the History of Taste* (Manchester, U.K.: Manchester University Press, 1994).

46. Interestingly, that kind of theory holds in other areas, notably the case of the Maya in Mexico and Central America, where the people on the reliefs do still exist, and the glyphic writing was finally deciphered on the basis of the modern language.

47. J. F. Coakley, *The Church of the East and the Church of England* (Oxford: Clarendon Press, 1992), 44, 375 n. 90.

48. Botta and Layard cannot possibly have imagined that by the end of the twentieth century replicas of the great winged bulls they unearthed would later appear as parade floats supporting the nationalistic aspirations of the Assyrian community in Chicago.

49. See Oleg Grabar, "Roots and Others," in Holly Edwards, ed., *Noble Dreams, Wicked Pleasures: Orientalism in America, 1870–1930*, 3–9 (Princeton, N.J.: Princeton University Press, 2000).

50. Bernard Heyberger and Chantal Verdeil, "Spirituality and Scholarship: The Holy Land in Jesuit Eyes (Seventeenth to Nineteenth Centuries)," in Heleen Murre-van den Berg, ed., *New Faith in Ancient Lands: Western Missions in the Middle East in the Nineteenth and Early Twentieth Centuries*, 19–41 (Leiden: Brill, 2006).

51. Yehoshua Ben-Arieh, "Holy Land Views in Nineteenth-Century Western Travel Literature," in Moshe Davis and Yehoshua Ben-Arieh, eds., *Western Societies and*

the Holy Land, 10–29, With Eyes Toward Zion III (New York: Praeger, 1991). On the Palestine Exploration Fund, see Haim Goren, "Scientific Organizations as Agents of Change: Palestine Exploration Fund, the *Deutsche Verein sur Erforschung Palästinas*, and Nineteenth-Century Palestine," *Journal of Historical Geography* 27 (2001): 153–165; and Burke O. Long, *Imagining the Holy Land: Maps, Models, and Fantasy Travels* (Bloomington: Indiana University Press, 2003).

52. The literature on the connection between proving the historical accuracy of the Bible and travel to the Holy Land is extensive and growing. See Ruth Kark, "Millenarism and Agricultural Settlement in the Holy Land in the Nineteenth Century," *Journal of Historical Geography* 9 (1983): 47–62; Ruth Kark, "Sweden and the Holy Land: Pietistic and Communal Settlement," *Journal of Historical Geography* 22 (1996): 46–67; Mahmoud Yazbak, "Templars [*sic*] as Proto-Zionists? The 'German Colony' in Late Ottoman Haifa," *Journal of Palestine Studies* 28 (1999): 40–54.

53. Mark Twain, *The Innocents Abroad, or the New Pilgrims' Progress* (Hartford, Conn.: American, 1869), chap. 48, quoted in David Klatzker, "American Christian Travelers to the Holy Land, 1821–1939," in Davis and Ben-Arieh, eds., *Western Societies and the Holy Land*, 73. See also Hilton Obenzinger, *American Palestine: Melville, Twain, and the Holy Land Mania* (Princeton, N.J.: Princeton University Press, 1999); and Milette Shamir, "'Our Jerusalem': Americans in the Holy Land and Protestant Narratives of National Entitlement," *American Quarterly* 55 (2003): 29–60.

54. On the Spaffords' American Colony, see Helga Dudman and Ruth Kark, *The American Colony: Scenes from a Jerusalem Saga* (Jerusalem: Carta, 1998), and Jane Fletcher Geniesse, *American Priestess: The Extraordinary Story of Anna Spafford and the American Colony in Jerusalem* (New York: Doubleday, 2008).

55. Quoted in Lyle L. Vander Werff, *Christian Mission to Muslims—the Record: Anglican and Reformed Approaches in India and the Near East 1800–1938* (South Pasadena, Calif.: William Carey Library, 1977), 163.

56. Quoted in Selim Deringil, *The Well-Protected Domains: Ideology and the Legitimation of Power in the Ottoman Empire, 1876–1909* (London: I. B. Tauris, 1999), 133–134.

57. Ibid., 91.

58. On the Alevi (Kizilbash), see Hans-Lukas Kieser, "Muslim Heterodoxy and Protestant Utopia: The Interaction Between Alevis and Missionaries in Ottoman Anatolia," *Die Welt des Islams* 41 (2001): 89–111.

59. Deringil, *The Well-Protected Domains*, 68–92; on the issue of apostasy, see Turgut Subasi, "The Apostasy Question in the Context of Anglo–Ottoman Relations, 1843–44," *Middle Eastern Studies* 38 (2002): 1–34.

60. Deringil, *The Well-Protected Domains*, 127–128.

61. In Gaza and Salt (Transjordan), the Ottomans built schools and forbade Muslims to attend Christian schools, but to no avail (Eugene L. Rogan, *Frontiers of the State in the Late Ottoman Empire: Transjordan 1850–1921* [Cambridge: Cambridge University Press, 1999], 143).

62. Quoted in Deringil, *The Well-Protected Domains*, 131. Regarding Islamic philanthropic associations, see Mahmoud Haddad, "Syrian Muslim Attitudes Toward Foreign Missionaries in the Late Nineteenth and Twentieth Centuries," in Tejirian

and Simon, eds., *Altruism and Imperialism*, 254–255; and Benjamin C. Fortna, *Imperial Classroom: Islam, the State, and Education in the Late Ottoman Empire* (New York: Oxford University Press, 2000).

63. Quoted in Rogan, *Frontiers of the State in the Late Ottoman Empire*, 146; see also Tibawi, "The Genesis and Early History of the Syrian Protestant College (Part II)," 202, 211.

64. Hermas J. Bergman, "The Diplomatic Missionary: John Van Ess in Iraq," *The Muslim World* 72 (1982), 185.

65. Janet Wallach, *Desert Queen: The Extraordinary Life of Gertrude Bell: Adventurer, Adviser to Kings, Ally of Lawrence of Arabia* (New York: Doubleday, 1995), 164.

66. Bergman, "The Diplomatic Missionary," 191.

67. Mark E. Bernstein, "An American Hero in Iran," *Princeton Alumni Weekly* 107 (May 9, 2007), 23.

68. Quoted in ibid., 24.

69. Ibid., 25.

8. World War I

1. Nikki R. Keddie, *Qajar Iran and the Rise of Reza Khan, 1796–1925* (Costa Mesa, Calif.: Mazda, 1999), 44–64.

2. Peter Hopkirk, *Like Hidden Fire: The Plot to Bring Down the British Empire* (New York: Kodansha International, 1994), 73–76.

3. Quoted in Keith David Watenpaugh, *Being Modern in the Middle East: Revolution, Nationalism, Colonialism, and the Arab Middle Class* (Princeton, N.J.: Princeton University Press, 2006), 119.

4. James L. Barton, "The Effect of the War on Protestant Missions," *Harvard Theological Review* 12 (1919), 4.

5. Roberto Mazza, "Churches at War: The Impact of the First World War on the Christian Institutions of Jerusalem, 1914–20," *Middle Eastern Studies* 45 (2009), 213.

6. Bradley Rainbow Hale, "The Soul of Empire: The Society of Missionaries of Africa in Colonial Algeria, 1919–1939," Ph.D. diss., University of Connecticut, 2005, 35.

7. Dominique Trimbur, "Le Destin des institutions chrétiennes européennes de Jérusalem pendant la première guerre mondiale," *Mélanges de Science Religieuse* 58 (2001): 3–29.

8. Michael B. Oren, *Power, Faith, and Fantasy: America in the Middle East, 1776 to the Present* (New York: W. W. Norton, 2007), 326–327.

9. President Wilson personally appointed Glazebrook, a former pastor from Georgia and Princeton Seminary professor, to the post (Oren, *Power, Faith, and Fantasy*, 356).

10. Eduardo Manzano Moreno and Roberto Mazza, *Jerusalem in World War I: The Palestine Diary of a European Diplomat—Conde de Ballobar* (London: Tauris,

2011), 21, 155–156; Jane Fletcher Geniesse, *American Priestess: The Extraordinary Story of Anna Spafford and the American Colony in Jerusalem* (New York: Doubleday, 2008), 242–243.

11. Barton, "The Effect of the War on Protestant Missions," 11.

12. John A. DeNovo, *American Interests and Policies in the Middle East, 1900–1939* (Minneapolis: University of Minnesota Press, 1963), 96.

13. Joseph L. Grabill, *Protestant Diplomacy and the Near East* (Minneapolis: University of Minnesota Press, 1971), 60.

14. Ibid., 67.

15. Bayard Dodge, *The American University of Beirut: A Brief History of the University and the Lands Which It Serves* (Beirut: Khayat's, 1958), 39.

16. L. Schatkowski Schilcher, "The Famine of 1915–1918 in Greater Syria," in John P. Spagnolo, ed., *Problems of the Modern Middle East in Historical Perspective: Essays in Honour of Albert Hourani* (Reading, U.K.: Ithaca Press, 1992), 234; Elizabeth Thompson, *Colonial Citizens: Republican Rights, Paternal Privilege, and Gender in French Syria and Lebanon* (New York: Columbia University Press, 2000), 19–23; DeNovo, *American Interests and Policies in the Middle East*, 91–92; Abigail Jacobson, "A City Living Through Crisis: Jerusalem During World War I," *British Journal of Middle Eastern Studies* 36 (2009): 73–92.

17. Fruma Zachs, "From the Mission to the Missionary: The Bliss Family and the Syrian Protestant College (1866–1920)," *Die Welt des Islams* 45 (2005), 278.

18. Quoted in Oren, *Power, Faith, and Fantasy*, 343.

19. Ibid., 326–328.

20. John Joseph, *Muslim–Christian Relations and the Inter-Christian Rivalries in the Middle East: The Case of the Jacobites in an Age of Transition* (Albany: State University of New York Press, 1983), 132; Michael Zirinsky, "American Presbyterian Missionaries at Urmia During the Great War," *Bibliothèque Iranienne* (2002): 1–22.

21. Joseph, *Muslim–Christian Relations and the Inter-Christian Rivalries in the Middle East*, 136.

22. Ibid., 136–138.

23. Ibid., 141.

24. Ibid., 143.

25. Ibid., 158.

26. Walter Russell Mead, *Special Providence American Foreign Policy and How It Changed the World* (New York: Routledge, 2002), 132–173; Oren, *Power, Faith, and Fantasy*, 376–377.

27. Grabill, *Protestant Diplomacy and the Near East*, 90–100; Zachs, "From the Mission to the Missionary," 281.

28. Howard Bliss's daughter married Cleveland Dodge's son Bayard, who became the third president of the Syrian Protestant College (American University of Beirut) (Grabill, *Protestant Diplomacy and the Near East*, 88–89).

29. Ibid., 80–88.

30. James L. Barton, *Story of Near East Relief (1915–1930): An Interpretation* (New York: Macmillan, 1930), 4.

31. Eleanor H. Tejirian, "Faith of Our Fathers: Near East Relief and the Near East Foundation—from Missions to NGO," in Eleanor H. Tejirian and Reeva Spector Simon, eds., *Altruism and Imperialism: Western Cultural and Religious Missions in the Middle East* (New York: Middle East Institute, Columbia University, 2002), 300.

32. Ibid., 301.

33. Robert L. Daniel, *American Philanthropy in the Near East, 1820–1960* (Athens: Ohio State University Press, 1970), 150. Following the merger of the Syrian–Palestine Relief Committee and the Persian committee into the Dodge committee at the behest of the Rockefeller Foundation, the name was changed yet again to "American Committee on Armenian and Syrian Relief" and finally to "Near East Relief."

34. Tejirian, "Faith of Our Fathers," 302.

35. Quoted in ibid., 303.

36. Oren, *Power, Faith, and Fantasy*, 382. Before the 1917 Russian Revolution, Constantinople had been promised to czarist Russia.

37. Thompson, *Colonial Citizens*, 60–61.

38. Grabill, *Protestant Diplomacy and the Near East*, 124–125; Oren, *Power, Faith, and Fantasy*, 378–379.

39. Grabill, *Protestant Diplomacy and the Near East*, 187.

40. Zachs, "From the Mission to the Missionary," 281–284.

41. Grabill, *Protestant Diplomacy and the Near East*, 155–156; Daniel, *American Philanthropy in the Near East*, 163; Zachs, "From the Mission to the Missionary," 284.

42. George Antonius, *The Arab Awakening: The Story of the Arab Nationalist Movement* (Philadelphia: Lippincott, 1939), 287.

43. See Michael Reimer, "The King–Crane Commission at the Juncture of Politics and Historiography," *Critique: Critical Middle Eastern Studies* 15 (2006): 129–150.

44. Grabill, *Protestant Diplomacy and the Near East*, 163.

45. Ibid., 70–71, 199.

46. Stuart E. Knee, "The King–Crane Commission of 1919: The Articulation of Political Anti-Zionism," *American Jewish Archives* 29 (1977), 47–52.

47. Report printed in *New York Times*, December 3, 1922; see Recommendations E and E1–3.

48. Grabill, *Protestant Diplomacy and the Near East*, 199–203. Wilson's detractors note that the president backtracked on his support of the Balfour Declaration. William Yale, observer for the State Department and resident agent for the Standard Oil Company, wrote a minority report in which he objected to the commission's findings, which he thought had been manufactured by anti-Zionists (Stuart E. Knee, "Anglo–American Relations in Palestine 1919–1925: An Experiment in *Realpolitik*," *Journal of American Studies of Turkey* 5 [1997], 6).

49. For more detail on the settlement of this boundary, see David Cuthell, "A Kemalist Gambit: A View of the Political Negotiations in the Determination of the Turkish–Iraqi Border," in Reeva Spector Simon and Eleanor H. Tejirian, eds., *The Creation of Iraq, 1914–1921*, 80–94 (New York: Columbia University Press, 2004).

50. DeNovo, *American Interests and Policies in the Middle East*, 132.

9. Setting the Agenda

1. Selim Deringil, *The Well-Protected Domains: Ideology and the Legitimation of Power in the Ottoman Empire, 1876–1909* (London: I. B. Tauris, 1999), 107.

2. John A. DeNovo, *American Interests and Policies in the Middle East 1900–1939* (Minneapolis: University of Minnesota Press, 1963), 258–260.

3. William R. Hutchison, *Errand to the World: American Protestant Thought and Foreign Missions* (Chicago: University of Chicago Press, 1987), 112–113.

4. Ibid., 125.

5. Clifton Jackson Phillips, "Changing Attitudes in the Student Volunteer Movement of Great Britain and North America," in Torben Christensen and William R. Hutchison, eds., *Missionary Ideologies in the Imperialist Era: 1880–1920* (Aarhus, Denmark: Aros, 1982), 137.

6. Ibid., 143.

7. Eleanor H. Tejirian, "Faith of Our Fathers: Near East Relief and the Near East Foundation—from Missions to NGOs," in Eleanor H. Tejirian and Reeva Spector Simon, eds., *Altruism and Imperialism: Western Cultural and Religious Missions in the Middle East* (New York: Middle East Institute, Columbia University, 2002), 305.

8. DeNovo, *American Interests and Policies in the Middle East*, 254.

9. From the ABCFM's annual report of 1923, quoted in ibid., 255.

10. Ibid., 259.

11. Ibid., 260–261.

12. Ibid., 235.

13. Ibid., 239.

14. Ibid., 333.

15. Elizabeth Thompson, *Colonial Citizens: Republican Rights, Paternal Privilege, and Gender in French Syria and Lebanon* (New York: Columbia University Press, 2000), 60–61.

16. Silvio Ferrari, "The Vatican, Israel, and the Question of Jerusalem (1943–1984)," *Middle East Journal* 39 (1985): 316–331; Anthony O'Mahony, "The Latins of the East: The Vatican, Jerusalem, and the Palestine Christians," in Anthony O'Mahony, ed., *The Christian Communities of Jerusalem and the Holy Land: Studies in History, Religion, and Politics*, 90–114 (Cardiff, U.K.: University of Wales Press, 2003).

17. Michael Marten, "Anglican and Presbyterian Presence and Theology in the Holy Land," *International Journal for the Study of the Christian Church* 5 (2005), 185–186.

18. DeNovo, *American Interests and Policies in the Middle East*, 346.

19. Ruth Kark, "The Impact of Early Missionary Enterprises on Landscape and Identity Formation in Palestine, 1820–1914," *Islam and Christian–Muslim Relations* 15 (2004), 217.

20. DeNovo, *American Interests and Policies in the Middle East*, 351.

21. Ibid.

22. Dexter Filkins, "Boys of Baghdad College Vie for Prime Minister," *New York Times*, December 12, 2005; see also Roderic D. Matthews and Matta Akrawi, *Education in Arab Countries of the Near East* (Washington, D.C.: American College on Education, 1949), 212–213.

23. DeNovo, *American Interests and Policies in the Middle East*, 355.

24. Ibid., 296–297.

25. The extent of the American College of Tehran's influence can be measured by the establishment of the Samuel Jordan Center for Persian Studies and Culture at the University of California, Irvine.

26. DeNovo, *American Interests and Policies in the Middle East*, 373.

27. Umar Ryad, "Muslim Response to Missionary Activities in Egypt: With a Special Reference to the al-Azhar High Corps of ĐUlama (1925–1935)," in Heleen Murre-van den Berg, ed., *New Faith in Ancient Lands: Western Missions in the Middle East in the Nineteenth and Early Twentieth Centuries*, 281–307 (Leiden: Brill, 2006); see also Heather Sharkey, "Empire and Muslim Conversion: Historical Reflections on Christian Missions in Egypt," *Islam and Christian–Muslim Relations* 16 (2005): 43–60; B. L. Carter, "On Spreading the Gospel to Egyptians Sitting in Darkness: The Political Problem of Missionaries in Egypt in the 1930s," *Middle Eastern Studies* 20 (1984): 18–35.

28. On the response by Rashid Rida, see Mahmoud Haddad, "Syrian Muslim Attitudes Toward Foreign Missionaries in the Late Nineteenth and Twentieth Centuries," in Tejirian and Simon, eds., *Altruism and Imperialism*, 253–274; for Egypt in particular, see Ryad, "Muslim Response to Missionary Activities in Egypt," 300–301.

29. Quoted in Ryad, "Muslim Response to Missionary Activities in Egypt," 296.

30. Sharkey, "Empire and Muslim Conversion."

31. Hutchison, *Errand to the World*, 77.

32. Heather Sharkey, *American Evangelicals in Egypt: Missionary Encounters in an Age of Empire* (Princeton, N.J.: Princeton University Press, 2008), 37.

33. William Ernest Hocking, *Re-Thinking Missions: A Laymen's Inquiry After One Hundred Years* (New York: Harper & Brothers, 1932), 25.

34. "World Council of Churches," *Wikipedia*, available at http://wikipedia.org/wiki/ World_Council_of_Churches.

35. Sharkey, *American Evangelicals in Egypt*, 185.

36. Ibid., 178.

37. Ibid., 203.

38. Ibid., 205.

39. Ibid., 218.

40. The ABCFM similarly changed its name several times and is now called "Global Ministries," and the American Episcopal Foreign Mission Board has now become "Episcopal Relief and Development." The shift in emphasis is clear. Even the Muslim–Christian encounter shifted from proselytization to "interfaith dialogue" and "respectful witness."

41. Sharkey, *American Evangelicals in Egypt*, 211.

42. DeNovo, *American Interests and Policies in the Middle East*, 343.

43. Ibid., 344.

44. Sharkey, *American Evangelicals in Egypt*, 193. See also Nancy Gallagher, *Quakers in the Israeli–Palestinian Conflict: The Dilemma of NGO Humanitarian Activism* (Cairo: American University in Cairo Press, 2007).

45. Silvio Ferrari, "The Holy See and the Postwar Palestine Issue: The Internationalization of Jerusalem and the Protection of the Holy Places," *International Affairs* 60 (1984), 268.

46. Jean Corbon, "The Churches of the Middle East: Their Origins and Identity from Their Roots in the Past to the Openness of the Present," in Andrea Pacini, ed., *Christian Communities in the Arab Middle East: The Challenge of the Future* (Oxford: Clarendon Press, 1998), 97.

47. NaÐim Ateek, *Justice and Only Justice: A Palestinian Theology of Liberation* (Maryknoll, N.Y.: Orbis, 1989).

48. O'Mahony, "The Latins of the East," 105.

49. Despite its name, the American Board of Missions to the Jews has no connection with the ABCFM. Since 1984, it has been known as the "Chosen People Ministries, Inc." See "Chosen People Ministries," *Wikipedia*, available at http://en.wikipedia.org/wiki/Chosen_People_Ministries, accessed March 11, 2011.

50. Quoted in Yaakov Ariel, "Evangelists in a Strange Land: American Missionaries in Israel, 1948–1967," *Studies in Contemporary Jewry* 14 (1998), 198–199.

51. David Little, "Religion and Global Affairs: Religion and U.S. Foreign Policy," *SAIS Review* 18 (1998), 26; Allen D. Hertzke and Daniel Philpott, "Defending the Faiths," *The National Interest* 6 (2000), 75; Donna Casata, "Congress Enters Unchartered Territory with Bill on Religious Persecution," *Congressional Quarterly Weekly Report* 55 (September 1997): 2121–2123.

52. Office of International Religious Freedom, U.S. Bureau of Democracy, Human Rights, and Labor, *Fact Sheet: History of the Office of International Religious Freedom* (Washington, D.C.: U.S. Department of State, April 16, 2001), no page numbers.

53. Jeremy T. Gunn, "A Preliminary Response to Criticisms of the International Religious Freedom Act of 1998," *Brigham Young University Law Review* 3 (2000), 854.

54. See the description of the Presbyterian Church World Mission at http://www.pcusa.org/worldmission, accessed December 21, 2009.

55. For the Global Ministries in Turkey, see http://globalministries.org/mee/countries/turkey/, accessed December 21, 2009.

56. See FABSIT's history at http://fabsit.org/about_history.php, accessed December 21, 2009.

57. See the description of FABSIT's partners at http://fabsit.org/about.partners.php, accessed December 21, 2009.

58. From the Global Ministries Web site at http://global ministries.org/mee/missionaries/american-board-schools-in-turkey.html, accessed December 21, 2009.

59. From the description of the Presbyterian Church World Mission at http://www.pcusa.org/worldmission, accessed December 21, 2009.

60. From the Global Ministries Web site at http://globalministries.org/mee/countries/egypt/, accessed December 21, 2009.

61. The Assemblies of God Web site is at http://worldmissions.ag.org, accessed December 21, 2009.

62. Carlton Coon, *Caravan: The Story of the Middle East* (New York: Holt, 1951).

Abrahams, Beth-Zion Lask. "James Finn: Her Britannic Majesty's Consul at Jerusalem Between 1846 and 1863." *Transactions of the Jewish Historical Society of England* 27 (1982): 40–50.

Abu El-Haj, Rifaʿat Ali. "The Social Uses of the Past's Recent Arab Historiography of Ottoman Rule." *International Journal of Middle East Studies* 14 (1982): 185–201.

Abu Lughod, Janet. *Before European Hegemony: The World System A.D. 1250–1350.* New York: Oxford University Press, 1989.

Adas, Michael. *Machines as the Measure of Men: Science, Technology, and Ideologies of Western Dominance.* Ithaca, N.Y.: Cornell University Press, 1989.

Aldrich, Robert. *Greater France: A History of French Overseas Expansion.* New York: Palgrave, 1996.

American Board of Commissioners for Foreign Missions, Near East Mission, ed. *Centennial of the Constantinople Station.* Constantinople: The Mission, 1931.

Anawati, Georges C. "Factors and Effects of Arabization and Islamization in Medieval Egypt and Syria." In Speros Vryonis Jr., ed., *Islam and Cultural Change in the Middle Ages,* 18–41. Wiesbaden, Germany: Otto Harrasowitz, 1975.

Anderson, Benedict. *Imagined Communities: Reflections on the Origin and Spread of Nationalism.* London: Verso, 1983.

Anderson, Olive. "The Growth of Christian Militarism in Mid-Victorian Britain." *English Historical Review* 86 (1971): 46–72.

Antonius, George. *The Arab Awakening: The Story of the Arab National Movement.* Philadelphia: Lippincott, 1939.

Arberry, A. J., ed. *Religion in the Middle East: Three Religions in Concord and Conflict*. New York: Cambridge University Press, 1969.

Ariel, Yaakov. "American Dispensationalists and Jerusalem, 1870–1918." In Yehoshua Ben-Arieh and Moshe Davis, eds., *Jerusalem in the Mind of the Western World, 1800–1948*, 123–134, With Eyes Toward Zion V. Westport, Conn.: Praeger, 1997.

——. "Evangelists in a Strange Land: American Missionaries in Israel, 1948–1967." *Studies in Contemporary Jewry* 14 (1998): 195–213.

Armajani, Yahya. "Christian Missions in Persia." In *Encyclopaedia Iranica* 5. Available at http://www.iranica.com/newsite/articles/unicode/v5f5/v5f5a018.html.

Armenian, Haroutune K. and Aftim Acra. "From Missionaries to the Endemic War: Public Health Action and Research at the American University of Beirut." *Journal of Public Health Policy* 9 (1988): 261–272.

Asbridge, Thomas. *The First Crusade: A New History—the Roots of Conflict Between Christianity and Islam*. New York: Oxford University Press, 2004.

Ateek, NaÐim. *Justice and Only Justice: A Palestinian Theology of Liberation*. Maryknoll, N.Y.: Orbis, 1989.

Atiya, Aziz S. *A History of Eastern Christianity*. 1967. Millwood, N.Y.: Kraus Reprint, 1991.

Atkin, Muriel. "Russian Expansion in the Caucasus to 1813." In Michael Rywkin, ed., *Russian Colonial Expansion to 1917*, 139–187. London: Mansell, 1988.

Baker, William J. "To Pray or to Play? The YMCA Question in the United Kingdom and the United States, 1850–1900." *International Journal of the History of Sport* 11 (1994): 42–62.

Baldwin, Marshall W. "Missions to the East in the Thirteenth and Fourteenth Centuries." In Kenneth M. Setton, ed., *A History of the Crusades*, 5:452–518. Madison: University of Wisconsin Press, 1985.

Balmer, Randall. *Encyclopedia of Evangelism*. Waco, Tex. Baylor University Press, 2004.

Baring-Gould, Sabine. "Onward, Christian Soldier." Music by Arthur S. Sullivan. Available at Hymnsite.com, http://www.hymnsite.com/lyrics/umh575.sht.

Barton, James L. "The Effect of the War on Protestant Missions." *Harvard Theological Review* 12 (1919): 1–35.

——. *Story of Near East Relief (1915–1930): An Interpretation*. New York: Macmillan, 1930.

Bashan, Eliezer. *The Anglican Mission and the Jews of Morocco in the Nineteenth Century* (in Hebrew). Ramat Gan, Israel: Bar Ilan University Press, 1999.

Beckingham, Charles F. and Bernard Hamilton, eds. *Prester John, the Mongols, and the Ten Lost Tribes*. Aldershot, U.K.: Variorum, 1996.

Ben-Ami, Aharon. *Social Change in a Hostile Environment: The Crusaders' Kingdom of Jerusalem*. Princeton, N.J.: Princeton University Press, 1969.

Ben-Arieh, Yehoshua. "Holy Land Views in Nineteenth-Century Western Travel Literature." In Moshe Davis and Yehoshua Ben-Arieh, eds., *Western Societies and the Holy Land*, 10–29, With Eyes Toward Zion III. New York: Praeger, 1991.

——. "Patterns of Christian Activity and Dispersion in Nineteenth-Century Jerusalem." *Journal of Historical Geography* 2 (1976): 49–69.

Ben-Arieh, Yehoshua and Moshe Davis, eds. *Jerusalem in the Mind of the Western World, 1800–1948*. With Eyes Toward Zion V. Westport, Conn.: Praeger, 1997.

Bergman, Hermas J. "The Diplomatic Missionary: John Van Ess in Iraq." *The Muslim World* 72 (1982): 180–196.

Berkey, Jonathan P. *The Formation of Islam: Religion and Society in the Near East, 600–1800*. New York: Cambridge University Press, 2003.

Bernstein, Mark E. "An American Hero in Iran." *Princeton Alumni Weekly* 107 (May 9, 2007): 23–25.

Bickers, Robert A. and Rosemary Seton, eds. *Missionary Encounters: Sources and Issues*. Richmond, U.K.: Curzon Press, 1996.

Bird, Jessalyn. "Crusade and Conversion After the Fourth Lateran Council (1215): Oliver of Paderborn's and James of Vitry's Missions to Muslims Reconsidered." *Essays in Medieval Studies* 21 (2004): 23–48.

Bodin, George L. "Joseph S. C. F. Frey, the Jews, and Early Nineteenth-Century Millenarianism." *Journal of the Early Republic* 1 (1981): 27–49.

Bohnstedt, John W. "The Infidel Scourge of God: The Turkish Menace as Seen by German Pamphleteers of the Reformation Era." *Transactions of the American Philosophical Society* (new series) 58 (1968): 1–58.

Boojamra, John L. "Athanasios of Constantinople: A Study of Byzantine Reactions to Latin Infiltration." *Church History* 48 (1979): 27–48.

Brecher, F. W. "Charles R. Crane's Crusade for the Arabs, 1919–39." *Middle Eastern Studies* 24 (1988): 42–55.

Brower, Daniel R. "Russian Roads to Mecca: Religious Tolerance and Muslim Pilgrimage in the Russian Empire." *Slavic Review* 55 (1996): 567–584.

Brower, Daniel R. and Edward J. Lazzerini, eds. *Russia's Orient Imperial Borderlands and Peoples 1700–1917*. Bloomington: Indiana University Press, 1997.

Brown, Peter. *The World of Late Antiquity AD 150–750*. New York: W. W. Norton, 1989.

Brown, Stewart J. *Providence and Empire 1815–1914: Religion, Politics, and Society in the United Kingdom 1815–1914*. New York: Longman, 2008.

Browne, Laurence. *The Eclipse of Christianity in Asia*. New York: Howard Fertig, 1967.

Brumett, Palmira. *Ottoman Seapower and Levantine Diplomacy in the Age of Discovery*. Albany: State University of New York Press, 1994.

Bulliet, Richard W. *Conversion to Islam in the Medieval Period: An Essay in Quantitative History*. Cambridge, Mass.: Harvard University Press, 1979.

——. *Islam: The View from the Edge*. New York: Columbia University Press, 1995.

——. "Process and Status in Conversion and Continuity." In Michael Gervers and Ramzi Jibran Bikhazi, ed., *Conversion and Continuity: Indigenous Christian Communities in Islamic Lands Eighth to Eighteenth Centuries*, 3–12, Papers in Mediaeval Studies no. 9. Toronto: Pontifical Institute of Medieval Studies, 1990.

Burke, Jeffrey C. "The Establishment of the American Presbyterian Mission in Egypt, 1854–1940: An Overview." Ph.D. diss., McGill University, 2000.

Burnet, David Staats, comp. *The Jerusalem Mission Under the Direction of the American Christian Missionary Society*. 1853. Reprint. New York: Arno Press, 1977.

Burns, Robert I., S.J. "Christian–Islamic Confrontation in the West: The Thirteenth Century Dream of Conversion." *American Historical Review* 76 (1971): 1386–1434.

Burr, David. "Antichrist and Islam in Medieval Franciscan Exegesis." In John Victor Tolan, ed., *Medieval Christian Perceptions of Islam: A Book of Essays*, 131–152. New York: Garland, 1996.

Burrows, Mathew. "*Mission Civilisatrice*': French Cultural Policy in the Middle East, 1860–1914." *Historical Journal* 29 (1986): 109–135.

Bush, John. "Education and Social Status: The Jesuit College in the Early Third Republic." *French Historical Studies* 9 (1975): 125–140.

Callahan, John J., S.J. *A Brief History of Jesuit Education*. Available at http://www. cheverus.org/upload/images/docs/jesuits/Brief_History_of_Jesuit_Education__ Callahan_f_632909075586888750.pdf.

Carmel, Alex. "The German Settlers in Palestine and Their Relations with the Local Arab Population and the Jewish Community, 1868–1918." In Moshe Ma'oz, ed., *Studies on Palestine During the Ottoman Period*, 442–465. Jerusalem: Magnes Press, 1975.

——. "The Political Significance of German Settlement in Palestine, 1868–1918." In Jehuda L. Wallach, ed., *Germany and the Middle East, 1835–1939*, International Symposium, April 1975, 45–71. Tel Aviv: Institute of German History, 1975.

——. "Russian Activity in Palestine in the Nineteenth Century." In Richard I. Cohen, ed., *Vision and Conflict in the Holy Land*, 45–77. New York: St. Martin's Press, 1985.

Carter, B. L. "On Spreading the Gospel to Egyptians Sitting in Darkness: The Political Problem of Missionaries in Egypt in the 1930s." *Middle Eastern Studies* 20 (1984): 18–35.

Casata, Donna. "Congress Enters Uncharted Territory with Bill on Religious Persecution." *Congressional Quarterly Weekly Report* 55 (September 1997): 2121–2123.

Chapman, Rupert L. "British–Holy Land Archaeology: Nineteenth Century Sources." In Moshe Davis and Yehoshua Ben-Arieh, eds., *Western Societies and the Holy Land*, 208–226, With Eyes Toward Zion III. New York: Praeger, 1991.

Chapman-Adisho, Annette Renee. "*Mission Civilisatrice* to Mandate: The French and Education in Syria and Lebanon." Master's thesis, University of Louisville, 1998.

Chiat, Marilyn J. and Kathryn L. Reyerson, eds. *The Medieval Mediterranean: Cross-Cultural Contacts*. St. Cloud, Minn.: North Star Press of St. Cloud, 1988.

Chilton, Bruce. *Rabbi Paul: An Intellectual Biography*. New York: Doubleday, 2004.

Coakley, J. F. *The Church of the East and the Church of England*. Oxford: Clarendon Press, 1992.

Cohen, Shaye J. D. "Conversion to Judaism in Historical Perspective: From Biblical Israel to Postbiblical Judaism." *Conservative Judaism* 36 (1983): 31–45.

Cole, Penny J. *The Preaching of the Crusades to the Holy Land, 1095–1270*. Cambridge: Medieval Academy of America, 1991.

Colley, Linda. *Britons: Forging the Nation 1707–1837*. New Haven, Conn.: Yale University Press, 1992.

——. *Captives*. New York: Pantheon, 2002.

Cook, James J. "Eugene Etienne and the Emergence of Colon Dominance in Algeria, 1884–1905." *Muslim World* 65 (1975): 39–53.

Coon, Carlton. *Caravan: The Story of the Middle East*. New York: Holt, 1951.

Corbon, Jean. "The Churches of the Middle East: Their Origins and Identity from Their Roots in the Past to the Openness of the Present." In Andrea Pacini, ed., *Christian Communities in the Arab Middle East: The Challenge of the Future*, 92–110. Oxford: Clarendon Press, 1998.

Cowdrey, H. E. J. "The Reform Papacy and the Origin of the Crusades." In H. E. J. Cowdrey, ed., *The Crusades and Latin Monasticism, 11th–12th Centuries*, 65–83. Aldershot, U.K.: Ashgate, 1999.

Cragg, Kenneth. *The Arab Christian: A History in the Middle East*. Louisville, Ky.: Westminster/John Knox Press, 1991.

——. "Being Made Disciples—the Middle East." In Kevin Ward and Brian Stanley, ed., *The Church Missionary Society and World Christianity, 1799–1999*, 120–143. Grand Rapids, Mich.: Eerdmans, 2000.

Cubitt, Geoffrey. *The Jesuit Myth: Conspiracy Theory and Politics in Nineteenth-Century France*. Oxford: Clarendon Press, 1993.

Curl, James Stevens. *Egyptomania: The Egyptian Revival—a Recurring Theme in the History of Taste*. Manchester, U.K.: Manchester University Press, 1994.

Cuthell, David. "A Kemalist Gambit: A View of the Political Negotiations in the Determination of the Turkish–Iraqi Border." In Reeva Spector Simon and Eleanor H. Tejirian, eds., *The Creation of Iraq, 1914–1921*, 80–94. New York: Columbia University Press, 2004.

Cutler, Allan. "The First Crusade and the Idea of Conversion." *Muslim World* 58 (1968): 57–71, 155–164.

Daniel, E. Randolph. *The Franciscan Concept of Mission in the High Middle Ages*. Lexington: University Press of Kentucky, 1975.

Daniel, Norman. *Islam and the West: The Making of an Image*. Oxford: Oneworld, 1993.

Daniel, Robert L. *American Philanthropy in the Near East, 1820–1960*. Athens: Ohio State University Press, 1970.

Daughton, J. P. *An Empire Divided: Religion, Republicanism, and the Making of French Colonialism 1880–1914*. New York: Oxford University Press, 2006.

Davis, Moshe and Yehoshua Ben-Arieh, eds. *Western Societies and the Holy Land*. With Eyes Toward Zion III. New York: Praeger, 1991.

Deguilhem, Randi. "Turning Syrians into Frenchmen: The Cultural Politics of a French Non-Governmental Organization in Mandate Syria (1920–1967)—the French Secular Mission Schools." *Islam and Christian–Muslim Relations* 13 (2002): 449–460.

Delaney, Carol. "Columbus's Ultimate Goal: Jerusalem." *Comparative Studies in Society and History* 48 (2006): 260–292.

DeNovo, John A. *American Interests and Policies in the Middle East 1900–1939*. Minneapolis: University of Minnesota Press, 1963.

Deringil, Selim. "'There Is No Compulsion in Religion': On Conversion and Apostasy in the Late Ottoman Empire: 1839–1856." *Comparative Studies in Society and History* 42 (2000): 547–575.

——. *The Well-Protected Domains: Ideology and the Legitimation of Power in the Ottoman Empire, 1876–1909*. London: I. B. Tauris, 1999.

Dockrill, Michael L. and J. Douglas Gould. *Peace Without Promise: Britain and the Peace Conferences, 1919–23*. London: Batsford Academic and Educational, 1981.

Dodge, Bayard. "American Educational and Missionary Efforts in the Nineteenth and Early Twentieth Centuries." *Annals of the American Academy of Political and Social Science* 401 (1972): 15–22.

——. *The American University of Beirut: A Brief History of the University and the Lands Which It Serves*. Beirut: Khayat's, 1958.

Dols, Michael. *The Black Death in the Middle East*. Princeton, N.J.: Princeton University Press, 1977.

Doumato, Eleanor A. "An Extra Legible Illustration of the Christian Faith: Medicine, Medical Ethics, and Missionaries in the Arabian Gulf." In Eleanor H. Tejirian and Reeva Spector Simon, eds., *Altruism and Imperialism: Western Cultural and Religious Missions in the Middle East*, 167–182. New York: Middle East Institute, Columbia University, 2002. Also published in *Islam and Christian–Muslim Relations* 13 (2002): 377–390.

Drijvers, Hans. "The Persistence of Pagan Cults and Practices in Christian Syria." In Nina G. Garsoian, Thomas F. Mathews, and Robert W. Thomson, eds., *East of Byzantium: Syria and Armenia in the Formative Period*, 35–43. Washington, D.C.: Dumbarton Oaks, 1982.

Dudman, Helga and Ruth Kark. *The American Colony: Scenes from a Jerusalem Saga*. Jerusalem: Carta, 1998.

Dueck, Jennifer M. "Educational Conquest: Schools as a Sphere of Politics in French Mandate Syria, 1936–1946." *French History* 20 (2006): 442–459.

Dvornik, Francis. *Byzantine Missions Among the Slavs: SS. Constantine-Cyril and Methodius*. New Brunswick, N.J.: Rutgers University Press, 1970.

Edbury, Peter and Jonathan Phillips, eds. *The Experience of Crusading*. Cambridge: Cambridge University Press, 2003.

Eldem, Edhem, Daniel Groffmann, and Bruce Masters, eds. *The Ottoman City Between East and West: Aleppo, Izmir, and Istanbul*. Cambridge: Cambridge University Press, 1999.

Eliav, Mordechai. "German Interests and the Jewish Community in Nineteenth Century Palestine." In Moshe Ma'oz, ed., *Studies on Palestine During the Ottoman Period*, 423–441. Jerusalem: Magnes Press, 1975.

Elsbree, Oliver Wendell. "The Rise of the Missionary Spirit in New England, 1790–1815." *New England Quarterly* 1 (1928): 295–322.

Elshakry, Marwa. "The Gospel of Science and American Evangelism in Late Ottoman Beirut." *Past and Present* 196 (2007): 173–214.

Endelman, Tod, ed. *Jewish Apostasy in the Modern World*. London: Holmes and Meier, 1987.

——. *Radical Assimilation in English Jewish History, 1656–1945*. Bloomington: Indiana University Press, 1990.

Epperson, Steven. "Dedicating and Consecrating the Land: Mormon Ritual Performance in Palestine." In Eli Lederhendler and Jonathan D. Sarna, eds., *America and*

Zion: Essays and Papers in Memory of Moshe Davis, 91–116. Detroit: Wayne State University Press, 2002.

——. *Mormons and Jews: Early Mormon Theologies of Israel*. Salt Lake City: Signature Books, 1992.

Farah, Caesar F. *The Politics of Interventionism in Ottoman Lebanon 1830–1861*. London: Centre for Lebanese Studies in association with I. B. Tauris, 2000.

——. "A Tale of Two Missions." In *Arabic and Islamic Garland: Historical, Educational, and Literary Papers Presented to Abdul-Latif Tibawi by Colleagues, Friends, and Students*, 81–91. London: Islamic Cultural Centre, 1977.

Feldman, Louis. "Was Judaism a Missionary Religion in Ancient Times?" In Menachem Mor, ed., *Jewish Assimilation, Acculturation, and Accommodations: Past Traditions, Current Issues, and Future Prospects*, 24–37. Millburn, N.J.: University Press of America, 1992.

Ferrari, Silvio. "The Holy See and the Postwar Palestine Issue: The Internationalization of Jerusalem and the Protection of the Holy Places." *International Affairs* 60 (1984): 261–283.

——. "The Vatican, Israel, and the Question of Jerusalem (1943–1984)." *Middle East Journal* 39 (1985): 316–331.

Figes, Orlando. *The Crimean War: A History*. New York: Metropolitan Books, 2010.

Filkins, Dexter. "Boys of Baghdad College Vie for Prime Minister." *New York Times*, December 12, 2005.

Finnie, David H. *Pioneers East*. Cambridge, Mass.: Harvard University Press, 1967.

Fishburn, Janet F. "The Social Gospel as Missionary Ideology." In Wilbert R. Shenk, ed., *North American Foreign Missions, 1810–1914: Theology, Theory, and Policy*, 217–242. Grand Rapids, Mich.: Eerdmans, 2004.

Fleischmann, Ellen. "Evangelization or Education: American Protestant Missionaries, the American Board, and the Girls and Women of Syria (1830–1910)." In Heleen Murre-van den Berg, ed., *New Faith in Ancient Lands: Western Missions in the Middle East in the Nineteenth and Early Twentieth Centuries*, 263–280. Leiden: Brill, 2006.

——. "The Impact of American Protestant Missions in Lebanon on the Construction of Female Identity, c. 1860–1950." *Islam and Christian–Muslim Relations* 13 (2002): 411–426.

——. "'Our Muslim Sisters': Women of Greater Syria in the Eyes of American Protestant Missionary Women." *Islam and Christian–Muslim Relations* 9 (1998): 307–323.

Foerster, Frank. "German Missions in the Holy Land." In Yehoshua Ben-Arieh and Moshe Davis, eds., *Jerusalem in the Mind of the Western World, 1800–1948*, 183–194, With Eyes Toward Zion V. Westport, Conn.: Praeger, 1997.

——. "The Journey of Friedrich Adolph Strauss to the Holy Land and the Beginnings of German Missions in the Middle East." In Martin Tamcke and Michael Marten, eds., *Christian Witness Between Continuity and New Beginnings: Modern Historical Missions in the Middle East*, 125–132. Berlin: Lit, 2006.

Forell, George W. "Luther and the War Against the Turks." *Church History* 14 (1945): 256–271.

Forse, James H. "Armenians and the First Crusade." *Journal of Medieval History* 17 (1991): 13–22.

Fortna, Benjamin C. *Imperial Classroom: Islam, the State, and Education in the Late Ottoman Empire*. New York: Oxford University Press, 2000.

Fowdon, Garth. *Empire to Commonwealth: Consequences of Monotheism in Late Antiquity*. Princeton, N.J.: Princeton University Press, 1993.

Fox, Robin Lane. *Pagans and Christians*. New York: Knopf, 1987.

France, John. *The Crusades and the Expansion of Catholic Christendom 1000–1714*. London: Routledge, 2005.

Frankel, Jonathan. *The Damascus Affair*. New York: Cambridge University Press, 1997.

Frazee, Charles A. *Catholics and Sultans: The Church and the Ottoman Empire, 1453–1923*. New York: Cambridge University Press, 1983.

Frend, W. H. C. "Christianity in the Middle East: Survey Down to A.D. 1800." In A. J. Arberry, ed., *Religion in the Middle East: Three Religions in Concord and Conflict*, 1:239–296. New York: Cambridge University Press, 1969.

Fromkin, David. *A Peace to End All Peace: The Fall of the Ottoman Empire and the Creation of the Modern Middle East*. New York: Henry Holt, 1989.

Gallagher, Nancy. *Quakers in the Israeli–Palestinian Conflict: The Dilemma of NGO Humanitarian Activism*. Cairo: American University in Cairo Press, 2007.

Garrett, Clarke. *Respectable Folly: Millenarians and the French Revolution in France and England*. Baltimore: Johns Hopkins University Press, 1975.

Garsoian, Nina G. "The History of Armenia." In Thomas F. Matthews and Roger S. Wieck, eds., *Treasures of Heaven*, 2–23. New York: Pierpont Morgan Library, 1994.

Garsoian, Nina G., Thomas F. Mathews, and Robert W. Thomson, eds. *East of Byzantium: Syria and Armenia in the Formative Period*. Washington, D.C.: Dumbarton Oaks, 1982.

Geldbach, Erich. "The German Protestant Network in the Holy Land." In Moshe Davis and Yehoshua Ben-Arieh, eds., *Western Societies and the Holy Land*, 151–169. With Eyes Toward Zion III. New York: Praeger, 1991.

Gelvin, James. "The Ironic Legacy of the King–Crane Commission." In David W. Lesch, ed., *The Middle East and the United States: A Historical and Political Reassessment*, 2nd ed., 13–29. Boulder, Colo.: Westview, 1996.

Geniesse, Jane Fletcher. *American Priestess: The Extraordinary Story of Anna Spafford and the American Colony in Jerusalem*. New York: Doubleday, 2008.

Gervers, Michael, and Ramzi Jibran Bikhazi, eds. *Indigenous Christian Communities in Islamic Lands, Eighth to Eighteenth Centuries*. Papers in Mediaeval Studies no. 9. Toronto: Pontifical Institute of Mediaeval Studies, 1990.

Gervers, Michael and James M. Powell, eds. *Tolerance and Intolerance: Social Conflict in the Age of the Crusades*. Syracuse, N.Y.: Syracuse University Press, 2001.

Gidney, W. T. *History of the London Society for Promoting Christianity Amongst the Jews: From 1809 to 1908*. London: London Society for Promoting Christianity Amongst the Jews, 1908.

Gilchrist, John. "The Lord's War as the Proving Ground of Faith: Pope Innocent III and the Propagation of Violence (1198–1216)." In Maya Shatzmiller, ed., *Crusaders and Muslims in Twelfth-Century Syria*, 65–83. Leiden: Brill, 1993.

——. "The Papacy and the 'Saracens.'" *International History Review* 10 (1988): 173–197.

Gillard, David. *The Struggle for Asia 1828–1914: A Study in British and Russian Imperialism*. London: Methuen, 1977.

Gilley, Sheridan and W. J. Sheils, eds. *A History of Religion in Britain: Practice and Belief from Pre-Roman Times to the Present*. Oxford: Blackwell, 1994.

Goffman, Carolyn McCue. "Masking the Mission: Cultural Conversion in the American College for Girls." In Eleanor H. Tejirian and Reeva Spector Simon, eds., *Altruism and Imperialism: Western Cultural and Religious Missions in the Middle East*, 88–119. New York: Middle East Institute, Columbia University, 2002.

Goffman, Daniel. *The Ottoman Empire and Early Modern Europe*. Cambridge: Cambridge University Press, 2002.

Goldman, Shalom. "The Holy Land Appropriated: The Careers of Selah Merrill, Nineteenth Century Christian Hebraist, Palestine Explorer, and U.S. Consul in Jerusalem." *American Jewish History* 85 (1997): 151–172.

Goodman, Martin. "Proselytising in Rabbinic Judaism." *Journal of Jewish Studies* 40 (1989): 175–185.

Goodwin, Jason. *Lords of the Horizons: A History of the Ottoman Empire*. New York: Holt, 1997.

Goren, Haim. "The German Catholic 'Holy Sepulchre Society': Activities in Palestine." In Yehoshua Ben-Arieh and Moshe Davis, eds., *Jerusalem in the Mind of the Western World 1800–1948*, 155–172, With Eyes Toward Zion V. Westport, Conn.: Praeger, 1997.

——. "Scientific Organizations as Agents of Change: Palestine Exploration Fund, the *Deutsche Verein sur Erforschung Palästinas*, and Nineteenth-Century Palestine." *Journal of Historical Geography* 27 (2001): 153–165.

Grabar, Oleg. "Roots and Others." In Holly Edwards, ed., *Noble Dreams, Wicked Pleasures: Orientalism in America, 1870–1930*, 3–9. Princeton, N.J.: Princeton University Press, 2000.

Gräbe, Uwe. "Mission and Proselytism as a Historical Background to a Contemporary Reformulation of Christian 'Presence and Witness' in the Middle East." In Martin Tamcke and Michael Marten, eds., *Christian Witness Between Continuity and New Beginnings: Modern Historical Missions in the Middle East*, 247–254. Berlin: Lit, 2006.

Grabill, Joseph L. *Protestant Diplomacy and the Near East*. Minneapolis: University of Minnesota Press, 1971.

Griffith, Sidney H. "The View of Islam from the Monasteries of Palestine in the Early Abbasid Period: Theodore Abu Qurrah and the *Summa Theologiae Arabica*." *Islam and Christian–Muslim Relations* 7 (1996): 9–28.

Gunn, Jeremy T. "A Preliminary Response to Criticisms of the International Religious Freedom Act of 1998." *Brigham Young University Law Review* 3 (2000): 841–865.

Haddad, Mahmoud. "Syrian Muslim Attitudes Toward Foreign Missionaries in the Late Nineteenth and Twentieth Centuries." In Eleanor H. Tejirian and Reeva Spector Simon, eds., *Altruism and Imperialism: Western Cultural and Religious Missions in the Middle East*, 253–274. New York: Middle East Institute, Columbia University, 2002.

Haddad, Robert M. "Conversion of Eastern Orthodox Christians to the Unia in the Seventeenth and Eighteenth Centuries." In Michael Gervers and Ramzi Jibran Bikhazi, eds., *Indigenous Christian Communities in Islamic Lands, Eighth to Eighteenth Centuries*, 449–459, Papers in Mediaeval Studies no. 9. Toronto: Pontifical Institute of Mediaeval Studies, 1990.

——. *Syrian Christians in Muslim Society: An Interpretation*. Princeton Studies on the Near East. Westport, Conn.: Greenwood Press, 1970.

Hale, Bradley Rainbow. "The Soul of Empire: The Society of Missionaries of Africa in Colonial Algeria, 1919–1939." PhD diss., University of Connecticut, 2005.

Hamdani, A. "Columbus and the Recovery of Jerusalem." *Journal of the American Oriental Society* 99 (1979): 39–48.

Hamilton, Alistair. *The Copts and the West, 1439–1822: The European Discovery of the Egyptian Church*. Oxford: Oxford University Press, 2006.

Hamilton, Bernard. *The Latin Church in the Crusader States: The Secular Church*. London: Varorium, 1980.

Hankins, James. "Renaissance Crusaders: Humanist Crusade Literature in the Age of Mehmed II." *Dumbarton Oaks Papers* 49 (1995): 111–207.

Harel, Yaron. *Syrian Jewry in Transition 1840–1880*. Oxford: Littman Library of Jewish Civilization, 2010.

Heffernan, Michael J. "The Parisian Poor and the Colonization of Algeria During the Second Republic." *French History* 3 (1989): 377–403.

Herrin, Judith. *Byzantium: The Surprising Life of a Medieval Empire*. Princeton, N.J.: Princeton University Press, 2008.

Hertzke, Allen D. and Daniel Philpott. "Defending the Faiths." *The National Interest* 6 (2000): 74–81.

Heyberger, Bernard. "Eastern Christians, Islam, and the West: A Connected History." *International Journal of Middle East Studies* 42 (2010): 475–478.

Heyberger, Bernard and Chantal Verdeil. "Spirituality and Scholarship: The Holy Land in Jesuit Eyes (Seventeenth to Nineteenth Centuries)." In Heleen Murre-van den Berg, ed., *New Faith in Ancient Lands: Western Missions in the Middle East in the Nineteenth and Early Twentieth Centuries*, 19–41. Leiden: Brill, 2006.

Hocking, William Ernest. *Re-Thinking Missions: A Laymen's Inquiry After One Hundred Years*. New York: Harper & Brothers, 1932.

Hocquet, Jean-Claude. "Venice and the Turks." In Stefano Carboni, ed., *Venice and the Islamic World 828–1797*, 36–51. New York: Metropolitan Museum of Art, 2007.

Hodder, Edwin. *The Life and Work of the Seventh Earl of Shaftesbury, K. G.* 3 vols. London: Cassell, 1888.

Hodges, Richard and David Whitehouse. *Mohammed, Charlemagne, and the Origins of Europe: Archaeology and the Pirenne Thesis*. Ithaca, N.Y.: Cornell University Press, 1983.

Hoffmann, Godehard. "Kaiser Wilhelm II und der Benediktinerorden." *Zeitschrift für Kirchengeschichte* 106, no. 3 (1995): 363–384.

Hopkirk, Peter. *The Great Game: On Secret Service in High Asia*. London: John Murray, 1990.

——. *Like Hidden Fire: The Plot to Bring Down the British Empire.* New York: Kodansha International, 1994.

Hopwood, Derek. "'The Resurrection of Our Eastern Brethren' (Ignatiev): Russia and Orthodox Arab Nationalism in Jerusalem." In Moshe Ma'oz, ed., *Studies on Palestine During the Ottoman Period*, 394–407. Jerusalem: Magnes Press, 1975.

——. *The Russian Presence in Syria and Palestine 1843–1914: Church and Politics in the Near East.* Oxford, U.K.: Clarendon Press, 1969.

Horden, Peregrine and Nicholas Purcell. *The Corrupting Sea: A Study of Mediterranean History.* Oxford, U.K.: Blackwell, 2000.

Hourani, Albert. *Arabic Thought in the Liberal Age: 1798–1939.* New York: Oxford University Press, 1970.

Housley, Norman. "Crusades Against Christians: Their Origins and Early Development, c. 1000–1216." In Peter W. Edbury, ed., *Crusade and Settlement*, 17–36. Cardiff, U.K.: University College of Cardiff Press, 1985.

——. "Jerusalem and the Development of the Crusade Idea, 1099–1128." In Benjamin Z. Kedar, ed., *The Horns of Hattin*, 27–40. Jerusalem: Yad Izhak Ben Zvi, 1992.

Howard, Harry N. "An American Experiment in Peacemaking: The King–Crane Commission." *Muslim World* 32 (1942): 122–146.

Howe, John. "The Nobility's Reform of the Medieval Church." *American Historical Review* 93 (1988): 317–339.

Hoyland, Robert C. *Seeing Islam as Others Saw It: A Survey and Evaluation of Christian, Jewish, and Zoroastrian Writings on Early Islam.* Princeton, N.J.: Darwin Press, 1997.

Hsia, P. po-Chia. *The World of Catholic Renewal.* Cambridge: Cambridge University Press, 1998.

Hummel, Thomas. "Between Eastern and Western Christendom: The Anglican Presence in Jerusalem." In Anthony O'Mahony, ed., *The Christian Communities of Jerusalem and the Holy Land: Studies in History, Religion, and Politics*, 147–170. Cardiff, U.K.: University of Wales Press, 2003.

Hutchison, William R. *Errand to the World: American Protestant Thought and Foreign Missions.* Chicago: University of Chicago Press, 1987.

Hyamson, Albert M. *The British Consulate in Jerusalem in Relation to the Jews of Palestine 1838–1914.* 2 vols. London: Jewish Historical Society of England and Edward Goldston, 1939.

Jackson, Peter. "The Crisis in the Holy Land in 1260." *English Historical Review* 376 (1980): 481–513.

——. "Hulegu Khan the Christian: The Making of a Myth." In Peter Edbury and Jonathan Phillips, eds., *The Experience of Crusading*, 2:196–213. Cambridge: Cambridge University Press, 2003.

Jacobson, Abigail. "A City Living Through Crisis: Jerusalem During World War I." *British Journal of Middle Eastern Studies* 36 (2009): 73–92.

Jenkins, Paul. "The Church Missionary Society and the Basel Mission: An Early Experiment in Inter-European Cooperation." In Kevin Ward and Brian Stanley, eds., *The Church Mission Society and World Christianity, 1799–1999*, 43–65. Grand Rapids, Mich.: Eerdmans, 2000.

Jeyaraj, Daniel. "Mission Reports from South India and Their Impact on the Western Mind: The Tranquebar Mission of the Eighteenth Century." In Dana L. Robert, ed., *Converting Colonialism: Visions and Realities in Missionary History, 1706–1914,* 21–42. Grand Rapids, Mich.: Eerdmans, 2008.

Joseph, John. *The Modern Assyrians of the Middle East: Encounters with Western Christian Missions, Archaeologists, and Colonial Powers.* Leiden: Brill, 2000.

——. *Muslim–Christian Relations and the Inter-Christian Rivalries in the Middle East: The Case of the Jacobites in an Age of Transition.* Albany: State University of New York Press, 1983.

Kaegi, Walter Emil, Jr. "Initial Byzantine Reactions to the Arab Conquest." *Church History* 38 (1969): 139–149.

Kaminsky, Uwe. "German 'Home Mission' Abroad: The *Orientarbeit* of the Deaconess Institution Kaiserwerth in the Ottoman Empire." In Heleen Murre-van den Berg, ed., *New Faith in Ancient Lands: Western Missions in the Middle East in the Nineteenth and Early Twentieth Centuries,* 191–209. Leiden: Brill, 2006.

Kane, Eileen M. "Pilgrims, Piety, and Politics: The Founding of the First Russian Ecclesiastical Mission in Jerusalem." In Martin Tamcke and Michael Marten, eds., *Christian Witness Between Continuity and New Beginnings: Modern Historical Missions in the Middle East,* 177–198. Berlin: Lit, 2006.

Kaplan, Robert D. *The Arabists: The Romance of an American Elite.* New York: Free Press, 1993.

Kark, Ruth. "The Contribution of Nineteenth Century Protestant Missionary Societies to Historical Geography." *Imago Mundi* 45 (1993): 112–119.

——. "The Impact of Early Missionary Enterprises on Landscape and Identity Formation in Palestine, 1820–1914." *Islam and Christian–Muslim Relations* 15 (2004): 209–235.

——. "Millenarism and Agricultural Settlement in the Holy Land in the Nineteenth Century." *Journal of Historical Geography* 9 (1983): 47–62.

——. "Sweden and the Holy Land: Pietistic and Communal Settlement." *Journal of Historical Geography* 22 (1996): 46–67.

Kark, Ruth, Dietrich Denecke, and Haim Goren. "The Impact of Early German Missionary Enterprise in Palestine on the Modernization and Environmental and Technological Change, 1820–1914." In Martin Tamcke and Michael Marten, eds., *Christian Witness Between Continuity and New Beginnings: Modern Historical Missions in the Middle East,* 145–176. Berlin: Lit, 2006.

Katz, David S. and Richard H. Popkin. *Messianic Revolutions: Radical Religious Politics to the End of the Second Millennium.* New York: Hill and Wang, 1998.

Katz, Itamar and Ruth Kark. "The Church and Landed Property: The Greek Orthodox and Patriarchate of Jerusalem." *Middle Eastern Studies* 43 (2007): 383–408.

Kaufman, Asher. *Reviving Phoenicia: In Search of Identity in Lebanon.* New York: I. B. Tauris, 2004.

Kedar, Benjamin Z. *Crusade and Mission: European Approaches Toward the Muslims.* Princeton, N.J.: Princeton University Press, 1984.

——, ed. *The Horns of Hattin.* Jerusalem: Yad Izhak Ben Zvi, 1992.

Keddie, Nikki R. *Qajar Iran and the Rise of Reza Khan, 1796–1925*. Costa Mesa, Calif.: Mazda, 1999.

Kedourie, Elie. "The American University of Beirut." *Middle Eastern Studies* 3 (1966): 74–88.

Kennedy, Hugh. *The Great Arab Conquests: How the Spread of Islam Changed the World We Live In*. Philadelphia: Da Capo Press, 2007.

Khater, Akram. "'God Has Called Me to Be Free': Aleppan Nuns and the Transformation of Catholicism in 18th-Century Bilad al-Sham." *International Journal of Middle East Studies* 40 (2008): 421–443.

Khodarkovsky, Michael. "The Conversion of Non-Christians in Early Modern Russia." In Robert Geraci and Michael Khodarkovsky, eds., *Of Religion and Empire: Missions, Conversion, and Tolerance in Tsarist Russia*, 115–143. Ithaca, N.Y.: Cornell University Press, 2001.

——. "Ignoble Savages and Unfaithful Subjects: Contrasting Non-Christian Identities in Early Modern Russia." In Daniel Brower and Edward Lazzerini, eds., *Russia's Orient: Imperial Borderlands and Peoples, 1700–1917*, 9–26. Bloomington: Indiana University Press, 1997.

——. "Of Christianity, Enlightenment, and Colonialism: Russia in the North Caucasus 1550–1800." *Journal of Modern History* 71 (1999): 394–430.

Kidd, Thomas S. *American Christians and Islam: Evangelical Culture and Muslims from the Colonial Period to the Age of Terrorism*. Princeton, N.J.: Princeton University Press, 2009.

Kiernan, V. "Evangelicalism and the French Revolution." *Past and Present* 1 (1952): 44–56.

Kieser, Hans-Lukas. "Mission as Factor of Change in Turkey (Nineteenth to First Half of Twentieth Century)." *Islam and Christian–Muslim Relations* 13 (2002): 391–410.

——. "Muslim Heterodoxy and Protestant Utopia: The Interaction Between Alevis and Missionaries in Ottoman Anatolia." *Die Welt des Islams* 41 (2001): 89–111.

Klatzker, David. "American Christian Travelers to the Holy Land, 1821–1939." In Moshe Davis and Yehoshua Ben-Arieh, eds., *Western Societies and the Holy Land*, 63–76, With Eyes Toward Zion III. New York: Praeger, 1991.

Klier, John D. "State Policies and the Conversion of Jews in Imperial Russia." In Robert P. Geraci and Michael Khodarkovsky, eds., *Of Religion and Empire: Missions, Conversion, and Tolerance in Tsarist Russia*, 92–112. Ithaca, N.Y.: Cornell University Press, 2001.

Kling, David W. "The New Divinity and the Origins of the American Board of Commissioners for Foreign Missions." *Church History* 72 (2003): 791–819.

Knee, Stuart E. "Anglo–American Relations in Palestine 1919–1925: An Experiment in *Realpolitik*." *Journal of American Studies of Turkey* 5 (1997): 3–18.

——. "The King–Crane Commission of 1919: The Articulation of Political Anti-Zionism." *American Jewish Archives* 29 (1977): 22–53.

Knobler, Adam. "Holy Wars, Empires, and the Portability of the Past: The Modern Uses of Medieval Crusades." *Comparative Studies in Society and History* 48 (2006): 293–325.

——. "Pseudo-Conversions and Patchwork Pedigrees: The Christianization of Muslim Princes and the Diplomacy of Holy War." *Journal of World History* 7 (1996): 181–197.

Krüger, Jürgen. "Wilhelm II's Perception of Sacrality." In Hélène Sader, Thomas Scheffler, and Angelika Neuwirth, eds., *Baalbek: Images and Monument 1898–1998*, 89–95. Stuttgart: Franz Steiner, 1998.

Laffey, John F. "The Roots of French Imperialism in the Nineteenth Century: The Case of Lyon." *French Historical Studies* 6 (1969): 78–92.

Landes, Richard. "The Fear of an Apocalypse Year 1000: Augustinian Historiography, Medieval and Modern." *Speculum* 75 (2000): 97–145.

Langohr, Vickie. "Colonial Education Systems and the Spread of Local Religious Movements: The Cases of British Egypt and Punjab." *Comparative Studies in Society and History* 47 (2005): 161–189.

Lapidus, Ira M. "The Conversion of Egypt to Islam." *Israel Oriental Studies* 2 (1972): 248–262.

Laskier, Michael M. *The Alliance Israélite Universelle and the Jewish Communities of Morocco, 1862–1962*. Albany: State University of New York Press, 1983.

Latourette, Kenneth Scott. *A History of the Expansion of Christianity*. 7 vols. New York: Harper & Brothers, 1937–1945.

Laurens, Henry. "Jaussen et les services de renseignement français." In G. Chatelard and M. Tarawneh, eds., *Antonin Jaussen: Sciences sociales occidentales et patrimoine arabe*, 23–35. Paris: Centre d'Études et de Recherches sur le Moyen-Orient Contemporain, 1999.

Lederhendler, Eli and Jonathan D. Sarna, eds. *America and Zion: Essays and Papers in Memory of Moshe Davis*. Detroit: Wayne State University Press, 2002.

Leest, Charlotte van der. "The Protestant Bishopric of Jerusalem and the Missionary Activities in Nazareth: The Gobat Years, 1846–1879." In Martin Tamcke and Michael Marten, eds., *Christian Witness Between Continuity and New Beginnings: Modern Historical Missions in the Middle East*, 199–211. Berlin: Lit, 2006.

Lerner, Robert E. "Medieval Prophecy and Religious Dissent." *Past and Present* 72 (August 1976): 3–24.

Lesch, David W., ed. *The Middle East and the United States: A Historical and Political Reassessment*. 2nd ed. Boulder, Colo.: Westview, 1996.

Levtzion, Nehemia. "Conversion to Islam in Syria and Palestine and the Survival of Christian Communities." In Michael Gervers and Ramzi Jibran Bikhazi, eds., *Conversion and Continuity: Indigenous Christian Communities in Islamic Lands Eighth to Eighteenth Centuries*, 289–312, Papers in Mediaeval Studies no. 9. Toronto: Pontifical Institute of Mediaeval Studies, 1990.

Lieven, Dominic. *Empire: The Russian Empire and Its Rivals*. New Haven, Conn.: Yale University Press, 2000.

Lipman, Vivian D. "Britain and the Holy Land: 1830–1914." In Moshe Davis and Yehoshua Ben-Arieh, eds., *Western Societies and the Holy Land*, 195–207, With Eyes Toward Zion III. New York: Praeger, 1991.

Little, David. "Religion and Global Affairs: Religion and U.S. Foreign Policy." *SAIS Review* 18 (1998): 25–31.

Long, Burke O. *Imagining the Holy Land: Maps, Models, and Fantasy Travels*. Bloomington: Indiana University Press, 2003.

Lückhoff, Martin. "Prussia and Jerusalem: Political and Religious Controversies Surrounding the Foundation of the Jerusalem Bishopric." In Yehoshua Ben-Arieh and Moshe Davis, eds., *Jerusalem in the Mind of the Western World 1800–1948*, 173–182, With Eyes Toward Zion V. Westport, Conn.: Praeger, 1997.

Macmillan, Margaret. *Paris 1919: Six Months That Changed the World*. New York: Random House, 2001.

MacMullen, Ramsay. *Christianizing the Roman Empire (A.D. 100–400)*. New Haven, Conn.: Yale University Press, 1984.

——. "Two Types of Conversion to Early Christianity." *Vigilae Christianae* 37 (1983): 174–192.

Mahdavi, Shireen. "Shahs, Doctors, Diplomats, and Missionaries in 19th Century Iran." *British Journal of Middle Eastern Studies* 32 (2005): 169–191.

Maier, Christoph T. *Preaching the Crusades: Mendicant Friars and the Cross in the Thirteenth Century*. Cambridge: Cambridge University Press, 1994

Makdisi, Ussama. *Artillery of Heaven: American Missionaries and the Failed Conversion of the Middle East*. Ithaca, N.Y.: Cornell University Press, 2008.

——. *The Culture of Sectarianism: Community, History, and Violence in Nineteenth Century Ottoman Lebanon*. Berkeley and Los Angeles: University of California Press, 2000.

——. "Reclaiming the Land of the Bible: Missionaries, Secularism, and Evangelical Modernity." *American Historical Review* 102 (1997): 680–713.

Maksoudian, Krikor H. "The Religion of Armenia." In Thomas F. Mathews and Roger S. Wieck, eds., *Treasures in Heaven*, 24–37. New York: Pierpont Morgan Library, 1994.

Ma'oz, Moshe, ed. *Studies on Palestine During the Ottoman Period*. Jerusalem: Magnes Press, 1975.

Maraval, Pierre. "The Earliest Phase of Christian Pilgrimage in the Near East (Before the 7th Century)." *Dumbarton Oaks Papers* 56 (2002): 63–74.

Marcus, Abraham. *The Middle East on the Eve of Modernity: Aleppo in the Eighteenth Century*. New York: Columbia University Press, 1989.

Marr, Timothy. *The Cultural Roots of American Islamicism*. New York: Cambridge University Press, 2006.

Marsden, George M. *Fundamentalism and American Culture*. 2nd ed. New York: Oxford University Press, 2006.

Marten, Michael. "Anglican and Presbyterian Presence and Theology in the Holy Land." *International Journal for the Study of the Christian Church* 5 (2005): 182–199.

——. *Attempting to Bring the Gospel Home: Scottish Missions to Palestine, 1839–1917*. London: Tauris Academic Studies, 2006.

——. "Imperialism and Evangelisation: Scottish Missionary Methods in Late 19th and Early 20th Century Palestine." *Holy Land Studies* 5 (2006): 155–186.

Martin, R. H. "United Conversionist Activities Among the Jews in Great Britain 1795–1815: Pan-Evangelicalism and the London Society for Promoting Christianity Amongst the Jews." *Church History* 46 (1977): 437–452.

Masters, Bruce. "The 1850 Events in Aleppo: An Aftershock of Syria's Incorporation in the Capitalist World System." *International Journal of Middle East Studies* 22 (1990): 3–20.

——. "Aleppo: The Ottoman Empire's Caravan City." In Edhem Eldem, Daniel Groffman, and Bruce Masters, eds., *The Ottoman City Between East and West: Aleppo, Izmir, and Istanbul*, 17–78. Cambridge: Cambridge University Press, 1999.

——. *Christians and Jews in the Ottoman Arab World: The Roots of Sectarianism*. New York: Cambridge University Press, 2001.

Mathews, Thomas F. and Roger S. Wieck, eds. *Treasures in Heaven*. New York: Pierpont Morgan Library, 1994.

Matthews, Roderic D. and Matta Akrawi. *Education in Arab Countries of the Near East*. Washington, D.C.: American College on Education, 1949.

Mazza, Roberto. "Churches at War: The Impact of the First World War on the Christian Institutions of Jerusalem, 1914–20." *Middle Eastern Studies* 45 (2009): 207–227.

Mead, Walter Russell. *Special Providence American Foreign Policy and How It Changed the World*. New York: Routledge, 2002.

Ménage, V. L. "The Islamization of Anatolia." In Nehemia Levzion, ed., *Conversion to Islam*, 52–67. New York: Holmes and Meier, 1979.

Meyendorff, John. "Byzantine Views of Islam." *Dumbarton Oaks Papers* 18 (1964): 113–132.

Miège, Jean-Louis. "Les Missions Protestantes au Maroc, 1875–1905." *Hespéris* 42 (1955): 153–186.

Miller, Jon. *The Social Control of Religious Zeal: A Study of the Organizational Contradictions*. New Brunswick, N.J.: Rutgers University Press, 1994.

Mirak, Robert. *Torn Between Two Lands: Armenians in America, 1890 to World War I*. Cambridge, Mass.: Harvard University Press, 1983.

Mitchell, Timothy. *Colonizing Egypt*. Berkeley and Los Angeles: University of California Press, 1991.

Moreno, Eduardo Manzano and Roberto Mazza. *Jerusalem in World War I: The Palestine Diary of a European Diplomat—Conde de Ballobar*. London: Tauris, 2011.

Muldoon, James. *Popes, Lawyers, and Infidels: The Church and the Non-Christian World, 1250–1550*. Philadelphia: University of Pennsylvania Press, 1979.

——. "Tolerance and Intolerance in the Medieval Canon Lawyers." In Michael Gervers and James M. Powell, eds., *Tolerance and Intolerance: Social Conflict in the Age of the Crusades*, 117–123. Syracuse, N.Y.: Syracuse University Press, 2001.

Murray, Jocelyn. *Proclaim the Good News: A Short History of the Church Missionary Society*. London: Hodder and Stoughton, 1985.

Murre-van den Berg, Heleen. "The Middle East: Western Missions and the Eastern Churches, Islam and Judaism." In Sheridan Gilley and Brian Stanley, eds., *The Cambridge History of Christianity*, vol. 8: *World Christianities c. 1815–c.1914*, 458–472. New York: Cambridge University Press, 2006.

——, ed. *New Faith in Ancient Lands: Western Missions in the Middle East in the Nineteenth and Early Twentieth Centuries*. Leiden: Brill, 2006.

——. "'Simply by Giving to Them Maccaroni . . .': Anti-Roman Catholic Polemics in Early Protestant Missions in the Middle East, 1820–1860." In Martin Tamcke and Michael Marten, eds., *Christian Witness Between Continuity and New Beginnings: Modern Historical Missions in the Middle East*, 63–80. Berlin: Lit, 2006.

Naby, Eden. "The Assyrians of Iran: Reunification of a 'Millet,' 1906–1914." *International Journal of Middle East Studies* 8 (1977): 237–249.

Neill, Stephen. *A History of Christian Missions*. 2nd ed. Revised by Owen Chadwick. New York: Penguin, 1986.

Neubert-Preine, Thorsten. "The Founding of German Protestant Institutions in Jerusalem During the Reign of Kaiser Wilhelm II." In Haim Goren, ed., *Germany and the Middle East: Past, Present, and Future*, 27–33. Jerusalem: Magnes Press, 2003.

——. "The Struggle Over the Muristan in Jerusalem as an Example of National-Confessional Rivalry in the 19th Century Middle East." In Martin Tamcke and Michael Marten, eds., *Christian Witness Between Continuity and New Beginnings: Modern Historical Missions in the Middle East*, 133–144. Berlin: Lit, 2006.

Nirenberg, David. *Communities of Violence: Persecution of Minorities in the Middle Ages*. Princeton, N.J.: Princeton University Press, 1996.

Noll, Mark A. *America's God: From Jonathan Edwards to Abraham Lincoln*. New York: Oxford University Press, 2002

——. *The Rise of Evangelicalism: The Age of Edwards, Whitefield, and the Wesleys*. Downers Grove, Ill.: InterVarsity Press, 2003.

Obenzinger, Hilton. *American Palestine: Melville, Twain, and the Holy Land Mania*. Princeton, N.J.: Princeton University Press, 1999.

O'Brien, Susan. "A Transatlantic Community of Saints: The Great Awakening and the First Evangelical Network, 1735–1755." *American Historical Review* 91 (1986): 811–832.

O'Donnell, J. Dean, Jr. *Lavigerie in Tunisia: The Interplay of Imperialist and Missionary*. Athens: University of Georgia Press, 1979.

Office of International Religious Freedom, U.S. Bureau of Democracy, Human Rights, and Labor. *Fact Sheet: History of the Office of International Religious Freedom*. Washington, D.C.: U.S. Department of State, April 16, 2001.

Okkenhaug, Inger Marie. "Education, Culture, and Civilization: Anglican Missionary Women in Palestine." In Anthony O'Mahony, ed., *The Christian Communities of Jerusalem and the Holy Land: Studies in History, Religion, and Politics*, 171–199. Cardiff, U.K.: University of Wales Press, 2003.

O'Mahony, Anthony, ed. *The Christian Communities of Jerusalem and the Holy Land: Studies in History, Religion, and Politics*. Cardiff, U.K.: University of Wales Press, 2003.

——. "The Latins of the East: The Vatican, Jerusalem, and the Palestinian Christians." In Anthony O'Mahony, ed., *The Christian Communities of Jerusalem and the Holy Land: Studies in History, Religion, and Politics*, 90–114. Cardiff, U.K.: University of Wales Press, 2003.

O'Mahoney, Anthony, with Göran Gunner and Kevork Hintlian, eds. *The Christian Heritage in the Holy Land*. London: Scorpion Cavendish, 1995.

Oren, Michael B. *Power, Faith, and Fantasy: America in the Middle East, 1776 to the Present*. New York: W. W. Norton, 2007.

Pacini, Andrea, ed. *Christian Communities in the Arab Middle East: The Challenge of the Future*. Oxford, U.K.: Clarendon Press, 1998.

Paul, Jim. "Medicine and Imperialism in Morocco." *MERIP Reports* 60 (1977): 3–12.

Perry, Yaron. *British Mission to the Jews in Nineteenth-Century Palestine*. London: Frank Cass, 2003.

Petricioli, Marta. "Italian Schools in Egypt." *British Journal of Middle Eastern Studies* 24 (1997): 179–191.

Phillips, Clifton Jackson. *Protestant America and the Pagan World: The First Half Century of the American Board of Commissioners for Foreign Missions, 1810–1860*. Cambridge, Mass.: Harvard East Asian Monographs, 1969.

Pinnington, John. "Church Principles in the Early Years of the Church Missionary Society: The Problem of the 'German' Missionaries." *Journal of Theological Studies*, new series, 20 (1969): 522–532.

Pirenne, Henri. *Mohammed and Charlemagne*. New York: Meridian Books, 1957.

Pomeranz, Kenneth. "Empire & 'Civilizing' Missions, Past and Present." *Daedalus* 134 (2005): 34–45.

Porter, Andrew. "'Commerce and Christianity': The Rise and Fall of a Nineteenth-Century Missionary Slogan." *Historical Journal* 28 (1985): 597–621.

——. "Evangelicalism, Islam, and Millennial Expectation in the Nineteenth Century." In Dana L. Robert, ed., *Converting Colonialism: Visions and Realities in Mission History*, 60–85. Grand Rapids, Mich.: Eerdmans, 2008.

——. "Missions and Empire c. 1873–1914." In Sheridan Gilley and Brian Stanley, eds., *The Cambridge History of Christianity*, 8:560–575. New York: Cambridge University Press, 2006.

——. *Religion Versus Empire? British Protestant Missionaries and Overseas Expansion, 1700–1914*. Manchester, U.K.: Manchester University Press, 2004.

Porterfield, Amanda. *Mary Lyon and the Mount Holyoke Missionaries*. New York: Oxford University Press, 1997.

Powell, James M. *Anatomy of a Crusade 1213–1221*. Philadelphia: University of Pennsylvania Press, 1986.

——. "The Papacy and the Muslim Frontier." In James M. Powell, ed., *Muslims Under Latin Rule, 1100–1300*, 175–203. Princeton, N.J.: Princeton University Press, 1990.

Prein, Philipp. "Mission to Arcadia: The Moravian Invention of an African Missionary Object as an Example of the Culture of German Nationalism and Colonialism." *German History* 16 (1998): 328–357.

Pringle, Denys. "Churches and Settlement in Crusader Palestine." In Peter Edbury and Jonathan Phillips, eds., *The Experience of Crusading*, 2:161–178. Cambridge, U.K.: Cambridge University Press, 2003.

Proctor, J. H. "Scottish Medical Missionaries in South Arabia, 1886–1979." *Middle Eastern Studies* 42, no. 1 (January 2006): 103–121.

Ragussis, Michael. *Figures of Conversion: "The Jewish Question" and English National Identity*. Durham, N.C.: Duke University Press, 1995.

Reid, Donald Malcolm. *Whose Pharaohs? Archaeology, Museums, and Egyptian National Identity from Napoleon to World War I*. Berkeley and Los Angeles: University of California Press, 2002.

Reimer, Michael. "The King–Crane Commission at the Juncture of Politics and Historiography." *Critique: Critical Middle Eastern Studies* 15 (2006): 129–150.

Renault, François. *Cardinal Lavigerie: Churchman, Prophet, and Missionary*. Trans. John O'Donohue. London: Athlone Press, 1994.

Richard, J. "Le Début des relations entre la papauté et les Mongoles de Perse." *Journal Asiatique* 237 (1949): 291–297.

Riggs, Rev. Charles T. "History of the Constantinople Station, 1831–1931." In American Board of Commissioners for Foreign Missions, Near East Mission, ed., *Centennial of the Constantinople Station*, 52–60. Constantinople: The Mission, 1931.

Riley-Smith, Jonathan. *The Crusades*. 2nd ed. New Haven, Conn.: Yale University Press, 2005.

——. "Islam and the Crusades in History and Imagination, 8 November 1898–11 September 2001." *Crusades* 2 (2003): 151–167.

——. *What Were the Crusades?* 3rd ed. San Francisco: Ignatius Press, 2002.

Robert, Dana L. "The 'Christian Home' as a Cornerstone of Anglo-Missionary Thought and Practice." In Dana L. Robert, ed., *Converting Colonialism: Visions and Realities in Mission History, 1706–1914*, 134–165. Grand Rapids, Mich.: Eerdmans, 2008.

——, ed. *Converting Colonialism: Visions and Realities in Mission History, 1700–1914*. Grand Rapids, Mich.: Eerdmans, 2008.

——. "The First Globalization: The Internationalization of the Protestant Missionary Movement Between the World Wars." *International Bulletin of Missionary Research* 26 (2002): 50–66.

——. "Introduction." In Dana L. Robert, ed., *Converting Colonialism: Visions and Realities in Mission History, 1700–1914*, 1–20. Grand Rapids, Mich.: Eerdmans, 2008.

——. "Mount Holyoke Women and the Dutch Reformed Missionary Movement, 1874–1904." *Missionalia* 21 (1993): 103–123.

Robinson, Chase F. *Empire and Elites After the Muslim Conquest and the Transformation of Northern Mesopotamia*. New York: Cambridge University Press, 2000.

Rodrigue, Aron. *French Jews, Turkish Jews: The Alliance Israélite Universelle and the Politics of Jewish Schooling in Turkey 1860–1925*. Bloomington: Indiana University Press, 1990.

——. *Images of Sephardi and Eastern Jewries in Transition: The Teachers of the Alliance Israélite Universelle, 1860–1939*. Seattle: University of Washington Press, 1993.

Rogan, Eugene L. *Frontiers of the State in the Late Ottoman Empire: Transjordan 1850–1921*. Cambridge, U.K.: Cambridge University Press, 1999.

Rogers, Richard Lee. "'A Bright and New Constellation': Millennial Narratives and the Origins of American Foreign Missions." In Wilbert R. Shenk, ed., *North American Foreign Missions, 1810–1914: Theology, Theory, and Policy*, 39–60. Grand Rapids, Mich.: Eerdmans, 2004.

Runciman, Steven. "The Pilgrimages to Palestine Before 1091." In Kenneth M. Setton, ed., *A History of the Crusades*, 1:68–80. Madison: University of Wisconsin Press, 1969.

Ryad, Umar. "Muslim Response to Missionary Activities in Egypt: With a Special Reference to the al-Azhar High Corps of *ÐUlama* (1925–1935)." In Heleen Murre-van den Berg, eds., *New Faith in Ancient Lands: Western Missions in the Middle East in the Nineteenth and Early Twentieth Centuries*, 281–307. Leiden: Brill, 2006.

Ryan, James D. "Missionary Saints of the High Middle Ages: Martyrdom, Popular Veneration, and Canonization." *Catholic Historical Review* 90 (2004): 1–28.

Rywkin, Michael, ed. *Russian Colonial Expansion to 1917.* London: Mansell, 1988.

Salt, Jeremy. "A Precious Symbiosis: Ottoman Christians and Foreign Missionaries in the Nineteenth Century." *International Journal of Turkish Studies* 3 (1985–1986): 59–64.

Sapir, Shaul. "The Anglican Missionary Societies in Jerusalem: Activities and Impact." In Ruth Kark, ed., *The Land That Became Israel: Studies in Historical Geography*, 105–119. New Haven, Conn.: Yale University Press, 1990.

Sarna, Jonathan D. "The Impact of Nineteenth-Century Christian Missions on American Jews." In Todd M. Endelman, ed., *Jewish Apostasy in the Modern World*, 232–254. London: Holmes and Meier, 1987.

Al-Sayegh, Fatma. "American Missionaries in the UAE Region in the Twentieth Century." *Middle Eastern Studies* 32 (1996): 120–139.

Schein, Sylvia. *Fideles Crucis: The Papacy, the West, and the Recovery of the Holy Land 1274–1314.* Oxford, U.K.: Oxford University Press, 1991.

——. "Gesta Dei per Mongolos 1300: The Genesis of a Non-Event." *English Historical Review* 94 (1979): 805–819.

Schilcher, L. Schatkowski. "The Famine of 1915–1918 in Greater Syria." In John P. Spagnolo, ed., *Problems of the Modern Middle East in Historical Perspective: Essays in Honour of Albert Hourani*, 229–258. Reading, U.K.: Ithaca Press, 1992.

Schütz, Edmond. "Armenia: A Christian Enclave in the Islamic Near East in the Middle Ages." In Michael Gervers and Ramzi Jibran Bikhazi, eds., *Conversion and Continuity: Indigenous Christian Communities in Islamic Lands Eighth to Eighteenth Centuries*, 217–236, Papers in Mediaeval Studies no. 9. Toronto: Pontifical Institute of Mediaeval Studies, 1990.

Scult, Mel. "English Missions to the Jews—Conversion in the Age of Emancipation." *Jewish Social Studies* 35 (1973): 3–17.

——. *Millennial Expectations and Jewish Liberties: A Study of the Efforts to Convert the Jews in Britain, up to the Mid–Nineteenth Century.* Leiden: Brill, 1978.

Sedra, Paul D. "John Lieder and His Mission in Egypt: The Evangelical Ethos at Work Among Nineteenth Century Copts." *Journal of Religious History* 28 (2004): 219–239.

——. "Modernity's Mission: Evangelical Efforts to Discipline the Nineteenth-Century Coptic Community." In Eleanor H. Tejirian and Reeva Spector Simon, eds., *Altruism and Imperialism: Western Cultural and Religious Missions in the Middle East*, 208–235. New York: Middle East Institute, Columbia University, 2002.

Setton, Kenneth M., ed. *A History of the Crusades.* 6 vols. Madison: University of Wisconsin Press, 1969–1990.

Sevcenko, Ihor. "Religious Missions Seen from Byzantium." *Harvard Ukrainian Studies* 12–13 (1988–1989): 7–27.

Shamir, Milette. "'Our Jerusalem': Americans in the Holy Land and Protestant Narratives of National Entitlement." *American Quarterly* 55 (2003): 29–60.

Sharkey, Heather. *American Evangelicals in Egypt: Missionary Encounters in an Age of Empire.* Princeton, N.J.: Princeton University Press, 2008.

——. "Empire and Muslim Conversion: Historical Reflections on Christian Missions in Egypt." *Islam and Christian–Muslim Relations* 16 (2005): 43–60.

Shatzmiller, Maya, ed. *Crusaders and Muslims in Twelfth-Century Syria.* Leiden: Brill, 1993.

Sheils, W. J., ed. *The Church and War: Papers Read at the Twenty-First Summer Meeting and the Twenty-Second Winter Meeting of the Ecclesiastical Society.* London: Blackwell, 1983.

Shenk, Wilbert R. "Reflections on the Modern Missionary Movement: 1792–1992." *Mission Studies* 9 (1992): 62–78.

Shields, Sarah D. *Mosul Before Iraq: Like Bees Making Five-Sided Cells.* Albany: State University of New York Press, 2000.

Shorrock, William I. "Anti-Clericalism and French Policy in the Ottoman Empire, 1900–1914." *European Studies Review* 4 (1974): 33–55.

Siberry, Elizabeth. "Missionaries and Crusaders, 1095–1274: Opponents or Allies?" In W. J. Sheils, ed., *The Church and War: Papers Read at the Twenty-First Summer Meeting and the Twenty-Second Winter Meeting of the Ecclesiastical Society,* 103–110. Oxford, U.K.: Blackwell, 1983.

Silberman, Neil Asher. *Between Past and Present: Archaeology, Ideology, and Nationalism in the Modern Middle East.* New York: Doubleday, 1989.

——. "'If I Forget Thee, O Jerusalem': Archaeology, Religious Commemoration, and Nationalism in a Disputed City, 1801–2001." *Nations and Nationalism* 7 (2004): 487–504.

Simon, Rachel. "Education." In Reeva Spector Simon, Michael Menachem Laskier, and Sara Reguer, eds., *The Jews of the Middle East and North Africa in Modern Times,* 142–164. New York: Columbia University Press, 2003.

——. "The Struggle Over the Christian Holy Places During the Ottoman Period." In Richard I. Cohen, ed., *Vision and Conflict in the Holy Land,* 23–44. New York: St. Martin's Press, 1985.

Simon, Reeva Spector. "The Case of the Curse: The London Society for Promoting Christianity Amongst the Jews and the Jews of Baghdad." In Eleanor H. Tejirian and Reeva Spector Simon, eds., *Altruism and Imperialism: Western Cultural and Religious Missions in the Middle East,* 45–65. New York: Middle East Institute, Columbia University, 2002.

Simon, Reeva Spector, Michael Menachem Laskier, and Sara Reguer, eds., *The Jews of the Middle East and North Africa in Modern Times.* New York: Columbia University Press, 2003.

Simon, Reeva Spector and Eleanor H. Tejirian, eds. *The Creation of Iraq, 1914–1921.* New York: Columbia University Press, 2004.

Smith, Eli and H. G. O Dwight. *Missionary Researches in Armenia: Including a Journey Through Asia Minor, and Into Georgia and Persia.* London: George Wightman, 1834.

Smith, Morton. "Pauline Worship as Seen by Pagans." *Harvard Theological Review* 73 (1980): 241–249.

Smith, Robert Michael. "The London Jews' Society and Patterns of Jewish Conversion in England, 1801–1859." *Jewish Social Studies* 43 (1981): 275–290.

Southern, R. W. *Western Views of Islam in the Middle Ages*. Cambridge, Mass.: Harvard University Press, 1962.

Spagnolo, J. P. "The Definition of a Style of Imperialism: The Internal Politics of French Educational Investment in Ottoman Beirut." *French Historical Studies* 8 (1974): 563–584.

——. "French Influence in Syria Prior to World War I: The Functional Weakness of Imperialism." *Middle East Journal* 23 (1969): 45–62.

Stanley, Brian. *The Bible and the Flag: Protestant Missions and British Imperialism in the Nineteenth and Twentieth Centuries*. Leicester, U.K.: Apollos, 1990.

——, ed. *Christian Missions and the Enlightenment*. Grand Rapids, Mich.: Eerdmans, 2001.

——. "Christian Responses to the Indian Mutiny of 1857." In W. J. Sheils, ed., *The Church and War: Papers Read at the Twenty-First Summer Meeting and the Twenty-Second Winter Meeting of the Ecclesiastical Society*, 277–289. London: Blackwell, 1983.

——. "'Commerce and Christianity': Providence Theory, the Missionary Movement, and the Imperialism of Free Trade, 1842–1860." *Historical Journal* 26 (1983): 71–94.

Stavrou, Theofanis George. "Russian Interest in the Levant 1845–1848." *Middle East Journal* 17 (1963): 91–103.

Stock, Eugene. *The History of the Church Missionary Society: Its Environment, Its Men, and Its Work*. 3 vols. London: Church Missionary Society, 1899.

Stockdale, Nancy L. "Biblical Motherhood: English Women and Empire in Palestine, 1848–1948." *Women's History Review* 15 (2006): 561–569.

——. "An Imperialist Failure: English Missionary Women and Palestinian Orphan Girls in Nazareth, 1864–1899." In Martin Tamcke and Michael Marten, eds., *Christian Witness Between Continuity and New Beginnings: Modern Historical Missions in the Middle East*, 213–232. Berlin: Lit, 2006.

Stockton, Ronald R. "Christian Zionism: Prophecy and Public Opinion." *Middle East Journal* 41 (1987): 234–253.

Stone, Frank Andrews. *Academies for Anatolia: A Study of the Rationale, Program, and Impact of the Educational Institutions Sponsored by the American Board in Turkey, 1830–1980*. Lanham, Md.: University Press of America, 1984.

Storrs, R. S. *A Sermon . . . at the Ordination of the Rev. Daniel Temple, and Rev. Isaac Bird*. Boston: n.p., 1822.

Stransky, Thomas. "Origins of Western Christian Missions in Jerusalem and the Holy Land." In Yehoshua Ben-Arieh and Moshe Davis, eds., *Jerusalem in the Mind of the Western World, 1800–1948*, 137–154, With Eyes Toward Zion V. Westport, Conn.: Praeger, 1997.

Subasi, Turgut. "The Apostasy Question in the Context of Anglo–Ottoman Relations, 1843–44." *Middle Eastern Studies* 38 (2002): 1–34.

Sullivan, Richard E. "Early Medieval Missionary Activity: A Comparative Study of Eastern and Western Methods." *Church History* 23 (1954): 17–35.

Tamcke, Martin and Michael Marten, eds. *Christian Witness Between Continuity and New Beginnings: Modern Historical Missions in the Middle East.* Berlin: Lit, 2006.

Tanner, Norman P. *The Councils of the Church: A Short History.* New York: Crossroad, 2001.

Tannous, Afif I. "Missionary Education in Lebanon: A Study in Acculturation." *Social Forces* 21 (1943): 338–343.

Tejirian, Eleanor H. "Faith of Our Fathers: Near East Relief and the Near East Foundation—from Missions to NGO." In Eleanor H. Tejirian and Reeva Spector Simon, eds., *Altruism and Imperialism: Western Cultural and Religious Missions in the Middle East*, 295–316. New York: Middle East Institute, Columbia University, 2002.

Tejirian, Eleanor H. and Reeva Spector Simon, eds. *Altruism and Imperialism: Western Cultural and Religious Missions in the Middle East.* New York: Middle East Institute, Columbia University, 2002.

Thompson, Elizabeth. *Colonial Citizens: Republican Rights, Paternal Privilege, and Gender in French Syria and Lebanon.* New York: Columbia University Press, 2000.

——. "Neither Conspiracy nor Hypocrisy: The Jesuits and the French Mandate in Syria and Lebanon." In Eleanor H. Tejirian and Reeva Spector Simon, eds., *Altruism and Imperialism: Western Cultural and Religious Missions in the Middle East*, 66–87. New York: Middle East Institute, Columbia University, 2002.

Thomson, Robert W. "Mission, Conversion, and Christianization: The Armenian Example." *Harvard Ukrainian Studies* 12–13 (1988–1989): 28–45.

Thorne, Susan. *Congregational Missions and the Making of an Imperial Culture in Nineteenth-Century England.* Stanford, Calif.: Stanford University Press, 1999.

Tibawi, A. L. *American Interests in Syria, 1800–1901: A Study of Educational, Literary, and Religious Work.* Oxford: Clarendon Press, 1966.

——. *British Interests in Palestine 1800–1901: A Study in Religious and Educational Enterprise.* London: Oxford University Press, 1961.

——. "The Genesis and Early History of the Syrian Protestant College (Part I)." *Middle East Journal* 21 (1967): 1–15

——. "The Genesis and Early History of the Syrian Protestant College (Part II)." *Middle East Journal* 21 (1967): 199–212.

Tolan, John V., ed. *Medieval Christian Perceptions of Islam: A Book of Essays.* New York: Garland, 1996.

——. *Saracens: Islam in the Medieval European Imagination.* New York: Columbia University Press, 2002.

Toth, Istvan Gyorgy. "Between Islam and Catholicism: Bosnian Franciscan Missionaries in Turkish Hungary, 1584–1716." *Catholic Historical Review* 89 (July 2003): 409–433.

Treitler, Leo. *With Voice and Pen: Coming to Know Medieval Song and How It Was Made.* New York: Oxford University Press, 2003.

Trimbur, Dominique. "Le Destin des institutions chrétiennes européennes de Jérusalem pendant la première guerre mondiale." *Mélanges de Science Religieuse* 58 (2001): 3–29.

——. "A French Presence in Palestine—Notre Dame de France." *Bulletin du Centre de Recherche Français de Jérusalem* 3 (1998): 117–140.

Tsimhoni, Daphne. *Christian Communities in Jerusalem and the West Bank Since 1948: An Historical, Social, and Political Study*. Westport, Conn.: Praeger, 1993.

Tudesco, James Patrick. "Missionaries and French Imperialism: The Role of Catholic Missionaries in French Colonial Expansion 1880–1905." Ph.D. diss., University of Connecticut, 1980.

Twain, Mark. *The Innocents Abroad, or the New Pilgrims' Progress*. Hartford, Conn.: American, 1869.

Tyerman, Christopher. *Fighting for Christendom: Holy War and the Crusades*. New York: Oxford University Press, 2004.

——. *God's War: A New History of the Crusades*. Cambridge, Mass.: Harvard University Press, 2006.

——. "The Holy Land and the Crusades of the Thirteenth and Fourteenth Centuries." In Peter W. Edbury, ed., *Crusade and Settlement*, 105–112. Cardiff, U.K.: University College of Cardiff Press, 1985.

Vander Werff, Lyle L. *Christian Mission to Muslims—the Record: Anglican and Reformed Approaches in India and the Near East, 1800–1938*. South Pasadena, Calif.: William Carey Library, 1977.

Verdeil, Chantal. "Between Rome and France, Intransigent and Anti-Protestant Jesuits in the Orient: The Beginning of the Jesuits' Mission of Syria, 1831–1864." In Martin Tamcke and Michael Marten, *Christian Witness Between Continuity and New Beginnings: Modern Historical Missions in the Middle East*, 23–32. Berlin: Lit, 2006.

——. "Travailler à la renaissance de l'Orient Chrétien: Les missions latines en Syrie (1830–1945)." *Proche-Orient Chrétien* 51 (2001): 267–316.

Vereté, Meir. "The Restoration of the Jews in English Protestant Thought." *Middle Eastern Studies* 8 (1972): 3–50.

Vryonis, Speros, Jr., ed. *Islam and Cultural Change in the Middle Ages*. Wiesbaden, Germany: Otto Harrassowitz, 1975.

Wallach, Janet. *Desert Queen: The Extraordinary Life of Gertrude Bell: Adventurer, Adviser to Kings, Ally of Lawrence of Arabia*. New York: Doubleday, 1995.

Wallach, Jehuda L., ed. *Germany and the Middle East, 1835–1939*. International Symposium, April 1975. Tel Aviv: Institute of German History, 1975.

Walls, Andrew F. *The Missionary Movement in Christian History: Studies in the Transmission of Faith*. Maryknoll, N.Y.: Orbis Books, 1996.

Waltz, James. "Historical Perspectives in Early Missions to Muslims." *Muslim World* 61 (1971): 170–186.

Ward, Kevin. "'Taking Stock': The Church Missionary Society and Its Historians." In Kevin Ward and Brian Stanley, eds., *The Church Mission Society and World Christianity, 1799–1999*, 15–42. Grand Rapids, Mich.: Eerdmans, 2000.

Ward, Kevin and Brian Stanley, eds. *The Church Mission Society and World Christianity, 1799–1999*. Grand Rapids, Mich.: Eerdmans, 2000.

Watenpaugh, Keith David. *Being Modern in the Middle East: Revolution, Nationalism, Colonialism, and the Arab Middle Class.* Princeton, N.J.: Princeton University Press, 2006.

——. "The League of Nations' Rescue of Armenian Genocide Survivors and the Making of Modern Humanitarianism, 1920–1927." *American Historical Review* 115 (2010): 1315–1339.

Weber, Eugen. *From Peasants Into Frenchmen: The Modernization of Rural France, 1870–1914.* Stanford, Calif.: Stanford University Press, 1976.

Webster, Gillian. "Elizabeth Anne Finn." *Biblical Archaeologist* (September 1985): 181–185.

Weiss, Gerhard. "The Pilgrim as Tourist: Travels to the Holy Land as Reflected in the Published Accounts of German Pilgrims Between 1450 and 1550." In Marilyn J. Chiat and Kathryn L. Reyerson, eds., *The Medieval Mediterranean: Cross-Cultural Contacts*, 119–131. St. Cloud, Minn.: North Star Press of St. Cloud, 1988.

Werth, Paul W. "From 'Pagan' Muslims to 'Baptized' Communists: Religious Conversion and Ethnic Particularity in Russia's Eastern Provinces." *Comparative Studies in Society in Society and History* 42 (2000): 497–523.

——. *The Margins of Orthodoxy: Missions, Governance, and Confessional Politics in Russia's Volga–Kama Region, 1827–1905.* Ithaca, N.Y.: Cornell University Press, 2002.

Whitehouse, David. *Mohammed, Charlemagne, and the Origins of Europe: Archaeology and the Pirenne Thesis.* Ithaca, N.Y.: Cornell University Press, 1983.

Whittow, Mark. *The Making of Byzantium, 600–1025.* Berkeley and Los Angeles: University of California Press, 1996.

Wickham, Chris. "The Mediterranean Around 800: On the Brink of the Second Trade Cycle." *Dumbarton Oaks Papers* 58 (2004): 161–174.

Williams, C. Peter. "British Religion and the Wider World: Mission and Empire, 1800–1940." In Sheridan Gilley and W. J. Sheils, eds., *A History of Religion in Britain: Practice and Belief from Pre-Roman Times to the Present*, 381–405. Oxford, U.K.: Blackwell, 1994.

——. "The Church Missionary Society and the Indigenous Church in the Second Half of the Nineteenth Century: The Defense and Destruction of the Venn Ideals." In Dana L. Robert, ed., *Converting Colonialism: Visions and Realities in Mission History, 1700–1914*, 86–111. Grand Rapids, Mich.: Eerdmans, 2008.

Yazbak, Mahmoud. "Templars as Proto-Zionists? The 'German Colony' in Late Ottoman Haifa." *Journal of Palestine Studies* 28 (1999): 40–54.

Zachs, Fruma. "From the Mission to the Missionary: The Bliss Family and the Syrian Protestant College (1866–1920)." *Die Welt des Islams* 45 (2005): 255–291.

——. "Toward a Proto-Nationalist Concept of Syria? Revisiting the American Presbyterian Missionaries in the Nineteenth-Century Levant." *Die Welt des Islams* 41 (2001): 145–173.

Zaka, Samy F. "Education and Civilization in the Third Republic: The University of Saint-Joseph, 1875–1914." Ph.D. diss., University of Notre Dame, 2006.

Zirinsky, Michael. "American Presbyterian Missionaries at Urmia During the Great War." *Bibliotheque Iranienne* (2002): 1–22.

——. "'Render Therefore Unto Caesar the Things Which Are Caesar's': American Presbyterian Educators and Reza Shah." *Iranian Studies* 26 (1993): 337–356.